POETIC ASSOCIATIONS

Poetic Associations

The Nineteenth-century English Poetry Collection of Dr. Gerald N. Wachs

Essays by Stephen Weissman, Stuart Curran, James Chandler

Entries by Stephen Weissman

Foreword by Catherine Uecker

Edited by Eric Powell

Project Management by Patti Gibbons

Research assistance by Eric Powell

Photography by Michael Kenny

Copyediting by Alexandra Bonfante-Warren

THE UNIVERSITY OF CHICAGO LIBRARY
Chicago 2017

Publication of this catalogue was generously underwritten
by the family of Dr. Gerald N. Wachs.

All illustrations are keyed to catalogue entry numbers

Contents

Foreword

This catalogue of the Gerald N. Wachs Collection of Nineteenth-Century Poetry is more than a description of the collection, it is the story of a partnership and friendship that spanned over forty years. The collaboration began in the early 1970s with an inspired purchase of a birthday gift at Ximenes Rare Books in New York (Byron's *Hebrew Melodies*, 1815), resulting in a collection of almost nine hundred titles by 2012. The collection was formed by Dr. Gerald N. Wachs (1937–2013), in collaboration with Stephen Weissman, the owner of Ximenes. In his essay and in many of the catalogue entries, the bookseller tells the history of how he and Gerald (Jerry) built the collection and became friends; in the process, he includes many entertaining tales of the pursuit of elusive titles. Two other essays accompany Stephen Weissman's in the catalogue. "Poetry's Empire: 'The Songs of Humanized Society,'" by James Chandler, Barbara E. & Richard J. Franke Distinguished Service Professor, Department of English; Director of the Franke Institute for the Humanities; and Chair of the Department of Cinema and Media Studies at the University of Chicago, explores the special significance of the English poetry of this time. "The Wachs Collection: An Introduction," by Stuart Curran, President, Keats-Shelley Association of America, and Professor Emeritus of the Department of English, University of Pennsylvania, presents the collector behind the collection.

The Wachs Collection focuses on English Romantic and Victorian poetry created in the era known as the Long Nineteenth Century (1789–1914). The books acquired for the collection are nearly all extraordinary in some way: they may boast remarkable provenances, display presentation inscriptions revealing personal associations, or, in certain cases, be among the very few known copies of a title. Works were also chosen for their condition, with preference given to pristine copies in their original paper-covered boards or publisher's bindings. Wachs and Weissman used volume 3, *1800–1900,* of *The New Cambridge*

Bibliography of English Literature (NCBEL; 1969–77) as their guide to build and organize the collection. As Weissman wrote in his essay, "Here, in one volume, was a well-defined universe, and a simple way of keeping track of progress." The collection also contains works not listed in the *NCBEL*, titles or authors not known to the *NCBEL* editors at the time of publication.

After Dr. Wachs's death in 2013, the collection was placed on deposit at the University of Chicago Library. Alice Schreyer, then Assistant University Librarian for Humanities, Social Sciences, and Special Collections and Curator of Rare Books, consulted with the Wachs family, and it was decided that the Library would produce a gallery exhibition, a permanent web exhibition, and a catalogue of the entire collection.

Organization of the Catalogue

As with the formation of the collection by Gerald Wachs and Stephen Weissman, the structure of the catalogue follows that of volume 3 of the *NCBEL*. Authors are grouped by period—early, mid-, and late nineteenth century—and then further subdivided by the categories of "major" or "minor." However, the forms of authors' names and their birth and death dates are, with a few exceptions, in accordance with the Library of Congress Name Authority File.

Acknowledgments

Thanks for their generosity go to Dr. Wachs's children, Deborah Wachs Barnes, Sharon Wachs Hirsch, Judith Pieprz, and Joel Wachs, who in 2015 donated two-thirds of the collection—nearly seven hundred volumes—to the University of Chicago. Many people in the Special Collections Research Center and the Library were key in the production of this catalogue. Eric Powell, a PhD candidate in the English Department, started this project as a graduate-student assistant, but because of his expertise in the area of nineteenth-century English poetry, his role quickly evolved to that of catalogue editor. Daniel Meyer, Director and University Archivist, coordinated the overall process; Patti Gibbons, Head of Collection Management and Preservation, managed all phases of the catalogue's production; Michael Kenny, the Library Preservation

Department's Photographer, photographed the selected publications that illustrate the catalogue; and Rare Books staff assisted with the bibliographic and collection questions that arose.

Catherine Uecker
Rare Books Librarian
Special Collections Research Center
University of Chicago Library

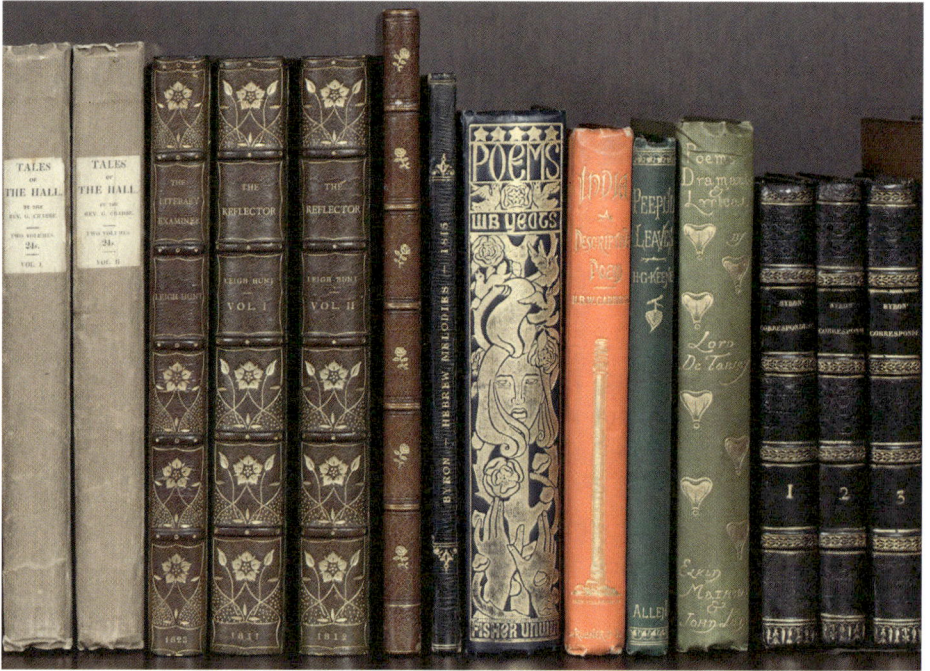

The Wachs Collection:
An Informal Chronology Stephen Weissman

The Gerald N. Wachs Collection of Nineteenth-Century Poetry came about because of an article in the December 8, 1969, issue of *New York Magazine*. Part of a series called "The Passionate Shopper," it consisted of a survey of the local antiquarian book scene, and included a few paragraphs on my shop, Ximenes Rare Books, which I had opened in the summer of 1965 on the fifth floor of a narrow little office building on West 45th Street, just off 5th Avenue. The article was written by a friend of mine, who did me the favor of making me sound rather less intimidating than such dominant figures in the trade as John Fleming and H. P. Kraus. At the age of thirty, I was presented as much the youngest of all the booksellers in town, and nothing if not talkative: "Ximenes is an admirable place for a beginning collector, or one of limited means. Books range from $10 up, and ten minutes of Weissman is better than five books on books."

Jerry was intrigued by the article, and put it to one side. The following March he arrived unannounced at my office, with the notion of finding a birthday present for his wife. I happened not to be very busy at the time, and we had a long chat, at the end of which he chose, as a suitable gift, a slightly battered but perfectly presentable first edition of Byron's *Hebrew Melodies*. This was priced at $75, and included "She Walks in Beauty like the Night," which seemed to both of us appropriate to the occasion.

Jerry lived in Short Hills, New Jersey, but he had a routine of coming into the city once a week, and in the months to follow he stopped by from time to time to find out a little more about the curious world of collecting old books. He was a collector by instinct, but had never gotten beyond such things as stamps and coins, or baseball cards. One way or another we got to know each other quite well, and at some point we discovered a common interest in playing duplicate bridge. We formed a partnership, and began to play once a week, in the afternoon and evening,

11

at a local club. Between sessions we would have dinner at a nearby Italian restaurant, and talk for a couple of hours about the afternoon's results, our bidding strategies, our work, our children, and life in general. Inevitably I would tell Jerry quite a lot about what was going on at the shop.

Jerry became more and more interested in the rare book business, not only in the books themselves, but also in the way they were bought and sold, and how they were priced. Soon he knew quite a bit about my purchases and sales, my colleagues, my catalogues, and my customers. One day, pretty much out of the blue, he raised the possibility of starting his own book collection, under my guidance. This sounded to me an appealing project, so we began to discuss the question of what exactly he would like to collect. We agreed from the start that neither of us had any enthusiasm for a collection based upon Jerry's professional world of dermatology, an area in which I had no experience and little interest. I think the first possibility Jerry raised was Charles Dickens, but my reaction to this was lukewarm, largely because it was such an old-fashioned and well-traveled topic that nothing new could be accomplished.

Another suggestion by Jerry was modern fiction, books by such writers as Hemingway and Fitzgerald. This notion I rejected out of hand, as I seldom handled anything printed after 1900, and had always been put off by the fact that much of the value of most modern first editions lay in their dust jackets. After a while, out of frustration, Jerry asked me to pick a subject I myself would like to collect. I thought about this for a bit, and then said that as his first purchase had been a Byron title, then perhaps nineteenth-century English poetry would be a good idea. This area at least had the advantage that interesting books were available, and were not necessarily all that expensive. And it was a field in which I had some experience, and a bit of expertise.

The next time Jerry came to the office I showed him a copy of volume 3 (1800–1900) of *The New Cambridge Bibliography of English Literature* (*NCBEL*), a recent revision of a standard guide first published in 1940. This was a reference book I had immediately acquired when it came out in 1969, and my copy was already filled with penciled ticks against any title I had ever had in stock. This bibliography, and my slightly compulsive habit of marking it up, drew an immediate response from Jerry.

Here, in one volume, was a well-defined universe, and a simple way of keeping track of progress.

Jerry was at that time working at the pharmaceutical company Schering-Plough, and had yet to go into private practice. He had, I suppose, a reasonable salary, but with four small children there was not a lot of disposable income. We agreed to proceed with an annual budget of $1,500. The whole scheme now seems a bit ludicrous, but we were young, and everything was possible.

We began in May 1971, with two books by Tennyson, both of which had appeared in Catalogue Five, issued shortly after my move to New York in the summer of 1965. For one reason or another they had failed to sell, and had remained in stock ever since. The first was the two-volume *Poems* of 1842, in a gift binding of the period, and signed by the poet's younger sister Mary, to whom he was very close. This was priced at $240, which even then did not seem a lot for a charming association copy of what was by any standard one of the great collections of nineteenth-century verse. The other title was something I had acquired for £30 at the first Sotheby's sale I ever attended in London, a copy of *Tiresias and Other Poems* (1885), inscribed by Tennyson to William Allingham, a younger poet who was his close friend for the better part of fifty years. The price for this was $150, but for Jerry I lowered it to $125.

This was a start, and we were both impatient to continue. In the coming weeks I revisited the office shelves and selected another three books, Tennyson's *Maud* (1855), and the two series of Browning's *Dramatic Idyls* (1879 and 1880). These were all in fine condition, and inexpensive: the Tennyson cost $30, and the two Browning titles were $15 each. From Jerry's point of view these acquisitions made sense. The *NCBEL* had, after all, provided us with a well-defined list of desiderata, and a logical goal was to get one of everything.

I was not so sure. To some extent Jerry and I were both stamp collectors by instinct, and shared a philatelic predilection for completeness. At the same time I was hesitant about applying the same principle to collecting books, not so much because there was anything inherently wrong with it, but more because of a general sense that there was a difference between filling shelves and filling the pages of an album. We discussed

13

this matter a good deal over the next few months. On the question of condition we were in full agreement that a high standard should be maintained, but my instinct was that for certain obviously common titles we should also hold out for inscribed copies, or copies with interesting provenance. Jerry was willing to go along with this requirement, albeit with a certain reluctance. In the end, we retained *Maud* and the two Browning titles in the collection, and never upgraded them, but there were to be very few other acquisitions of this sort in the future.

A few months later, in January 1972, I had a stroke of luck. I was at that time in the habit of making periodic forays into New England, and on this occasion I stopped in to see a New Hampshire bookseller named Dick Mills, who also dealt, with some considerable success, in old pictures and furniture. I did not know him very well, but on this visit he could not have been more welcoming. I was allowed to look wherever I liked, including in various desk drawers, where many of the smaller books were tucked away. Nothing was priced, but when Mills did give me prices, I rather wished I had pulled out more. I drove away in high spirits, with a box of about forty books, of considerable variety and charm. There was one little gem printed in London in 1652 entitled *Pseuchographia Anthropomagica*, by someone calling himself Agricola Carpenter. Included in this bit of philosophical nonsense were a number of commendatory poems, the last signed "J. M.," but I had to admit that it was not likely that Milton would have begun, "What stupefactive opium did infect / The protoplasts intuitive intellect."

More importantly, there were two obvious titles for Jerry. One was Coleridge's first book, a slim verse play called *The Fall of Robespierre*, printed in Cambridge in 1794. I'd never seen a copy before, and this one was in fine condition, in a collector's binding by Sangorski & Sutcliffe, and complete with a leaf at the end containing proposals for print-ing by subscription "Imitations from the Modern Latin Poets," an early Coleridge project that came to nothing. For this I paid $150, which even in those days seemed ridiculous. The other was also a first book, Chris-tina Rossetti's *Verses*, privately printed by her father in 1847, when she was sixteen. I knew vaguely that this was rare on the market, and this copy, in a pretty morocco binding by Riviere, had the added feature of

14

an autograph letter by the author tipped in, written in the mid-1860s to a somewhat disreputable art "agent" named Charles Augustus Howell, who had attached himself to the Rossetti family. The letter begins, "Please don't forbid me the pleasant duty of thanking you for so precious a collection of stamps." This book was priced $250, and could hardly have been more appropriate for Jerry and me, given our philatelic bias.

With the acquisition of these two books we both now felt that our project was properly under way. There arose at the same time the question of what I was to charge Jerry for them. The only other copy I could find of *The Fall of Robespierre* to appear on the market in recent times was one sold at the Louis Silver sale at Sotheby's in 1965 for £140, or $392, but that one lacked the important and appealing final leaf. Clearly the copy from Dick Mills, seven years later, was much more valuable; a retail price of something in the order of $1,000 to $1,500 would not have been unreasonable. We talked about the pricing of the Coleridge at some length, and eventually settled on a figure of $450 as a fair compromise, by which I tripled my money, and Jerry acquired an attractive book at less than half the going rate. This early episode set a pattern for the future. Jerry had a genuine interest in the workings of the book trade, so I always told him where each book came from, and what it cost; somehow the price to Jerry always seemed obvious. One benefit of our arrangement, of course, was that because I had a guaranteed buyer, I could afford to pay a full retail price for an appropriate title, and simply pocket whatever trade discount I had been given.

At auction we agreed to a fee of 10 percent of the hammer price, as was customary for commission bids. Our first auction purchase was a rare and curious novel called *Edmund Oliver*, printed in Bristol in 1798, which I had spotted in a minor Sotheby Parke Bernet sale in December 1972. The author was Charles Lloyd, an erratic young friend of Coleridge, and the plot was a thinly disguised account of Coleridge's brief and unhappy experiment in soldiering, as a volunteer in the 15th Light Dragoons. Coleridge was embarrassed and outraged by the publication of this book, and his friendship with Lloyd cooled. As we had already made a beginning with Coleridge, and as Lloyd himself was classified in the *NCBEL* as a "minor" poet, this seemed a most desirable title for our purposes, especially because the copy on offer was in fine condition, and had formerly been owned by two of the most famous American book collectors, Robert Hoe and A. Edward Newton. I remember conveying my enthusiasm to several of my younger colleagues who showed up at the sale, and as a result when the lot came up no one bid against me, and *Edmund Oliver* was acquired for $200. This happy result had an amusing sequel. About three years later I bought a shelf of old novels in New England, which included, amazingly enough, another copy of *Edmund Oliver*, in a slightly battered old binding. I offered it to the Pforzheimer Library for $600, which was perfectly reasonable, but the librarian turned it down, as he could not see why he should have to pay three times the price the last copy had fetched at auction.

Over the next few years we proceeded with caution. Or perhaps it would be more accurate to say that I was cautious, and Jerry was patient. There was plenty of nineteenth-century verse on the market, so that the principal dilemma was one of selection. Most of the books that were available were not hugely expensive, and an annual budget that gradually edged up to about $5,000 was sufficient to add about twenty-five books a year, more or less one every two weeks. Titles were added singly, rather than in clusters, and the collection began to grow slowly and steadily, rather than by leaps and bounds. There was no particular strategy; with lots to choose from, I suppose I just picked out books that took my fancy.

Gradually we began to refine the limits of the collection. A critical decision involved whether or not to include letters and manuscripts. I had no problem with doing this, but Jerry was not keen, as autograph material seemed to him somehow to blur the limits of what we were trying to do, and aside from anything else, the acquisition of a letter gave us nothing to tick off in the *NCBEL*. To be completely honest, I could see his point; I liked checking off titles just as much as he did.

We also adopted a rule that for writers who were classified as poets, all titles, even those in prose, were admissible. For those who were listed in the *NCBEL* as prose writers, only their verse would be included; it seemed to make no sense to acquire the novels of Walter Scott, or the art criticism of Ruskin. Very early on, however, we opted to elevate Leigh Hunt and Walter Savage Landor to the rank of poets; they had both, after all, published a good deal of verse, and their books were both affordable and amusing to collect. In hindsight it seems a bit absurd for us to have made such intricate decisions when only a handful of books had actually been purchased, but we were full of enthusiasm for our collaboration, and to some extent poring over lists of titles and authors made up for the fact that we did not have a lot of money to spend.

The question of condition was a little more difficult to resolve, for both of us. It was easy enough to say, as we had done at the start, that only fine copies would be admitted to the collection, but what exactly did this mean? For the vast majority of Victorian books the answer was, broadly speaking, simple. For these the overriding requirement was that copies be in a well-preserved publisher's binding, either cloth or printed wrappers. Essentially we both wanted the books to look nice on the shelf, and, with a limited budget and much to choose from, it was not difficult to pass up shabby copies, no matter how rare the title or evocative the provenance.

For the Romantic period the situation was a little different. Postwar collectors had been taught, by such authorities as Michael Sadleir, to place a premium on "original" condition, which meant that for the early nineteenth century the most desirable copies were those preserved in a publisher's binding of paper boards, with a printed paper label on the spine. The problem was that these bindings were by their very nature fragile, and subject over time to a certain degree of wear and tear. We took the position very early on that books in worn original boards were unacceptable, and that rebound copies were often a reasonable alternative. These could be either in attractive and well-preserved leather bindings of the period, or, occasionally, in more recent bindings for collectors by such craftsmen as Bedford or Riviere. The latter bindings had become unfashionable, but we both thought them rather attractive.

For certain famous Romantic titles, the premium necessary to buy copies in original boards simply seemed excessive. The three books by Keats published in his lifetime, for example, were added to the collection early on, but they were all rebound. Copies of Keats in boards were by no means unobtainable, but they demanded a considerable premium, and it seemed somehow a waste of money to go after what so many other collectors had already possessed. That being said, we did in time acquire, with patience and often a bit of luck, a substantial number of titles in original boards, many of them in a spectacular condition.

We were both fascinated by rarity, but the truth is that in the 1970s there was not a lot to go on for nineteenth-century books, aside from auction records or the odd author bibliography, and a general feel that comes from experience, either by visiting shops and looking at shelves, or reading catalogues. It was possible to write to the Library of Congress and ask for the locations of copies held in North American libraries as recorded by the National Union Catalogue, and these were duly sent back on a printed slip, but the process was a bit cumbersome, and I seldom took advantage of it. Every now and then, however, something would turn up that just looked rare. In 1976, for example, on one of my British buying trips, I stopped in to see Ted Hofmann, an American expatriate more or less my own age and with a similar background, who had set up shop near Sevenoaks, in Kent. Ted had in stock a copy of the first separate edition of Tennyson's *Charge of the Light Brigade* (1855), a four-page quarto printed specifically for circulation to soldiers in the Crimea. The poem had been collected a few months earlier in *Maud, and Other Poems*, which we already had, but the text there had been somewhat watered down, and lacked its most famous line, "Someone had blundered." Ted had bought this separate printing for next to nothing in the autograph department at Goodspeed's, in Boston, where it had been thrown in as an extra in a folder containing an inconsequential Tennyson letter. He was able to determine that only a handful of copies had survived, but as his cost was virtually zero, the price was reasonable, and the leaflet was added to Jerry's collection for just under $1,000. In the years since, I have seen only two other copies. One surfaced in New York at the Marjorie Wiggins Prescott sale in 1981, where it fetched the astonishing hammer price of $18,000, from a rogue bidder whom none of us had ever seen before; this copy reappeared at auction in 1984, where the price fell to a more sober $9,000, which was a bit disappointing as far as Jerry and I were concerned, but we were hardly crestfallen. By coincidence another copy cropped up in the trade at almost the same time at about the same price, but it was severely trimmed, and as far as we were concerned hardly counted. It has been more than thirty years now, and no other copy has come on the market.

In the early years we made few purchases at auction. We followed the major sales with great intensity, but we simply did not have the funds to compete. At the Stockhausen sale at Sotheby Parke Bernet in New York, in 1974, I made a noble effort to secure a set of page proofs of Robert Browning's *Red Cotton Night-Cap Country* (1873), "with extensive corrections in Browning's hand," but wound up as the underbidder at $2,500; the buyer was the Armstrong Browning Library at Baylor University, who no doubt would have paid a lot more. The only lot we did manage to get was a fine copy in boards of Shelley's *Laon and Cythna* (1818), for $950; this book had an appealing and slightly unexpected provenance, as it had once been in the celebrated Britwell Court library, known chiefly for its extraordinary holdings of early English printing. Something like Wordsworth's first publication, *An Evening Walk* (1793), was beyond our means at $3,750. The situation was pretty much the same at the Borowitz sales, at the same venue, in 1977–78. Here our most aggressive bid was on a copy of Shelley's *Epipsychidion* (1821), one of his best poems despite the rather daunting title. This we lost at $2,800, which turned out to be rather lucky, as I had somewhat overestimated the book's rarity; another copy, just as good, turned up two years later for less than a thousand dollars. Byron's *Waltz* (1813) was unaffordable at $5,250; a similar copy was purchased seven years later at more or less the same price. In the end our only Borowitz purchases were, for $375, a very fine copy of Browning's *Men and Women* (1855), which had belonged to one of the Lushington brothers, who were close friends of Tennyson, and a couple of Leigh Hunt rarities, which I extracted from a sixty-four-volume set of first editions uniformly bound in blue morocco by Riviere. The Leigh Hunt lot cost me $1,900 for stock, which was rather a bargain, so that the books for Jerry were modestly priced.

By the time of the Arthur Houghton sales at Christie's in London, in 1979 and 1980, we were becoming a little more competitive. The collection ought to have been given to Harvard, but he sent his books and manuscripts to auction, some ten years before his death. The two sales presented a dazzling array of English literature, much of it acquired through the legendary Dr. Rosenbach, and I arranged my schedule to attend both sessions, essentially as a spectator.

There were only a small number of lots of possible interest to Jerry. Lot 13, for example, in the first session, was Matthew Arnold's first publication, a Rugby School–prize poem called *Alaric at Rome*, printed anonymously in 1840, and long considered one of the black tulips of nineteenth-century verse. This copy, in a Riviere binding, lacked the printed wrappers, but I was willing to overlook this flaw, as this was a title I feared we might never see again. The estimate was £600 to £800. I was in the habit of writing bids in my catalogue in code, in the event, admittedly a bit far-fetched, that a rival was looking over my shoulder, and I see now that for this lot I put down a limit of "br–," which meant £1,500 (my code word was "bankruptcy," with $b = 1$, $a = 2$, and so on). We weren't even close: *Alaric at Rome* was knocked down to Rosenbach's successor, John Fleming, for £3,400. Happily, we were eventually able to acquire, more than twenty years later, a much better copy, with the wrappers preserved, bearing a presentation inscription.

We did, however, secure three Houghton books. The first, for £700, was a copy of Robert Browning's second book, *Paracelsus* (1835), whose binding of dark gray paper boards was in an astonishing state of preservation. In the second session we acquired, for £800, a copy of Coventry Patmore's *Angel in the House* (1854–56) presented to the noted photographer Julia Margaret Cameron; the two volumes were in a very attractive black morocco gift binding of the period, with the recipient's name stamped in gilt on the front covers, and the text contained, as the catalogue pointed out, "numerous important alterations and additions in the author's hand." Patmore is perhaps no longer a name to conjure with, but his *Angel in the House* was highly regarded in its day, and the fact that he and Mrs. Cameron were both members of Tennyson's inner circle made this copy, for our purposes, ideal. Near the end of the sale was a small run of Wordsworth, beginning with indifferent copies of the 1798 and 1800 editions of *Lyrical Ballads*. What caught my eye, however, was a copy of his *Two Addresses to the Freeholders of Westmorland* (1818), published during the course of a local election campaign in which he had taken a great interest. I knew that this little book, printed in Kendal in the

Lake District, was rare, and I marked my catalogue "t / c" (£800 to £900), a bit over the high estimate of £600. I well remember the scene. As this long and fiercely contested sale was drawing to a close, many members of the trade were getting up to leave, and the auctioneer was speeding up the pace. When the lot came up, it was quickly knocked down to me for an opening bid of £280; I have since observed that Wordsworth never does as well as he should in sales arranged alphabetically by author. The Houghton books added to Jerry's collection illustrate rather neatly the three principal criteria for inclusion we had established early on: immaculate condition (Browning), spectacular provenance (Patmore), and absolute rarity (Wordsworth). We were, to be sure, still operating on a small scale, but we were making progress.

Over time, certain books that were both famous and common presented a special challenge. Clearly there was a place in the collection, for example, for significant editions of *Lyrical Ballads*, in which Wordsworth and Coleridge to some extent established the parameters of Romantic verse. Copies of the earliest form of the 1798 first edition, with a Bristol imprint on the title page, were effectively unobtainable; I still have never seen a copy on the open market, and even if one had turned up, it would have been unaffordable. Copies with the cancel London title page, on the other hand, were plentiful enough in the 1970s, but one way or another after ten years I had never gotten around to buying one; such copies as I saw were either too expensive, or were not in good enough condition. The same was true of the equally important two-volume edition of 1800, with Wordsworth's celebrated Romantic manifesto printed for the first time, as the preface.

We used to talk about such things frequently. By 1980 there were a couple of hundred books on the shelves, and the notion of a gap in the collection was beginning to have some meaning. And by this time Jerry, of course, knew a lot more about what we were trying to do. His focus, quite understandably, tended to be on the *NCBEL*'s "major" poets, and titles like Shelley's *Adonais* and FitzGerald's *Rubáiyát* began to recur in our book chat as desiderata. The lack of *Lyrical Ballads* in any form became something of a standing joke.

Finally, in 1982, an opportunity arose. The occasion was the sale at Christie's in New York of the collection of English and American literature belonging to Dr. Gerald E. Slater. Jerry Slater was something of a shooting star in the rare book firmament. He first came to my attention as a major buyer at the Borowitz sale in 1977, and within a year he had become a regular customer. Slater was one of those people who caught on quickly to what collecting was all about, and by and large the books he chose to buy were well selected. He had money to spend, and broad interests, so that before long we were frequently in touch, to the extent that my first Jerry, I think, began to be a little jealous of another Jerry appearing on the scene. After a little more than five years, however, the Slater collection came to an abrupt halt, which led to a dispersal at auction.

Considering how recently the books had been acquired, the auction results were not too bad, with a number of books selling for rather more than Slater had paid for them. Our focus was on the second half of the sale, devoted to the nineteenth and twentieth centuries, though its emphasis was more on fiction than verse. Halfway through, we acquired a copy of Keats's *Poems* (1817), his first book, in a simple but not unattractive mid-Victorian binding. I thought it rather charming that an early owner had neatly written "first edition" on the title page. This was not, in my experience, a common phrase for what was then still a recent book, and there was in its use a certain irony, as none of Keats's three books had been reprinted in his lifetime. We got this copy for $1,200, less than half what I had been prepared to pay, and a fraction of what a copy in original boards would have cost.

Near the end of the sale was a copy in original boards of the second edition of *Lyrical Ballads* (1800). In this case a binding in boards was a real temptation, as the description cited a remark by George Healey, in his catalogue of the Wordsworth collection at Cornell that "no copy with paper labels entirely intact is known to me." Slater's copy was in exceptional condition, and the paper labels were perfect; here at last was something out of the ordinary, and I put down a limit of $3,000, against an estimate of $1,500 to $2,000. That we only had to pay $1,600 seemed to confirm my notion that Wordsworth, coming at the end of the alphabet, never fetches as much at auction as he is worth. That being said, a copy at the Bradley Martin sale eight years later, whose labels were definitely not "entirely intact," sold for $13,000.

To chart the growth of Jerry's collection by his purchases at auction is rather misleading, as most of what we acquired came from other sources in the trade. Within a few months of the Slater sale I stumbled across, where I cannot remember, an extraordinary copy of the first American edition of *Lyrical Ballads*, printed in Philadelphia in 1802. I had never before paid any attention to American printings on Jerry's behalf, but in this case it seemed worth making an exception, as the book represented the first appearance of Romantic poetry in the United States. This set was printed on paper of unusually high quality for an American book at the start of the nineteenth century, and was preserved in a beautiful Philadelphia binding of the period. I had no idea at the time what a lucky find this was. In the years since, I have seen a few more copies of this book, but these have all been printed on thin paper, and bound two volumes in one. It now appears, though the details are murky, that the Philadelphia publisher, James Humphreys, printed a small number of copies, perhaps for subscribers, on expensive paper. There are, in fact, a few other examples of this practice, most notably the *Federalist* (1788), but its application to such an experimental book as *Lyrical Ballads* is very surprising. Further research is required, but I strongly suspect that Jerry's copy is the finest one in existence. A year later we were at last able to add as well the first edition of 1798, in a collector's binding by Riviere; as with *Edmund Oliver*, Charles Lloyd's novel about Coleridge, this bore the bookplate of A. Edward Newton, whose books and articles played such a key role in the popularization of book collecting in the United States. The condition of the books in Newton's own library had long since become rather old-fashioned, but for Jerry and me his copies had a certain resonance.

Over the course of the 1980s we made steady progress, and by the end of the decade there were about four hundred titles on the shelves in New Jersey. For each book, as it was acquired, I provided Jerry with a typed description. These contained copy-specific details of binding, condition, provenance, and bibliographical niceties, along with general notes on the author and text. The latter gradually became more and more sophisticated, as my grasp of the period matured, and as Jerry's familiarity with the authors we were pursuing increased. In 1983, I purchased a newly published microfiche set of the National Union Catalogue, which allowed me to add, for some of the rarer titles, locations of copies in major North American libraries. I kept a set of photocopies of all the descriptions in the office. In a way these were, for me, the collection, as I rarely saw the books themselves in Short Hills.

However little we depended on auctions, it is nonetheless fair to say that certain ones did serve as marker buoys in charting the progress of the collection, none more so than the sale of "highly important" English literature from the library of H. Bradley Martin, which took place at Sotheby's in New York on April 30 and May 1, 1990. The dispersal of this library had begun the year before with a series of sales devoted to an extraordinary collection of ornithology, followed by sales in January 1990 of Americana and children's books. But it was the English literature, of course, that was important as far as Jerry was concerned. Bradley Martin's holdings were diverse, but he had a special passion for what were then known as "Hayward titles," after an exhibition at the National Book League in London in 1947, orchestrated and catalogued by John Hayward, a prominent bibliophile and the editor of the *The Book Collector*. Hayward had assembled a display of 346 "first and early editions of works of the English poets from Chaucer to the present day," and in time Bradley Martin had found copies of most of them, including virtually everything from the nineteenth century.

I had come to know Bradley quite well during the last few years of his life, when he got into the habit of dropping by my office on East 69th Street from time to time, to buy the odd book, or often just to chat about recent acquisitions or forthcoming sales, for which he sometimes gave me bids. After his death I was called in by his lawyers to do an estate appraisal of his English and American literature. My instructions were, somewhat unusually, to try to predict what the books would fetch at auction, and as a result I had to examine them rather more closely than I would normally have done. I'd never been keen on appraisal work, but this was a special challenge, and aside from anything else, there were a number of books that Jerry and I had a serious interest in.

24

By this time Jerry was well established in private practice, and had significantly more money to spend on his collection. When the catalogue of Bradley's English literature appeared, Jerry and I spent hours going over all the lots of possible interest, trying to decide which we most wanted, and to devise some sort of strategy for the sale. In the end Jerry came up with an overall budget of $50,000, which represented a major step up in financial terms. We had never even discussed such a figure before, but at the same time it was nowhere near enough to buy everything we wanted. In the end we could do little more than hope for the best. We were both in a state of high excitement. When I stopped by the office the morning of the sale, the woman who worked for me handed me a three-by-five card with a few last-minute phone messages. I still have the card tucked inside the front cover of my catalogue; one of the messages reads, "Dr. Wachs called—Good luck. Spend money."

I had quite a few other commission bids, and had marked a substantial number of lots as possible purchases for stock, so I was pretty busy throughout the sale. For Jerry's purposes, by the luck of the alphabet, there was nothing of great interest until some seventy-five lots had gone under the hammer and we were well into the Bs. Then came *The Improvisatore, in Three Fyttes*, by Thomas Lovell Beddoes, published at Oxford in 1821, when the author was only eighteen. This was a book Jerry and I had discussed, as Beddoes is classified in the *NCBEL* as a major poet, and this, his first book, is also a Hayward title, which is why, of course, it was in the Bradley Martin collection. I had appraised the book at $1,000, but by the time of the sale I had decided that this was too low, perhaps much too low, partly because I was unable to find a record of another copy for sale in recent years, and partly because this particular copy was in a very appealing black morocco binding of the period, and bore on the title page the signature of the author's aunt, the well-known Irish novelist Maria Edgeworth. From our point of view it would have been hard to ask for anything more: a major poet, a Hayward title, a great rarity, a beautiful copy, a perfect provenance. The mark in my catalogue reflects a mixture of enthusiasm and uncertainty. What it reads is "ar++/ k," which means "$2,500 plus a couple of bids, but maybe go up to $4,000." In fact I got the book for $4,000 hammer; with the gallery premium and

25

my commission we had spent $4,800, and were off and running. This remains the only copy of the book I have ever seen for sale.

About seventy-five lots later came a copy of Byron's *Curse of Minerva* (1812), a satire on the removal of the Elgin Marbles from Greece, printed in a small number of copies for private circulation, and a notorious rarity. I had appraised this for $25,000, but for some reason Sotheby's had estimated it only at $5,000 / $7,000; when I bought it for $14,000 hammer, it seemed rather a bargain, even though it was by some margin the most expensive book we had as yet acquired. This, too, remains the only copy I have ever seen on the market. We went on to get a number of other exceptionally nice books, including one of my favorites in the entire collection, a copy of the first edition of the most famous of all poetry anthologies, Palgrave's *Golden Treasury* (1861), inscribed by England's leading critic, Matthew Arnold, to his counterpart in France, Charles-Augustin Sainte-Beuve, with a long letter about the history of English verse tucked in. By the end of the sale I had spent something like $50,500, and Jerry's collection had taken a major leap forward.

There were at the same time a number of disappointments, which gives an idea of how far we had progressed, and how far we still had to go. I let a nice copy of FitzGerald's *Rubáiyát* go at $13,000, even though this was a title Jerry particularly wanted, on the grounds that another copy was bound to turn up. Toward the end of the sale were two very rare prose pamphlets by Shelley, *An Address to the Irish People* (1812), appraised by me at $40,000 but estimated by Sotheby's at only $10,000 / $15,000, and *A Proposal for Putting Reform to the Vote*, by "the hermit of Marlow," appraised at $45,000 but estimated to bring $15,000 / $20,000. These were two titles I feared we would never see again. Despite the fact that by this time I had used up Jerry's budget, I recklessly went ahead and bid on them, with fear and trembling. In each case I wound up the underbidder, at $30,000 and $33,000. I found out later that they had been purchased for Harry Oppenheimer, the South African diamond magnate, who was also a book collector, with a penchant for the Romantic poets. We were not in his league.

Nor could we compete for two exceptional first books, Elizabeth Barrett Browning's *Battle of Marathon* (1820), which fetched $45,000, which I thought was quite reasonable, and Robert Browning's *Pauline* (1833), which sold for a more robust $70,000, almost exactly what I had appraised it for. Books like these were as yet in the realm of fantasy.

Jerry had by this time acquired a couple of small adjacent apartments in a new high-rise on Broadway, just opposite Lincoln Center, which he rented out on short leases. Not long after the Bradley Martin sale, he decided to knock down the connecting wall and turn them into a single apartment for his own use. The important thing from my point of view was that he also decided to move his book collection into the city, and to this end he had special shelving made, with glass doors. When the books arrived we unpacked them together and arranged them on the shelves, roughly in *NCBEL* order. Some weeks later Jerry did an inventory check, just to make sure everything was in place. It turned out one book was missing, a nice copy of James Hogg's *Queen Hynde* (1825); a search of the shelves in New Jersey proved fruitless, and in the end we decided that we must have left it at the bottom of one of the cartons in which the books had been packed for transit.

The new setting was a bit startling, to put it mildly. Jerry's apartment was on the thirty-second floor. The front door opened onto a large room decorated entirely in black and white, with the odd splash of bright red, and dominated by what was then called an "entertainment center," consisting largely of an enormous television screen with speakers on either side. Down a corridor to the left, past the bedroom, was a rather narrow room that had been turned into a kind of office, and it was here, along the two facing longer walls, that the books were housed. There were now more than four hundred titles in the collection, and the effect of seeing them arrayed in surroundings that were essentially minimalist, and pervasively modern, was curiously pleasing. Now for the first time I could literally see what had been achieved over the course of twenty years; this physical sense of the books was inspiring, as was the fact that there was a lot of empty space on the shelves.

About this time we began to discuss the possibility of having some kind of exhibition. The obvious venue was, of course, the Grolier Club, to which I had belonged for as long as I had known Jerry. I had taken him there any number of times, but somehow he had never shown much interest in becoming a member, though he had for some time been amply qualified, as a book collector. Now, however, he had a good reason to join, so we set about gathering the necessary letters of recommendation and arranging an interview. Everything went according to plan, and Jerry was admitted to membership in 1993.

We were soon able to book space in the small exhibition room on the second floor of the club, for January to March 1995. In fact the room was not all that small, and I was apprehensive at first that we might not have enough nice things to fill it up. In the end I picked out almost 150 titles, which proved to be about the right number. The show began in the hall as one emerged from the elevator, where there were two large glass cases suitable for about thirty broadsides and pamphlets. Almost the first thing to meet the eye was our most recent acquisition, a copy of *Fare Thee Well!* (1816), the poem Byron wrote on the occasion of his controversial separation from his wife. As T. J. Wise had once described this original printing as "practically impossible to acquire," Jerry and I were pleased to show it off. The rest of the books were attractively arranged in roughly chronological order around the main room. The exhibit had a slightly cluttered look, which I found appealing, and not inappropriate for a collection that was essentially textual, rather than visual, in its focus.

To accompany the exhibit I had prepared a printed catalogue, which I called a "progress report," containing a lightly annotated checklist of the entire collection. To this I asked Jerry to contribute a foreword, not knowing quite what to expect, as I had never actually seen anything he had written. What he came up with was completely genuine, and rather charming in a self-deprecating sort of way. He included a quotation that he had stumbled across during a visit to Wordsworth's Dove Cottage. It was from James Beresford's *Bibliosophia* (1810), defining its title, and Jerry's passion, as "an appetite for collecting books—carefully distinguished from, wholly unconnected with, nay absolutely repugnant to, all idea of reading them." The truth is that Jerry knew rather more about what we were doing than he let on.

The timing of the exhibit was fortunate in that it coincided with the annual meeting of the Bibliographical Society of America, a number of whose members showed up for drinks on opening night. I think Jerry was a little taken aback to see, for the first time, people looking at his books who knew something about them and appreciated his collection. It was also a new experience to meet acquisition librarians from such venerable institutions as Harvard, Yale, and Princeton, a few of whom were quick to express envy at seeing the odd title not represented in their collections. To possess something that someone else would like to own is, of course, one of the joys of collecting, but it was not a pleasure that Jerry had as yet felt. I remember that Bill Cagle, then the director of the Lilly Library, took away a copy of the checklist that I had prepared, and sent it back a month later diligently marked up against the library's holdings; much to our satisfaction, there were a surprising number of titles that the Lilly did not have.

Not long after the exhibition Jerry allowed his membership in the Grolier Club to lapse. We never really discussed why he did this, but I suppose on the simplest level the club, from his point of view, had served its purpose. About the same time he became involved in the American branch of the Keats-Shelley Association, of which he was for many years the treasurer. Jerry had also for some time been active in the Baker Street Irregulars, and was sufficiently knowledgeable about the exploits of Sherlock Holmes to be assigned the task of compiling an annual quiz with a high degree of difficulty for meetings of the New York chapter. At some point he also began to collect Sherlockiana. I never really became involved in this pastime, but I could see books and pamphlets accumulating at a rapid rate in a small back room. It was not long before this new collection was quite substantial; Jerry used to say that he would sell it if I ever found something really good in the way of nineteenth-century poetry, but I always assumed he was joking.

In the spring of 1996 I closed my shop. My wife, a Londoner, had decided that ten and a half years in New York were quite enough, and we agreed to move to England. Within a year we had acquired a large house in a village about thirty miles west of Oxford, and a few miles from the source of the Thames, which ran along the bottom of our garden. Here, there was plenty of room for me to work from home. Neither Jerry nor I had any idea what to expect from the abrupt relocation of Ximenes, but as it turned out new titles were acquired more or less as if nothing had happened. When I visited New York, which was two or three times a year, I always stayed with Jerry, and slept on a spectacularly uncomfortable convertible sofa, surrounded by his books. Inevitably we had long discussions about the progress of the collection, and for the first time the possibility was raised of one day publishing a proper catalogue. Jerry was very keen on the project, and I began in a desultory fashion to update and amplify some of my earlier descriptions.

In 2001, Jerry suddenly announced that he had sold his Sherlock Holmes collection. He had by then managed to acquire virtually all the obvious rarities, and had reached the point where there was little of interest still to find. His decision to sell proved to be rather well timed, as it coincided with the rapid expansion of the Internet, which provided an ideal platform for the sale of old books. I don't think anyone in the book trade realized how quickly the market would change. At first, booksellers with large inventories experienced an explosion of sales, as the listing of titles on such sites as Bibliocity began to reach a much larger customer base than had ever been possible in the past. All too soon, however, the presence of multiple copies on offer, often of titles once thought to be scarce, inevitably resulted in a downward cascade of prices. The most immediate effect was upon specialist booksellers, who found it difficult to charge a premium for their expertise. A well-defined field like Sherlockiana was a perfect example of this phenomenon; had Jerry waited five years longer to sell his collection, he might well have had trouble getting half what he had been paid.

In any event, Jerry now had a substantial sum of money to spend, which in his mind had always been earmarked for his poetry collection. His notion, which made sense, was to spend it on one great book. These were the circumstances that led us to revisit the question of the two Browning first books, at the sale of which in the Bradley Martin auction eleven years earlier we had been merely spectators. Both, as it happened, were still in the hands of a private collector, who, in his retirement, had begun to sell some of his books. The situation was pretty straightforward. Both were available, at more or less the same price, but we could afford only one of them. Which to choose?

Elizabeth Barrett's father had privately printed her *Battle of Marathon* (1820) in an edition of fifty copies for her fourteenth birthday. Of the fifteen copies known to survive, only the Bradley Martin copy, inscribed to her grandmother, is in a private collection. Robert Browning's *Pauline* was issued by the well-known London booksellers Saunders and Otley when he was twenty-one. There is no reliable record of the print run, but the book attracted little notice, and many unsold copies were returned to the young author, who later destroyed them. The latest census, in 1984, lists twenty-three copies (not thirty-eight, as stated by Sotheby's, whose cataloguers inadvertently conflated the locations of both Browning titles); again, all but the Bradley Martin copy belong to institutional libraries (though the Turnbull copy in New Zealand was stolen in 1940, and has never resurfaced). In the end we went for absolute rarity, condition, and charm, and chose *The Battle of Marathon*. Aside from anything else, the binding of *Pauline* was rather worn.

In the spring of 2002, I heard on the grapevine that Simon Nowell-Smith's books were coming up for sale. This was exciting, and a bit worrying. Simon was, of course, already a major name in the world of book collecting and bibliography when I first came into the trade in the 1960s, and he gradually became a very occasional customer. At some point in the late 1970s he paid a visit to my office in New York, during the course of which he invited me to come see his books in Headington, on the outskirts of Oxford. As the focus of Simon's collection was as close to Jerry's as any I had as yet encountered, I was keen to find out what he had, so I took up his offer on my next buying trip to England. As it turned out, there was much to see and much to talk about. Simon's house became a regular stopping-off point during the early 1980s.

As a younger man, Simon had been a keen collector of a number of writers, including Henry James and a group he called "the four Georges" (Borrow, Eliot, Meredith, and Gissing). These collections, however, had been sold off over the years, partly because they were essentially complete, and partly because the proceeds made it possible to pursue other areas of interest. In his later years, Simon chose to concentrate on English poetry, from the Romantic period to World War I. By the time I got to know him, he was in the habit of selling off batches of minor titles to fund the acquisition of major rarities, and as a result Jerry already owned a handful of books with the Nowell-Smith book label, which I had picked up in the course of my wanderings.

Simon's first wife had died in 1977, a year or two before I first met him. In 1986 he married again, and one way or another we lost touch with one another. Simon died ten years later, after spending his last three years in a nursing home. He had left his books to his widow, but no one I knew had any idea where she was, or what she intended to do with them.

In the end it turned out, much to my surprise, that the collection had been sold to the London firm Bertram Rota Ltd., specializing in modern literature. As soon as I found out about this, I rang the owner, Anthony Rota, whom I knew, and asked what was going to be done with the books. Anthony told me that a substantial catalogue was planned, and that his son Julian was in charge of it. When I asked if I could see the books, I was told that they were all at Julian's house in Kintbury, a village near Newbury in Berkshire, about half an hour from where I lived. I got the impression that the catalogue was imminent.

I don't think I had ever met Julian before, but I figured there was nothing to lose by giving him a call. When we spoke, I gave him a brief history of Jerry's collection. His response was sympathetic, and he invited me to come over the next day to see the books. That evening I got in touch with Jerry, who responded with great enthusiasm; he told me that I should buy whatever I could, and that he would find the money somewhere. I realized that despite my various visits to Headington, I had only a very general idea of what I might find.

As it happened, the timing was ideal. The books were all priced, and the catalogue had been written, but it had not yet gone to press. A handful of titles had already been sold to a couple of private collectors, but basically everything was still available, and Julian was happy for me to pick out whatever I wanted. My experience had been over the years that in situations like this it was common to give various major libraries a head start, but happily this was not the case for the Nowell-Smith books. They were all arranged on shelves alphabetically by author, and I sat down to go through them one by one. The collection was not as large as I had feared. Leaving aside the twentieth century, there were about six hundred titles, which was roughly the same number Jerry had.

First came a group of seven titles by William Allingham, who was someone of possible interest, but the books all seemed rather expensive, especially a copy of his first book, *Poems* (1850), at £1,750. I decided to leave them, at least for the time being. There were a dozen Matthew Arnold titles, but nothing we were missing. The first thing I saw that I felt we had to have was a nice copy of *Orra: A Lapland Tale* (1822), by the Dorset poet William Barnes; this was something I had never seen before, and it seemed very reasonable at £425. I had already picked out half a dozen titles by the time I reached T. E. Brown, who had written a number of rather sophisticated poems in the Manx dialect, much admired by such contemporaries as George Eliot and Robert Browning. Simon had had a particular interest in Brown, and had published a checklist of his first editions in *The Book Collector* in 1962. His holdings included four of the earliest titles–three printed in Douglas, on the Isle of Man, and one in Cockermouth, in Cumbria, on the mainland, not far away. These regional imprints were all obviously very rare, and seemed cheap at prices ranging from £150 to £400. I particularly liked the Cockermouth imprint, a poem called *Christmas Rose*; Simon's copy had been heavily marked up by Brown himself for a Macmillan reprint in standard English, to make the rather racy text acceptable to a wider Victorian audience.

As I went on I was able to fill in a number of gaps in Jerry's collection by such major writers as Byron, Coleridge, Leigh Hunt, Shelley, and Tennyson. I added half a dozen titles by Walter Savage Landor, who was one of Simon's favorites, but someone whose early works I had found especially difficult to acquire. My general feeling was that Jerry's books were, on the whole, in better condition than Simon's, but in a few cases I decided to upgrade. Simon's copy of Charles Lloyd's first book, *Poems on Various Subjects* (1795), was very attractive in original boards, and much better than Jerry's disbound copy. By the time I was finished I had selected about sixty titles. There were a number of things I had rejected on the basis of price, but not so many that I felt any great sense of frustration. I came across a few things Jerry already had that I thought had been underpriced, and I suggested to Julian, as much out of gratitude as anything else, that he mark these up. The one I particularly remember was Arthur Hallam's *Timbuctoo* (1829), an unsuccessful entry in a Cambridge poetry competition won by his new friend Tennyson. Jerry had acquired a copy a few years earlier, and at the time the only other example I could locate was at Yale. Julian hadn't paid much attention to this unassuming pamphlet, and had marked it a few hundred pounds. At my suggestion he added the phrase "extremely rare," and raised the price to £10,000, rather more, I am sure, than what I had suggested. When the catalogue came out, however, there was an order from a private collector; the copy reappeared some years later at auction, and is now at Harvard.

The Nowell-Smith purchases were exciting, to be sure, but it was at the same time a relief to see that they did not overwhelm what we already had. In the years to follow, our pace of acquisition slowed a bit, not from any lack of enthusiasm, but because there were simply, among the major writers at least, fewer gaps to fill. That being said, there were still some notable additions to follow, such as Wordsworth's first two poems, Coleridge's *Fears in Solitude*, Byron's *Euthanasia*, Shelley's *Adonais*, Arnold's *Alaric at Rome*, and, at last, FitzGerald's *Rubáiyát*. Jerry used to amuse himself from time to time by compiling a "top ten" want-list, but the truth is that most of the titles he came up with were either unobtainable, or unaffordable, or both. There really wasn't much point in listing Byron's first book, *Fugitive Pieces* (1806), known in three copies, or Shelley's *Necessity of Atheism* (1811), which would have cost a fortune in the unlikely event a copy came on the market. When Jerry asked me for a realistic want-list, I found it difficult to come up with one. I might have started out with something like Coleridge's *Ode on the Departing Year* (1796), which was potentially affordable (though something we never managed to find), but it was difficult to think of another nine titles of comparable allure. There were a few gaps in Jerry's holdings of writers like Byron or Browning, but these tended to be common titles, and relatively minor ones, and they inspired little sense of urgency.

That being said, there was no sense in which either of us thought of the collection as complete. The whole notion of "completeness," in fact, had long since become irrelevant. What was much more important, though I don't think either of us actually put this into words, was not the collection's size, but its shape. In the beginning, I had attributed Jerry's preference for the major poets to inexperience, but in time I came to share his bias, albeit with a certain reluctance, as I found many of the minor writers amusing to explore. We could, in theory, have added hundreds if not thousands of lesser titles, even within the limits of the *NCBEL*, but it became clear to both of us that to do this would alter the nature of the collection. One way or another a balance between major and minor writers had evolved that we both felt was somehow appropriate.

In 2007, Jerry turned seventy, and I followed suit a year later. The pace of acquisitions gradually slowed to about one title a month, as opposed to one a week, as had been the pattern in prior years. It was not at all that we had lost interest in the collection, but rather that our focus had begun to change. Jerry had no particular concern about what would happen to the books, as he had for a long time taken the position that they would simply be left to his children, to be dealt with as they pleased. His principal concern was that there should be some sort of printed record of what we had achieved together. I had much sympathy for this notion, and began, in a haphazard way, to revisit some of our earliest acquisitions and bring the descriptions I had provided up to date. Over the next few years, Jerry returned again and again to the idea of creating a proper catalogue of the books; this, it became clear, was what he truly wanted.

As I began to look at the collection as a whole, it was difficult not to wonder at the odd trajectory we had followed. A theme had been chosen pretty much at random, and yet somehow we had managed to create a picture of an era in which seemingly everyone was obsessed by verse, employing the technology of print to communicate in a manner not dissimilar to the use of electronic media in the present day. But Jerry and I were not, after all, serious readers of nineteenth-century poetry. What the collection had become was not an expression of a passion for literature, but more an exercise in social history.

This exercise did involve an element of scholarship, which could at times be entertaining, as books were acquired with evocative provenance, or revealing annotations. There was one slightly comical occasion a long time ago, when I came across a book published in 1848 called *Poems and Songs*, by "E. H. B." It is cited in the *NCBEL*, and elsewhere, as the first appearance in print of Edward Henry Bickersteth, who went on to become a distinguished Anglican clergyman, and a prolific writer of popular hymns. The only trouble was that this copy bore a presentation inscription at the front "by the son of the authoress," whose gender was confirmed in the text by such poems as "A Mother to Her Sleeping Child," and "A Mother to Her Son on His Birthday." Only recently, some thirty years later, the hint provided by Jerry's copy led Angela Phippen, a researcher in Sydney, to find a specific reference to the book in an obituary for the prominent nineteenth-century lawbook publisher Henry Butterworth, which appeared in *The Gentleman's Magazine* in January 1849; it turns out that the "E. H. B." who wrote the poems in Jerry's book was his wife, Elizabeth Henry Butterworth. In the end we managed to find a significant number of books that had elements of scholarly interest, ranging from inserted letters not previously published, to hitherto unexamined manuscript revisions and annotations. No doubt there are other discoveries to be made, and conundrums to be solved.

But Jerry was in no sense an academic, and his primary motivation was not the scholarly potential of his books. He was, essentially, a collector, and as a result of our collaboration I became a collector by proxy. The historical record of book collecting is rather less well documented than one might expect. Over the years, many of the best collections have been either absorbed into larger institutional holdings or dispersed at auction; whatever printed record survives tends to be more a list of titles than a narrative of how and why they were acquired.

A notable exception is Michael Sadleir's *XIX Century Fiction: A Bibliographical Record Based on His Own Collection* (1951), which has a long preface entitled "Passages from the Autobiography of a Bibliomaniac." Sadleir was a publisher by profession, a writer by avocation, and a scholar by instinct, but more than anything else he was an incomparable book collector. He was fascinated by such things as condition and rarity. In the early 1930s a collection came on the market from a country house called Mount Bellew in the west of Ireland. The library consisted entirely of books published between 1770 and 1830, virtually all of which were in a remarkable state of preservation, as Sadleir describes in his preface: "Practically without exception the books were not only in wrappers or boards as issued ... but as clean and new as the day they had first appeared. ... Indeed it would hardly be possible to over-state the perfection of Bellew condition or the excitement of those Bellew days, with parcels from Dublin trickling in and immaculate treasures slowly encumbering my table." This is the language, and these are the emotions, of a collector.

It is no longer possible to collect nineteenth-century books on the scale that could be achieved when Sadleir was active. The supply from country-house libraries has been pretty much exhausted, and virtually all that did emerge in the past is now to be found in institutional libraries. The principles, however, that Sadleir followed, in what he modestly called his "hobby," remain germane. Books from Mount Bellew have now essentially vanished from the market, but about twenty-five years ago I stumbled across one remnant of the library, a two-volume anthology called simply *Selection of Poems*, published in 1808 and printed in Newark, not far from Byron's ancestral home at Newstead Abbey. Of the editor, Charles Snart, little is known, but he appears to have been one of those enthusiasts of verse with which the century was richly populated. His anthology includes many of his own poems, and some by his friends, along with others by such major figures as Samuel Rogers, Robert Southey, and Coleridge. But far more important than the text was the physical condition of this set, with the light blue paper boards, white paper backstrips, and printed paper labels in a Mount Bellew state of perfection. Charles Snart does not appear in the *NCBEL*, but there was without doubt a place for him in Jerry's collection, if only as an act of homage to a master.

Sadleir characterized himself as a bibliomaniac, but in a way the epithet is misleading, as the pastime he described is something more appealing than a mere obsession: "The hunt was a delight and the examination of my captures an education." The metaphor of the chase strikes a chord. This, if anything, is what Jerry and I were up to in our pursuit of nineteenth-century poetry, in original state, as issued. To what extent we succeeded, the catalogue of the collection will testify.

The Wachs Collection:
An Introduction   Stuart Curran, *President, Keats-*
Shelley Association of America, and Emeritus Professor, University of
Pennsylvania Department of English

Gerald N. Wachs, hereafter Jerry (as he was universally known), joined
the Board of Directors of the Keats-Shelley Association of America in
1986, the year before I was appointed to the same body. As a fellow
Director and subsequently also serving as its President, I had a continu-
ing interrelation with Jerry for more than a quarter century, until his
untimely death in 2013. This body holds two meetings a year, and Jerry,
though a physician with a large practice, never missed one of them. He
brought dedication, solicitude for the Association's well-being, and good
counsel to our gatherings, and also something else, an almost ingenuous
enthusiasm for the poets we revere and an abiding sense that, though
he was by no means averse to critical analysis and scholarly investiga-
tion of them, they were not merely subjects for academic study but had
been bequeathed to successive generations as enduring treasures, and
that it was his good fortune, like others in the English-speaking world,
to have inherited that singular trust. Extending that fervor to authors
across the long nineteenth century, in 1970 he embarked—with the
dedicated assistance of Stephen Weissman, the deeply knowledgeable
owner of Ximenes Rare Books, who compiled this masterful catalogue
of the Wachs Collection—on a forty-year voyage of discovery that culmi-
nated in the most substantial private assemblage of nineteenth-century
British poetry that we are ever again likely to encounter, one that is as
distinguished in its depth as it is wide-ranging in its scope.

When we became acquainted, Jerry had already moved from New
Jersey, where he had established his medical practice, to Manhattan,
where he occupied a home with a commanding view of the Lincoln
Center Plaza. There, in what would have been intended by the architects
as an internal study, he constructed his library. So serious was he as a

39

guardian, so careful a conservator, that his books were not lodged on open shelves but rather were enclosed in climate-controlled cabinets with wooden doors. It was not at all a large room. There was nothing palatial in its appointments to complement the rarity of its contents. Rather, it was a simple, even austere setting. But then Jerry opened the cabinets housing his collection, and the spectacle flashed before one's eyes: all of Keats, all of Shelley (except the very early juvenile poems), a great swath of Byron, a plentiful sweep of Hunt over his long career. Those were only the Younger Romantics–the line of treasures went on and on, from one end of the century to the other, as rare to the sight as in its contents.

When Jerry proposed this endeavor to himself, it was probably not as quixotic an enterprise as it might seem today. For one thing, a generation ago he was functioning within a highly traditional focus. Great literature, in the understanding that had prevailed until around the 1840s, had always been synonymous with poetry. Even in the Victorian period, when novelists were celebrities, and some of them, like Dickens, became very rich, it was first Wordsworth, then Tennyson, and finally Browning who were crowned with laurels and elevated to the cultural status of sage. Then, on a practical level as well, in the 1970s older collections were still customarily broken up at the end of their collectors' lives and sold at auction rather than bequeathed to libraries. In addition, comparatively speaking, noteworthy editions were still reasonably priced. The impediment to a collector, with rare exceptions, was not finding a particular book, but, as the Wachs Collection exemplifies, in finding *the* particular copy that stood out. The process is sharply delineated by the catalogue entry for Robert Browning's two volumes of *Dramatic Idyls*: "This book and the next were added to the collection at a very early stage; we soon decided that there needed to be something special about copies of common titles of this sort to make them worthy of inclusion." Observing this principle, the preceding four items in the poet's oeuvre are all presentation copies in Browning's hand. In the case of Matthew Arnold, Jerry managed over time to acquire ten separate presentation copies, which must constitute something of a record. Where such close association of book to author might not be feasible, Jerry could fall back on the family circle: the Tennyson holdings here are thus centered.

There was a third element that, for better or worse, allowed Jerry to imagine the long-term feasibility of his project: the decision to undertake his pursuit mainly within the boundaries established by *The New Cambridge Bibliography of English Literature* (NCBEL), whose 1969 revision would have seemed in all respects current when Jerry started seriously collecting two years later. There was at the time no real alternative. The various catalogues of books in English at this point were ambitious but, beyond their alphabetical organization, unsystematic; the *English Short-Title Catalog* (ESTC) had yet to be extended into the eighteenth century; and attempts to recover a complete nineteenth-century record of publications in English were still years off. So, the *NCBEL* at least offered an informed template from which to project a framework for collecting. At the same time, it was formulated around the authorial canon of midcentury, which in many ways was both ahistorical and arbitrary in its judgments. Thus, for example, Walter Scott, celebrated by Francis Jeffrey in the August 1810 *Edinburgh Review* notice of "Lady of the Lake" as a poet who "has manifestly outstripped all his competitors in the race of popularity; and stands already upon a height to which no other writer has attained in the memory of any one now alive," was classified as a minor writer of verse and barely noticed in the Wachs Collection, whereas Leigh Hunt, who is historically of less significance but is designated by the *NCBEL* as major, is amply accommodated—indeed, with some extremely rare and important prose documents over and above an ample array of his poems. The canon of "British" (as distinguished from "English") poetry of the nineteenth century has undergone a seismic shift in the nearly half century since the *NCBEL* was published. Most notably this has involved the recovery of once central, but over time marginalized, women authors: in the Wachs Collection, among Romantic poets Mary Robinson is represented by one publication, *Lyrical Tales*, whose very title suggests that its interest is dictated by its association with Wordsworth and Coleridge; Charlotte Smith, the obsessive psychological orientation of whose *Elegiac Sonnets* marks the inception of Romanticism in Britain, is notable for her absence; and Jane Taylor, inventor of a strikingly modern vernacular style, appears only incidentally among the youthful poets of Josiah Conder's *Associate Minstrels*. Both Elizabeth

41

Barrett Browning and Christina Rossetti are richly represented in the collection, but such contemporary figures as Eliza Cook, Emily Hickey, Amy Levy, Constance Naden, and Augusta Webster, who are now widely anthologized, were not even on the historical horizon when the *NCBEL* was compiled.

Even given the limitations within the field of knowledge that constricted Jerry as he contemplated this lifelong enterprise, however, the fourth critical aspect to the assembling of this collection was his approach to it as a lover of books rather than as a scholar of the field. The nineteenth century in English studies has long been plagued by a sharp division, as the customary capitalizations by their nature acknowledge, between Romanticists and Victorianists. The former tend to see their subjects as rooted in the eighteenth century but forecasting late twentieth-century values (or in the case of Byron's "Don Juan" even current postmodernism). Victorianists tend to start with Victoria and to look forward, so to speak, to her eldest son, Edward. But a collection that refuses such clear distinctions tells a somewhat different story, bridging divisions rather than magnifying them. One of the clear results is that the Wachs Collection as a whole represents a remarkable excursion through the material history of the nineteenth-century book of poetry. Quartos give way to octavos then to duodecimos, as the reading public expands and the prices drop; illustrations begin to accumulate with the advances in lithography. Then, in the later Victorian period comes the invention of the rare book as marketable commodity. The compulsive forger Thomas Wise, who is much commented on as the catalogue reaches its third phase, exemplifies the extreme manifestation of a common phenomenon, the veneration of the book as mystified artifact. The most amazing quotation to be found in Weissman's erudite commentary may be that of Charles Dodgson (Lewis Carroll) in planning for the distribution of his ingenious nonsense poem "The Hunting of the Snark," first published in an enormous edition of ten thousand for a presumptive eager general public. But that public is not where Dodgson focused his interest as he instructed his publisher, Macmillan, to produce an entire secondary run of copies: "'100 in red and gold, 20 in dark blue and gold, 20 in white vellum and gold,' along with 'four miscellaneous covers to be used in binding 4 copies for me.' The following year he described these special bindings in a letter to Maud Standen: 'I have had them bound in various coloured cloths with a ship and bell-buoy in gold: e.g. light blue, dark blue, light green, dark green, scarlet (to match Alice), and, what is perhaps prettiest of all, white i.e. a sort of imitation vellum which looks beautiful with the gold.'"

Observing the complexity of these instructions, we are apt to forget that the object involved—that is to say, the particular poem here so fancifully gussied up—was written to make no sense in a normative linguistic environment. Dodgson contemplated a book reduced (or elevated, perhaps, in his perspective) to the status of visual artifact, only liminally connected with the conventional verbal import of a piece of writing.

"The Hunting of the Snark," as encountered here, presents an extreme case of decoration as substance. But it also provides a lens through which to perceive how valuable is the final third of the Wachs Collection, in its material features, for deepening our understanding of the history of book design. The rarer the particularized copies in the collection the more useful they are for the study of the book as aesthetic object or for more clearly delineating the attempt, which begins intermittently with the pre-Raphaelites in the 1850s and grows exponentially across the ensuing decades and into the early twentieth century, to merge verbal and visual elements, the sister arts of poetry and design. These are rare books in the most refined sense; like Blake's illuminated works they are irreducible objects, each with its vital integrity. Each must be seen as a whole: felt; hefted; marveled at, first page by page and then as an overall objet d'art. Such books may be seen as wholly resistant to the threat posed by modern technology to democratize the distinctive nature of rare books and to eradicate their privileged status.

That is to say, at one point what we today designate as rare books were often essential documentary records. A poet like Wordsworth often revised poems from one printing to the next, so that by the time he prepared what was presumed to be the final, authoritative edition, the original form of the poem had been altered in crucial ways. A modern "authoritative" edition will customarily give us all the variants, edition by edition, eliminating the need to return to the succession of versions of the text in one volume after another. There are, of course, limits to such a variorum presentation. In the case of Robert Southey, he so significantly rewrote his poems every time he republished them that, for instance, the "Joan of Arc" of the final authorized edition in 1837, revised one last time when Southey was a calcified reactionary, is a substantially different work from the almost seditious first edition of 1796. (That first edition is also an overtly feminist text, as we are reminded in the Wachs Collection by a gift of the original printing from "the Ladies of Llangollen," Lady Eleanor Butler and Sarah Ponsonby, to the "Swan of Litchfield," Anna Seward.) With such disparate versions of a poem there can never be a definitive text. Still, even with this complication, the growth of digital libraries means that, if all editions of this poem are not yet fully and universally available to any reader at any time or place, it is just a matter of time before the lacunae will be filled in. What does that then mean for the practical application of a great collection of rare books such as the one Jerry Wachs spent more than forty years assembling?

We could answer such a question by reverting to the obvious sense of proximity to genius when we come face to face with the original *Lyrical Ballads*, or what Wordsworth in his "Mutability" sonnet called the "unimaginable touch of Time," when we contemplate the materiality of its original light blue boards. It is theoretically possible even in the twenty-first century that we will find in a rare-book library a never-before-discerned variant. Two years ago, by chance, I discovered in the Huntington Library a copy of Shelley's London imprint of *The Cenci* in which the standard "Second Edition" on the title page had been replaced with a colophon. Solving the mystery of why Charles Ollier, Shelley's publisher, would reset an entire title page still eludes me, even as it remains a gnawing question. Such an interrogation of necessity leads us into the actual conditions and even exigencies of the publishing world as it was then constituted and so on into an ever-widening circle of scholarly inquiry: the smallest typographical detail may thus potentially harbor major repercussions. The Wachs Collection, if paradoxically we pursue its contents beyond the examples of the great masterpieces it contains, does this as well and in many different ways.

Let me suggest some of these that are, of course, tailored to my own personal interests. When Jerry acquired his copies of Coleridge's two periodicals, *The Friend* and *The Watchman,* exceedingly rare in their complete runs, they had already been published in the multi-volume Bollingen edition of that writer's complete works, so, beyond their rarity, his copies were not necessarily to be thought of in terms of utility. But Jerry's runs of two ephemeral periodicals in which Keats (and in the latter case also Hazlitt) published, *Annals of the Fine Arts* and *The Champion,* allow any curious scholar to understand how their contents and general intellectual bearing might contextualize Keats's writings, both in poetry and prose, and to pursue the subject by browsing around the periodical's issues. Institutions have since digitized the *Annals* and deposited the files in the Hathi Trust, so, with some difficulty caused by being confined to a page-by-page perusal, this kind of investigation is now available in a digital form as well. *The Champion,* however, is likely to elude such publication because of its very rarity and to necessitate access to the actual text for a similar pursuit for Keats (and, it should be said, for Hazlitt as well).

Association and presentation copies can be useful for tracing biographical connections, for establishing a hierarchy of family relationships or friendships, and the like, but they can also tell us something crucial about an author of whom we might not have been aware. It is a matter of conjecture, for instance, when Shelley gave a copy of *The Revolt of Islam* to Maria Gisborne, an old friend of Godwin's, who resided with her husband, John, in Livorno, but its existence testifies to the poet's continuing esteem after his removal to Italy for what history has denominated his least successful major venture, as well as to his sense that its entrenched political and social radicalism would be acceptable to Gisborne's principles. The additional fact that the copy bears the Buxton Forman bookplate provokes interesting questions about its provenance that are detailed in the commentary. An even larger question surrounds the truly remarkable copy of the first printing in 1839 of Blake's *Songs of Innocence and of Experience,* which was a gift to Robert Browning at a crucial stage in his development, between the publications of *Paracelsus* (1835) and *Sordello* (1840). Although the "historical tragedy" *Stafford* intervened in 1837, here in his twenties Browning seemed to be embarking on a career of long narratives distanced from contemporary concerns. Yet it is at this very point that Browning's poetic orientation markedly changed to the portrayal of subtle inner dynamics, enjoining the reader's participation in plumbing the psychological recesses of characters speaking in monologue. Shelley's early influence on Browning has been long acknowledged, but this copy of Blake has the capacity to startle one into asking whether Blake's nuanced voicings in the *Songs*, so complex in their seeming simplicity, so demanding of the reader's responsiveness to unassuming signals, might have had a formerly unacknowledged be-cause undeterminable influence on Browning's maturing preoccupation with how experience forms and deforms character and how perception transforms reality. That Browning often juxtaposed complementary or contrasting perspectives, culminating in the brilliant multiple frames of *The Ring and the Book*, might also indicate Blake's influence.

Balancing the assemblage of major works by major authors in the Wachs Collection is a counter-thrust toward a historical residuum, where the catalogue determines that a volume constitutes the single copy known of a particular text. To have a work so distinguished is a boon to scholars who would be hard put to identify such relics from a source like *WorldCat*. Two of these volumes are by Tennyson: his *Ode on the Opening of the Exhibition, 1862* and Henry Irving's acting edition of *Becket*. Although the works in question are known, these particular imprints have not been, and thus they must have an impact, even if a minor one, on the historical record. In another case, one that perhaps underscores the fragility of all printed texts, the title page of a volume of verse known in only this single copy refers to an earlier publication by the same poet that apparently has not survived.

Of comparable rarity and of much greater scholarly utility, it might be said, are texts in this collection that bear authorial additions to the manuscript. Such a text can be useful for mapping disparate cultural landscapes, as is the case with a fascinating item in the collection, Thom-as Edward Brown's *Christmas Rose*, a narrative poem in Manx dialect, which in this authorial copy was being transformed for re-publication through the main-stream firm of Macmillan. Its reader can observe the remarkable overlay of the original, at times racy, diction in dialect with Brown's attempts to render it into acceptable standard English and at the same time conform to a stricter Victorian code of values, plus the Macmillan editor's blue-penciling to make certain no blush whatsoever would be raised upon the countenance of the Mayfair maiden who might peruse it in the proper metropolis. There are also in the collection several more substantial manifestations of authorial rethinking. It may be thought that the numerous revisions to William Watson's *Ode on the Day of the Coronation of King Edward VII* are unlikely to return that text to the pride of place it occupied in 1902; still, they are preserved in this collection. Of much greater moment, however, are texts by two poets of real prominence. The rarest of all volumes in the Wachs Collection is its copy of Elizabeth Barrett's youthful venture into sanguinary Homerics, *The Battle of Marathon,* which was the last example of this privately printed production of a sixteen-year-old prodigy still in private hands. It appears from other copies that Barrett continuously reworked the poem even after it was printed. In this copy there are a further twenty-four alterations not known before. In the same key, two different texts from Landor's long poetic career, *Poetry* (1802) and *Heroic Idyls* (1863), bear extensive revisions: the latter is a proof copy the rewritings in which were never incorporated into the final published version. Clearly, these are revisions in both instances that will need to be assimilated to the scholarly record.

There are, to my mind, two documents in the Wachs Collection that are truly exhilarating to come upon. One of these might seem to many decidedly obscure, Thomas Doubleday's *Sixty-five Sonnets . . . [and] a Few Miscellaneous Poems*, published in 1818. I first encountered this volume while writing *Poetic Form and British Romanticism* (1986). Doubleday was by no means the only then unknown author I encountered in researching that study, but he impressed me with the assuredness of the craft displayed in this collection of sonnets. The examples lack the compressed depth of his major contemporaries, but they are, in the aggregate, works of significant art, looking forward, in ways that, say, Keats and Wordsworth do not, to the tonalities of Victorian word-painting in the sonnet form. I printed one in that study, and the Feldman-Robinson collection, *A Century of Sonnets* (2002), printed another three, so Doubleday may be said to have made at least a cameo appearance on the modern poetic stage. But it turns out that he was not alone in this venture, that one William Greene shared the volume, having contributed twenty-seven sonnets to it and five further poems among the miscellany at the end. If we have hardly yet given Doubleday credit as a poet of genuine merit, nothing at all appears known of this co-author (who, for all we know, could be the person responsible for the four sonnets reprinted in our time). The manuscript notes in this volume are not significant just because they add previously unknown information about its contents but also because they suggest that if Doubleday's minor fame is to be resuscitated, it would appear that we will have to locate Mr. Greene in the process. This volume in the Wachs Collection offers us a literary puzzle well worth solving.

Something of the same intimation of discovery surrounds the volume put together from numerous ephemeral publications by Richard Monckton Milnes, gathering writings from the group of twelve young literary men at Trinity College, Cambridge, in the late 1820s who designated themselves as the Apostles. Of these, of course, it was Tennyson who went on to gain preeminence as major poet and laureate. The multiple contents of Milnes's unique volume, however, allow us to contextualize Tennyson within the group, to read, for example Arthur Henry Hallam's submission of *Timbuctoo* for the Chancellor's Gold Medal in 1829, which was won by the eighteen-year-old Tennyson with a poem by the same title. Among the prizes here is the first English edition of Shelley's *Adonais* (1829), which the Apostles had printed in Cambridge. There is probably such a wealth of new material in this volume as to allow a much fuller account of the influences on, as well as the activities and cultural range of the individuals comprising, the Cambridge Apostles.

Because the nineteenth century in British literature has been so rigidly demarcated between Romanticism and Victorianism, the decade and a half following the death of Byron in 1824 remains far too little comprehended. Richard Cronin's *Romantic Victorians, 1824–1840* (2001) endeavored to fill the void, but, though a fine study, it concentrates heavily on the writers whom we understand in retrospect to have been major.

48

Such an approach has the tendency to reproduce the faults of the *NCBEL*, taking for granted and thus reinforcing rather than testing prior categories. As the Milnes compilation of ephemeral writing by the Cambridge Apostles suggests, the Wachs Collection documents this period with a particular richness, and the organization of the catalogue is of a signal value in that it allows scholars who wish to pursue the various literary dynamics of these years a concentrated survey from which to begin new thinking. That may also be the case in the late decades of the century as well, when the elderly Browning and Tennyson, though beyond their prime, were still held in such high regard that it was difficult for younger writers to find a station in British culture from which to project new voices. In retrospect, the obvious new energy is Anglo-Irish in its impetus, mainly stemming from Wilde and Yeats, though Hopkins (and later and in prose Joyce) are likewise characteristic of this vital cultural exuberance. But that there were many competing voices (and visions) in the 1880s and '90s is amply documented by the Wachs Collection.

Others perusing this catalogue will discover further riches that I have not remarked in this brief survey of what Jerry Wachs accomplished through forty years of devoted collection. His stipulation that every addition to his library have some truly distinctive feature means that the collection is not just of rare books but of genuine treasures. That in this late day there is so much that is new, even where there is so much that is major, is a testament to how valuable was that decision in ensuring a library of enduring magnitude and importance.

Poetry's Empire: "The Songs of Humanized Society"

James Chandler, *Barbara E. & Richard J. Franke Distinguished Service Professor, Department of English; Director, Franke Institute for the Humanities; and Chair of the Department of Cinema and Media Studies at the University of Chicago*

It is an honor and a pleasure to contribute to this catalogue. It is an honor because of the distinguished collection of Dr. Gerald N. Wachs that it documents and celebrates. It is a pleasure both because of the treasures that Dr. Wachs managed to assemble and because of the beauties of the exhibition that was so thoughtfully mounted to provide a sense of it. It is also a distinct personal pleasure to be involved in this project. To prepare for writing this essay, I, too, spent some time working in the closed stacks of the Special Collections Research Center, University of Chicago Library, where the larger part of the Wachs Collection is housed, nearly seven hundred books strong. Wonderful as it was to browse those many shelves of rare books, there was an added dimension for me in this experience, for my first job at the University of Chicago was in fact here at Special Collections. This was long ago, in the dark backward and abysm of time when I was in graduate school. I'd been hired to write copy for an exhibition catalogue by the legendary Robert Rosenthal, then head of Special Collections in the still-spanking-new Regenstein Library. The exhibition (also sponsored by the Library Society) displayed some of the most important items in the collection of Helen and Ruth Regenstein. Writing them up was a dream job for a graduate student in English: I was paid a decent wage to hole up in Special Collections reading great books in original editions and determining how best to comment on them in a short space.

It brought back fond memories to return to that place recently for the first time in more than forty years. Remembering my experience with the marvelous Regenstein collection, I was struck by an interesting

51

difference between it and the one that Dr. Wachs had already begun to undertake at that time. For while the great Regenstein collection offers literary treasures that range over all of literature since the advent of the printed book, the Wachs Collection reveals a personal intellectual passion with a distinct subject and scope. Clearly, Dr. Wachs came to the determination at some point that British poetry of the long nineteenth century would be his mission. And his fidelity to that mission is evident in the way the collection took shape over the years. It is an edifice carefully crafted, literary brick by literary brick, to do justice to that great poetic corpus that stretches over the decades from William Blake to the early work of his great Anglo-Irish admirer, William Butler Yeats.

It must be said that Dr. Wachs chose his subject very well in the first place. The achievement of British poets in the nineteenth century is one of the cultural wonders of the modern world, like theater in the Elizabethan period and Dutch painting in the seventeenth century. Or, to stay with the nineteenth century, we might compare it to German music of that epoch, or French painting, or Italian opera. In all these cases, to be sure, one finds supreme accomplishments on the part of certain artists, writers, or composers: William Shakespeare and Ben Jonson, Rembrandt van Rijn and Johannes Vermeer, Gioacchino Rossini and Giuseppe Verdi, Gustave Courbet and Paul Cézanne, Ludwig van Beethoven and Johannes Brahms. But one also finds an enormous range of impressive work by myriad diverse hands representing, as it were, the robust creative culture from which the greatest work emerged. So it is, too, for nineteenth-century Britain. One finds towering figures like William Wordsworth and Lord Byron, or John Keats and Alfred Tennyson, or Percy Shelley and Robert Browning, but also a vast and diverse array of poets who published work that, in a different time and place, might have stood out even more visibly in historical retrospect. Some of these other poets, like Thomas Moore and Felicia Hemans, were widely known and read in their own moment. Others, like John Clare, the working-class poet haunted by mental illness, have been discovered and promoted in the years since. Even Blake, a case similar to Clare's, was relatively little known in his day until he was later championed by Algernon Charles Swinburne, also represented in the collection, and then by Yeats. It is part of Gerald Wachs's genius as a collector that he seems to have grasped all this very well. He recognized this body of poetry for the extraordinary thing that it is, and he understood something of its pyramidal structure, not least its wide, strong base.

For some of the great artistic efflorescences I listed above, we can readily find explanations of how they came about. For the great epoch of Dutch art in the seventeenth century, we can look to Simon Schama's *Embarrassment of Riches*. For the age of Rossini and Verdi in Italian opera, there is Carolyn Abbate and Roger Parker's *History of Opera*. But what about the extraordinary production of verse composition in nineteenth-century Britain? How might we begin to account for that? This is the question I mean to address in what follows.

ꝯ PART 1: UNACKNOWLEDGED LEGISLATORS

Any such explanation must begin at the beginning, with the period we call Romantic. Poetry of that era is dominated first by the generation that came of age at about the time of the French Revolution—Blake, Robert Burns, Wordsworth, Samuel Taylor Coleridge, Sir Walter Scott, Anna Laetitia Barbauld—and then by the generation that followed close upon them—Byron, Moore, Shelley, Keats, and Hemans. What were the conditions that made possible their great revolutions in poetry—large and small, high and low, near and far—that ramified through the century that followed and beyond?

In the first place, I would suggest, it has something to do with sheer talent, and literature, especially poetry, attracted persons of enormous talent in this early period. If one considers the Romantic poets counted as "major" in Dr. Wachs's ranking, just about all of them initially understood themselves to be in quest of other careers. Blake was a committed painter and engraver. Wordsworth went to Cambridge to pursue a career in law. Coleridge went to the same university to study for the ministry. William Hazlitt, who later reported being taken by his father, when still a boy, to see Coleridge preach in the mid-1790s, was initially going to be an art critic. In the next generation, Byron, supremely gifted as he was in so many ways, seemed destined for a career in politics at the time he gave his maiden addresses to the House of Lords in 1812. At the other end of the spectrum from the aristocratic Byron was Keats, the lowest-born of the so-called major Romantics, who matriculated at Guy's Hospital in South London to pursue a career in medicine. Four years before Keats's premature death from consumption at the age of twenty-six, such aspirations had long given way to his passion for writing poetry.

Keats's friend Shelley, three years his senior, lived only slightly longer, dying in a boating mishap in Italy at the age of twenty-nine. Shelley's case is especially telling, for his intellectual talents in *many* areas were of the highest order. He had an exceptional command of languages, including Greek and Latin. His translation of Plato's *Symposium* was standard until the twentieth century. He was well versed in both the history of philosophy and in economic issues such as monetary policy. His early work in

54

the natural sciences has been remarked upon by no less an authority than Alfred North Whitehead, who declared, in *Science and the Modern World*, that if Shelley had stayed with his early experimental work at Eton and Oxford he would have been "a Newton among Chemists." For all this, Shelley is known to posterity mainly as a poet, and that is because it was poetry to which he eventually dedicated the extraordinary energies of his brief life.

As it happens, Shelley also wrote one of the most beautiful and impassioned accounts of his vocation in 1821, one year before his death, in *A Defence of Poetry*:

> For the literature of England, an energetic development of which has ever preceded or accompanied a great and free development of the national will, has arisen as it were from a new birth. . . . The most unfailing herald, companion, and follower of the awakening of a great people to work a beneficial change in opinion or institution, is poetry. At such periods there is an accumulation of the power of communicating and receiving intense and impassioned conceptions respecting man and nature. . . . It is impossible to read the compositions of the most celebrated writers of the present day without being startled with the electric life which burns within their words. They measure the circumference and sound the depths of human nature with a comprehensive and all-penetrating spirit, and they are themselves perhaps the most sincerely astonished at its manifestations, for it is less their spirit than the spirit of the age. Poets are the hierophants of an unapprehended inspiration, the mirrors of the gigantic shadows which futurity casts upon the present, the words which express what they understand not, the trumpets which sing to battle and feel not what they inspire: the influence which is moved not, but moves. Poets are the unacknowledged legislators of the World.

This is heady stuff from the then-twenty-eight-year-old prodigy, who was one of the first to proclaim the distinctive achievements of the poets of his time. Moreover, his high claims for poetry help to convey a sense of what was then at stake in the commitment to this vocation. Note, too, that, underlying these words, one can find remnants of Shelley's explorations in fields that led him to becoming a poet. The phrase "electric life," for example, denotes a concept still relatively novel in 1821, one that Shelley became conversant with because of his scientific pursuits. Nor did he keep it to himself: the idea of life's being animated by electricity was, after all, the premise of his wife Mary's famous novel about a mad scientist called Frankenstein just three years before. In an earlier draft of the *Defence,* Shelley backed up his claim about the relationship between poetry and political freedom with an extraordinary piece of writing that intertwined the history of poetry and the history of politics since the Greeks, once again showing his high competence for other life pursuits.

The conviction about poetry's distinctive powers was shared by many writers of this moment, but the question was not pursued in hermetic isolation. Journals of the day hotly debated the tendencies and merits of volumes of verse alongside discussions of the great issues of this tumultuous age. It was, after all, an age when *print in general* came to be recognized as having a certain kind of power, when the book, the newspaper, the pamphlet were understood to reach and to move increasingly literate multitudes. Here we might think of Thomas Paine's *Common Sense* (1776), in the context of the American Revolution, or, in the context of the French Revolution, the 1789 pamphlet by the Abbé Sieyès—*Qu'est-ce que le Tiers État* (What is the Third Estate?)—which most historians consider an important trigger for the political chain of events that unfolded in Paris in 1789. It is telling in this respect that the older Hazlitt, looking back on this period from the vantage point of 1825 in his *Spirit of the Age,* would summarize the work of this time in a series of essays about, precisely, its most important *authors.* Three years later, reviewing the age for his *Life of Napoleon* (1828), Hazlitt would begin with a pronouncement that makes the unspoken premise of *The Spirit of the Age* quite explicit: "The French Revolution might be described as a remote but inevitable result of the invention of the art of printing."

France is not England, however, and printing is not poetry, so we still have some work to do to account for the extraordinary achievement that Gerald Wachs sought to capture with his impressive collection of books. This work requires us to engage with two larger and more complicated facts about Britain on the threshold of the nineteenth century. One is its distinctive position in the world as a modern commercial economy by

1800—even already by then an *industrializing* commercial economy. The other is its vast global empire, which in spite or because of the loss of the American colonies in 1783 was entering a new phase of political and cultural reach, not least in its power to extend the use of the English language around the world. In turning to those complex developments and their bearing on English poetry, I will focalize them somewhat through the eyes of Wordsworth. He is, after all, the poet who would come to be recognized throughout the century as the dominant voice of a certain vernacular and nationalist tendency in British poetry—a role Byron, by contrast, was too deliberately cosmopolitan and contrarian to play.

LYRICAL BALLADS,

WITH

Arabella Crawfurd from C.J.C.

15th March 1801

OTHER POEMS.

IN TWO VOLUMES.

By W. WORDSWORTH.

Quam nihil ad genium, Papiniane, tuum!

VOL. I.

SECOND EDITION.

LONDON:

PRINTED FOR T. N. LONGMAN AND O. REES, PATERNOSTER-ROW,

BY BIGGS AND CO. BRISTOL.

1800.

It is a credit to those who put this exhibition together that the first edition of Wordsworth and Coleridge's *Lyrical Ballads* is given its own separate case. Although its immediate reception was not earthshaking, *Lyrical Ballads* came to be understood as marking a watershed moment in the history of British poetry and it cast an especially long and strong shadow forward in the nineteenth century. Thousands of pages of ink have been spilled explaining the meaning of this fascinating publication–this literary *event*. For present purposes, I want to zero in on two points: one is that these volumes are explicitly framed as addressing a certain moment of British modernity, and the other that they are involved in a project of remedial archaism, a marked return to the style of an earlier time or a more primitive moment.

One way into the problem is to see how Wordsworth related his great poetic purposes at the close of the eighteenth century to the crisis he saw unfolding "at the present day." His account of this crisis and its causes, much influenced by conversations with his partner, Coleridge, stands as one of the earliest modern instances of what, in contemporary academic terms, we might now call cultural analysis within the framework of "critical media studies":

> For a multitude of causes unknown to former times are now acting with a combined force to blunt the discriminating powers of the mind, and unfitting it for all voluntary exertion to reduce it to a state of almost savage torpor. The most effective of these causes are the great national events which are daily taking place, and the encreasing [sic] accumulation of men in cities, where the uniformity of their occupations produces a craving for extraordinary incident which the rapid communication of intelligence hourly gratifies. To this tendency of life and manners the literature and theatrical exhibitions of the country have conformed themselves. The invaluable works of our elder writers, I had almost said the works of Shakespear [sic] and Milton, are driven into neglect by frantic novels, sickly and stupid German Tragedies, and deluges of idle and extravagant stories in verse.

Wordsworth was obliged to find a way for his poetry to sensitize his readers because of the condition into which they have been cast by his-

59

torically unprecedented social and cultural conditions. The litany may look familiar to us now—urbanization, the monotony of the modern workplace, political upheavals, technological speedup, even what we might now call "new media"—but few poets, indeed few persons, were thinking in such terms before Wordsworth. Standing on the threshold of the nineteenth century, in the nation with the most advanced commercial and manufacturing economy in the world, Wordsworth produced here an extraordinary act of cultural stocktaking to explain the motivation of his own poetic experiments.

The analysis is not, of course, *altogether* of his own making. His term for the contemporary condition—"torpor"—is borrowed from a somewhat earlier analysis along some of the same lines in what might seem an unlikely source: Adam Smith's *Wealth of Nations*, which laid the groundwork for the modern field of political economy. In the often-neglected book five of that work, Smith, writing a quarter of a century before Wordsworth, offered this analysis of the effect of the division of labor on individual workers:

> The man whose whole life is spent in performing a few simple operations, of which the effects, too, are, perhaps, always the same, or very nearly the same, has no occasion to exert his understanding, or to exercise his invention in finding out expedients for removing difficulties which never occur. He naturally loses, therefore, the habit of such exertion, and generally becomes as stupid and ignorant as it is possible for a human creature to become. The torpor of his mind renders him, not only incapable of relishing or bearing a part in any rational conversation, but of conceiving any generous, noble, or tender sentiment, and consequently of forming any just judgment concerning many even of the ordinary duties of private life.

Smith's twentieth-century reputation as unconcerned with the moral effects of commercial modernity, together with Wordsworth's disparaging remarks about him in print, has masked Wordsworth's debts to *The Wealth of Nations*. But the coupling of the key terms in their respective analysis—exertion and torpor—is hard to dismiss as coincidental.

Wordsworth also borrowed something from another older contemporary, Erasmus Darwin, who was part of that Lunar Society in Birmingham that helped to launch the so-called First Industrial Revolution two decades earlier. Grandfather of Charles, this Darwin was a theorist of psychological stimulation whose thinking carried some influence in that time. One of his case studies was borrowed for the experimental ballad "Goody Blake and Harry Gill," about a guilty man whose teeth will not stop chattering. In the preface to *Lyrical Ballads*, Wordsworth expanded on Darwin's analysis to include the effects of urbanization and communication technology, and, more to the point, he coupled this entire account with a wholesale critique of cultural production in his moment. Wordsworth roundly attacked the literature and theater of the late eighteenth century–singling out gothic fiction, Sturm-und-Drang theater, and sensationalizing ballads–for their tendency to cater to rather than combat the kind of "craving" that the social world of his moment had generated. To crave, in this context, is to be in need of outrageous stimulation. It is to be incapable of excitement without it. It is not to be able, in the relevant sense, "to feel."

Looking back on the previous half-century or so from 1850, on the occasion of Wordsworth's death, Matthew Arnold compared that poet's achievement with the only two contemporaries who could rival him in all of Europe:

> Ah! since dark days still bring to light
> Man's prudence and man's fiery might,
> Time may restore us in his course
> Goethe's sage mind and Byron's force;
> But where will Europe's latter hour
> Again find Wordsworth's healing power?
> Others will teach us how to dare,
> And against fear our breast to steel;
> Others will strengthen us to bear–
> But who, ah! who, will make us feel?

Byron teaches courage and Johann Wolfgang von Goethe teaches wisdom, both ancient virtues that date from the time of the Greeks. These virtues have surfaced and resurfaced over a long course of time. Odds are, suggested Arnold, they will again. What Wordsworth teaches is not easily captured in the classical lexicon of virtue that gives us, say, republican

61

bravery and Stoic philosophical resignation. What Wordsworth teaches is something more contemporary or recent in its provenance, something that Arnold intimated may in fact be singular, not replicable. It is not classical virtue. It may be closer to traditional Christian charity, but it is not that either. It is something more elusive, a power of healing that comes of a certain kind of feeling. And this has to do with Wordsworth's relation to the fact of modernity, with Britain's status at the turn of the century as the most advanced society in the world.

What exactly does it mean to say that Britain was the most "advanced" society in the world? The full explanation of such a claim can be found in lots of very readable books, such as the late Roy Porter's *Creation of the Modern World*. Suffice it to say here that from 1688 to 1800 Britain underwent a series of what might be called "soft revolutions" in a number of moments and domains. The first is the so-called Glorious Revolution itself, in which the British Parliament permanently displaced the monarch as the effective sovereign power in the kingdom. That momentous event was followed by the establishment of the Bank of England, which saw the emergence of a modern credit system in England and with it the idea of a new secular form of "futurity" (to use one of Shelley's favorite terms for a post-Christian eschatology). In the following decades Britain underwent further hugely transformative changes: the Union with Scotland; the new network of coffee houses and newspapers and with it the new "public sphere" of modern British life; extraordinary advances in naval and military power; the great theoretical advances of the Scottish Enlightenment; and, not least, the First Industrial Revolution, spurred by the work of the Lunar Society of Birmingham, including that of James Watt, inventor of the steam engine, and in its wake the network of manufactories and delivery systems that became a template for the Second Industrial Revolution some decades later.

The effects of this period of rapid and self-conscious development were explicitly registered in works of the Scottish Enlightenment, such as *The Wealth of Nations*. It was in this period, too, that Britain was poised to become, as William St. Clair has put it, a "reading nation." In London, the number of presses increased fourfold over the course of the eighteenth century. This did not reflect a similar rise in printed books or in readers, a surge that came in at the end of the eighteenth century, especially with the push for literacy from organizations like the working-class London Corresponding Society, and that was sustained through the nineteenth.

Wordsworth and Coleridge were well aware that they launched their poetic experiments at a pivotal moment for English readers. Two years before Wordsworth wrote his preface, Coleridge published a poem called "Fears in Solitude" (1798), written on the occasion of a threatened invasion of England's south coast by revolutionary France. (A copy of the first edition appeared in the exhibition at the Special Collections Research Center in 2015.) The poem offers a meditation on what we might call the new media of that moment and their effects on readerly sensibilities, and, in turn, on the politics of war:

> We send our mandates for the certain death
> Of thousands and ten thousands! Boys and girls,
> And women that would groan to see a child
> Pull off an insect's leg, all read of war,
> The best amusement for our morning meal!

The transformative poetry that Wordsworth and Coleridge produced could not be more explicit in situating itself in relation to this new military-industrial-*and*-media context that was Britain at the turn of the nineteenth century. Their precociousness is indeed astonishing.

But why would Wordsworth and Coleridge turn to "poetry," of all things, for the solution to the large problem they were coming to identify? This is in fact a question they themselves raised. In the 1800 preface to their joint venture, Wordsworth put it this way: "When I think upon this degrading thirst after outrageous stimulation I am almost ashamed to have spoken of the feeble effort with which I have endeavoured to counteract it." Almost, yes, but not quite. Wordsworth placed his hope in the enduring powers of poetry to keep us whole, to make us whole again, yet the gambit is a tricky one. Wordsworth was in the position of Cordelia at the beginning of *King Lear*, after Regan and Goneril have raised the rhetorical stakes with false claims and flattering calculations. What can the true voice of feeling have to say in such a circumstance?

For Cordelia, the answer was, "Nothing, my lord." For Wordsworth and Coleridge, nothing would not do. Their solution was to cast their lot with poetry, and in particular on what they both took to be poetry's powerful ancient resources. This committed them, I want to argue, to the somewhat paradoxical project of undertaking novel experiments in poetic archaism.

Archaism is an important and elusive notion, and one with particular relevance for the self-conscious modernity of nineteenth-century Britain. Archaism involves the deployment of forms and styles recognizable as primitive to readers or observers in a given moment. What often makes the use of archaism elusive to *later* observers—ourselves in relation to Wordsworth and Coleridge, say—is that the power to recognize it can be dulled with the passage of time. To take an example familiar to literary historians: Scott turned from a successful career in poetry in 1814 to produce *Waverley*, which many consider the first historical novel. In *Waverley*, everything depends on a fine-tuned interplay between the now and the then—between the present moment of 1805 and "sixty years since," when Scotland's highland clans staged their last-ditch effort to assert feudal claims in modern Britain. One reason that Scott's fiction lost its interest over time was that twentieth-century readers were no longer capable of seeing the play of archaism in the novels. At a certain *later* historical distance, Scott's "now" of 1805 and his "then" of 1745 had begun to merge into one time. We can even forget that Edmund Spenser's *Faerie Queene* was itself archaic in the sophisticated Elizabethan culture of the 1590s. Knights did not go pricking across the plain in the age of Shakespeare's urbane Globe Theatre.

Wordsworth and Coleridge found inherent in the very idea of poetry special resources for anachronism, and these had to do with two different aspects of verse composition: for shorthand we can call these "orality" and "residuality." As for the first, the origins of poetry in the media of the mouth and the ear, this was an emerging fact in the world of British poetics that Wordsworth and Coleridge inhabited. The late eighteenth century marked the beginning of a serious antiquarian movement that deepened interest in ancient forms of poetry, including studies in the Homeric epics and in less grand forms of oral composition. It would have been well understood by Wordsworth and Coleridge that verse

64

was associated in the first instance with preliterate media for cultural memory and transmission, with rhyme and meter serving mnemonic functions making it possible to perform important cultural functions. Oral poetry was, for the first societies, or for contemporary societies that had not yet been transformed by print, simply how the business of cultural memory largely got done. It was, in part, the association of the ballad with oral culture that led Wordsworth and Coleridge to seize on the ballad as the paradigmatic genre for their revolution in poetry. The "Advertisement" for the 1798 edition announced that they were going to save Britain's overheated, too-rapidly modernized culture from itself by returning printed poetry to its oral roots, to "the language of *conversation* in the middle and lower classes of society." Owen Barfield once termed this phenomenon "colloquial archaism."

If one kind of poetic archaism thus involves moving downward, so to speak, to a lower layer in the archaeology of media, another involves moving backward in the history of a practice. When the Pre-Raphaelites undertook their work in both painting and poetry some decades later, they committed to such a rolling back of the artistic clock. That is, they reversed the course of the history of symbolism to return to the state of painting and especially painterly symbolism as it was before the adverse intervention, as they saw it, of Raphael. This is a good way to understand what Coleridge did in "Christabel," or indeed in "The Rime of the Ancient Mariner," his primary contribution to the *Lyrical Ballads* project. "The Rime" is thus a "literary ballad" imagined as having been composed or transcribed in the late sixteenth century, with a Neoplatonic gloss from the late seventeenth century added later to create the version of the poem that we all know, with its distinctive sense of historical layering. "The Rime of the Ancient Mariner" might be said to dramatize most conspicuously the announced commitment of the authors of *Lyrical Ballads* to "the spirit of the elder writers" in Britain—that is, to a kind of *literary* archaism. In both cases, whether in "colloquial archaism" or in "literary archaism"—in the movement downward or backward—the effort is to effect a return to nature. The presumption is that such a restorative return can rescue a practice in danger of decadence or corruption. This new, paradoxical paradigm—the "literary ballad"— played out over the decades thence in ways that became important to Keats, Christina Rossetti, Swinburne, Thomas Hardy, Yeats, and beyond. (In our time, an archaic ballad like Bob Dylan's "Girl from the North Country" arguably belongs in this tradition.)

My suggestion, then, is that the Britain of the turn of the nineteenth century, in spite or because of its modernity, was deeply invested in archaic forms, especially in poetry, and that this is especially so for a central line of poetry developed by Wordsworth and Coleridge. It is part of what would constitute their importance to British poetry for decades to come, and part of what made poetry so central in British culture generally in this period. As I have already hinted, Coleridge's part of the bargain in partnering to produce *Lyrical Ballads* was primarily to explore the capacities of literary archaism, while at the start Wordsworth was more interested in colloquial archaism: the language of *conversation*. Eventually, though, Wordsworth synthesized the two dimensions of archaism, and this is perhaps one reason why his influence is so much greater than Coleridge's.

There is no more influential English poem in the nineteenth-century than the great lyric that is Wordsworth's first great ode—"Intimations of Immortality from Recollections of Early Childhood"—first published in *Poems in Two Volumes* (1807). Its complexities are rich and daunting, but a look at its famous opening can briefly serve to illustrate some of the points I have been making about archaism and modernity in this formative moment:

> There was a time when meadow, grove, and stream,
> The earth, and every common sight,
> To me did seem
> Apparell'd in celestial light,
> The glory and the freshness of a dream.
> It is not now as it has been of yore;—
> Turn whereso'er I may,
> By night or day,
> The things which I have seen I now can see no more.
>
> The Rainbow comes and goes,
> And lovely is the Rose,
> The Moon doth with delight

> Look round her when the heavens are bare;
> Waters on a starry night
> Are beautiful and fair;
> The sunshine is a glorious birth;
> But yet I know, where'er I go,
> That there hath passed away a glory from the earth.

Like Wordsworth's equally well-known (and exactly contemporary) sonnet that begins "The world is too much with us," the ode announces itself as a poem about the condition of existential modernity—a confrontation with a present experience drained of joy and meaning. To read it carefully is to see that the announced themes of loss and lapsed time are played out not only in a dizzying set of grammatical tense shifts. Some of the most important effects of Wordsworth's rich poetry in terms of time and memory are achieved with his play with tenses, not unlike the opening of Marcel Proust's *À la Recherche du Temps Perdu*. But if one looks more closely still, one sees that these are interlaced with stylistic shifts between archaic and nonarchaic ways of writing verse. The poem itself can be understood as addressing the problem of how poetry can be composed in the face of such anomie.

Part of the point of the opening stanzas is to show the poet struggling to begin his poem, but failing to do so as he moves among those different stylistic forms ("Turn whereso'er I may"; "But yet I know."). In that second stanza, for example:

> The Moon doth with delight
> Look round her when the heavens are bare;

The shift to present tense involves a grammatical archaism, "doth," that signals the larger stylistic archaism of this naïve and primitive lyric utterance. It's as if the mini-lyric that begins "The Rainbow comes and goes" were in quotation marks. The poet says: I can try to reinhabit the past world by way of archaism and write a lyric like this, but my modern skepticism won't allow me to sustain it. Something similar happens in section 3 in a pastoral, archaic register with the poet's lines about the lamb's bounding about to the tabor's sound. (It would be possible, with more time, to discuss this poem in relation to the distinction Friedrich

Schiller worked out in Germany a few years earlier in his seminal book *On the Naïve and Sentimental in Poetry* [1795].)

The larger point for the "Intimations" ode is that these poetic trials of various styles, archaic and otherwise, become the poet's own version of what he would later momentarily criticize in the young child he would describe. The child is presented as puzzlingly seeking to grow up too fast by inhabiting various forms of life, a wedding or a festival, a morning or a funeral, and so the young poet-in-the-making finds a métier: "unto this his frames his song / . . . as if his whole vocation / Were endless imitation." This leads the speaking poet to the central question of the poem, posed directly to the child in some of the most beautiful lines ever written in English. "Thou little child," the speaker asks:

> Why with such earnest pains dost thou provoke
> The Years to bring the inevitable yoke,
> Thus blindly with thy blessedness at strife?
> Full soon thy Soul shall have her earthly freight,
> And custom lie upon thee with a weight,
> Heavy as frost, and deep almost as life!

But in the poem's great peripeteia in the following stanza—"O joy that in our embers / Is something that doth live"—all this is changed, as the poet discovers the possibility of joy and meaning precisely in the child's wish to speed up time and risk loss. It is a joy, the poet explains, not for the child's "simple creed" but for his *skepticism,* our skepticism, an inherent mistrust of nature's satisfactions that the poet comes to see is implicit in both the child's and the poet's acts of imitation. By a familiar Wordsworthian move, then, we are ultimately invited to return to the poem's beginning and see that beginning in a new light, one in which the poet's apparently failed trying-on of archaic forms is likewise re-deemed—redeemed in spite or because of a doubt about the capacity of mere nature to satisfy our deepest longings.

⚓ PART 3: BRITANNIA RULES THE WAVES

As I've already suggested, this kind of redemptive effort became central for Britain in its precocious modernity all through the nineteenth century, though the great corpus of poetry is just one example of this. Ian Duncan has noted the extraordinary fact that this same Britain in the 1790s, for all its modern advances, developed a fascination with a certain kind of narrative archaism that took shape in the great flurry of gothic novels in that decade. Looking forward into nineteenth-century fiction, we might also think of the British novel's preoccupation with a certain premodern provinciality in Jane Austen, the Brontës, George Eliot, and Hardy. Even Britain's great novelist of urban modernity, Charles Dickens, worked out his sketches of contemporary London by way of an all-but-compulsive attraction to the out-of-the-way and the idiosyncratic: the archaic world of the provincial countryside often available for retreat, as in the conclusion to *Great Expectations*.

Nonetheless, poetry might be said to matter here most of all, because of the fact of what, borrowing from the exhibition's title, we might call poetic associations. Wordsworth himself made the point explicitly in the preface to *Lyrical Ballads* when he spelled out the implications of the very fact of poetic composition: "It is supposed, that by the act of writing in verse an Author makes a formal engagement that he will gratify certain known habits of association. . . . I will not take upon me to determine the exact import of the promise which by the act of writing in verse an Author in the present day makes to his Reader; but I am certain it will appear to many persons that I have not fulfilled the terms of an engagement thus voluntarily contracted." The associations that constitute the payoff of the poetic contract, the connotations of the specific measures and usages of verse practice, inevitably draw us into residual resonances, preexisting modes of feeling. The sonnet, the ballad, the ode, the song: all these poetic forms involve conventions that have prior histories—histories that are mobilized in "the act of writing in verse." Such resources, as Wordsworth and Coleridge recognized, gave poetry a special role in the effort to address Britain's problematic acceleration into social and cultural novelty.

The first context, then, for understanding why precisely Britain should have had this century-long literary efflorescence, and what precisely poetry had to do with it, is that of British modernity in relation to what I have called archaism. The second context, to which I now turn more briefly, is that of the British Empire, a vast enough subject that I can treat it only telegraphically in this connection. The largest frame to put around the issue is to say that on the eve of its great century of poetic production, Britain took its place in a succession of powerful (and of course overlapping) overseas empires that began with Portugal under Prince Henry, extended to Spain in the period of the Armada and the Conquistadors, Holland in the seventeenth century, and in heated rivalry with France in a series of struggles throughout the eighteenth century. By 1813, and certainly by 1815 with Napoleon's final defeat at Waterloo, Britain stood preeminent among the world's imperial powers. (That is, after all, one reason why so much of the world now speaks English.) For, even as Britain was losing its American colonies, it was securing its position in other parts of the globe: in India the British victory over the Mughals at the Battle of Plassey in 1776 set the terms for almost two centuries of British rule in South Asia; Captain Cook reached Australia in 1771; and the first convicts were sent to Botany Bay there in 1788. The British secured their power in Canada and other parts of the eventual commonwealth in this same period. And even as the American colonies pronounced their political independence, their cultural dependency on Britain remained strong for decades—these are battles Ralph Waldo Emerson was, of course, still fighting in the mid-nineteenth century.

How consciousness of the role of British culture in the wider world was registered in the printed record is something that can be determined in many ways. Early-nineteenth-century reviewers, for example, in what became something of a refrain, would trumpet the reach of British poets to the shores of the farthest rivers of the empire, to the Mississippi and the Ganges. But consciousness of the imperial project shows as well in locations that might surprise us, especially when it comes to poetry. One such place worth visiting briefly is the seemingly *domestic* epic in which Wordsworth invested more of his time and energy than any other, "The Recluse," a poem with a long first section, not completed or published in Wordsworth's lifetime, celebrating the poet's arrival "home at Grasmere." "The Recluse" was a massive epic for contemporary Britain, on which Wordsworth began work at the turn of the century, about the same time he was working on *Lyrical Ballads*. The second part of this epic was published in 1814 under the title *The Excursion*; itself a long poem in nine books, it was the only major part of "The Recluse" that would be published in his lifetime. It became a monument of nineteenth-century British poetry, admired by Keats, disparaged by the Shelleys, mocked by Byron. (Knowing its importance, of course, Dr. Wachs acquired a rare edition of it for his collection.)

Wordsworth explained the relation of *The Excursion* to the larger "Recluse" project in a preface and he appended some verses intended to serve, as he put it, as a kind of prospectus to the entire work. In these verses, Wordsworth announced, with a refined sense of existential

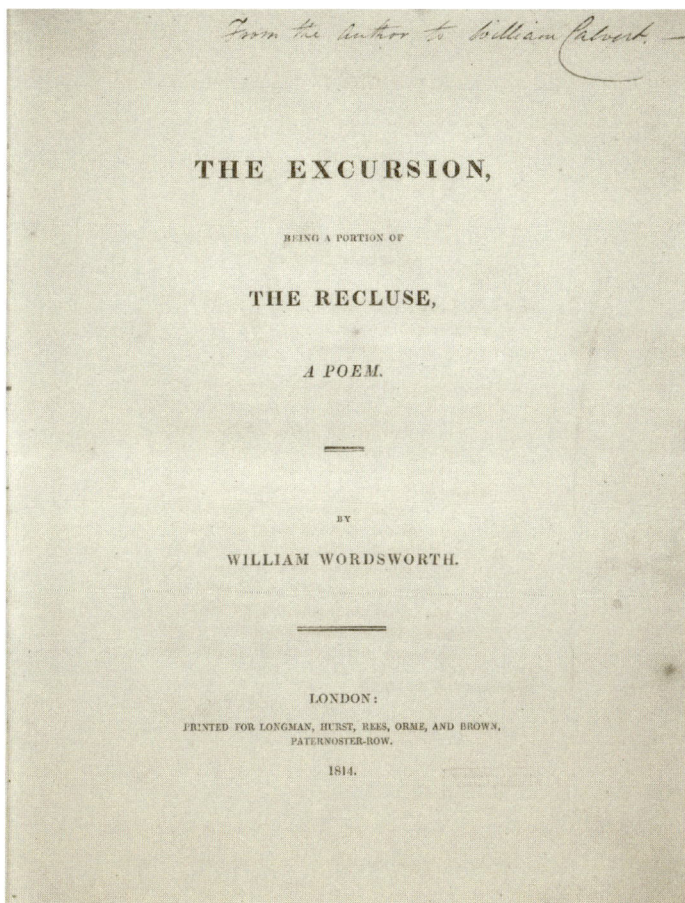

ITEM 16

THE EXCURSION,

BEING A PORTION OF

THE RECLUSE,

A POEM.

BY

WILLIAM WORDSWORTH.

LONDON:
PRINTED FOR LONGMAN, HURST, REES, ORME, AND BROWN,
PATERNOSTER-ROW.
1814.

modernity, that his would be an epic of a post-Enlightenment world, one that would take the human mind, rather than the ordered cosmos, as its starting point: "My haunt, and the main region of my Song." And this challenge meant that he would confront difficulties unknown even to Milton when he produced Britain's greatest epic to date, *Paradise Lost*. Even though Wordsworth marked his difference from Milton, his new epic is in a sense actually constituted by an extended archaism: for the entire poem is not only composed in Miltonic blank verse but is also riddled with residual tropes and topoi in what Wordsworth and Coleridge called the "the spirit of the elder poets."

The Excursion tells the story of a poet's encounter with various figures in a rural landscape—a priest, a reclusive atheist, and above all a garrulous peddler called the Wanderer, who narrates the stories that inform the life-world of the countryside. By the end of the nine books, and many stories in verse of "low and rustic life," the Wanderer escorts his guests to a high hill, in the manner of the prospect poem, stock and trade of English poetry, and waxes expansive with a vision of how British culture, and British poetry in particular, is likely to transform not only Britain itself but all the world, to the farthest reaches of its unrivaled naval and military prowess:

> Change wide, and deep, and silently performed,
> This Land shall witness; and, as days roll on,
> Earth's universal Frame shall feel the effect
> Even 'till the smallest habitable rock,
> Beaten by lonely billows, hear the songs
> Of humanized Society; and bloom
> With civil arts, that shall breathe forth their fragrance,
> A grateful tribute to all-ruling Heaven.
> From Culture, universally bestowed
> On Albion's noble Race in freedom born;
> From Education, from that humble source,
> Expect these mighty issues.

In his influential *Minute on Indian Education* (1833), Thomas Macaulay famously declared that the many shelves of Sanskrit literature were not worth a single volume of Shakespeare, advocating English as the standard language of education in South Asia. Macaulay's was a policy with massive ramifications for the modern world. It was perhaps the origin of what the Chinese now call "soft power." But here Wordsworth, two decades earlier, was already urging Britain, and specifically English poetry, to assume what he took to be its destined role in shaping a global cultural hegemony.

No wonder British men and women of talent were drawn to such an enterprise. They were drawn to the public sphere of print in general, to be sure, but they were drawn to composing poems, "songs / Of humanized Society," precisely because of the new role that poetry had come to be assigned in Britain's emerging civilizing mission. That word "humanized" is a complex term in this context and Wordsworth was clearly invoking both of its evolving senses around the year 1800. One is to make human, another is to make "humane"—that is, given sensibility, human kindness. In light of what I discussed above about Wordsworth's and Coleridge's new deployment of poetic archaism as a response to the *de*humanizing tendencies of British modernity, a certain paradox about the role of poetry in the age of Britain's highest imperial ascendency begins to come into view.

On the one hand, for writers as distinct as Smith and Wordsworth, Britain's advanced position in the world meant that its own city dwellers had to be saved from its newly industrialized commercial modernity. They had to be saved with the poetry capable of restoring them to their humanity by way of a return to nature in the archaizing gesture. But when facing outward to its widening cultural empire, that same poetry was asked to perform a different kind of humanizing function for the wider world reached by Britain's vast network of ships. It was asked to bring civilization to places that never knew it in the first place, places that included not only India, Australia, and America and the islands that dot the oceans that connect them.

In this latter, imperial context, it is hard not to be struck by Wordsworth's claim in the preface to *Lyrical Ballads* that the "causes, unknown to former times" hurtling Britain into modernity tended to reduce British subjects "to a state of almost savage torpor." In *Lyrical Ballads*, the healthy primitivism of the new literary ballad counteracts the decadent primitivism of the new urban insensitivity. In *The Excursion*, a decade and a half later, these same lyrical ballads writ large—as Britain's "songs / Of humanized Society"—were envisioned as the redemptive solution for "savage torpor" in its literal sense, as it was encountered by Britain's maritime imperialism on even the last habitable rock, beaten by the lonely billows.

In short, what Arnold later called "the healing power" of this poetry—its capacity to "make us feel"—must be understood *both* in relation to Britain's advanced modernity *and* paradoxically in relation to the far ends of the earth in what we might now call "the developing world." This goes some way, I hope, in explaining the sense of mission that helped produce the remarkable body of poetry represented in the Wachs Collection. Was Dr. Wachs aware of this aspect when he began collecting some decades ago? One cannot know for sure, but it is worth mentioning that one of the most valuable aspects of the collection are the holdings in nineteenth-century English poetry published in India both before and after Macaulay's 1833 *Minute*. And these holdings, I suspect, will prove to be among the most valuable for working scholars who come to consult the collection in future years.

The Gerald N. Wachs Collection of Nineteenth-century English Poetry

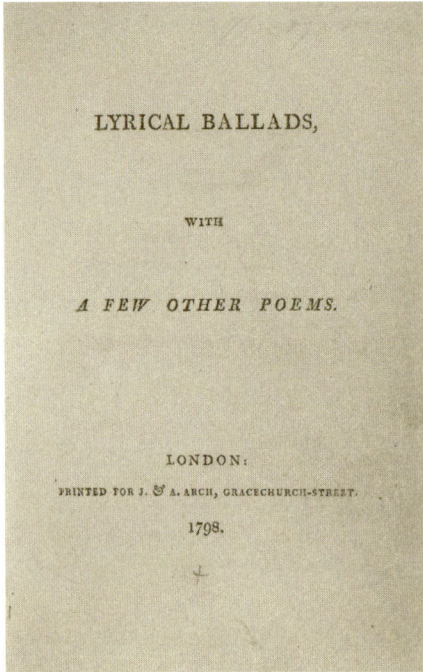

LYRICAL BALLADS,

WITH

A FEW OTHER POEMS.

LONDON:
PRINTED FOR J. & A. ARCH, GRACECHURCH-STREET.

1798.

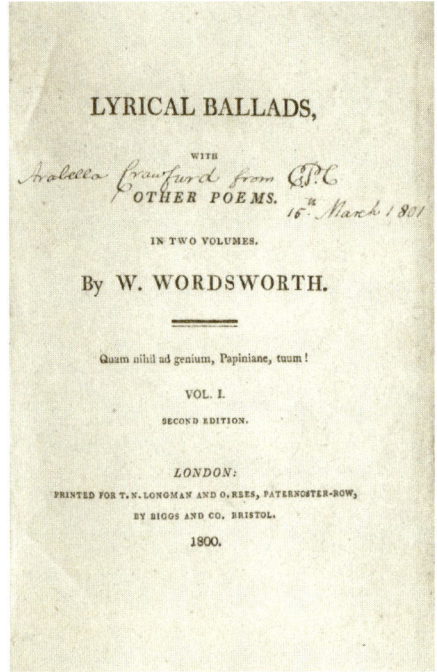

LYRICAL BALLADS,

WITH

Arabella Crawfurd from C.P.C
16ᵗʰ March 1801

OTHER POEMS.

IN TWO VOLUMES.

By W. WORDSWORTH.

Quam nihil ad genium, Papiniane, tuum!

VOL. I.

SECOND EDITION.

LONDON:
PRINTED FOR T. N. LONGMAN AND O. REES, PATERNOSTER-ROW,
BY BIGGS AND CO. BRISTOL.

1800.

ITEM 10   ITEM 11

The Early Nineteenth Century

℘ MAJOR POETS

SAMUEL ROGERS (1763–1855)

1. [Rogers, Samuel.] Verses written in Westminster Abbey, after the funeral of the Right Hon. Charles James Fox, October 10, 1806. [Colophon:] London: T. Bensley, printer, n.d. [1806]. 8vo, two leaves, removed from an album.

> An early owner has identified the authorship on the first page. The only other copies located are at the British Library, Harvard, and Wellesley College. Acquired in 1994.

2. [Rogers, Samuel.] Jacqueline. A poem. London: printed for T. Cadell and W. Davies; by W. Bulmer and Co., 1814. 12mo, bound with Part I of *Italy* (1822; no. 4), early blue straight-grained morocco.

> Shortly after this poem was printed, Rogers decided to publish it jointly with Byron's "Lara"; copies of this separate edition were never offered for public sale. The withdrawal of the printing is confirmed by the fact that the publisher's imprint on the title page has been crossed out in pencil. This copy is inscribed, "From the Author" on the half-title. Acquired in 1972.

3. Rogers, Samuel. Human life, a poem. London: John Murray, 1819. 8vo, original drab boards, printed paper label.

> First octavo edition; first published in quarto earlier the same year. For this printing three lines were added to the poem, and two of the notes were expanded. The Simon Nowell-Smith copy. Acquired in 2002.

4. [Rogers, Samuel.] Italy, a poem. Part the first. London: printed for Longman, Hurst, Rees, Orme, and Brown, 1822. Sm. 8vo, bound with *Jacqueline* (1814; no. 2).

> Rogers did not acknowledge his authorship of this poem until it was reprinted the following year by John Murray.

5. Rogers, Samuel. Italy, a poem. Part the second. London: John Murray, 1828. Sm. 8vo, early blue straight-grained morocco. Acquired in 1972.

6. Rogers, Samuel. The poetical works of Samuel Rogers. London: Edward Moxon, 1848. 12mo, original orange-brown cloth.

> This copy is inscribed on the front flyleaf, "Algernon C. Swinburne, from his affec. mother, Sept. 18th, 1849." Swinburne's early education had been carefully orchestrated by his parents, particularly his mother, Lady Jane Swinburne, who was a woman of considerable accomplishments. Soon after Easter, in 1849, when he had just turned fourteen, Swinburne was sent to Eton. About the same time, his mother took him to visit Samuel Rogers in London; the old man laid his hand on Algernon's head, and said, "I think that you will be a poet too." This volume was given to Swinburne when he was taken to the Lake District to meet Wordsworth, whose poetry the boy had attacked at school. Wordsworth was very gracious to his young critic, and said that he did not think Algernon "would forget" him, whereupon Swinburne burst into tears. This evocative association copy turned up in Australia. Acquired in 2001.

7. [Auction catalogue.] Catalogue of the very celebrated collection of works of art, the property of Samuel Rogers, Esq., deceased; comprising ancient and modern pictures; drawings and engravings; Egyptian, Greek, and Roman antiquities; Greek vases; marbles, bronzes, and terracottas, and coins; also, the extensive library; copies of Rogers's poems, illustrated; the small service of plate and wine: which will be sold by auction by Messrs. Christie and Manson. [London: 1856.] [Bound with:] Catalogue of the collection of Greek & Roman coins, early Italian medals, and medallions, &c. &c. of the late Samuel Rogers, Esq., which will be sold at auction by Messrs. Christie and Manson. [London: 1856.] Two vols. in one, 8vo, contemporary calf.

> The sale catalogues of the poet's art collections and library, auctioned five months after his death, which realized more than £45,000. Rogers was not a serious book collector, but in a long lifetime of accumulation he inevitably acquired some fine things, including a good George Washington manuscript, a first edition of the *Lusíadas*, an edition of Garth's *Dispensatory* (1703) with annotations by Pope, and a botanical work with notes by Rousseau.
>
> Remarkable testimony to his extensive literary friendships can be seen in the fact that among the 2,132 lots that made up the library proper, there were no fewer than 476 presentation copies, beginning with the poems

of Robert Bloomfield in 1802, and including inscribed books by such writers as Byron, Moore, Scott, Beckford, Crabbe, Southey, Babbage, Carlyle, Dickens, Herschel, Bulwer Lytton, Macaulay, Ruskin, and Tennyson. Of particular charm is lot 558, a set of Samuel Johnson's *Lives of the Poets* in ten volumes (1779), described as "the first book purchased by Mr. Rogers"; Rogers had attended the sale of Johnson's library in 1782. With the contemporary book label of Charles Rugge-Price. Acquired in 2007.

WILLIAM WORDSWORTH (1770–1850)

8. Wordsworth, William. An evening walk. An epistle; in verse. Addressed to a young lady, from the lakes of the north of England. London: printed for J. Johnson, 1793. 4to, brown morocco, by Sangorski & Sutcliffe.

> Wordsworth's first book, published at the age of twenty-three; his *Descriptive Sketches*, advertised on the last page as "just published," was in fact printed slightly later the same year. Writing in 1927, Wise described this quarto as "an extremely rare book." Approximately twenty copies can now be located. This is the Bradley Martin copy, purchased at the sale of his library in 1999 by James O. Edwards, who has added his book label. Acquired in 2008.

9. Wordsworth, William. Descriptive sketches. In verse. Taken during a pedestrian tour in the Italian, Grison, Swiss, and Savoyard Alps. London: printed for J. Johnson, 1793. 4to, half calf and marbled boards.

> Wordsworth's second book. He never reprinted the poem in this form; in later collections of his verse it is both revised and truncated. The Simon Nowell-Smith copy. Acquired in 2008.

10. [Wordsworth, William, and Samuel Taylor Coleridge.] Lyrical ballads, with a few other poems. London: printed for J. & A. Arch, 1798. Sm. 8vo, red morocco, by Riviere.

> Second issue, as usual, with the title page a cancel. No copy with the original Bristol title page ("printed by Biggs and Cottle, for T. N. Longman") was ever seen by us for sale, but had one emerged it would no doubt have been unaffordable. With the bookplates of Roderick Terry and A. Edward Newton. Acquired in 1983.

11. Wordsworth, William [and Samuel Taylor Coleridge]. Lyrical ballads, with other poems. London: printed for T. N. Longman and O. Rees; by

Biggs and Co. (Bristol), 1800. Two vols., sm. 8vo, original light blue boards, drab paper backstrips, printed paper labels.

> Second edition. Vol. 1 contains the first printing of Wordsworth's celebrated preface, a kind of Romantic manifesto, in which he explains in detail the theoretical basis of his new sort of poetry. The poems in the second volume are all new, and all are by Wordsworth. G. H. Healey, in *The Cornell Wordsworth Collection* (1957), says that "no copy with paper labels entirely intact is known to me." The labels in this set are perfect. This is a much better copy than Bradley Martin's, also in boards, which sold in 1990 for $14,300. There is a presentation inscription on each title page, "Arabella Crawfurd from C. P. C. 16 March, 1801." The signature "Mrs. Crawfurd" is on each front cover. The Gerald E. Slater copy. Acquired in 1982.

12. Wordsworth, William [and Samuel Taylor Coleridge]. Lyrical ballads, with other poems. Philadelphia: printed and sold by James Humphreys, 1802. Two vols., 12mo, contemporary tree calf, spines in six compartments with starburst devices in gilt, contrasting red and green morocco labels.

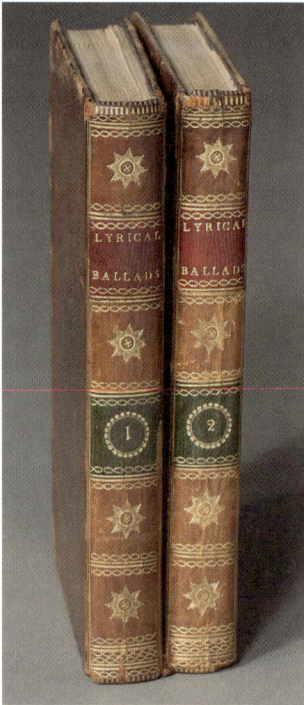

ITEM 12

> First American edition. The first appearance of Romantic poetry in the United States. A publisher's "advertisement" at the front of the first volume reveals that this set was published by subscription, and that considerable care was taken with the text. Humphreys also explains that the revisions made by Wordsworth for the latest London edition (the third edition, of 1802) necessitated a certain delay in the Philadelphia printing. The poems in vol. 1, however, are presented in the order in which they had originally appeared, and "The Convict," which Wordsworth had dropped in 1800, is still present. This copy, in a beautifully preserved Philadelphia binding of the period, is printed on paper of unusually high quality; the great majority of copies were printed on thinner paper, and bound two volumes in one. On the front flyleaf of vol. 1 is the penciled signature "Miss Fanny Vaux"; in vol. 2 the signature is that of George Vaux. Acquired in 1982.

13. Wordsworth, William [and Samuel Taylor Coleridge]. Lyrical ballads, with pastoral and other poems. London: printed for Longman, Hurst, Rees, and Orme, by R. Taylor and Co., 1805. Two vols., 12mo, contemporary green half morocco and marbled boards.

> Fourth (and last) edition. Included are a substantial number of revisions to the text of various poems; also present is the much revised and expanded text of Wordsworth's celebrated preface, as first published in the second edition of 1800. Acquired in 1996.

14. Wordsworth, William. Poems, in two volumes. London: printed for Longman, Hurst, Rees, and Orme, 1807. Two vols., 12mo, contemporary calf.

> With the book label of Viscount Mersey, Bignor Park, and his penciled note of acquisition from the bookseller Macleish, for £12 10s. Acquired in 1992.

15. Wordsworth, William. Concerning the relations of Great Britain, Spain, and Portugal, to each other, and to the common enemy, at this crisis; and specifically as affected by the Convention of Cintra: the whole brought to the test of those principles, by which alone the independence and freedom of nations can be preserved or recovered. London: printed for Longman, Hurst, Rees, and Orme, 1809. 8vo, bound with another work, contemporary half calf and marbled boards.

> Wordsworth's first published prose work, a passionate statement of political outrage, which was seen through the press by Thomas De Quincey. The title of this book, as first set in type, began *The Convention of Cintra . . .* , and Wordsworth's name did not appear. Three copies of this original issue are known, two of which belonged to De Quincey himself (British Library and Swarthmore), and one that was owned by Charles Lloyd (Berg Collection, New York Public Library). As published, however, the book bore a new title page with a much longer title and Wordsworth's name; also added was an errata leaf, and a two-page prefatory "Advertisement," dated May 20, 1809. There was one other last-minute change, to alter a phrase that Wordsworth feared too extreme. Bound in at the front of this volume is a pamphlet on currency depreciation by the political economist William Huskisson (1811). On a flyleaf is the inscription "J. T. Coleridge, C. C. C., Oxon, June 1811." The owner was Sir John Taylor Coleridge (1790–1876; see no. 34), a nephew of Samuel Taylor Coleridge. Acquired in 2007. A copy

of this scarce Wordsworth title had been purchased by Ximenes at the Arthur Houghton sale in 1980, but was not added to the collection because the binding was in poor condition. It took another twenty-seven years to find a suitable example.

16. Wordsworth, William. The excursion, being a portion of The Recluse, a poem. London: printed for Longman, Hurst, Rees, Orme, and Brown, 1814. 4to, early Victorian green calf, binder's ticket of Charles Thurnam and Sons, Carlisle.

In this copy, Y1 has not been canceled, and the two missing lines of verse have been supplied in manuscript. There are three other manuscript corrections in the same neat hand, on pp. 104, 149, and 195; the second of these is the same one Wordsworth himself made in a copy belonging to Benjamin Haydon, now at Cornell. This copy is inscribed on the title page, "From the Author to William Calvert"; the inscription is apparently in the hand of the recipient. Calvert, the son of a steward to the Duke of Norfolk, was one of Wordsworth's closest schoolboy friends, and one with whom the poet kept in touch. When Wordsworth returned from France in the summer of 1793, he stayed with Calvert on the Isle of Wight. The next year Wordsworth went with his sister, Dorothy, to the Lake District, and stayed at Calvert's farm near Keswick. He also visited Calvert's brother Raisley at Penrith. Raisley Calvert's health was failing, and he died of consumption soon afterward, leaving Wordsworth a legacy of £900; these funds enabled Wordsworth to avoid going into the church or the law. With the signature of Raisley Moorsom, Ramsdean (1948). Acquired in 1984.

17. Wordsworth, William. The brothers, a pastoral poem. New York: published by Richard Scott, 1815. 16mo, original mustard printed wrappers.

First separate edition; first published in *Lyrical Ballads* (1798). The second printing of Wordsworth in America. The only other known copy of this small pamphlet, at Cornell, lacks the printed wrappers, which have advertisements at the back for a miscellany of other recent publications. Acquired in 1993.

18. Wordsworth, William. The white doe of Rylestone; or the fate of the Nortons. A poem. London: printed for Longman, Hurst, Rees, Orme, and Brown; by James Ballantyne and Co. (Edinburgh), 1815. 4to, half brown morocco. Acquired in 1971.

19. [Barker, Mary, with William Wordsworth.] Lines addressed to a noble lord; (his Lordship will know why,) by one of the small fry of the Lakes. London: printed by W. Pople, 1815. 8vo, sewn, as issued.

A privately printed pamphlet, largely in verse, and one of the earliest separate pieces of Byroniana, whose significance and importance have only recently been discovered. Robert Southey met the author, Mary Barker, in Portugal in 1796, when he was only twenty-one; he was clearly captivated. The two appear to have kept in touch, and in 1814 Miss Barker was living next door to Southey and his entourage at Greta Hall in the Lake District. Here she became friendly with Wordsworth and his sister, Dorothy, and by October she was staying at Rydal Mount. At about this time Southey and Wordsworth were visited by the Scottish poet James Hogg ("the Ettrick Shepherd"), who showed around a letter he had received from Byron in which the "Lakers" were dismissively characterized as "Pond Poets." Miss Barker took great offence, and resolved to reply in verse. Surviving correspondence reveals that Wordsworth was persuaded to help, though his reluctance to participate is palpable.

The poem consists of sixteen stanzas, varying in length from ten to sixteen lines. Of these, Wordsworth contributed a couplet to stanza 8, and wrote most or all of stanzas 12 to 16; he was also clearly much involved in the opening stanza, and other words and phrases show his influence as well, but the details remain uncertain. The lines specifically about Byron are virtually all by Miss Barker; Wordsworth, by contrast, appears to have been less keen on a direct confrontation with his younger rival. The pamphlet ends with a fanciful seven-page critique of an article by Francis Jeffrey in *The Edinburgh Review*, in which Byron had been described as "England's leading poet." As far as one can tell, this critique is all by Mary Barker. Acquired in 2003.

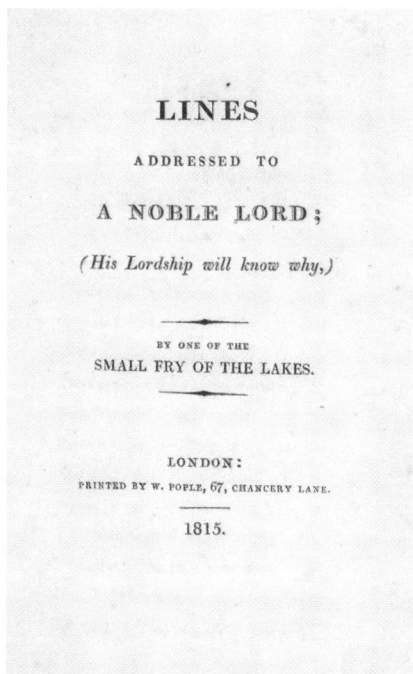

LINES

ADDRESSED TO

A NOBLE LORD;

(His Lordship will know why,)

BY ONE OF THE
SMALL FRY OF THE LAKES.

LONDON:
PRINTED BY W. POPLE, 67, CHANCERY LANE.

1815.

ITEM 19

83

20. Wordsworth, William. Poems by William Wordsworth: including lyrical ballads, and the miscellaneous pieces of the author. With additional poems, a new preface, and a supplementary essay. London: printed for Longman, Hurst, Rees, Orme, and Brown, 1815. Two vols. in one, 8vo, bound uniformly with a second volume containing six later Wordsworth first editions, nineteenth-century green morocco, by John Clarke of London.

> The first collected edition of Wordsworth's poetry, containing everything published previously save for *The Excursion*, along with some new poems, and a long new preface. These volumes came from the private collection of Michael Papantonio, a proprietor of Seven Gables Bookshop in New York. With the earlier bookplate of Charles Douglas Halford. Acquired in 1989.

21. Wordsworth, William. A letter to a friend of Robert Burns: occasioned by an intended republication of the account of the life of Burns, by Dr. Currie; and of the selection made by him from his letters. London: printed for Longman, Hurst, Rees, Orme, and Brown, 1816. 8vo, bound second in a volume of two works, contemporary polished calf.

> Bound in at the front is a collection of previously unpublished poems by Burns, printed in Glasgow in 1801. This volume was originally in the library of the poet and collector John Mitford, and bears his notes on the front flyleaf, along with two signatures, one of 1816, the other of May, 1826. It later passed to Richard Monckton Milnes, editor of Keats's *Poetical Works*, and bears the book label of his son Robert Crewe-Milnes, 1st Marquis of Crewe. Acquired in 1983.

22. Wordsworth, William. Thanksgiving ode, January 18, 1816. With other short pieces, chiefly referring to recent public events. London: printed by Thomas Davison; for Longman, Hurst, Rees, Orme, and Brown, 1816. 8vo, bound third in a volume of six titles (see no. 20).

23. [Wordsworth, William.] Westmorland election. To the independent freeholders, of the county of Westmorland. Kendal: Airey and Bellingham, printers, n.d. [1818]. Sm. folio, broadside.

> A hitherto unlocated Wordsworth broadside, signed at the end, "A Friend to Consistency," and dated January 30, 1818. This is Wordsworth's first contribution to the debate surrounding a parliamentary election in West-

morland. The text of this letter has long been known from its appearance in a local newspaper, *The Kendal Chronicle*, for Jan. 31, 1818; a reference appears in Wordsworth's correspondence to the letter also having been printed as a "handbill," but until now, no copy has surfaced. Whether the newspaper text, and the text of this broadside, are identical, has not as yet been determined.

In 1818, Henry Brougham (later Lord Brougham) came forward to challenge Lord Lonsdale's practice of nominating the two county members of Parliament for Westmorland; these were, in the election of that year, his sons William, Viscount Lowther, and Colonel Henry Lowther. This was a time, following the end of the years of war with France, of economic distress and political ferment among the working classes. Even Westmorland experienced some of this disaffection, and because of Brougham's unexpected intervention in local affairs, the county became for a brief time the center of a political storm. Wordsworth was both a supporter and a beneficiary of the landed interest. In 1805, Lord Lonsdale had made him a present of £800 toward the purchase of some land, and in 1813, he had obtained for the poet the post of distributor of stamps for Westmorland. Wordsworth also had a genuine attachment to Lord Lonsdale and his family, and when he first learned of a challenge to the Lowther interest, he quickly became passionately involved. This broadside first surfaced at an auction in North Yorkshire, where it was purchased by the booksellers James Burmester and Chris Johnson. Included in the lot were nine other broadsides relating to the same election, all printed in Kendal and most of them similarly unlocated; one is a direct response to Wordsworth. Acquired in 2001.

The other broadsides are as follows:

(a) Kendal, Jan. 26, 1818. At a meeting of the freeholders of the county of Westmorland, resident in and near the town of Kendal, held this day, John Wakefield, Esq. in the chair; the following resolutions were unanimously agreed to. Kendal: printed by R. Lough, n.d. [1818]. Folio, broadside.

John Wakefield was the chairman of Brougham's election committee. He and his brother Jacob were Quaker woolen manufacturers and owned a bank in Stricklandgate; they were Brougham's most powerful supporters in Kendal. On February 13, Wordsworth had dinner with John Wakefield; he got on well with Wakefield's son who, Wordsworth reported, found his father's conduct in the campaign "very violent." No other copy of this broadside has been found.

(b) Hall, George. To the independent freeholders of the county of Westmorland. Kendal: printed by Richard Lough, n.d. [1818]. Folio, broadside.

Dated February 10, 1818. A statement by the secretary of Brougham's committee, pointing out to freeholders that they need not be bound by promises of support for the Lowther candidates made before they knew that Brougham would stand. Hall also urges freeholders not to be bullied by the argument that if they vote for one of the Lowther candidates, they must also vote for the other (as argued by Wordsworth). Unrecorded.

(c) Kendal, 11th Feb., 1818. Westmorland election. Kendal: printed by Richard Lough, n.d. [1818]. Folio, broadside.

This broadside repeats the charge that Viscount Lowther was a placeman living at the taxpayer's expense. Writing to Lord Lonsdale on February 14, Wordsworth refers to it as "that inflammatory handbill." It was this abusive and personal attack that prompted him to take up his pen again. On February 19, he sent a copy of the broadside to Lord Lonsdale, and reported that he had submitted two letters in rebuttal to the editor of *The Kendal Chronicle*, signed "A Friend to Truth." These, along with other material, were published in pamphlet form as *Two Addresses to the Freeholders of Westmorland* (no. 24). Unrecorded.

(d) Hall, George. Independence of Westmorland. By order of Mr. Brougham's committees at Appleby. Kendal: printed by Richard Lough, n.d. [1818]. Folio, broadside.

Dated 12 Feb., 1818. A report of the results of canvassing, noting a strong increase among those "plumping" for Brougham. Unrecorded.

(e) Berry, William, Jun. To the public. Kendal: printed by Richard Lough, n.d. [1818]. Sm. folio, broadside.

Dated 16 Feb., 1818. Signed at the end by William Berry, presumably the Mr. Berry, a town clerk, included in a list of Kendal attorneys written out by Dorothy Wordsworth, which Wordsworth sent to Lord Lonsdale. His father is described as "canvassing for Mr. Brougham." The Brougham committee here denies responsibility for the Kendal riot on February 11. The Lowther party is accused of the indiscriminate distribution of ale to the populace the day before, "in consequence whereof the town became greatly disturbed through the whole of that night." There is another copy of this broadside at Cornell, where it is incorrectly described as opposing Brougham.

(f) Emancipation of Westmorland. The following address to the independent freeholders of Westmorland not appearing in *The Kendal Chronicle*

WESTMORLAND ELECTION.

TO THE

Independent

FREEHOLDERS,

OF THE

County of Westmorland.

Gentlemen,

It is reported that certain of the Freeholders who had promised their support to the present Members for the County, now that a Canvass has commenced for another Individual, are inclined to split their votes in his favour. But this practice, I trust, will scarcely prevail in a county so distinguished for the intellectual discernment of its Inhabitants as Westmorland; and for their frank, warm, decisive, and generous attachment to their Friends, and to the Cause which they espouse. Here are two parties, not merely of different, but of *opposite* political principles,—what inconsistency, then, would those persons be involved in, what absurdity would they fall into, who, by dividing their suffrages lend their support, as they imagine, to both! Such conduct if it were *equally* advantageous to both Parties would be of no use to either.

But it is not so; and if any one vote in this manner, from a notion that he is acting judiciously and impartially, a moment's reflection will show, first, that impartiality in a case of this sort, where the principles, as has been observed above, are *opposite*, reflects no honour on his judgement; and next, that by so doing he would *not* be acting impartially, but directly the reverse; as he would favour the new Candidate who stands *single* in opposition to the *two* present Members whose interests are the same, in the proportion of two to one. I say nothing of the merits of the respective principles, it is enough that those principles are diametrically opposed to each other; and I I am anxious for the credit of my Countrymen; I am desirous that they should retain their ancient character for good sense, and for cordial, honest, and unreserved attachment to the persons whom they regard, and to the side which they take.—Men who divide themselves between two parties, run great risk of forfeiting the esteem of both. The present state of things would indeed render indecisive conduct of great importance to the new Candidate, but, though he will be glad of such assistance, he will not be *proud* of it; and as to the present Members, he who is not *entirely* with them is *against* them.

A FRIEND TO CONSISTENCY.

Westmorland, Jan. 30, 1818.

AIREY AND BELLINGHAM, PRINTERS, KENDAL.

ITEM 23

87

KENDAL, 21st Feb. 1818.

EMANCIPATION
OF
WESTMORLAND.

The following Address to the Independent Freeholders of Westmorland not appearing in the KENDAL CHRONICLE of this morning as was expected, Mr. Brougham's Committee here adopt this mode of presenting it to the Public.

To the Independent Freeholders of Westmorland.

GENTLEMEN,

A writer under the signature of "A Freeholder," whose letter is dated February 4th, 1818, has furnished an elaborate article (the first in the last No. of the Chronicle) in favour of the present Members. This "Freeholder" is evidently a writer by profession.—He has furnished lexicographical articles on the words " submit," and " with-held," which Mr. Brougham's Committee at Kendal cannot do less than enter into a blank leaf in their dictionaries. It surely must be considered as a great condescension in one " who understands mankind, and knows the heights and levels of human nature, by which the course of the streams of social action is determined," to drill the Kendal Committee in the use of words; and to tell them how they ought to have expressed themselves, how they ought to have drawn up their resolutions. The stilts upon which this " Freeholder" stalks, and the suddenness with which he comes down from them, would lead one to suppose that he wished the leading Resolutions to be expressed in Blank verse, and the minor Resolutions to hop into Lyrical measure. Independent Freeholders, what miserable work is this! The contest at present going on in your County, is not respecting the construction of a sentence, nor of a Resolution, but it is respecting a fundamental Constitutional Principle. The *Bill of Rights* has said that " *Elections shall be free*," and the Law has said " *that no Peer of Parliament shall interfere in Elections*." Now these are two fundamental principles, and, I ask you, Freeholders of Westmorland, have not these two principles been shamefully and habitually violated by the influence of the House of Lowther for half a century? The Kendal Committee say right, when they say that the preponderating influence of one family has " *with-held* " from them the elective franchise for half a century—the Kendal Committee say right, when they say " it is impossible any longer to submit," &c. for the accumulated grievance of half a century has become intolerable. The terms *submit* and *with-held* may give offence to courtly ears, the question for you to determine is not, are these terms *elegant* or *inelegant*, but are they *just* and *true?*

Freeholders, you can have no *personal* hostility to the present Members, for you are strangers to their persons; by their votes and their consequences only do you know them—You have no quarrel with the Earl of Lonsdale, or his private character, or his splendid hospitalities, or his private benevolences; *you object to his interference with the freedom of your election, because he is a Peer of the realm.* You do not object to " the voice of gratitude being not loud out of delicacy to the benefactor," but you do object to the voice of gratitude attempting to put down the voice of Patriotism. By the way, this " voice of gratitude" bespeaks the author as one who has the Noble Earl for his " Benefactor," and it is fitting that the voice of gratitude should be heard, but not to influence others at an election! Let this Freeholder stand forth in his own name, and it may be found perhaps that he has substantial reasons for his attachment, that he holds a situation worth holding under the House of Lowther. But, Freeholders of Westmorland, there are not patent places for all of you! What is now going on in the County is like a lottery puff—all prizes and no blanks; but it will turn out in the issue, that the promises are the blanks, and the benefits conferred are the prizes. The Office of Distributor of Stamps, for instance, is one of the good things not of every day occurrence.

But this Freeholder builds his strongest appeal on the *argumentum ad misericordiam*—

" With humble suit, and lowly dirty, He comes to move all hearts to pity."

" They are there (says he) because no one else had presented himself." Like flies in amber—not that they have any right to be there, but the question is, how they got there? The *argumentum ad misericordiam* is one which no one sets himself to answer—" 'tis true 'tis pity, and pity 'tis, 'tis true." In correcting the phraseology of " the misbegotten knaves in Kendal Green," he says, " words to that effect would surely have given the sense of this resolution, as proceeding from men of cool reflection, and offered nakedly to the considera-

tion of minds which, it was desired should be kept in a similar state." Now if this means *my thing*, taken in its obvious sense it means " it was desired that minds should be kept in a *similar* state," *i. e.* in a state of nakedness ! prob ! pudor ! Let the " Freeholder" again and again correct his own composition before he revises the resolutions of the Kendal Committee.

This Freeholder exemplifies in his own person how debasing to the human mind is a familiarity with corruption. Let him speak for himself—" as to our own County, that man most surely be strangely prejudiced who does not perceive how desirable it is that some powerful individual should be attached to it, *who, by his influence with Government, may facilitate the execution of any plan which may tend to its especial benefit.*" The attention of Government is, or ought to be, equally awake to the representatives of every county who have plans to propose, for the especial benefit of that county, be it small or great. Does the " Freeholder" mean to say, that the connection of the especial benefit to flow from each plan, is not sufficient to insure every facility which Government can afford them, but that some secret, undefined, undue influence, possessed by such men as the present Members, is necessary for this purpose ? This is well understood. The connection of the Minister with the Ministerial members is a kind of give and take. " I support your measures, you give me places for myself or friends." Such are the ways and the wages of corruption. Such the flagrant wrong and intolerable *sedignity* inflicted on our native County.—But if this be the " Freeholder's" meaning, is not the influence of the Lord Lieutenant with Government sufficient ? Is there any place in the Stamp Office, Customs, or Excise given away in Westmorland that is not bestowed through the hands of the noble Earl ? or is not one Lowther representative sufficient ? " The junior Lord is said to have spoken for his brother at Kendal, on the 11th instant, (while "he found an echo in every breast !") surely then he might act for his brother.

Freeholders of Westmorland ! barter not your birthright for a mess of pottage, nor *for* a mess of promises. Firmly, peaceably, and perseveringly come forward in favour of Mr. Brougham. Be the first to condemn and to suppress the riotous proceedings which disgraced the Burgh of Kendal on the 11th inst. Even from that occurrence the present members should learn wisdom—the people are not with them, therefore let them not mark the people with talking of " free, unbiassed, and independent support." Even the Lowther ale fermented against them in the ungrateful stomachs of those who drank it — Even the poor Irish labourer remembered in his drink that he had a country dear to him—as an Irishman, his country is as dear as his heart's blood—and that the Ministerial measures which the two members and their party supported have been an unbroken series of insult and oppression, and misgovernment and wrong, to poor Ireland ! When the lethargy (of which Mr. Wyberg spoke at Appleby) is to be thrown off, some convulsive effort may be expected, before the man is broad awake—the accumulated *wrong* and *iniquity* of half a century cannot be put off as quietly and complacently as a placeman turns his coat.

Freeholders ! let us see when the " man of the people " comes amongst you whether any *special* constables be necessary to keep the peace !

True loyalty consists in an attachment and obedience to the laws. The Constitution of King, Lords, and Commons is dear to you as your homes and household, and you wish to see all these estates entire and not one encroaching upon the other. The friends of Mr. Brougham, are the friends of their aged and venerable King, of an hereditary and high minded nobility, of an independent House of Commons.—They love them all, and are ready to shed their last drop of blood in their defence. Freeholders ! in chusing who shall represent you in the Commons House of Parliament, take care that the oligarchy of Lords does not tread on the privileges of the Commons—chuse for yourselves—one of yourselves—a native and a Freeholder of Westmorland, and let every valley and mountain of old Westmorland ring with the cry of—" Brougham and Independence."

A WESTMORLAND BLUE.

Feb. 19th, 1818.

Printed by Richard Lough, Fish-Market, Kendal.

88

of this morning as was expected, Mr. Brougham's committee here adopt this mode of presenting it to the public. To the independent freeholders of Westmorland. Kendal: printed by Richard Lough, n.d. [1818]. Tall folio, broadside.

Dated 21 Feb., 1818, and signed at the end, "A Westmorland Blue." A substantial text, containing an elaborate answer to Wordsworth's letter to *The Kendal Chronicle* dated "February 4th" (presumably a mistake for February 14th), under the signature "A Freeholder." This broadside, despite the mistake in the date, is clearly a response to Wordsworth's article, and contains amusing allusions to his identity. The "Freeholder" is described as "evidently a writer by profession," and is teased for his particularity about language: "The stilts upon which this 'Freeholder' stalks, and the suddenness with which he comes down from them, would lead one to suppose that he wished the leading resolutions to be expressed in blank verse, and the minor resolutions to hop into lyrical measure. . . . Independent freeholders, what miserable work is this?" There is another copy of this broadside at Cornell, where it is incorrectly described as opposing Brougham.

(g) Brougham, Henry. Mr. Brougham's second address. To the independent freeholders of the county of Westmorland. House of Commons, Monday evening. Kendal: printed by Richard Lough, n.d. [1818]. Folio, broadside.

Dated February 21st, 1818. Brougham rallies his supporters to the cause. Unrecorded.

(h) A caution. Kendal: printed by Richard Lough, n.d. [1818]. Slip ballad, printed on one side.

An undated prose address to freeholders, signed "A Kendal-Ward Man," followed by "A New Song," in four verses. The points raised in the prose letter are similar to those in item (b), above. Unrecorded.

(i) Westmorland contest. Kendal: printed by Richard Lough, n.d. [1818]. Folio, broadside.

An undated text, signed "A True Friend of Peace, Truth, and Good Order," and responding to a "large handbill" issued by the supporters of Lowther (probably not, in this case, Wordsworth). Presumably printed at about the same time as item (e), above. Unrecorded.

24. [Wordsworth, William.] Two addresses to the freeholders of Westmorland. Kendal: printed by Airey and Bellingham, 1818. 8vo, later nineteenth-century black morocco.

> With the bookplate of George Lillie Craik. This elusive pamphlet was acquired at the Arthur A. Houghton sale in 1980. The modest hammer price of £280 (just over $650) reflects the fact that there were only a few lots to go in the auction, and everyone was getting up to leave. Writers like Wordsworth sometimes do not fare as well as might be expected at auctions whose arrangement is strictly alphabetical.

25. [Wordsworth, William.] Westmorland election. An address to the freeholders of the county of Westmorland, elucidating the claims of the several candidates to the suffrages of the freeholders. By a friend to the constitution of England. Carlisle: printed and sold by B. Scott, and Messrs. Airey and Bellingham (Kendal), 1818. 8vo, early Victorian maroon morocco, covers ruled in gilt and blind, title in gilt on the front cover within an elaborate frame.

> Another attack by Wordsworth on Brougham's candidacy in the Westmoreland parliamentary election of 1818. This tract was wholly unknown until its discovery by T. J. Wise, who first described it in his Ashley Catalogue in 1930. The text still appears not to have been properly studied, nor has it been reprinted. Aside from Wise's copy in the British Library, one other is now recorded at Cornell, where it was evidently added to the library's Wordsworth Collection in 2009. The binding of this copy is unusually ornate and very striking, but, rather surprisingly, there is no sign of prior ownership. Acquired in 2011.

26. Wordsworth, William. Peter Bell, a tale in verse. London: printed by Strahan and Spottiswoode; for Longman, Hurst, Rees, Orme, and Brown, 1819. 8vo, bound first in a volume with four other titles, contemporary half calf, by W. Clarke of London.

> First edition. This copy is inscribed on the half-title, "From the author." The inscription appears to be in the hand of Wordsworth's sister, Dorothy. Included in this volume are a first edition of Wordsworth's *The Waggoner* (1819; no. 27), a second edition of Byron's *Beppo* (1818; no. 121), and the two "fragments" of a piece of Byroniana entitled *What Have We Got?* (1820; no. 183). Acquired in 1979. A second copy of *Peter Bell* is bound fourth in a volume with five other Wordsworth titles (see no. 22).

27. Wordsworth, William. The waggoner, a poem. To which are added, sonnets. London: printed by Strahan and Spottiswoode; for Longman, Hurst, Rees, Orme, and Brown, 1819. 8vo, bound second in a volume with no. 26.

> A second copy in the collection is bound fifth in a volume with no. 22.

28. Wordsworth, William. The river Duddon, a series of sonnets: Vaudracour and Julia: and other poems. To which is annexed, a topographical description of the country of the lakes, in the north of England. London: printed for Longman, Hurst, Rees, Orme, and Brown, 1820. 8vo, bound first in a volume with no. 22.

29. Wordsworth, William. Ecclesiastical sketches. London: printed for Longman, Hurst, Rees, Orme, and Brown, 1822. 8vo, bound sixth in a volume with no. 22.

30. Wordsworth, William. Memorials of a tour on the continent, 1820. London: printed for Longman, Hurst, Rees, Orme, and Brown, 1822. 8vo, bound second in a volume with no. 22.

31. Wordsworth, William. The poetical works of William Wordsworth. Complete in one volume. Paris: published by A. and W. Galignani, 1828. 8vo, contemporary rose calf, by R. Hering & Muller (signed at the foot of the spine).

> An unauthorized collection, one of a number of such volumes of Romantic poetry issued by Galignani. With a fine frontispiece portrait by J. J. Wedgwood after R. Carruthers; preceding the text is an original memoir of the author. The signed Parisian binding is very attractive. Acquired in 1994.

32. Wordsworth, William. Yarrow revisited, and other poems. London: printed for Longman, Rees, Orme, Brown, Green, & Longman; and Edward Moxon, 1835. 12mo, original drab boards, printed paper label.

> This binding is presumably earlier than those with cloth backstrips; a twelve-page publisher's catalogue at the front is not noted in any of the copies in the Wordsworth Collection at Cornell. This is an immaculate copy. With the bookplate of Alfred A. Bethune-Baker of Lincoln's Inn ("from his books, 1891"). Acquired in 1974.

33. Wordsworth, William. The poetical works of William Wordsworth. A new edition. In six volumes. London: Edward Moxon, 1836–7. Six vols., 8vo, original dark green cloth.

> An important collected edition, with which Wordsworth was much involved; many of the poems have been substantially revised. Acquired in 1971.

34. [Wordsworth, William.] Kendal and Windermere Railway. Two letters reprinted from the Morning Post. Revised, with additions. Kendal: printed by R. Branthwaite and Son, n.d. [1845]. 12mo, bound second in a volume with eleven other titles, later nineteenth-century half green morocco.

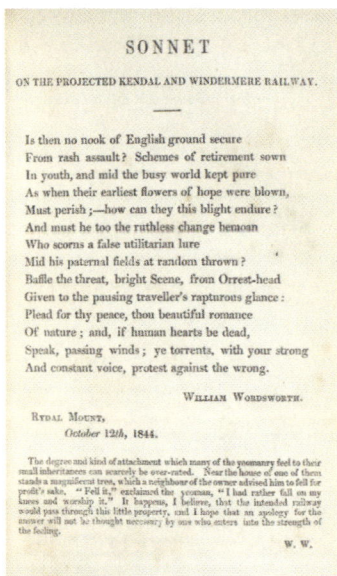

ITEM 34

First issue, with the imprint containing only the name of the Kendal printer; most copies have a cancel title page, with a London imprint. This pamphlet begins with Wordsworth's sonnet of protest, "On the Projected Kendal and Windermere Railway," an early and rather charming literary response to the clash between the progress of technology and the need to preserve the landscape and environment. This copy is signed on the title page, "J. T. Coleridge, Montague Place, Jany. 28, 1845." The owner was Sir John Taylor Coleridge (1790–1876), a nephew of Samuel Taylor Coleridge and a prominent jurist. He was a friend of Wordsworth, and close as well to Thomas Arnold and such prominent figures in the Oxford Movement as Pusey, Newman, and Keble. This volume, which has several other similar inscriptions, comes from the library of the Coleridge family at Chanter's House, Ottery St. Mary, Devon, where S. T. Coleridge was born. The library was for the most part undistinguished; at some point in 2006 a number of boxes of books were removed and sold to Yale. This is one of a handful of volumes not included in that transfer; for another, see no. 15. Acquired in 2006.

35. Wordsworth, William. The poems of William Wordsworth, D.C.L., Poet Laureate, etc., etc. London: Edward Moxon, 1845. Large 8vo, original purple cloth.

"A new edition." A highly important collected edition, as Wise points out: "For this edition Wordsworth again thoroughly revised the text of his poems, and a number of pieces made their first appearance in its pages." With the signature on the first page of an inserted publisher's catalogue of Helen Aldridge, dated Feb. 12, 1846. Acquired in 2003.

36. Wordsworth, William. [Cover title:] Ode on the installation of His Royal Highness Prince Albert as Chancellor of the University of Cambridge. London: printed, by permission, by Vizetelly Brothers and Co.; published by George Bell, n.d. [1847]. 4to, original white glazed wrappers, printed in gold.

> First published edition; preceded by a very rare printing done at Cambridge for distribution prior to the ceremonies. This is one of Wordsworth's last publications, and one of the few poems he wrote specifically in accordance with his duties as Poet Laureate. The text is enclosed within color-printed borders (red, gold, and blue); the wood-engraved portrait of Prince Albert was printed by a process called glyphography. Acquired in 1981.

37. Wordsworth, William. The prelude, or growth of a poet's mind; an autobiographical poem. London: Edward Moxon, 1850. 8vo, original purple cloth.

> This book was published shortly after the poet's death. It is not an uncommon title, but is rather difficult to find in nice condition. Acquired in 1993.

38. Wordsworth, William. The prose works of William Wordsworth. For the first time collected, with additions from unpublished manuscripts. Edited, with preface, notes and illustrations, by the Rev. Alexander B. Grosart, St. George's, Blackburn, Lancashire. London: Edward Moxon, Son, and Co., 1876. Three vols., 8vo, original bright green cloth.

> An important collection, printing much material for the first time. Acquired in 1982.

39. [Anon.] The dead asses. A lyrical ballad. London: printed for Smith and Elder, 1819. 8vo, disbound.

A parody of Wordsworth's attempts to deal in verse with very homely subjects, using plain and unpoetic language; facetiously signed "W. W." at the end. This is a very early Smith and Elder publication; they had begun their long partnership as booksellers in 1816, but did not begin to publish until 1818. Acquired in 1977.

40. [Jewsbury, Maria Jane.] Phantasmagoria; or, sketches of life and literature. London: printed for Hurst, Robinson and Co.; and Archibald Constable and Co. (Edinburgh), 1825. Two vols., 12mo, contemporary half calf.

THE POET'S FATE.

We poets in our youth begin in gladness,
But thereof comes in the end, despondency and madness.

WORDSWORTH

I.

WHAT is the Poet's fate?—In Life's young spring
His soul expandeth like a flower in the sun,
Smiling, and smiled on by each living thing
As though it ne'er would be a withered one:—
Or, like a bird in its first flight to heaven
Giving forth music with a spendthrift's joy,
As though such precious stores of both were given,
That joy could never change! nor music ever cloy!

II.

Awhile, a little while,—and then depart
His fond imaginings, and inward gladness;
Feelings that twined like flowers around his heart
Are plucked by time, or trodden down by sadness!

ITEM 40

The author's first book, dedicated to Wordsworth, with a prefatory poem addressed to him. Maria Jane Jewsbury was born in 1800, in a town near the Derbyshire and Leicestershire border. Dorothy Wordsworth found the new author "a young woman of extraordinary talents"; William expressed admiration for her literary criticism. The collection includes a substantial number of poems, a few short stories, a fairy tale called "Zerinda," and a series of literary essays, several of which satirize the contemporary scene. As a result of this book Jewsbury was invited to stay with the Wordsworths at Kent's Bank, Lancashire, in July 1825. Here she began a close relationship with the poet's daughter Dora, with whom she carried on an extensive correspondence. Jewsbury married in 1832, and went with her husband to India, where she died of cholera the following year. Acquired in 2006.

41. [Powell, Thomas.] Attempts at verse. London: George Mann, 1836. 12mo, original green cloth.

> The author's first book, published anonymously when he was twenty-seven, and effusively dedicated to Wordsworth, with his permission. For the next seven or eight years Powell and Wordsworth exchanged many letters; Powell sent the poet books, and gifts of Stilton cheese. Powell's later career was curious, to say the least. He had a wide acquaintance in literary circles, but at the same time was involved in episodes of embezzlement and forgery. In 1849, he made his way to New York, where he found work as a journalist and editor. At one point he published a biographical sketch of Charles Dickens, whom he had known slightly. Dickens was outraged by the inaccuracies in this article, and the ensuing dispute led to a libel suit, in which Powell unsuccessfully claimed damages of $10,000. Powell died in Newark, New Jersey, in 1887; according to some authorities, he committed suicide. Only two other copies of this book have been located, at the Lilly Library (Indiana) and Cornell; in neither case is Powell's authorship noted. This copy is inscribed on the title page, "To Miss Jane Lough, with the author's love." On the back pastedown is a second inscription, in a slightly shaky hand, which reads, "Georgy Lough from her affectionate friend Mr. Powell, 1842 (made by himself)." Acquired in 2001.

42. [Wordsworth, William.] William Wordsworth. At a meeting held at the house of Mr. Justice Coleridge, on Monday the 13th of May, the Lord Bishop of London in the chair, it was resolved—That a subscription be raised to do honour to the memory of William Wordsworth, and that a committee be appointed to carry this object into effect. The committee having met at the same place on the 10th of June, A. J. P. Howe, Esq., M.P. in the chair, it was resolved:—That the object of the subscription be I. To place a whole-length effigy of Wordsworth in Westminster Abbey. II. If possible to erect some monument to his memory in the neighbourhood of Grasmere, Westmoreland. [London: 1850.] 4to, single sheet, folded.

> This four-page leaflet records the proceedings involved in creating a monument to Wordsworth, who had died on April 23, 1850. The last two pages contain a list of subscriptions already in hand, beginning with Queen Victoria and Prince Albert (£50). This copy was found in a batch of Coleridge family papers (see no. 34). Acquired in 2007.

THE

F A L L

OF

ROBESPIERRE.

AN

HISTORIC DRAMA.

BY S. T. COLERIDGE,

OF JESUS COLLEGE, CAMBRIDGE.

𝕮𝖆𝖒𝖇𝖗𝖎𝖉𝖌𝖊:

PRINTED BY BENJAMIN FLOWER,

FOR W. H. LUNN, AND J. AND J. MERRILL ; AND SOLD
BY J. MARCH, NORWICH.

1794.

[PRICE ONE SHILLING.]

43. Coleridge, Samuel Taylor [and Robert Southey]. The fall of Robespierre. An historic drama. Cambridge: printed by Benjamin Flower, for W. H. Lunn, and J. and J. Merrill; and sold by J. March (Norwich), 1794. 8vo, red morocco, by Sangorski & Sutcliffe.

> Coleridge's first book. Major portions of this verse drama were in fact written by Robert Southey, though he is not mentioned on the title page. A leaf of advertisements at the end contains proposals for printing by subscription "Imitations from the Modern Latin Poets," a book that never appeared. Acquired in 1972.

44. Coleridge, Samuel Taylor. Conciones ad populum. Or addresses to the people. N.p. [Bristol]: 1795. 8vo, bound with *The Plot Discovered* (no. 45), red morocco, by R. Nelson.

> Coleridge's third publication, consisting of two political lectures delivered to audiences in Bristol, where Coleridge and Southey were living at the time. The stance is vehemently anti-Pitt. With a bookplate bearing the crest of the Russell Clan (Stirlingshire), and the motto "Que sara sara" (*sic*). Acquired in 1978.

45. Coleridge, Samuel Taylor. The plot discovered; or an address to the people, against ministerial treason. Bristol: 1795. 8vo, bound with *Conciones ad Populum* (no. 44).

46. Coleridge, Samuel Taylor. Poems on various subjects. London: printed for G. G. and J. Robinsons [sic]; and J. Cottle (Bristol), 1796. 8vo, maroon morocco, by Zaehnsdorf.

> Three poems are by Charles Lamb, and are signed with his initials; part of another poem is by Robert Southey, as the preface explains. With the book label of Alfred Nathan. Acquired in 1975.

47. Coleridge, Samuel Taylor. [Caption title:] The watchman. No. 1. Tuesday, March 1, 1796. Bristol: published by the author; and sold by the booksellers and newscarriers in town and country, n.d. [1796]. [With:] Nos. II–X. Bristol: published by the author; and by Parsons (London), n.d. [1796]. 8vo, nineteenth-century half calf.

A complete run of a periodical published for about two and a half months at eight-day intervals. Most of the essays, reviews, and original poems are by Coleridge himself, though there were other contributors as well, such as the physician Thomas Beddoes and the young Irish versifier Thomas Dermody (several poems). There were few subscribers; Coleridge notes in his *Biographia Literaria* that his maidservant used unsold copies for lighting fires. On the front flyleaf is the early signature of John J. Lightfoot; at the back is the stamp of the Derby Mechanics' Institute. Acquired in 1978.

48. Coleridge, Samuel Taylor. Fears in solitude, written in 1798, during the alarm of an invasion. To which are added, France, an ode; and Frost at midnight. London: printed for J. Johnson, 1798. 4to, marbled wrappers.

Acquired in 2001. This was the first copy of this twenty-three-page quarto to come on the market in more than thirty years. Another surfaced in 2007 at a provincial sale in England.

49. Coleridge, Samuel Taylor, translator. The Piccolomini, or the first part of Wallenstein, a drama in five acts. Translated from the German of Frederick Schiller by S. T. Coleridge. London: printed for T. N. Longman and O. Rees, 1800. [Bound with, as issued:] The death of Wallenstein. A tragedy in five acts. Translated from the German of Frederick Schiller by S. T. Coleridge. London: printed for T. N. Longman and O. Rees, by G. Woodfall, 1800. 8vo, contemporary half red morocco.

With the early signature on the title page and manuscript book label of Francis Trench (1757–1829) of Sopwell Hall (co. Tipperary). The Simon Nowell-Smith copy. Acquired in 2002.

50. Coleridge, Samuel Taylor. The friend; a literary, moral, and political weekly paper, excluding personal and party politics, and the events of the day. Conducted by S. T. Coleridge, of Grasmere, Westmoreland. Penrith: printed and published by J. Brown [imprints vary], n.d. [1809–10]. 8vo, nineteenth-century dark blue morocco.

A complete set of the original twenty-eight issues, numbered 1–27, with an unnumbered ("supernumerary") part between nos. 20 and 21. When Coleridge launched this periodical he had 632 subscribers, but his measured, logical approach to metaphysical theory was too difficult for most of his readers, and the audience dropped off sharply. Included are some significant contributions by Wordsworth, including three essays, some sonnets, and an early fragment of *The Prelude*. On the front pastedown is the bookplate of the Victorian novelist William Hale White; a number of neat penciled notes may be in his hand. With the later bookplate of Sir Harry Newton. Acquired in 2007.

51. Coleridge, Samuel Taylor. The friend; a series of essays. London: printed for Gale and Curtis, 1812. 8vo, red morocco, by R. Nelson.

First edition in book form, with a general title page and short preface. For this reissue it was necessary to reprint the first twelve numbers, as no supply of original sheets remained. Coleridge took this opportunity to make considerable changes, but he retained the original dates and imprints. Acquired in 1978.

52. Coleridge, Samuel Taylor. Remorse. A tragedy. London: printed for W. Pople, 1813. 8vo, red morocco, by Riviere.

The prologue is by Charles Lamb. With the bookplate of Lenore and James Marshall. Acquired in 1973.

53. Coleridge, Samuel Taylor. Christabel: Kubla Khan, a vision; The pains of sleep. London: printed for John Murray, by William Bulmer and Co., 1816. 8vo, original drab wrappers.

This is Lady Caroline Lamb's copy, with her jottings on p. 19. There she has written her first name twice; her full name once; her husband, William's, name several times; and the evocative name "Adolphe"; there is also a curious and slightly odd drawing of a half-length figure. The year 1816 was an important one for Lady Caroline. She was a clever and high-spirited woman, whose infidelities were the subject of scandal. Her celebrated affair with Byron had broken off in 1813, and by 1816 she was on the verge of divorce, though there was a last-minute reconciliation. The same year she also published *Glenarvon*, a roman à clef in which Byron plays a major role; the book caused a sensation. "Adolphe" is undoubtedly an allusion to the famous novel by Madame de Staël's lover, Benjamin Constant, which had also been published in London in 1816. With the later manuscript ownership label of Harry B. Smith, "from my Sentimental Library." This copy does not appear in the printed catalogue of that library, but many of the books he owned were not included. With the earlier bookplate of Col. F. Grant, and a small book label of Mary Elizabeth Hudson. Acquired in 1974.

But vainly thou warrest,
For this is alone in
Thy power to declare,
That in the dim forest
Thou heard'st a low moaning,
And found'st a bright lady, surpassingly fair :
And didst bring her home with thee in love and in
charity,
To shield her and shelter her from the damp air.

To sheild her and shelter her

William Lamb

William

Caroline

Caroline

Caroline Lamb

ADOLPH

William Lamb

54. Coleridge, Samuel Taylor. Biographia literaria; or biographical sketches of my literary life and opinions. London: Rest Fenner, 1817. Two vols., 8vo, original boards, printed paper labels.

> With the stenciled book labels of J. Carter, M.A., F.A.S. The Gerald E. Slater copy. Acquired in 1982.

55. Coleridge, Samuel Taylor. "Blessed are ye that sow beside all waters!" A lay sermon, addressed to the higher and middle classes, on the existing distresses and discontents. London: printed for Gale and Fenner; J. M. Richardson; and J. Hatchard, 1817. 8vo, maroon morocco, by Zaehnsdorf, original drab printed wrappers bound in.

> This copy is inscribed by Coleridge on the inside front wrapper as follows: "For a provincial Lady, who requested through a common Friend–(N. B. from the same county). A haughty Graff? Graff? That's what Germans call / their Counts. Haughty enough most of them are, Lord knows. / What can a Lady want one for, I wonder! / 'Nonsense! she means your name' Ho! is that all? / Bear witness, then my Hand, that here I under- / write, S. T. Coleridge, Scribe in verse & prose." The recipient has been tentatively identified as Eliza Aders, or Mrs. Charles Aders, the wife of a German merchant. In the text, Coleridge has made a dozen substantial manuscript additions, emendations, and deletions. With the bookplate of John Gribbel, whose library was sold at auction in New York in 1945. This copy is no. 8 in a list of fifteen annotated and inscribed copies recorded in Collected Works, vol. 6, ed. R. J. White (1972), where it is described as "not located" since the Gribbel sale. It had in fact been acquired by the American collector Halsted B. Vander Poel, the literary portion of whose library was dispersed at Christie's London on March 3, 2004.

56. Hurwitz, Hyman. [Title in Hebrew.] A Hebrew dirge, chaunted in the Great Synagogue, St. James's Place, Aldgate, on the day of the funeral of her Royal Highness the Princess Charlotte. By Hyman Hurwitz, master of the Hebrew Academy, Highgate: with a translation in English verse, by S. T. Coleridge, Esq. London: printed by H. Barnett; and sold by T. Boosey; Lackington, Allen, and Co.; Briggs and Burton; and H. Barnett, 1817. 8vo, red morocco, by R. Nelson.

> Hyman Hurwitz was a Polish Jew who settled in England and became professor of Hebrew at the University of London. He and Coleridge were

ISRAEL'S LAMENT.

MOURN, Israel! Sons of Israel, mourn!
Give utt'rance to the inward throe!
As wails, of her first Love forlorn,
The Virgin clad in robes of woe.

Mourn the young Mother, snatch'd away
From Light and Life's ascending Sun!
Mourn for the Babe, Death's voiceless prey,
Earn'd by long pangs and lost 'ere won.

קִינַת יְשֻׁרוּן

אֱלִי יְשֻׁרוּן וּבְנֶיהָ!
כְּמוֹ אִשָּׁה בְּחֶבְלֶיהָ;
וְכִבְתוּלָה חֲגוּרַת־שָׂק
עֲלֵי בַּעַל נְעוּרֶיהָ.
אֵלִי וכו

עֲלֵי גְבִירָה, אֲשֶׁר נִפְטְרָה
בְּעוֹדָהּ בִּנְעוּרֶיהָ,—
וְעַל בֶּן רַךְ, אֲשֶׁר נִלְקַח,
וְהֻרְבָּה מַכְאֹבֶיהָ.
אֵלִי וכו

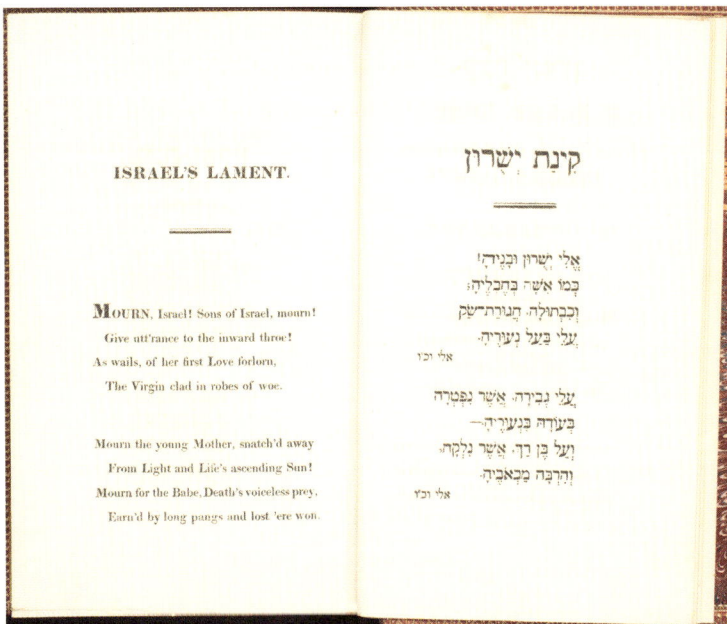

close friends. This pamphlet is printed in the Hebrew manner, back to front, with facing English and Hebrew text. Acquired in 1978.

57. Coleridge, Samuel Taylor. Sibylline leaves: a collection of poems. London: Rest Fenner, 1817. 8vo, contemporary calf. Acquired in 1995.

58. Coleridge, Samuel Taylor. Zapolya: a Christmas tale, in two parts: the prelude entitled "The Usurper's Fortune"; and the sequel entitled "The Usurper's Fate." London: printed for Rest Fenner, 1817. 8vo, late nineteenth-century cloth.

This copy is inscribed by Coleridge on the half-title in the form of a very long letter to John Gibson Lockhart, identified only as the anonymous author of *Peter's Letter to His Kinfolk*, published in 1819. Lockhart was then a young writer of promise, in his midtwenties, and about to become the close friend and son-in-law of Walter Scott. He was by this time a contributor to *Blackwood's Magazine*, and had published in 1817 a hostile review of Coleridge's *Biographia Literaria*. Presumably Lockhart's authorship of this essay was unknown to Coleridge. With five substantive corrections by Coleridge in the text. A bookseller's note at the end indicates that this copy had appeared at the Arthur Young sale at Sotheby's in 1896 (£14, to Pearson); the penciled signature of Alfred T. White on the front flyleaf is dated December 1896. Acquired in 1985.

59. Coleridge, Samuel Taylor. The friend: a series of essays, in three volumes, to aid in the formation of fixed principles in politics, morals, and religion, with literary amusements interspersed. London: printed for Rest Fenner, 1818. Three vols., 8vo, contemporary calf.

> "New edition," with substantial additions and revisions; in fact the second edition in book form. With the signature "Geo. Barclay" in vol. 1, dated 1889, and the later armorial bookplates of John W. Lucas. Acquired in 1982.

60. Coleridge, Samuel Taylor. The poetical works of S. T. Coleridge, including the dramas of Wallenstein, Remorse, and Zapolya. London: William Pickering, 1828. Three vols., 8vo, original red cloth, printed paper labels.

> Only 250 copies were printed. With the nineteenth-century bookplates of Albert R. Graves. Acquired in 1993.

61. Coleridge, Samuel Taylor. Specimens of the table talk of the late Samuel Taylor Coleridge. London: John Murray, 1835. Two vols., 8vo, original purple cloth.

> Edited by Coleridge's nephew, Henry Nelson Coleridge. Acquired in 1973.

62. Coleridge, Samuel Taylor. The poems of Samuel Taylor Coleridge. Edited by Derwent and Sara Coleridge. London: Edward Moxon, 1852. [With:] The dramatic works of Samuel Taylor Coleridge. Edited by Derwent Coleridge. London: Edward Moxon, 1852. Two vols., 8vo, contemporary purple morocco.

> The first collected edition of Coleridge's poetry as edited by his children. This set is inscribed in the first volume to William Wordsworth's widow: "In piam memoriam. Mrs. Wordsworth from Sara Coleridge with her kindest regards. Forwarded Oct. 16th, 1852, by Derwent Coleridge." The inscription is in Derwent's hand; his sister had died just as the volume of poetical works was about to appear. Wordsworth's wife lived to 1859; on the title page of each volume is a further inscription, dated August 17, 1860, by one of Wordsworth's sons, presenting the books to his wife ("M. Wordsworth from her husband"). Acquired in 1974.

63. [Allsop, Thomas, editor.] Letters, conversations and recollections of S. T. Coleridge. London: Edward Moxon, 1836. Two vols., 8vo, original dark green cloth.

> The compiler was widely known as Coleridge's favorite disciple. Acquired in 1982.

64. Cole, Owen Blayney. Christabel concluded, a Christmas tale. Portishead: 1860. 12mo, original glazed printed wrappers.

> A continuation of Coleridge's poem, which he famously left unfinished; Coleridge did, however, leave behind some notes on his intentions, and these are reprinted here. Cole was born in Ireland in 1808, and published his first book in Dublin in 1846. All his later verse, of which there was a fair amount, was printed in Portishead, in Somerset. Laid in is a small broadside poem, *To the Memory of Gilbert Stephens, Esq.*, printed there in 1866. Two copies of this 1860 pamphlet are located, at Cambridge University and Harvard. Acquired in 1990.

65. [Anon.] The farrago: or the lucubrations of Counsellor Bickerton, Esquire. Oxford: 1816. Two numbers, 8vo, recent wrappers.

> A complete run of a short-lived university periodical. The first number is devoted entirely to a review of Coleridge's *Christabel*, which had just been published. The anonymous reviewer was not impressed: "On no occasion has Mr. Coleridge appeared in so degraded and degenerate a light as in the present publication." Of "Kubla Khan" he thought so little that it was not found necessary "to give any detailed account." The second number consists largely of a review of Byron's *Poems*, also printed in 1816. Again, the critic is negative: "None of the poems contained in it will contribute to the exaltation of his poetical character; while many, we are sorry to say it, must operate much to his prejudice as an Englishman." Only two sets of these two numbers are located, at the British Library and the Bodleian; Yale has a copy of the second number. Acquired in 1978.

66. Sandford, Mrs. Henry. Thomas Poole and his friends. London: Macmillan and Co., 1888. Two vols., 8vo, original black cloth.

> Thomas Poole was a tanner by profession, and entirely self-taught. He first met Coleridge in 1794, at about the time Coleridge and his circle were

involved in the Pantisocracy project. A close friendship resulted, and in 1796 Poole became one of the principal backers of *The Watchman*; in one issue, Coleridge printed Poole's essay on the slave trade. Poole continued to supply funds in later years; in 1809 he provided money for *The Friend*, and he subsequently paid for part of Hartley Coleridge's education at Oxford. He saw Coleridge for the last time in 1834, and died three years later. This biography, by a descendant, is the chief source for Poole's life. Coleridge figures prominently throughout, and there are substantial extracts from his correspondence. Acquired in 2000.

67. Wise, Thomas James. A bibliography of the writings in prose and verse of Samuel Taylor Coleridge. London: printed for the Bibliographical Society by Richard Clay & Sons, Ltd., 1913. 8vo, original gray boards, cloth spine.

> This is a presentation copy, inscribed at the front, "H. Buxton Forman Esq. From his very sincere friend, Thos. J. Wise." Laid in is a copy of a typed letter from Wise to Forman, dated December 23, 1913, partly about this book. With Buxton Forman's bookplate. There is a penciled note in the hand of Michael Papantonio, of Seven Gables Bookshop, reading, "Not for sale." Bibliographies as a rule are not included in this checklist, but this one seemed worth recording. Acquired in 1981.

ROBERT SOUTHEY (1774–1843)

68. Southey, Robert, and Robert Lovell. Poems: containing The Retrospect, odes, elegies, sonnets, &c. By Robert Lovell, and Robert Southey, of Balliol College, Oxford. Bath: printed by R. Crutwell, and sold by C. Dilly (London), 1795. 8vo, green morocco, by Riviere.

> Southey's first book, preceded only by his anonymous collaboration with Coleridge in *The Fall of Robespierre* (1794; no. 43). Lovell was an early participant in the Pantisocracy movement, initiated by Southey and Coleridge. He died of a fever in 1796. One sonnet in this book is by Coleridge. With the book label of R. Percy Alden. Acquired in 1972.

69. Southey, Robert. Joan of Arc, an epic poem. Bristol: printed by Bulgin and Rosser, for Joseph Cottle; and Cadell and Davies, and G. G. and J. Robinson (London), 1796. 4to, contemporary calf, rebacked.

> Southey's first independently published book. This copy is inscribed by the recipient on the title page, "Anna Seward. The gift of the Right Honourable

Lady Eleanor Butler and Miss Ponsonby. Jany. 1797." Eleanor Butler and Sarah Ponsonby first met sometime in the late 1770s, and soon formed a friendship of unusual intensity. They resolved to live together in seclusion, and over their families' protests, they made their way to the north of Wales, where they settled in a cottage in Llangollen Vale. Here they remained, without spending a single night away from home, for some fifty years. Their eccentric manners, particularly their habit of dressing in a very mannish style, gave them wide notoriety, and they became something of a tourist attraction. Among their earliest admirers was Anna Seward, a poet known as "the Swan of Lichfield." In 1796, Seward wrote and published a poem in honor of the couple, entitled "Llangollen Vale." With the later signature of Roger Senhouse (1957). Acquired in 1979.

70. Southey, Robert. Poems. Bristol: printed by N. Biggs, for Joseph Cottle; and G. G. & J. Robinson (London), 1797. 8vo, contemporary calf, binder's ticket of C. Smith of Bath.

With the early signature on the front flyleaf "Edw. Combe." Acquired in 1991.

71. Southey, Robert. Letters written during a short residence in Spain and Portugal. . . . With some account of Spanish and Portugueze poetry. Bristol: printed by Bulgin and Rosser, for Joseph Cottle; and G. G. and J. Robinson (London); and Cadell and Davies (London), 1797. 8vo, contemporary calf, binder's ticket of C. Smith of Bath.

The text is interspersed with original poetry, translations, and Spanish verse. This copy is bound without a half-title or final leaf of advertisements; its purchase despite the missing leaves represents a rare departure from the standards adopted for the collection, but the ticketed provincial binding was hard to resist. With the signature "Edw. Combe," dated 1798. Acquired in 1993.

72. Southey, Robert. Joan of Arc. Bristol: printed by N. Biggs, for Joseph Cottle; and sold in London by T. N. Longman, 1798. Two vols., large 8vo, contemporary calf, rebacked.

Second edition, substantially revised, with numerous additional notes; first published as a quarto in 1796 (no. 69). This is one of reportedly only twelve copies on large and fine paper; the source for the statement of limitation has not as yet been discovered. This copy is inscribed by the author on the half-title of vol. 1, "Mr. Lamb from Robert Southey, June 13, 1798." Charles

Lamb and Southey were brought together through a common friendship with Coleridge. At the time these volumes were inscribed the relationship was in its early stages, but it was soon to intensify. The Simon Nowell-Smith copy. Acquired in 2002. Also in the collection is a copy of this edition on ordinary paper, in contemporary calf, acquired in 1981.

73. [Southey, Robert, editor.] The annual anthology. Bristol: printed by Biggs and Co., for T. N. Longman and O. Rees (London), 1799–1800. Two vols., 8vo, early nineteenth-century marbled boards, purple cloth spines, printed paper labels.

> The poems here are all new. Besides Southey himself, the most important contributor is Coleridge, with no fewer than twenty-seven poems, including "This Lime-Tree Bower My Prison." There are also poems by Joseph Cottle, Humphry Davy, George Dyer, Charles Lamb, Charles Lloyd, Robert Lovell, Amelia Opie, Mary Robinson, and Francis Wrangham. A third volume was planned but never appeared. This set is one of a few printed on large and thick paper. The title page of vol. 2 is signed by William Taylor (1765–1836), poet, man of letters, and a scholar of contemporary German literature, who was in fact the moving spirit behind this anthology. He met Southey early in 1798, and suggested that Southey compile an annual collection of original verse. Taylor himself contributed to both volumes; indeed the first piece in vol. 1 is his "Topographical Ode." Taylor has made several manuscript corrections in the text. The Borowitz copy (sold, with no mention of provenance, at Sotheby Parke Bernet, November 15, 1977, for $350, to Maggs). Acquired in 1989.

74. Southey, Robert. Thalaba the destroyer. London: printed for T. N. Longman and O. Rees, by Biggs and Cottle (Bristol), 1801. Two vols., 8vo, original pale blue boards, white paper backstrips, pink printed paper labels. Acquired in 1987.

75. [Southey, Robert, with Samuel Taylor Coleridge.] Omniana, or horæ otiosiores. London: printed for Longman, Hurst, Rees, Orme, and Brown, 1812. Two vols., 12mo, contemporary half calf.

> A collection of 246 short essays, of which 45 are by Coleridge, and are marked as his in the index with an asterisk; the project as a whole, however, was conceived and executed by Southey. With the early bookplates of S. M. Threipland. Acquired in 1993.

76. [Southey, Robert.] A summary of the life of Arthur Duke of Wellington, from the period of his first achievements in India, to his invasion of France, and the decisive battle of Waterloo, June 18, 1815. Dublin: printed for George Mullens [sic], 1816. 4to, contemporary green straight-grained morocco, covers gilt with a border of oak and shamrock leaves surrounding a central panel filled with a large Grolieresque design in blind, spine and inner dentelles gilt, a.e.g., by George Mullen of Dublin.

> This copy is in an exceptional Irish binding by the publisher of the book; for another example of Mullen's work, see no. 89. From the private collection of Michael Papantonio, of Seven Gables Bookshop. Acquired in 1989.

77. Southey, Robert. The poet's pilgrimage to Waterloo. London: printed for Longman, Hurst, Rees, Orme, and Brown, 1816. 12mo, original gray boards, printed paper label.

> With "Cambusmore" on the title page in an early hand. Acquired in 1976.

78. Southey, Robert. Essays, moral and political. Now first collected. London: John Murray, 1832. Two vols., 8vo, original drab boards, purple cloth spines, printed paper labels.

> With an early signature ("Revd. Wm Hull") in vol. 1; both volumes bear the signature of Maurice H. Fitzgerald (April 4, 1933). Acquired in 1997.

79. [Auction catalogue.] Catalogue of the valuable library of the late Robert Southey, Esq., LL.D., Poet Laureate. Which will be sold by auction, by order of the executors, by Messrs. S. Leigh Sotheby & Co. London: Compton and Ritchie, printers, n.d. [1844]. 8vo, old half calf.

> The sale catalogue of the most extensive English literary library of the first half of the nineteenth century. At the time of his death, Southey owned some fourteen thousand books; he described his collection as "the richest library that ever was possessed by a poor man." The catalogue contains 3,861 lots, which fetched just under £3,000. What has since become the most celebrated portion of the collection, the books bound in colored cotton prints by Southey's wife and daughters, and known as "the Cottonian library," does not appear in the sale catalogue, possibly because the books so bound were generally of lesser value. This copy has been neatly rubricated throughout, with the buyers' names and prices entered in the margins. With the early signature of Jane (?) Wells, Bristol, on the title page. Acquired in 2006.

80. Southey, Robert. Oliver Newman: a New-England tale (unfinished): with other poetical remains. By the late Robert Southey. London: Longman, Brown, Green, & Longmans, 1845. 8vo, original dark green cloth.

This book was published posthumously and seen through the press by Herbert Hill. This is the dedication copy, inscribed "from the editor" on the front flyleaf, and signed by William Wordsworth on the title page; on the page opposite, the verso of the half-title, is "Wm. Wordsworth, Rydal Mount," apparently in the hand of his wife, Mary. The printed dedication is "to William and Mary Wordsworth, the old and dear friends of Robert Southey." Wordsworth succeeded Southey as Poet Laureate, albeit with some reluctance. Acquired in 2002.

81. Southey, Robert. The life of Wesley; and rise and progress of Methodism. London: Longman, Brown, Green, and Longmans, 1846. Two vols., 8vo, original plum cloth.

Third edition, with additions; the first two editions had appeared in 1820. This edition was edited by the author's son, Rev. Charles Cuthbert Southey, a curate in Cockermouth. Included for the first time are voluminous notes made by Coleridge in a copy of a prior edition. With the signature of Sarah P. Pratt in each volume, dated 1847. Acquired in 2004.

Southeyana

82. Colling, Mary Maria. Fables and other pieces in verse. . . . With some account of the author, in letters to Robert Southey, Esq. Poet Laureate, etc. by Mrs. Bray. London: printed for Longman, Rees, Orme, Brown, and Green, 1831. 8vo, contemporary half calf.

First edition. Mary Maria Colling was born in Tavistock, Devon, in 1803. She was the daughter of Edmund Colling, a husbandman. She was sent to a school to learn to knit and sew, but managed to teach herself to read as well. This was her only book. It was seen into print by the well-known novelist Anna Eliza Bray; almost half the book is devoted to three long letters from Bray to Southey. Acquired in 1990.

83. Jones, John. Attempts in verse, by John Jones, an old servant: with some account of the writer, written by himself: and an introductory essay on the lives and works of our uneducated poets, by Robert

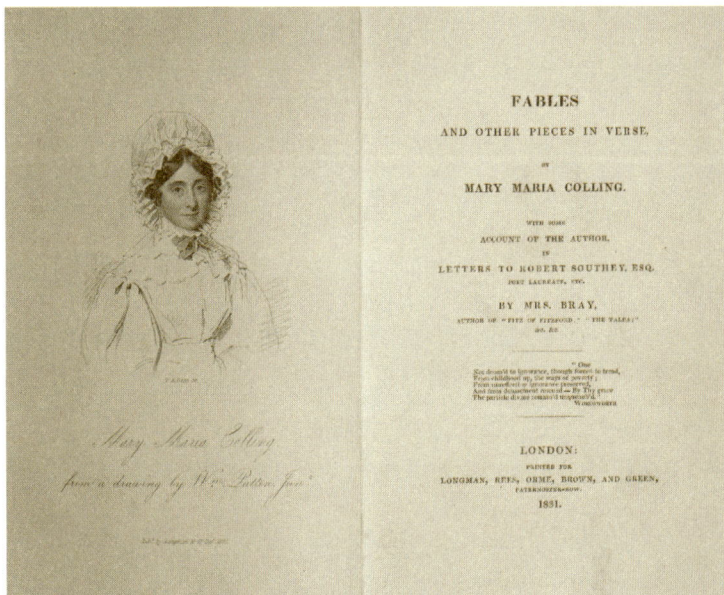

Southey, Esq., Poet Laureate. London: John Murray, 1831. 8vo, original gray boards, printed paper label.

> Southey's essay occupies about half the book. This was a "subscription copy," as indicated by the spine label, and sold for 10s. 6d. The owner was James Robson, whose name appears in the eight-page list of subscribers ("Crake Hall, Bedale"); his signature is on the title page. Acquired in 1993. Also in the collection is another copy, in original purple cloth, with a printed paper label (an early use of publisher's cloth). This copy is half an inch taller, and is also priced at 10s. 6d. Acquired in 1975.

84. Northey, Bob [pseud.]. The apostate bard; a mock-heroic dramatic poem: in two acts. By Bob Northey, Esq. To which is added, Fire, famine, and slaughter: a war eclogue. London: printed and published by E. Giles; sold also by E. Wilson; and all other booksellers in town and country, 1817. 8vo, original blue printed wrappers.

> An attack in verse on Robert Southey for having retreated from the radical opinions of his youth. Three copies are located, at the British Library, UCLA, and Pennsylvania. Acquired in 1981.

THOMAS CAMPBELL (1777–1844)

85. Campbell, Thomas. The pleasures of hope; with other poems. Edinburgh: printed for Mundell & Son; and for Longman & Rees, and J. Wright (London), 1799. 8vo, original marbled boards.

> The author's first book. On the front pastedown is the signature of Eliza Rose, Kilravock Castle, dated 1799. Rose was the 19th (and first female) Baron of Kilravock in Nairnshire, a friend of Robert Burns, and a keen book collector. A major portion of her substantial Scottish library was acquired by the bookseller Martin Hamlyn, of Peter Murray Hill, in the spring of 1969 (see also no. 405); a great many of the books were in fine original boards. The Abel E. Berland copy (purchased from Ximenes, ca. 1970). Acquired in 2001.

86. Campbell, Thomas. Inaugural discourse . . . on being installed Lord Rector of the University of Glasgow, Thursday, April 12th, 1827. Glasgow: John Smith and Son; Bell and Bradfute (Edinburgh); and Henry Colburn (London), 1827. 8vo, disbound.

> This copy is inscribed by Campbell on the half-title to Archibald Brown. Acquired in 1992.

87. Campbell, Thomas. Letters to the students of Glasgow, on the epochs of literature. . . . Letter I [–VII]. London: Henry Colburn, 1827. 8vo, disbound.

> A complete set. The seven parts were printed separately, but the pagination is continuous. Acquired in 1992.

88. Campbell, Thomas. Poland: a poem. . . . To which are added, Lines on the View from St. Leonard's. Extracted from the Metropolitan Magazine for June and July, 1831. London: printed for James Cochrane and Co., 1831. 8vo, original stiff light green printed wrappers. Acquired in 1996.

THOMAS MOORE (1779–1852)

89. Moore, Thomas, translator. Odes of Anacreon, translated into English verse, with notes. London: printed for John Stockdale, 1800. 4to, contemporary full red morocco, elaborate wide gilt borders with an interior

border in blind, broad turn-ins, decorated in gilt and blind, spine gilt, a.e.g., red and gold silk marker, by George Mullen of Dublin, with his binder's ticket.

> Thomas Moore's first book, in a beautiful Irish binding of the period; for another example of George Mullen's work, see no. 76. This copy is signed on the title page by John La Touche, Jun.; on the front pastedown is the armorial bookplate of his father, John La Touche, whose name appears in the list of subscribers, along with four other members of this family of prominent Dublin bankers (the family included Rose La Touche, who was later to become intimately involved with Ruskin). With the later bookplate of Henry J. B. Clements, with a manuscript note on the verso of the front flyleaf, "Bt. at the Gennadius sale at Sotheby's, March 28, 1895." The Simon Nowell-Smith copy. Acquired in 2002.

90. [Moore, Thomas.] The poetical works of the late Thomas Little, Esq. [pseud.]. London: printed for J. and T. Carpenter, 1801. 8vo, contemporary red morocco.

> Moore's first collection of original verse. With an old ownership stamp, "Loretto, Cheltenham," and the later book label of the noted bibliographer Graham Pollard (1903–1976). Acquired in 1978.

91. [Moore, Thomas.] The poetical works of the late Thomas Little, Esq. [pseud.]. London: printed for J. and T. Carpenter, 1802. 8vo, original pale blue boards, drab paper backstrip.

> Second edition. With a new dedication, to "J. At––ns––n," and slight revisions. Acquired in 1993.

92. Moore, Thomas. Epistles, odes, and other poems. London: printed for James Carpenter, 1806. 4to, contemporary half calf.

> Moore's third book. Acquired in 1979.

93. [Moore, Thomas.] Corruption and intolerance: two poems. With notes. Addressed to an Englishman by an Irishman. London: printed for J. Carpenter, 1808. [Bound with:] [Moore, Thomas.] The sceptic: a philosophical satire. London: printed for J. Carpenter, 1809. Two vols. in one, 8vo, contemporary half calf. Acquired in 1985.

94. [Moore, Thomas.] Intercepted letters; or, the twopenny post-bag. To which are added, trifles reprinted. By Thomas Brown, the younger [pseud.]. London: printed for J. Carr, 1813. 8vo, original pink boards, printed paper label.

> With the signature of William Sewell on the title page. The Graham Pollard copy. Acquired in 1978.

95. [Moore, Thomas.] Lines on the death of — — from the Morning Chronicle of Monday August 5, 1816. Ascribed to a personage of the highest poetic talent, and to gratify the anxious curiosity of the public, re-published, without note or comment. London: printed for W. Hone, 1816. 8vo, disbound.

A bitter poem on the death of the playwright Richard Brinsley Sheridan, whose last days were spent in poverty. This copy is inscribed on the title page, "Rice to his friend Tamsine" (Moore is identified as the author in the same hand). The donor was James Rice (1791–1832), the son of a prosperous lawyer and a close friend of both John Hamilton Reynolds and Benjamin Bailey. Together the three young men for several years carried on a flirtation with three sisters whose surname was Leigh, and who lived in the picturesque village of Salcombe Regis in Devon. The recipient of this poem was one of the sisters, Thomasine, nicknamed Tamsine (or Tamsin). The young group was much interested in literature, and its members circulated a

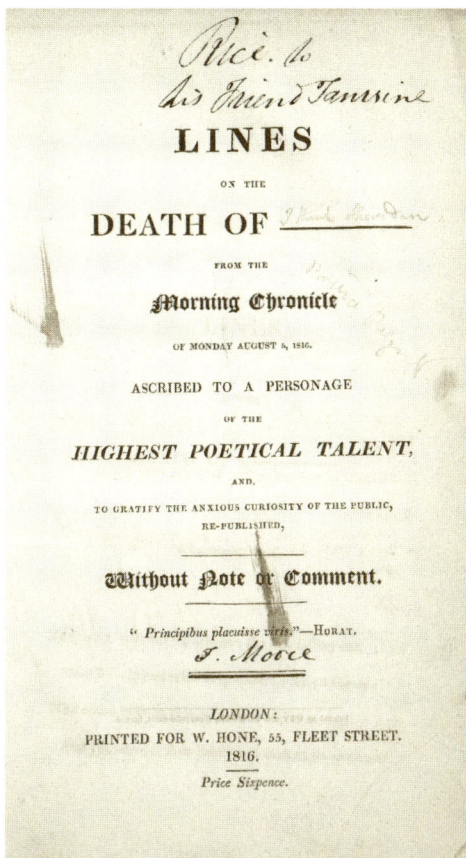

ITEM 95

113

good deal of verse to one another, both original and printed. In 1817, Rice was introduced by Reynolds to Keats, and in late June 1819 he accompanied Keats to Shanklin, on the Isle of Wight, where they spent a month, sharing a room. In the 1830s, Rice and Reynolds formed a law partnership, and he acted as a solicitor for both Fanny Keats and George Keats. He died of consumption at the age of forty. Acquired in 2011 (see no. 341).

96. Moore, Thomas. Lalla Rookh, an oriental romance. London: printed for Longman, Hurst, Rees, Orme, and Brown, 1817. 4to, contemporary olive green straight-grained morocco, richly paneled in gilt, with a border of interlaced fillets enclosing a frame of lyres and foliated scrolls, pointillé ground cartouche stamped with a wreathed lyre at the center, spine gilt, inner dentelles tooled in gilt and blind, crimson doublures and flyleaves, edges gilt and gauffered with an Oriental floral motif, by Dawson & Lewis.

> With the early monogram of the Countess of Bessborough on the front flyleaf. Later morocco book labels of Robert Hoe and Cortlandt F. Bishop. Acquired at auction from the library of Mrs. J. Insley Blair, a portion of which was sold in New York in 2004.

97. Moore, Thomas. Irish melodies . . . with an appendix, containing the original advertisements, and the prefatory letter on music. London: printed for J. Power; and Longman, Hurst, Rees, Orme, and Brown, 1821. 8vo, original gray boards, printed paper label.

> First authorized edition; an unreliable piracy had appeared in Dublin the year before. These songs had been published as sheet music at intervals, beginning in 1808. They are here printed for the first time simply as poetry; included is "'Tis the Last Rose of Summer." With the signature of William Bird, dated 1821, on the front pastedown. Acquired in 1973.

98. Moore, Thomas. Letters and journals of Lord Byron: with notices of his life. London: John Murray, 1830. Two vols., 4to, original gray-green cloth, printed paper labels.

> The most important early memoir of Byron, by his close friend and fellow poet. Moore had the benefit of access to Byron's manuscript autobiography; this precious document he subsequently destroyed. Acquired in 1983.

99. [Moore, Thomas.] The Fudges in England; being a sequel to the "Fudge Family in Paris." By Thomas Brown the younger [pseud.], author

of "The Twopenny Post-Bag," etc., etc. London: printed for Longman, Rees, Orme, Brown, Green, & Longman, 1835. 8vo, original drab boards, printed paper label.

> Moore's last book of poetry. In 1835 he received a government pension, and his career as a poet effectively came to an end, though he lived until 1852; in his final years he suffered from dementia. Acquired in 2006.

JAMES HOGG (1770–1835)

100. Hogg, James. The pilgrims of the sun; a poem. Edinburgh: printed for William Blackwood; and sold by J. Murray (London), 1815. 8vo, original gray boards, printed paper label.

> The H. Bradley Martin copy, with his penciled note on the front pastedown, "7 Gables, May 1969, £15 (Peter Murray Hill)." Acquired in 1990.

101. Hogg, James. The Jacobite relics of Scotland; being the songs, airs, and legends, of the adherents to the house of Stuart. Collected and illustrated by James Hogg. Edinburgh: printed for William Blackwood; and T. Cadell and W. Davies (London), 1819. [With:] Second series. Edinburgh: printed for William Blackwood; and T. Cadell and W. Davies, 1821. Two vols., 8vo, contemporary olive green morocco, by J. Clarke.

> From the noted library of William Beckford, which was inherited by his son-in-law, the 10th Duke of Hamilton, and dispersed in a series of auctions in 1882–83. Later in the collection of John David Drummond, 17th Earl of Perth (1907–2002). Acquired in 2004.

102. Hogg, James. Queen Hynde. A poem, in six books. London: printed for Longman, Hurst, Rees, Orme, Brown, and Green; and William Blackwood (Edinburgh), 1825. 8vo, original drab boards, dark blue cloth spine, printed paper label.

> Laid in is a two-page letter, quarto, with an integral address leaf, to the Earl of Buchan, dated July 28, 1814. In this letter, Hogg refuses an invitation to attend a dedication ceremony and commemoration of the death of the Scottish national hero Sir William Wallace: "Believe me, the occasion is quite congenial with my own sentiments. . . . The memory of the hero of Scottish liberty cannot be lost in that country which he bled to save." Acquired in 1982. This book was later lost in transit in the course of moving the collection from New Jersey to New York.

103. [Byron, George Gordon, Lord.] Poems on various occasions. Newark: printed by S. & J. Ridge, 1807. 8vo, contemporary tree calf.

> Byron's second book, which adds twelve poems to and deletes one from the suppressed *Fugitive Pieces* of the year before; the earlier book is effectively unobtainable, as only four copies are known. Of this new collection, one hundred copies are said to have been printed; the volume was never offered for sale, nor was it reviewed. This copy has an interesting provenance, as it bears the handstamp "Leacroft" on the front pastedown. The Leacroft family were Byron's neighbors at Southwell, and Byron is known to have had an intermittent flirtation with Julia Leacroft from 1804 to 1806. Local gossip had it that some of the more amorous of his early poems were addressed to Julia. "To Lesbia," which was originally called "To Julia," was certainly composed for her, and she is the best candidate for several others as well. According to John Cam Hobhouse, Julia's parents, who regularly received Byron at their house and sponsored amateur theatricals in which he performed, "winked at an intercourse" between Byron and their daughter, "in hopes of entangling them in an unequal marriage" (Marchand, *Life*, 1, p. 124). In the very month of publication of *Poems on Various Occasions* Byron seems to have appreciated the risks of the relationship, for he wrote three times to Julia's brother, Captain John Leacroft, specifically to cut it off, and narrowly avoided a duel. This copy of his book must have already been in the Leacroft household. The neat pencilings, including a reference in the margin beside one poem to "a copy given . . . in 1806," may well be in Julia's hand. The manuscript correction to "Love's Last Adieu" (p. 126) is probably by Byron himself, as in Augusta Byron's copy. Acquired in 1993.

104. Byron, George Gordon, Lord. Hours of idleness, a series of poems, original and translated, by George Gordon, Lord Byron, a minor. Newark: printed and sold by S. and J. Ridge; sold also by B. Crosby and Co.; Longman, Hurst, Rees, and Orme; F. and C. Rivington; and J. Mawman (all London), 1807. 8vo, red morocco, by Bedford.

> Byron's third book, and the first to be widely circulated; included are forty poems, of which twelve were new. With the armorial bookplate of John Leveson Douglas Stewart (1842–1887), whose library was sold at Sotheby's in 1888. Acquired in 2004.

105. [Byron, George Gordon, Lord.] English bards, and Scotch reviewers. A satire. London: printed for James Cawthorn, n.d. [1809]. 12mo, original drab printed boards.

> This poem was written by Byron as a reply to a contemptuous notice of his *Hours of Idleness* in *The Edinburgh Review*. It was also his first great poetical success; Cawthorn reprinted the book many times, often without Byron's knowledge or authorization, to meet a continuing demand. On the front flyleaf of this copy is a bibliographical footnote in an early hand: "This is the first edition of Lord Byron's foremost satire. It differs in many lines from the subsequent editions. W. H." Acquired in 1996.

106. [Byron, George Gordon, Lord.] Euthanasia. [London: printed by Thomas Davison, 1812.] 8 pp. 4to, included in an imperfect copy of cantos 1–2 of *Childe Harold* (1812), contemporary olive green straight-grained morocco, covers elaborately decorated in gilt and blind, spine gilt, a.e.g., pink silk doublures and endpapers (worn, inner stitching broken).

> The second copy known of a celebrated, if somewhat controversial, Byron rarity, and the only example to survive in its intended surroundings. When the first two cantos of *Childe Harold* were being printed, Byron decided to include in the volume, as a supplement, a series of lyrical poems, and these were duly placed at the end, preceded by a fly-title ("Poems"), on pp. (165)–200; the volume then concludes with an appendix of material relating to the title poem (pp. 201–26), followed by a leaf of advertisements. Two additional poems, "Euthanasia" and "Stanzas," were at the last moment suppressed, only to be restored, along with four further poems, in the second edition of *Childe Harold*, an octavo printed later in 1812.
>
> This sequence of events is discussed by T. J. Wise in the preface to the first volume of his bibliography of Byron, published in 1933, and in this context he reports the existence of a "unique" volume in the possession of the California collector William Andrews Clark. This volume, elaborately bound in red morocco and substantially padded with blank leaves, contained "eight pages of letterpress ... accompanied by a note dated February 20th, 1813, addressed by Byron to an unnamed correspondent." The eight numbered pages consisted of a quarto printing of "Euthanasia" and "Stanzas." Wise goes on to characterize this assemblage in quite contradictory terms: "Both printed leaves and written letter are genuine. But they are in no way related, and placed together as they are, and the former described as a privately printed Byron *princeps*, I fail to see how the book can be

regarded as other than a 'Fake.'" This harsh epithet appears to derive from a bit of unpleasantness:

Mr. Clark was good enough to send the volume to me for personal examination, and acquainted me with the identity of the dealer—an obscure American bookseller whose name it is kindest to withhold—from whom he had purchased it. To this individual I wrote politely, asking him for information as to the source from which he had obtained his treasure. He replied in a letter intended to be impudent but really only amusing, in which he told me I was "an arrogant Englishman who knew nothing whatever about books; that the printed leaves had been found bound up in a copy of the quarto *Childe Harold*; but that as regards the letter he declined to afford any information, and should refuse to correspond upon the subject." Although the onus of proof that the "pamphlet" is what it pretends to be rests with him, he has not produced one shred of evidence in support of his claim.

Wise goes on to surmise that the printed leaves formed part of a proof copy of *Childe Harold*, and says that had they been allowed to remain in the volume in which they were found, and had the letter been left in the album from which it had obviously been removed, "they would have formed objects of interest." In the preface to the second volume of his Byron bibliography, published later the same year, Wise returns at length to the question of this "fake." With the help of Arthur Swann, the printed leaves had been traced to an auction at the American Art Association, in New York, on March 18–19, 1930 (lot 62), where a copy of the first edition of *Childe Harold* was offered, with the eight pages of "Euthanasia" bound in at "the end," along with an inlaid octavo reprint of *The Giaour* ("new edition," 1813). This lot was purchased at the sale for $110 by C. W. Cavanaugh of the Pegasus Bookshop, acting on behalf of a bookseller in Maple, Wisconsin, named George A. Van Nosdall, who proceeded to extract the eight pages of "Euthanasia," bind them up with the letter, and sell the result on to Clark for $2,500. Wise concludes that Van Nosdall was able to produce a "spurious" first edition by what must have been an accidental survival of "a proof sheet," which was once, Wise again implies, part of a larger set of proofs for *Childe Harold*. This conclusion, however, is false. Until the present example turned up, no other example of these eight pages had ever been found, but a single copy of the same pages in uncorrected proof state does survive, at the Huntington Library. The Clark printing of "Euthanasia" is identical to the Huntington proof, but for "Stanzas," the two versions differ; the Clark copy has "shew" in l. 62, as opposed to "show," and in several lines an unaccented *e* in a past participle was inserted, where in the Huntington proof the *e* is elided. These differences, along with the

1

EUTHANASIA.

1.

WHEN Time, or soon or late, shall bring
The dreamless sleep that lulls the dead,
Oblivion! may thy languid wing
Wave gently o'er my dying bed!

2.

No band of friends or heirs be there,
To weep, or wish, the coming blow:
No maiden, with dishevell'd hair,
To feel, or feign, decorous woe.

fact that the pages in question are numbered 1 to 8, suggest that a small number of copies of "Euthanasia" and "Stanzas" were in fact printed in final form, and that at least two of them were, for whatever reason, bound up with copies of *Childe Harold*.

One puzzle, at least, remains. The binding of the volume sold in 1930 is described as follows: "Green straight grain morocco, gilt back and sides, gilt edges, doublures and end-papers of pink watered silk." The entry adds that a few pages are "slightly foxed," and that the final leaf of advertisements is "wanting." The present copy, surprisingly, is in what seems to be an identical binding, with identical pink silk doublures and endpapers. In this case, however, not only is the advertisement leaf missing, but pp. 221–26 have been removed as well, though the facsimile plate of a Romaic letter is still present at the end. There seem to be two possibilities. The first is that this volume is the same as that sold in 1930, and the fact that the inner stitching is broken, and that many leaves are now loose, is the result of the removal of "Euthanasia" from the back of the volume by Van Nosdall, who failed to notice that a second set of these pages was present in the interior. The other, more plausible, but nonetheless odd, scenario is that the sheets of "Euthanasia" were for some reason preserved in a few copies, which were bound in 1812, or not long afterward, in quite elegant straight-grained morocco. No provenance is given for the volume sold in 1930. In the present example, there is an inscription on the front flyleaf to Dorothea Oakes from Mr. Young, apparently dated 1864 (the third digit is obscured by an inkblot).

Whether or not "Euthanasia" qualifies as an *editio princeps*, as defined by Wise, is a matter of semantics. The fact that the four leaves are separately paginated strongly argues for some sort of independent status; they are, in any case, in no sense "spurious," or "fake." In this instance, the leaves are in fine condition; the volume as a whole is, as stated, rather worn and partly broken, with several leaves of *Childe Harold* missing at the end, and a number of others a bit frayed, or loose. In this context, however, as Wise puts it, the first printing of "Euthanasia" is indeed an object of great interest. Acquired in 2004 from James Burmester, who discovered this volume at a provincial auction in England, in a large lot of miscellaneous early printings of Byron, consigned by a major West End bookseller.

107. [Byron, George Gordon, Lord.] The curse of Minerva. London: printed by T. Davison, 1812. 4to, olive green morocco.

A satire in verse on Lord Elgin and the removal from Greece of the Elgin marbles. Byron decided not to publish the poem in deference to Lord Elgin and his friends, and contented himself with printing a handful of copies for private distribution. The exact number of copies printed is unclear, though an entry in the Murray ledgers indicates a figure of one hundred. This copy was once in the collection of the great Yale collector Chauncey Brewster Tinker, who purchased it after the sale of George D. Smith's stock at the Anderson Galleries in 1920. Tinker later acquired a copy with the original wrappers bound in, and sold this one. In 1934 it was sold, again in New York, as part of the library of Roderick Terry; in 1951 it resurfaced at a Parke-Bernet sale of the stock of the New York bookseller Gabriel Wells. It was subsequently in the stock of Seven Gables Bookshop (acquired in 1975); they sold it to H. Bradley Martin, at whose sale it was acquired in 1990. No other copy has appeared at auction for more than fifty years.

108. [Byron, George Gordon, Lord.] Waltz: an apostrophic hymn. By Horace Hornem, Esq. [pseud.]. London: printed by S. Gosnell; for Sherwood, Neely, and Jones, 1813. 4to, red morocco, by Riviere.

This poem was for Byron something of an experiment, which is why he adopted a pseudonym. After a rather lukewarm reception, Byron disowned the poem entirely. A small cache of uncut copies was discovered at some time in the mid-nineteenth century, and most surviving examples, including this one, are from this source. With the bookplate of William Waldorf, Viscount Astor, of Hever Castle, Kent. Acquired in 1984.

109. Byron, George Gordon, Lord. The Giaour, a fragment of a Turkish tale. London: printed by T. Davison, for John Murray, 1813. [Bound with:] Byron, George Gordon, Lord. The Giaour, a fragment of a Turkish tale. . . . The fourteenth edition. London: printed for John Murray, 1815. Two vols. in one, 8vo, early half dark green straight-grained morocco.

This volume combines the first and "last" editions of the first of Byron's Oriental poems. The first edition is one of what must have been a small number of copies printed on fine paper, with a Whatman watermark; ordinary copies are on thinner unwatermarked paper. The presence of a fourteenth edition is unusual, but not without significance. Byron from the first kept revising and expanding his poem, so that what was originally 685 lines became in the end 1,334; this 1815 printing is the last of the early separate editions. This volume is from the Carlingford library, and must have been bound about 1850. Acquired in 1990.

110. Byron, George Gordon, Lord. The bride of Abydos. A Turkish tale. London: printed by T. Davison, for John Murray, 1813. [Bound with:] Byron, George Gordon, Lord. The corsair, a tale. London: printed by Thomas Davison, for John Murray, 1814. [Bound with, at the front:] Byron, George Gordon, Lord. The giaour, a fragment of a Turkish tale. . . . Seventh edition, with some additions. London: printed by Thomas Davison, for John Murray, 1813. Together three vols. in one, 8vo, contemporary red straight-grained morocco.

> The first edition of *The Bride of Abydos* is a second issue, with the errata corrected and without the errata slip. The first edition of *The Corsair* is also a second issue (of four), with the last eight pages of miscellaneous poems excised, and no imprint at the foot of p. 100. In the third issue, "The end" was added, and, in the fourth issue, the last eight pages were restored. The seventh edition of *The Giaour* presents Byron's final text, with 119 new lines, and the first appearance of a long series of notes at the end. Acquired in 1985.

111. Byron, George Gordon, Lord. The corsair, a tale. London: printed by Thomas Davison, for John Murray, 1814. 8vo, original blue wrappers.

> The same variant as the copy in no. 110. The blue wrappers are unusual; all copies cited by Wise and others seem to be in drab wrappers, as were used for most of Byron's shorter poems. On the title page is the contemporary signature of Ric. (?) Arnold. The Simon Nowell-Smith copy. Acquired in 2002.

112. [Byron, George Gordon, Lord.] Ode to Napoleon Buonaparte. London: printed for John Murray, by W. Bulmer and Co., 1814. 8vo, original brown printed wrappers.

> Second edition; first printed earlier the same year. With the book labels of Frederick Spiegelberg and Jerome Kern (sold at Anderson Galleries, January 8, 1929, for $17.50). Acquired in 1981.

113. [Byron, George Gordon, Lord, and Samuel Rogers.] Lara, a tale. Jacqueline, a tale. London: printed for J. Murray, by T. Davison, 1814. 8vo, original drab boards, printed paper label.

> Byron's poem "Lara" appears here for the first time; the contribution by Rogers had already been printed privately (see no. 2). Acquired in 1980.

114. Byron, George Gordon, Lord. Hebrew melodies. London: printed for John Murray, 1815. 8vo, contemporary dark blue straight-grained morocco.

As issued in wrappers, *Hebrew Melodies* had, inserted at the end, two half-titles and two title pages, to enable Byron's various pamphlet poems to be bound up in two volumes. In this copy these insertions have, naturally enough, been discarded. The collection also includes a very worn copy in original drab wrappers, in which these leaves are preserved, along with a four-page catalogue of Murray's advertisements, dated June 1815; this was the first title acquired from me by Gerald (Jerry) Wachs (in 1970), before standards of condition had been set, and a copy in a well-preserved and rather beautiful binding of the period—quite an unusual occurrence for a Byron title of this sort—was deemed a suitable replacement (or companion). Acquired in 1981.

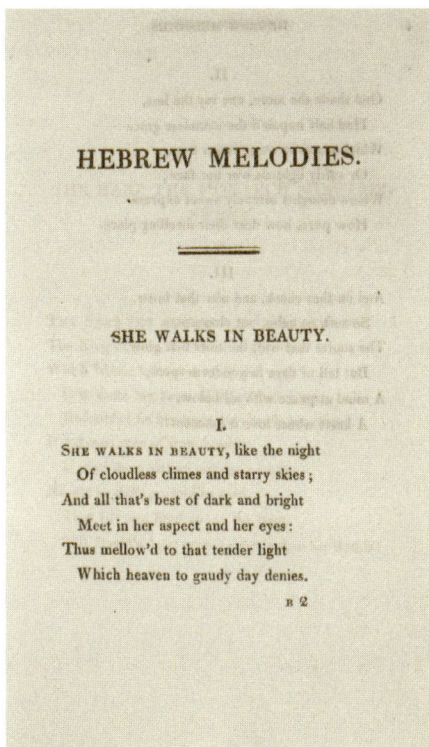

HEBREW MELODIES.

SHE WALKS IN BEAUTY.

I.

SHE WALKS IN BEAUTY, like the night
Of cloudless climes and starry skies;
And all that's best of dark and bright
Meet in her aspect and her eyes:
Thus mellow'd to that tender light
Which heaven to gaudy day denies.

B 2

ITEM 114

115. Byron, George Gordon, Lord. Childe Harold's pilgrimage, a romaunt: and other poems. London: printed for John Murray, 1815. [With:] Childe Harold's pilgrimage. Canto the third. London: printed for John Murray, 1816. [Bound with:] Childe Harold's pilgrimage. Canto the fourth. London: John Murray, 1818. Together three volumes in two, 8vo, contemporary diced calf, gilt, spines elaborately gilt, black morocco labels, green printed binder's ticket of A. Weightman in Penrith.

Tenth edition of cantos 1 and 2, the last to be published as a single unit. Included is one new poem (pp. 263–65), "On the Death of Sir Peter Parker,

123

Bart." Also present are the six poems added to the second edition of 1812, and the nine poems that appeared for the first time in the seventh edition of 1814. First edition of cantos 3–4. The ticketed provincial binding is very attractive. This copy is signed on each title page, "Charlotte & Sarah Crackanthorpe, Augst. 1818." They were the daughters of William Wordsworth's uncle, his mother's brother Christopher Crackanthorpe, with whom he did not get along; they lived in Newbiggin Hall, in Westmoreland. Acquired in 1989.

116. [Byron, George Gordon, Lord.] The siege of Corinth. A poem. Parisina. A poem. London: printed for John Murray, 1816. 8vo, original drab wrappers.

This copy was exported to Ireland for sale, and has the attractive orange bookseller's label of Richard Milliken of Dublin on the front wrapper. The Simon Nowell-Smith copy. Acquired in 2002.

117. [Byron, George Gordon, Lord.] Fare thee well! [London: 1816.] 4to, two leaves, folded, as issued.

This famous poem was written on the occasion of Lord Byron's separation from his wife, just prior to his final departure for the Continent. "'Fare Thee Well,' written with tears, it is said, the marks of which still blot the manuscript, expostulates pathetically with his wife for inflicting a 'cureless wound.'"–Leslie Stephen in the *DNB*. The precise circumstances of Byron's failed marriage have ever since been a source of controversy. Available evidence seems to indicate that *Fare Thee Well!* was first printed privately in a very small edition. A note from Byron to the printer, Thomas Davison, now in the Tinker Collection at Yale, almost certainly refers to this poem: "Mr. Davison. Print me 50 copies of the enclosed on quarto pot paper–& send the account to me–which I will discharge." The number of surviving copies is consistent with this limitation. At present, the following are recorded: (1) British Library (measuring 9 3/4 x 7 3/4 in.); (2) Leeds; (3) John Murray Archive; (4) Yale (the Tinker copy, measuring 9 5/8 x 7 5/8 in.); (5) Illinois (apparently mutilated, with the second leaf excised, and four lines from p. 3 mounted at the foot of p. 2); (6) Princeton; (7) New York Public Library; (8) a copy sold at Sotheby's in 1972 to Sawyer, presumably for Harry Oppenheimer in South Africa; (9) a copy sold at Phillips in 1979 to Blackwell's, offered for sale for many years and finally sold to the bookseller C. C. Kohler of Dorking, for inclusion in a collection of Romantic poetry that was subsequently sold to an institution en bloc; this copy was severely cut down to octavo size; (10) a copy from the library of the 5th Marquis Camden, also cut down to octavo size, and bound at the back of *Hours of Idleness* (1807), sold at Bloomsbury Book Auctions in 2010 for £26,400. One further copy, from the Huth library and later in the collection of John A. Spoor, may be one of those listed above. As is correct, the Wachs copy is printed on paper watermarked "J. Green / 1815." The measurements are 9 13/16 x 8 in., which probably indicates that it is entirely untrimmed. "Practically impossible to acquire."–T. J. Wise (who did not himself own a copy). Acquired in 1994.

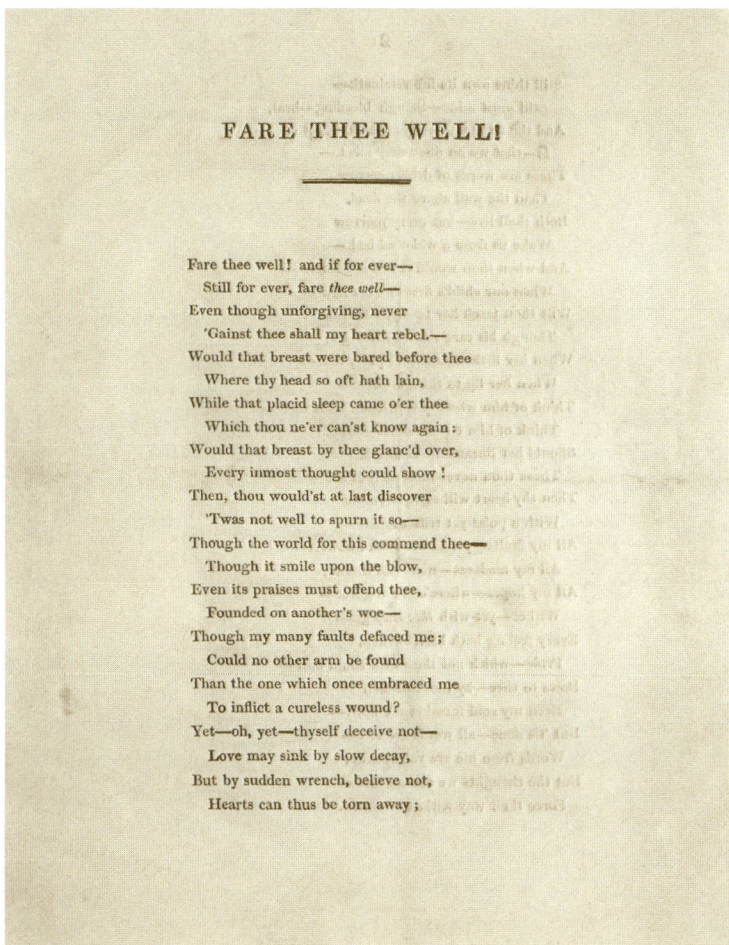

FARE THEE WELL!

Fare thee well! and if for ever—
    Still for ever, fare *thee well*—
Even though unforgiving, never
    'Gainst thee shall my heart rebel.—
Would that breast were bared before thee
    Where thy head so oft hath lain,
While that placid sleep came o'er thee
    Which thou ne'er can'st know again:
Would that breast by thee glanc'd over,
    Every inmost thought could show !
Then, thou would'st at last discover
    'Twas not well to spurn it so—
Though the world for this commend thee—
    Though it smile upon the blow,
Even its praises must offend thee,
    Founded on another's woe—
Though my many faults defaced me;
    Could no other arm be found
Than the one which once embraced me
    To inflict a cureless wound?
Yet—oh, yet—thyself deceive not—
    Love may sink by slow decay,
But by sudden wrench, believe not,
    Hearts can thus be torn away ;

118. [Byron, George Gordon, Lord.] Monody on the death of the Right Honourable R. B. Sheridan, written at the request of a friend, to be spoken at Drury Lane Theatre. London: printed for John Murray, 1816. 8vo, blue morocco, by Riviere.

> There are three variants of this poem. In the first, the first line of text on p. 11 begins, "To weep the vanished beam." In some copies, "weep" was changed to "mourn," but the setting is otherwise the same. In a subsequent issue, as here, the setting of type on p. 11 was tightened up, and the final four lines of text, from p. 12, were moved to the bottom. All variants have three pages of Murray's advertisements at the end. According to Wise, 750 copies of the first edition were printed; by the standard of Byron titles at this period, this was a relatively small number. With the armorial bookplate of Oliver Nowell Chadwyck-Healey. Acquired in 1981.

119. Byron, George Gordon, Lord. Manfred, a dramatic poem. London: John Murray, 1817. 8vo, original drab wrappers.

> This copy is an early issue, without a quotation from Hamlet on the title page. Byron had specifically requested this quote, but Murray forgot to include it, and the first copies run off did not have it; most copies are of the so-called third issue, and have the quotation. Of the early copies two variants are known, of uncertain sequence, one with the printer's imprint on the verso of the title page, and one, as here, with the imprint on the verso of the half-title. "Possession of either variant is a true reason for a collector's pride."–Francis Randolph, *Studies for a Byron Bibliography* (1979), p. 64. Acquired in 1993.

120. [Byron, George Gordon, Lord.] Beppo, a Venetian story. London: John Murray, 1818. 8vo, original dark drab wrappers.

> One of Byron's best poems, and the first to use ottava rima, a verse form he later employed in *Don Juan*. Only 500 copies of this anonymous first edition were printed, and it is now one of the more difficult of the major Byron titles to find, especially in fine original condition; as a comparison, *Manfred*, in 1817, was printed in 6,000 copies, and *Mazeppa*, in 1819, in 8,000 copies. The Simon Nowell-Smith copy. Acquired in 2002.

121. [Byron, George Gordon, Lord.] Beppo, a Venetian story. London: John Murray, 1818. 8vo, bound third in a volume with three other titles.

> Second edition; the text of the first edition has not been changed. Also bound in are first editions of Wordsworth's *Peter Bell* (1819; no. 26) and

The Waggoner (1819; no. 27), and the two parts of a parody of Byron called *What Have We Got?* (1820; no. 183). Acquired in 1979.

122. Byron, George Gordon, Lord. The prisoner of Chillon. A poem. Lausanne: Hignou & Company, booksellers, 1818. 8vo, original pink printed wrappers.

First separate edition; first printed in London with "other poems" in 1816. A pirated edition for English-speaking readers on the Continent, probably tourists visiting the castle where the poem is set. The frontispiece of Chillon was engraved after a design by J. Wezel. On the recto of the frontispiece is the signature of Sir C[harles] Macdonald Lockhart, 2nd Baronet (1799–1832), who succeeded his father to the title in 1816. Acquired in 2012.

123. Byron, George Gordon, Lord. Childe Harold's pilgrimage. A romaunt, in four cantos. London: John Murray, 1819. Two volumes, small 8vo, original drab boards, green cloth spines, printed paper labels.

First collected edition. This printing was produced when the supply of individual cantos was exhausted. Acquired in 1973.

124. Byron, George Gordon, Lord. Mazeppa, a poem. London: John Murray, 1819. 8vo, original drab wrappers.

Included is a prose piece called "A Fragment," concerning a mysterious death in Smyrna; this was begun by Byron on the same night that Mary Shelley started *Frankenstein*. Acquired in 1987.

125. [Byron, George Gordon, Lord.] Don Juan. London: printed by Thomas Davison, 1819. 4to, contemporary olive green straight-grained morocco.

The first two cantos of Byron's major poem, and the only cantos printed in this large format. In all 1,500 copies were printed, of which 150 were destroyed, or "wasted," after the book had been reprinted in octavo; subsequent cantos were all printed in both octavo and duodecimo formats. Murray's hesitancy to publish this poem is clearly indicated by the absence of his name in the imprint. "In 1823, with several more cantos already written and ready to be published, Byron broke with Murray who had been his publisher since he woke and found himself famous with *Childe Harold's Pilgrimage, a Romaunt*, in 1812. He had never been sympathetic to Murray's policy of high prices which cut him off from most of his potential audience."—William St Clair, *The Reading Nation in the Romantic Period* (2004), p. 323. Acquired in 1993.

126. [Byron, George Gordon, Lord.] Don Juan. A new edition. London: printed by Thomas Davison, 1819. [With:] Don Juan. Cantos III, IV, and V. London: printed by Thomas Davison, 1821. [With:] Don Juan. Cantos VI.--VII.--and VIII. London: printed for John Hunt, 1823. [With:] Don Juan. Cantos IX.--X.--and XI. London: printed for John Hunt, 1823. [With:] Don Juan. Cantos XII.--XIII.--and XIV. London: printed for John Hunt, 1823. [With:] Don Juan. Cantos XV. and XVI. London: printed for John and H. L. Hunt, 1824. Together six volumes, 8vo, original boards, printed paper labels; vol. 1 is in pale green boards, vol. 2 in drab boards with a tan backstrip, and vols. 3–6 in drab boards.

> First octavo edition of the first two cantos, first edition, largest format, of the rest. When John Murray reprinted the first two cantos of *Don Juan*, he did so at first as a large octavo, priced at 9s. 6d.; a year later, in 1820, he added an edition in a smaller octavo format, priced at 7s. These Wise refers to as "large paper," or "demy octavo," and "small paper," or "foolscap octavo."

When Leigh Hunt and his brother assumed publication of the poem in 1823, these two formats were maintained, and a third, much smaller one, was added (the so-called "common" edition). Surviving records indicate that Murray printed 1,500 copies of the large-paper edition of cantos 3–5; the number of small-paper copies is not known. For the large-paper edition of cantos 6–8 and cantos 9–11, the print run was also 1,500 copies; for the small-paper edition of these two volumes, the print runs were 3,000 and 2,500 copies, respectively. No records have been found for the last two volumes, but the size of the editions was no doubt comparable. Despite these figures, copies on large paper are now a good deal more common than those on small paper. The price of 9s. 6d. appears on the spine label of each volume in this set. Acquired in 1983.

127. [Byron, George Gordon, Lord.] Don Juan. London: printed by Thomas Davison, 1820. [With:] Don Juan. Cantos III, IV, and V. London: printed by Thomas Davison, 1821. [With:] Don Juan. Cantos VI.–VII.–and VIII. London: printed for John Hunt, 1823. [With:] Don Juan. Cantos IX.–X.– and XI. London: printed for John Hunt, 1823. [With:] Don Juan. Cantos XII.–XIII.–and XIV. London: printed for John Hunt, 1823. [With:] Don Juan. Cantos XV. and XVI. London: printed for John and H. L. Hunt, 1824. Together six volumes, 8vo (vols. 1–2) and 12mo (vols. 3–6), original boards, printed paper labels; vols. 1, 3, 4, and 6 are in drab boards, vols. 2 and 5 in blue boards with a drab paper backstrip.

> First small octavo edition of the first two cantos, first "small-paper" edition of the rest (see no. 126). The price of 7s. appears on the spine label of each volume in this set. With the early signature of W. D. Sneyd on each front pastedown, and the later bookplates of Herbert Brennon. Acquired in 1987.

128. [Byron, George Gordon, Lord.] Don Juan. . . . With a preface, by a clergyman. London: printed by and for Hodgson & Co., 1822. 12mo, original gray boards, printed paper label.

> An unusual, pirated edition of cantos 1–5, published a year before Byron began to produce further installments. The "clergyman" who wrote the preface has not been identified. His tone is lighthearted and conversational, and the text is intended to persuade the reader that Byron's poem was not, as was widely believed, "licentious," but in fact a work of considerable Christian moral content. Byron's poetical manner is also praised: "The Southeyans, the Wordsworthians, and the whole tribe of their canting and

childish admirers, are sinking into oblivion; and we are gradually returning to the true *tact*, (although, to use the words of our author, 'That modern phrase appears to me sad stuff,') or true poetical feeling, with which the admirers of Milton, Dryden, and Pope have ever been inspired." There is also a comment on the many unauthorized editions: "We have had editions of all sorts and sizes; from the original superb quarto, to the shabby 'two-penny trash,' or weekly instalment of about twenty-four duodecimo, badly printed pages." In fact, the present edition was no doubt very inexpensive; a contemporary owner matched it up with a volume containing the Hunt printings of cantos 6–16 in the "common" (or cheapest) edition (see no. 129). With a frontispiece portrait. This volume has a contemporary ownership stamp with the initials *HCO* and the motto "Bear and forbear" (the same stamp is in no. 129). Acquired in 1998.

129. [Byron, George Gordon, Lord.] Don Juan. Cantos VI.–VII.–VIII. London: printed for John Hunt, 1823. [Bound with:] Don Juan. Cantos IX.–X.–XI. London: printed for John Hunt, 1823. [Bound with:] Don Juan. Cantos XII.–XIII.–XIV. London: printed for John Hunt, 1823. [Bound with:] Don Juan. Cantos XV. and XVI. London: printed for John Hunt, 1824. Together four volumes in one, 12mo, original gray boards.

The so-called "common" edition of Byron's masterpiece, printed in a very small format, and sold at a shilling a volume; there was no comparable edition of cantos 1–5. The stated purpose of this printing was "to prevent piracy," and indeed most of the unauthorized editions of cantos 1–5 had been produced, by such booksellers as William Benbow, in a similarly small format. Both Wise and Randolph cite records of sixteen thousand copies having been printed of the first of these volumes, and seventeen thousand copies of the second; no records survive for the other two. These numbers seem scarcely credible, as copies are now very rare; this is the only set ever seen for sale. As first issued, the "common" editions were bound in tan printed wrappers. The copies here seem to have been bound up for sale in boards as a single volume, to match an 1822 pirated edition of cantos 1–5, in exactly the same size (no. 128). Acquired in 1998.

130. Byron, George Gordon, Lord. Marino Faliero, Doge of Venice. An historical tragedy, in five acts. With notes. The prophecy of Dante, a poem. London: John Murray, 1821. 8vo, original light brown boards, printed paper label.

With the contemporary signature of J. H. Smith, and the recent bookplate of Harry Barhr Smith. Acquired in 1972.

131. [Byron, George Gordon, Lord.] The age of bronze; or, carmen seculare et annus haud mirabilis. London: printed for John Hunt, 1823. 8vo, original drab wrappers. Acquired in 1978.

132. Byron, George Gordon, Lord. The island, or Christian and his comrades. London: printed for John Hunt, 1823. 8vo, original tan wrappers.

> A narrative poem about the mutiny on the *Bounty*, adapted from accounts by Captain Bligh and Will Mariner. With the signature of John P. Boileau, Jun. (1794–1869), dated "London, June 18, 1823"; in 1838 he was created a baronet, of Tacolnestone Hall, Norfolk. Acquired in 1976.

133. Byron, George Gordon, Lord. Werner, a tragedy. London: John Murray, 1823. 8vo, original drab wrappers.

> With the recent bookplate of Gerald P. Mander, Tettenhall Wood, Staffordshire. Acquired in 1979.

134. Byron, George Gordon, Lord. The deformed transformed; a drama. London: printed for J. and H. L. Hunt, 1824. 8vo, original tan wrappers. Acquired in 1991.

135. Byron, George Gordon, Lord. The miscellaneous poems. London: Benbow, printer and publisher, 1825. 12mo, contemporary dark green straight-grained morocco, covers elaborately decorated in gilt, spine gilt, a.e.g.

> First edition of this collection. A gathering of fifty-three poems. This is the last of a group of pirated editions issued by the somewhat disreputable bookseller William Benbow, beginning in 1821 with *Waltz, English Bards*, and the opening cantos of *Don Juan*. Benbow had a particular affinity for the poetry of Byron and Shelley, and all his various editions were printed, as here, in exceptionally small type. Bound in at the back, in an unidentified hand, is a transcript of Byron's "Maid of Athens." A particularly nice example of Benbow's handiwork, in a very pretty morocco binding of the period. Acquired in 2004.

136. Byron, George Gordon, Lord. Lamento del Tasso . . . Recato in Italiano da Michele Leoni. Pisa: presso Niccolò Capurro co' caratteri di F. Didot, 1818. 4to, nineteenth-century half brown morocco and marbled boards (original drab wrappers bound in).

> First edition in Italian of *The Lament of Tasso*, with the English text on facing pages; Byron's poem had first appeared the year before. Michele Leoni was a prolific translator of English literature, and had already produced versions of Milton's *Paradise Lost*, and a number of plays by Shakespeare. Byron was in Venice when he received a copy of this book, and he sent Leoni a gracious letter of thanks, referring with humility to his translations of "the most classical of our poets." Leoni went on to produce an Italian version of the fourth canto of *Childe Harold*. This copy is inscribed on the title page, "To Mrs. Somerville, from the translator." Acquired in 2001.

137. Byron, George Gordon, Lord. A volume of four early German translations, as described below. V.p.: 1819–1821. Together four vols. in one, 12mo, contemporary green morocco, covers elaborately decorated in gilt with wide borders and a central urn, spine richly gilt with a variety of ornaments including a lyre, red morocco label, rose endpapers, a.e.g.

> A beautiful collection of rare titles, as follows:
>
> (a) Byron, George Gordon, Lord. Lara. Eine Erzählung von Lord Byron. Im Versmasse des Originals übersetzt von Dr. Adrian. Frankfurt am Main: bei Johann David Sauerländer, 1819.
>
> First edition in German, and the first translation into any language; the poem had first appeared in 1814. The translator, Johann Valentin Adrian (1793–1864), taught at Rödelheim and Stuttgart before becoming associate professor of modern languages and literature at the University of Giessen in 1823; in 1824 he was appointed the university's first librarian. In 1830–31 he edited a twelve-volume collected edition of Byron in German.
>
> (b) Byron, George Gordon, Lord. Der Gauer Bruchstück einer Türkischen Erzählung. Von Lord Byron. . . . Nach der siebenter Englischen Ausgabe im Deutschen metrisch bearbeitet. Berlin: bey Ferdinand Dümmler, 1819.
>
> First edition in German of *The Giaour*; translated from the seventh edition of 1813 (with final additions, same year as the first edition). The translator's preface, dated May 24, 1819, is unsigned, but the translation has been attributed to Moritz Ludwig Wilhelm von Schoeler (b. 1771).

(c) Byron, George Gordon, Lord. Lord Byron's Gefanger von Chillon und Parisina nebst einem Anhang seiner lyrischen Gedichte, übersetzt durch Paul Graf von Haugwitz. Breslau: gedrucket und in Commission bei W. G. Kord, 1821.

Possibly the first edition in German of both poems; a different translation of the two poems, with others, by Julius Körner, was published in Zwickau the same year.

(d) Byron, George Gordon, Lord. Lord Byron's Erzählungen. Mit einem Versuch über Dichters Leben und Schriften von Dr. Adrian. Frankfurt am Main: bei Johann David Sauerländer, 1820.

First edition of this selection. Included are two translations, separately published in 1819, of *The Bride of Abydos* and *Lara*, along with *Der Blutsauger*, a translation of *The Vampyre* by Dr. Polidori, but here attributed to Byron. With a fifty-two-page review of Byron's life and writings by Johann Valentin Adrian, dated "Frühling [spring] 1819."

On the front flyleaf of this volume is the signature of Gertrud Koenig, dated 1901. This volume was acquired in 2011.

138. Byron, George Gordon, Lord. Manfred. Oversat af P. F. Wulff. Kjobenhavn: forlagt af Universitets-Boghandler Brummer; trokt i der Poppske Bogtrykkerie, 1820. 12mo, original pink printed stiff wrappers.

First edition in Danish. Acquired in 1980.

139. Byron, George Gordon, Lord. Manfred. Trauerspiel von Lord Byron. Teutsch von Adolf Wagner. Leipzig: F. A. Brockhaus, 1819. 12mo, original blue printed boards, printed paper label.

First edition in German. With an additional title page in English, and the English text on facing pages. At the end is a twenty-one-page section of Adolf Wagner's "Anmerkungen"; these notes refer at length to Goethe's judgement of the whole body of English poetry. Byron was unable to read German, and sent a copy of this translation to Richard Belgrave Hoppner, referring to the "plaguy long dissertation at the end of it," and asking if he could find "some poor Italian German scholar" who could translate it into English or Italian. This was duly achieved, and it was as a result of reading Goethe's opinions of English poetry that Byron decided to dedicate *Marino Faliero* to him. Byron sent the dedication to his publisher, John Murray, in October 1820; this was later suppressed, and one to Douglas Kinnaird was put in its place. Acquired in 2007.

Note: *Not included in the following list are titles by such writers as Thomas Moore, Leigh Hunt, and John Cam Hobhouse, which are listed separately by author. For another very early and truly remarkable piece of Byroniana, see above, under Wordsworth (no. 19).*

140. [Anon.] Another Cain. A poem. London: sold by Messrs. Hatchard and Son, 1823. 8vo, half blue morocco, by Tout.

A poetical attack on Byron's *Cain*, which was published in 1821 and quickly became the object of numerous attacks for its godlessness. This poem, in fact, has the same title as a long verse drama published in 1822 by William Battine (he is wrongly identified as the author on the front pastedown of this copy). The preface here, however, reveals that the author was a woman. Acquired in 1987.

141. B., F. H. An address to the Right Hon. Lord Byron, with an opinion on some of his writings. London: printed and published by Wetton and Jarvis, n.d. [1817]. 8vo, blue wrappers.

Second edition; first printed earlier the same year. A poem in blank verse inspired by the recent appearance of Byron's *Manfred*. The author regrets that the expression of Byron's genius is confined to a malevolent world, and urges him to seek inspiration in subjects of a higher order. The writer's identity has remained obscure, beyond the initials, which appear as a monogram on the title page. Acquired in 2011.

142. [Brougham, Henry.] Critique, from *The Edinburgh Review*, on Lord Byron's poems. Which occasioned "English Bards and Scotch Reviewers." London: printed by W. T. Sherwin, 1820. 8vo, original dark blue printed wrappers.

The first separate printing of a famous review of Byron's *Hours of Idleness*, which was, as the title page indicates, the occasion for a notable reply. The text was first published in 1808; the reason for this separate printing is not entirely clear. Brougham was a prolific and versatile contributor to *The Edinburgh Review* for a number of years. He went on to become an important Whig political leader, and served for a time as lord chancellor. Acquired in 1990.

143. [Byron, Anne Isabella (Milbanke) Byron, Baroness.] Remarks occasioned by Mr. Moore's notices of Lord Byron's life. [London: 1830.] 8vo, disbound.

An account by Byron's wife of the tumultuous events surrounding their permanent and legal separation in January 1816, written by her to correct the account provided by Thomas Moore in his recently published biography. Wise cites a letter written by Lady Byron to a friend in March 1830, in which she speaks of this pamphlet as follows: "My wish is to place the copy only in the hands of those who will make a discreet use of it, and prevent the possibility of its insertion in the newspapers at present. I think I shall not send out more than a dozen at first. Moore's is dispatched." This copy would appear to be one of those twelve, as it is inscribed on the front to Lord Holland; Holland House was, of course, at the very heart of the Whig aristocracy with which Byron himself, while he was still in England, was associated. Lady Byron may have decided eventually to give her pamphlet wider circulation, as it was reprinted in a slightly smaller typeface later the same year (condensed from fifteen pages to thirteen pages); there was also what appears to be a pirated edition, entitled *A Letter to Thomas Moore*. The rarity of this original printing is difficult to assess, as various sources do not make a clear distinction between the fifteen-page first edition and the thirteen-page reprint. Acquired in 2005.

144. Byron, Major George Gordon [pseud.], editor. [Wrapper title:] The inedited works of Lord Byron, now first published from his letters, journals, and other manuscripts, in the possession of his son, Major George Gordon Byron. Part I [–II]. New York: G. G. Byron; R. Martin, n.d. [1849]. Two parts, 8vo, original green printed wrappers.

A remarkable literary imposture. Major Byron, who also used the name De Gibler, first appeared on the scene in London in 1848, offering for sale, in a devious way, what purported to be a collection of autograph letters by Byron and Shelley. These documents were forgeries, and the Major's claim of consanguinity with Byron a fraud. The Major (or Colonel as he was sometimes called) in fact appears to have sprung up in the United States, and was clearly not, as he asserted, the son of a secret marriage between Byron and a certain Spanish lady. Some of the letters were purchased by the bookseller William White, in spite of his doubts as to their authenticity. Major Byron proceeded to advertise a forthcoming publication based upon his possessions, but he was evidently deterred by a growing cloud of public

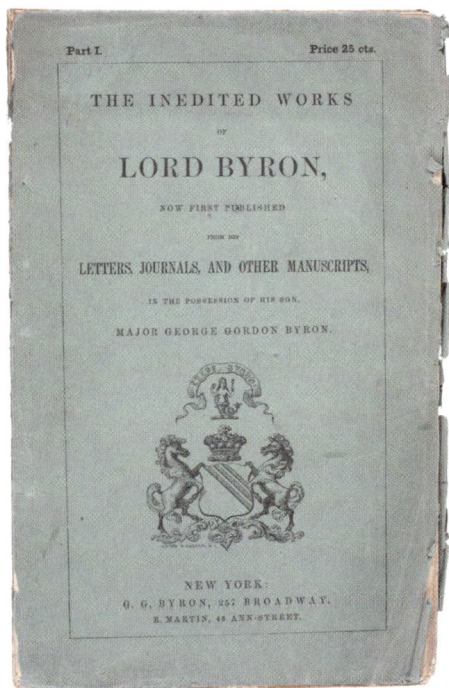

Part I.   Price 25 cts.

THE INEDITED WORKS

OF

LORD BYRON,

NOW FIRST PUBLISHED

FROM HIS

LETTERS, JOURNALS, AND OTHER MANUSCRIPTS,

IN THE POSSESSION OF HIS SON,

MAJOR GEORGE GORDON BYRON.

NEW YORK:
G. G. BYRON, 257 BROADWAY.
R. MARTIN, 48 ANN-STREET.

ITEM 144

suspicion, and he decamped to New York for the inauguration of his project.

His *Inedited Works* began to appear in monthly parts, with the work planned for completion in four volumes. Publication ceased after the appearance of only two parts, no doubt because Major Byron was once again threatened with exposure; the cessation of his project was so abrupt that the second part ends in the middle of a sentence. The printed wrappers here contain a prospectus for the whole; also laid in is a small broadside advertisement for the project, reprinted from its appearance in a New York newspaper. The text consists of a mixture of genuine material, culled from old sources and embellished with new anecdotes, and Major Byron's fabrications. The purported Byron letters that had been purchased by White were sold by him to John Murray in 1849. In 1851, Major Byron sent some forged manuscripts of Keats and Shelley to auction at Sotheby's, where they were purchased by Edward Moxon. Moxon then published a volume of the Shelley letters, with an introduction by Robert Browning, but he was forced to withdraw the book from sale when the fact was revealed that some of the letters were forgeries (see no. 476). Copies of Major Byron's aborted project are rare; no other set of these two parts has ever been seen for sale. Acquired in 1983.

145. Castelar y Ripoli, Emilio. Life of Lord Byron and other sketches. By Emilio Castelar. Translated by Mrs. Arthur Arnold. London: Tinsley Brothers, 1875. 8vo, original green cloth.

> First edition in English; first published in Madrid in 1873. An account of Byron's life, by a prominent and prolific Spanish aristocrat, statesman, and man of letters. Acquired in 1996.

146. [Catalogue.] A catalogue of a collection of books, late the property of a nobleman, about to leave England on a tour, including the large plates to Boydell's Shakespeare, 2 vol. proof impressions, red morocco.-

136

-Birch's General Dictionary, 10 vol. --Moreri, Dictionnaire Historique, 10 vol.--Lavater's Physiognomy, 5 vol. morocco.--Sophocles Brunckii, 2 vol. russia.--Malcolm's History of Persia, 2 vol. russia.--Dryden's Works, 18 vol. large paper, russia.--Beauties of England, 11 vol.--Cobbett's Parliamentary Debates, 31 vol.--State Trials, 21 vol. And some Romaic books of which no other copies are in this country. And a large skreen covered with portraits of actors, pugilists, representations of boxing matches, &c. Which will be sold by auction, by Mr. Evans, at his house, No. 26, Pall-Mall, on Friday, April 5, and following day. [London: 1816.] 8vo, recent wrappers.

ITEM 146

[2]

13 Conjuration du Duc d'Orleans, 3 vol. *Par.* 1796. Levis,
    Souvenirs et Portraits, 1813. Mémoires de la Margue-
    ritte de Bareith, 2 vol. and 7 more.
14 Biographical Dictionary, 11 vol. wanting vol. 8, and various
    others.
15 Saugnier and Brisson's Voyage to Africa, 1792. Walker's
    Voyages, 2 vol. 1760. Memoir of the Queen of Etruria,
    1814. Journey to Paris, 1814. Penrose's Journal,
    4 vol. 1815.
16 Despotism, or Fall of the Jesuits, 2 vol. 1811. Anecdotes
    of the French Nation, 1794, and 12 more.
17 Veneroni's Italian Grammar, 1812, and 9 School Books.
18 Xenophontis Cyropœdia Hutchinsoni, 1797 Ciceronis Ora-
    tiones Selectæ, Delphini, 1803. Demosthenis Orationes
    Selectæ, 1791.
19 Italian and English Dictionary, 1806. Veneroni's Italian
    Grammar, 1806. Graglia's Guide to Italian, 1803.
    Zotti's Italian Vocabulary.--4 vol.
20 Anquetil, Louis XIV. La Cour et le Regent, 4 vol. *Par.* 1789
21 Art of Tormenting, *russia*,   -   -   -   1806
22 Adams's Summary of Geography and History, *russia*,   1802
22* Ancient British Drama, 3 vol.   -   -   1810
23 Arabian Nights, by Scott, 6 vol. LARGEST PAPER, *with an
    additional set of plates inserted, green morocco*,   1811
23* Anderson's British Poets, 14 vol.   -   -   1795
24 Alciphronis Epistolæ, Gr. et Lat., Bergleri,   Lips. 1715
24* Æschylus a Porson, 2 vol. *russia*,   -   Glasg. 1806
25 Æschylus a Schutz, 3 vol. *russia*,   -   Halæ, 1798
25* Aristotelis Poetica a Tyrwhitt,   -   Oxon. 1794
26 Anacreon a Forster, *morocco*,   -   Lond. 1802
26* Anacreon by Moore, 2 vol. *russia*,   -   1800
27 Account of the most celebrated Pedestrians,   -   1813
28 Ariosto, Orlando Furioso, 4 vol.   -   Livorn. 1806
29 ————————————. 5 vol.   -   Par. 1786
30 Byron's (Lord) Hebrew Melodies,   -   1815
31 Another Copy,   -   -   -   1815
32 Another Copy,   -   -   -   1815
33 Another Copy,   -   -   -   1815
34 Beaumont and Fletcher's Works, with notes by Weber, 14 vol.
    1812
35 British Drama, 5 vol.   -   -   1804
36 British Novelists, with prefaces by Mrs. Barbauld, 50 vols.
    1810
37 British Essayists, by Chalmers, 45 vol.   -   1808
38 Beloe's Anecdotes of Literature, 2 vol.   -   1807
39 Boswell's Life of Johnson, 4 vol.   -   -   1807

137

A thirteen-page auction catalogue for the dispersal of Byron's library upon his flight from England in 1816. A copy of this catalogue in the British Library is fully priced, with the names of the buyers. The collection brought £723 12s. 6d., and the principal buyer was Byron's publisher John Murray, who acquired 96 out of the 383 lots; some of these were purchased on behalf of Mrs. Leigh and Samuel Rogers, and possibly for John Cam Hobhouse, who is known to have spent £34 at the sale, but whose name does not appear as a buyer. Byron's friend Scrope Davies, the gambler, also attended the sale, and bought 10 lots. In the present copy, the lots purchased by Murray are marked with an *M*; there are a few discrepancies between the markings here and those in the British Library copy. There are few clues to the ownership of these books, beyond the presence of four copies of *Hebrew Melodies* and fifteen copies of Thurston's *Illustrations of Lord Byron's Corsair*. The anonymity of this sale no doubt accounts for the rarity of the catalogue; four other copies are located, at the British Library, Harvard, Huntington, and Pennsylvania. Acquired in 1977.

147. [Anon.] Childe Harold's pilgrimage to the Dead Sea: Death on the Pale Horse: and other poems. London: printed for Baldwin, Cradock, and Joy, 1818. 8vo, disbound.

These poems were once carelessly attributed to Byron, but a footnote to the first of them makes it clear that they were merely written under his influence. Authorship has sometimes been attributed to Laura Sophia Temple (1763–after 1820), who had published three collections of verse between 1805 and 1812. This pamphlet was published at about the same time as canto 4 of *Childe Harold*. Acquired in 1977.

148. [Anon.] A critique on the genius and writings of Lord Byron, with remarks on Don Juan. Norwich: printed by and for John Stacy, and sold by all other booksellers, 1820. 8vo, original drab printed wrappers.

The authorship of this vituperative essay has been attributed to the publisher, Stacy, but the evidence is meager. On the front wrapper the signature of Rev. Neville White has been crossed out, and the signature of Joseph Neville White has been added below. Acquired in 1990.

149. Dallas, Robert Charles. Correspondence of Lord Byron, with a friend, including his letters to his mother, written from Portugal, Spain, Greece, and the shores of the Mediterranean, in 1809, 1810 and 1811. Also recol-

lections of the poet. By the late R. C. Dallas, Esq. The whole forming an original memoir of Lord Byron's life, from 1808 to 1814. And a continuation and preliminary statement of the proceedings by which the letters were suppressed in England, at the suit of Lord Byron's executors. Paris: published by A. and W. Galignani, 1825. Three vols., 12mo, contemporary calf.

> First published (and first complete) edition. R. C. Dallas was connected to Byron by the marriage of his sister to Byron's uncle, George Anson Byron. Dallas introduced himself to Byron after the publication of *Hours of Idleness*, and the two men stayed in contact for some time; Dallas sometimes acted on Byron's behalf in dealing with his publishers. In time Byron became bored with Dallas, and the relationship faltered. In 1824, Dallas arranged to publish in London an account of Byron's early life, but before the printing of the book could be completed, an injunction was obtained by Byron's executors, John Cam Hobhouse and Charles Hanson, to halt the project. Hobhouse and Hanson did not object to what Dallas proposed to publish, but they were afraid of the appearance of other, less innocent, portions of Byron's correspondence, and wished to establish the principle of executors' control. Dallas refused to compromise, and decided to get around the injunction by using the letters in his possession for the basis of a volume of recollections. Dallas died before this new volume was printed, but it was seen through the press, late in 1824, by his son, Rev. A. R. C. Dallas. Dallas also arranged for the original work to be printed in Paris the following year, beyond the reach of the English courts. These three volumes do, in fact, contain letters and other Byroniana of the highest importance. Acquired in 1987.

150. Delavigne, Jean François Casimir. Messénienne sur Lord Byron. Bruxelles: chez J. Coché-Mommens, imprimeur, n.d. [1824]. 8vo, bound seventh in a volume of eight titles relating to Byron (see no. 177).

> Apparently a Belgian piracy; first published in Paris in 1824, and twice reprinted there later the same year. A poetical tribute to Byron, by one of the most popular French poets of the day. This copy is signed on the title page by the forger Major Byron ("Geo. Gordon Byron"). Acquired in 1997.

151. [Anon.] Don Juan. Cantos XVII. and XVIII. London: printed for the booksellers, by Duncombe, n.d. [1825]. 12mo, original dark gray wrappers.

> One of a number of spurious continuations of Byron's masterpiece, the last two genuine cantos of which had first appeared in 1824 (the year of his death). Acquired in 1992.

139

152. [Anon.] Don Juan: with a biographical account of Lord Byron and his family; anecdotes of his Lordship's travels and residence in Greece, at Geneva, &c. Including, also, a sketch of the vampyre family. Embellished with a portrait of his Lordship, from an original drawing. . . . Canto III. London: printed for William Wright, 1819. 8vo, original gray boards, printed paper label.

> A poem of 144 stanzas in ottava rima, not so much a continuation of Byron's poem as a hostile and bitter account of Byron's life, purportedly written by Byron himself. Byron is variously called "Lord Harold," "Lord Beppo," and "Lord Squander." The "vampyre family" is the group of English expatriates living at Geneva, including Percy and Mary Shelley; p. 68 contains a reference to *Frankenstein*. With the contemporary signature of E. J. Shirley on the front cover, and an early orange ticket of S. Garrod's Circulating Library, No. 30, Paddington Street, London. Acquired in 1984.

153. Driver, Henry Austen. Harold de Burun. A semi-dramatic poem; in six scenes. London: printed for Longman, Rees, Orme, Brown, Green, and Longman, 1835. 8vo, contemporary calf.

> A remarkable verse play, whose two leading characters are Harold and Percy, characters closely based on Byron and Shelley. This is the dedication copy, inscribed on a front flyleaf, "To the Right Honourable Sir John Cam Hobhouse, Bart. from the author. May 27th, 1835." The printed dedication to Hobhouse describes him as "the early friend and intimate associate of the illustrious Byron." Acquired in 1996.

154. [Anon.] An elegy on the death of Lord Byron; intended as an humble but sincere tribute to the exalted virtues and brilliant talents of that much lamented nobleman: to which is prefixed, a dedicatory address, containing a feeble but well intentioned appeal on behalf of suffering Greece, stimulating to active exertions the friends of liberty in support of the glorious effort she is now making to shake off the galling chains of Ottoman oppression. Respectfully inscribed to the students of Cambridge University. London: sold at the Royal Academy, and by all booksellers, n.d. [1824]. 8vo, bound third in a volume of eight titles relating to Byron (see no. 177).

> An effusive tribute to Byron, both as a poet and as a supporter of Greek independence. The title page is printed within a mourning border. The only copy located is at the Boston Atheneum, where it is, curiously, dated 1885. Acquired in 1997.

155. [Anon.] Harold the exile. London: *******, 1819. Three vols., 12mo, contemporary half calf.

> First edition. An epistolary novel satirizing Byron, Lady Caroline Lamb, and other contemporaries. Michael Sadleir points out that this book was unique in his experience in having an imprint consisting only of asterisks; a leaf of advertisements makes it clear that the publisher was Henry Colburn. Acquired in 1972.

156. Lamartine, Alphonse Marie Louise de. Le dernier chant du pélerinage d'Harold. Paris: Dondey-Dupré père et fils; Ponthieu, 1825. 8vo, bound eighth in a volume of eight titles relating to Byron (see no. 177).

> Second edition (of four, all published the same year). A long verse continuation of Byron's *Childe Harold*, continuing the story up to the point of the hero's death (and no doubt inspired by Byron's own death). Acquired in 1997.

157. Lamartine, Alphonse Marie Louise de. The French poem of the celebrated Alphonse de la Martine, entitled Man, addressed to Lord Byron, translated into English verse, with the original text, by C. Hicks. Whitby: printed and published by R. Kirby, 1837. 8vo, original limp boards, purple cloth spine, printed paper side label.

> First edition in English; with the parallel version in French. The French text of this poem had originally appeared in *Méditations poétiques* (1820). With the early book label of John Earnshaw. Acquired in 1978.

158. [Lamb, Lady Caroline.] Glenarvon. London: printed for Henry Colburn, 1816. Three vols., 12mo, contemporary half red morocco.

> Lady Caroline's first book, a rhapsodical tale that attained some notoriety for its caricature portrait of Byron, with whom she had some years earlier been passionately infatuated. Lady Caroline was excitable and extravagant to the point of madness, and Byron had soon found her an embarrassment; his remark on the portrait of himself in the book, in a letter to Moore, is well known: "As for the likeness, the picture can't be good—I did not sit long enough." Acquired in 1991.

159. [Le Bas, Charles Webb.] Review of the life and character of Lord Byron. Extracted from the British Critic for April, 1831. London: printed for J. G. & F. Rivington, 1833. 8vo, contemporary calf.

A virulent attack on Byron, in the form of reviews of various biographies of him that were published in a journal whose readership was largely clerical. The reviewer, C. W. Le Bas, was an able clergyman who wrote widely for a number of periodicals, and served for some years as the principal of the East India College in Haileybury. The book edition was intended for a wider audience, as a new six-page preface explains. This copy is inscribed on a front flyleaf, "Written by Professor Le Bas of Haileybury College. Re-edited by me Edmund Mortlock." Mortlock appears not to have been hitherto identified as the editor of this volume; he also published a number of sermons, from the 1830s to the 1860s. Acquired in 2003.

160. [Anon.] A letter to R. W. Elliston, Esq. (lessee of the Theatre Royal Drury Lane) on the injustice and illegality of his conduct, in representing Lord Byron's tragedy of Marino Faliero: with some hints on the general management of his theatre. London: printed for John Lowndes, n.d. [1821]. 8vo, disbound.

> Byron's play had been produced at Drury Lane, against his wishes, on April 25, 1821; a court injunction prevented further performances until April 30. The author of this pamphlet, who signs himself "A Steady Observer," protests against the disregard of Byron's wishes. Acquired in 1983.

161. [Lockhart, John Gibson, probable author.] Letter to the Right Hon. Lord Byron. By John Bull [pseud.]. London: printed by and for William Wright, 1821. 8vo, bound sixth in a volume of eight titles relating to Byron (see no. 177).

> One of the most interesting and amusing of all pieces of Byroniana, consisting essentially of a review of the literary world of the Romantics, by Walter Scott's young son-in-law, who went on to become a major Scottish novelist and critic. Byron himself was quite amused by this pamphlet: "I have just read John Bull's letter. It is diabolically well written and full of fun and ferocity. I must forgive the dog, whoever he is. I suspect three people: one is Hobhouse, the other Mr. Peacock, and lastly Israeli [Isaac D'Israeli]. There are parts very like Israeli. . . . There is something too of the author of the Sketch-book [Washington Irving] in the style." Shortly afterward Shelley wrote to Peacock, telling him of Byron's suspicion, but Peacock replied, "As to the pamphlet signed John Bull, I certainly did not write it. I never even saw it, and do not know what it was about." Lockhart's authorship is now generally accepted; that being said, a copy in the Pforzheimer Library bears

an improbable contemporary manuscript ascription to Jeremy Bentham. This copy is signed on a blank leaf preceding the half-title by the forger Major Byron ("Geo. Gordon Byron"). Acquired in 1997.

162. Louvet, Édouard. Byron et la liberté, hymne de mort. Paris: imprimé chez Paul Renouard, 1824. 8vo, bound fifth in a volume of eight titles relating to Byron (see no. 177).

> This copy is signed on the half-title by the forger Major Byron ("Geo. Gordon Byron"). Acquired in 1997,

163. Mott, Mrs. Isaac Henry Robert. Sacred melodies, preceded by an admonitory appeal to the Right Honourable Lord Byron, with other small poems. London: printed for the author, 24, Dover Street, and 92, Pall Mall; and published by Francis Westley, 1824. 8vo, nineteenth-century half calf.

> The author's husband was a composer and music teacher, whose works are listed in an advertisement leaf at the end; Mott appears to have published no other book. In a preliminary six-page "advertisement" addressed to Lord Byron, the author laments the perversion of the poet's talents, particularly as displayed in *Don Juan* and *Cain*. The theme is continued in her "Admonitory Appeal," a poem of 451 lines, with accompanying notes. The rest of the book was also inspired by Byron: "The Sacred Melodies were originally written for the author's private use, being adapted from the Hebrew Melodies of Nathan and Braham. The metre of Lord Byron's words has been carefully preserved." The first poem in this section is an imitation of "She Walks in Beauty." With the large armorial bookplate of Gilbert Compton Elliot. Acquired in 2004.

164. [Murray, John.] Notes on Captain Medwin's Conversations of Lord Byron. [London: 1824.] 8vo, nineteenth-century red cloth.

> A privately printed response to Thomas Medwin's recent *Journal of the Conversations of Lord Byron at Pisa*. Byron's publisher was offended by the remarks about him recorded by Medwin, and he replies here by quoting extensive passages from Byron's letters in his possession. With the old book label of F. J. Sebley. Acquired in 1978.

165. Nathan, Isaac. Fugitive pieces and reminiscences of Lord Byron: containing an entire new edition of the Hebrew Melodies, with the addition of several never before published; the whole illustrated with critical,

historical, theatrical, political, and theological remarks, notes, anecdotes, interesting conversations, and observations, made by that illustrious poet: together with his lordship's autograph; also some original poetry, letters and recollections of Lady Caroline Lamb. London: printed for Whittaker, Treacher, and Co., 1829. 8vo, contemporary red morocco.

> Nathan was a London Jew of Polish descent. His introduction to Lord Byron in 1814 led to their collaboration on the "Hebrew Melodies" (1815–19), for which Nathan adapted ancient Jewish chants to Byron's poems. Acquired in 1996.

166. Newcastle Literary and Philosophical Society. A small group of printed ephemera relating to Byron, comprising two small quarto broadsides, one four-page pamphlet, and two related small printed notices. Included are:

> (a) Wawn, Charles N. Newcastle Literary and Philosophical Society. Don Juan. To the editor of the Newcastle Courant. Newcastle: printed by Edw. Walker, Jan. 25, 1820. 4to, broadside.
>
> Part of a controversy over whether or not a Newcastle subscription library should add to its shelves a copy of the first two cantos of *Don Juan*, published in 1819. Wawn here proposes that the book be banned.
>
> (b) [Anon.] Notice. [Newcastle: 1820.] 4to, broadside.
>
> A satirical thrust at a forthcoming meeting of the Society, at which the purchase (or apparently repurchase) of *Don Juan* was to be proposed and voted upon.
>
> (c) [Z., A.] Fragment of a prophetic report of the debate which will take place on Tuesday, Feb. 1st, 1820, at the room of the Lit. & Phil. Society, Newcastle upon Tyne, on Mr. B——tt's motion for the repurchase of the poem called Don Juan. [Newcastle: 1820.] 8vo, two leaves.
>
> A satirical poem; the unidentified author was evidently very young.
>
> (d) Two printed notices, both dated February 1, 1820, postponing the meeting in question because of the death of George III.
>
> No other copies have been located of any of these pieces. Acquired in 1983.

167. [Norton, Andrews, attributed author.] A review of the character and writings of Lord Byron. London: Sherwood Gilbert and Piper, 1826. 8vo, contemporary black morocco.

An early American attack on Byron, first published in *The Atlantic Monthly* (October 1825), and here printed for the first time in book form, with a substantial new preface. The authorship of this book has commonly been attributed to the man of letters and biblical scholar Andrews Norton (father of the more famous Charles Eliot Norton), but a copy at Yale bears an ascription to Willard Phillips. Acquired in 1990.

168. Palma di Cesnola, Alerino, Count. Greece vindicated; in two letters, by Count Alerino Palma; to which are added, by the same author, critical remarks on the works recently published on the same subject, by Messrs. Bulwer, Emerson, Pecchio, Humphreys, Stanhope, Parry, & Blaquiere. London: printed for the author, and sold by James Ridgway, 1826. 8vo, original drab boards, printed paper label.

> An account of various aspects of the Greek independence movement, by a contentious Italian participant living in exile in England; there are frequent references to Byron and his role in the insurgency. Palma di Cesnola had served under Napoleon; he was the father of Luigi Palma di Cesnola, an archaeologist who settled in America and was the first director of the Metropolitan Museum of New York. This copy is inscribed on the front pastedown, "To the Captain J. S. Crosbie with esteem, the author." With the signature of Commodore Crosbie, dated August 1826. Acquired in 2005.

169. [Anon.] A poetical epistle to Lord Byron. London: printed for John Miller; by B. M'Millan, 1816. 8vo, bound second in a volume of eight titles relating to Byron (see no. 177).

> A description in verse of Byron as an "Ungentle Bard," emphasizing his satanic genius; written upon the occasion of his departure from England. This copy is signed on the half-title by the forger Major Byron ("Geo. Gordon Byron"). Acquired in 1997.

170. [Anon.] The radical triumvirate, or, infidel Paine, Lord Byron, and surgeon Lawrence, colleaguing with the patriot radicals to emancipate mankind from all laws human and divine. With a plate—engraved for their instruction. A letter to John Bull, from an Oxonian resident in London. London: published by Francis Westley; sold also by J. Hatchard; E. Wilson; G. Greenland; Evans; and all other booksellers; printed by G. Hazard, 1820. 8vo, disbound.

An intemperate attack on "atheists and infidels of the present day." The last part of this fifty-page pamphlet is devoted to remarks on Byron's *Don Juan*, the first two cantos of which had just appeared; Byron is characterized as a poet capable of great beauty, who spoils his lines with "disgusting" blasphemy. With a satirical engraved frontispiece, "designed and drawn by Miss F. V. Parkyns," showing "sceptics instructed by the untutored South Sea Islanders." Acquired in 1992.

171. Reade, John Edmund. Italy: a poem, in six parts: with historical and classical notes. London: Saunders and Otley, 1838. 8vo, original purple cloth.

An imitation of *Childe Harold*. Reade published a number of volumes of verse, all of which show the influence of Byron. He was not averse to plagiarism, and freely borrowed sentiments and phrases from works he admired, by both Byron and such writers as Walter Scott, William Wordsworth, George Croly, and even Ben Jonson. This is the dedication copy, inscribed on the half-title, "To the Right Honble. Sir Robert Peel Bart M.P. &c. &c. &c. With the highest sentiments of respect from the author, May 26, 1838. Dover St. 21, Piccadilly." The printed dedication is on pp. v–vi; at the front is Peel's armorial bookplate. Acquired in 1984.

172. [Anon.] A reply to Fare Thee Well!!! Lines addressed to Lord Byron. London: printed by Plummer and Brewis, for R. S. Kirby, 1816. 8vo, disbound.

One of several poems responding to Byron's separation from his wife. This one purports to be by Lady Byron herself, and expresses mock compassion for his frailties, as well as an acknowledgment of his "matchless talent." Acquired in 1977.

173. Shaw, John. A volume containing three titles, two of them parodies of *Don Juan*. Three vols. in one, 8vo, contemporary black morocco.

Included are the following:

(a) Shaw, John. Woolton Green: a domestic tale; with other miscellaneous poems. Liverpool: printed by Perry and Metcalfe; and sold by the booksellers, and Robins and Sons (London), 1825.

The title page describes the author as living in Throstle Nest, Walton, near Liverpool. He was evidently a provincial actor, as he is also listed as "late of the Theatres Royal, York, Hull, Newcastle-upon-Tyne, &c."

(b) [Anon.] Don Juan. Canto XVII. Liverpool: printed by Perry and Metcalfe, and sold by all the booksellers, 1824.

First edition. A humorous continuation. No other copy has been located.

(c) Shaw, John. Don Juan. Canto XVIII. Liverpool: printed by Perry and Metcalfe, and sold by all the booksellers, 1825.

A second humorous continuation of *Don Juan*, similarly unlocated. The author is noted on the title page as the "author of Woolton Green." This volume is inscribed on a front flyleaf, "Presented by the author to James Hargraves Esq. as a small tribute of gratitude for past favours. June 21st, 1826." Acquired in 1996.

174. [Shelley, Mary.] Valperga: or, the life and adventures of Castruccio, prince of Lucca. By the author of "Frankenstein." London: printed for G. and W. B. Whittaker, 1823. Three vols., 12mo, original pale blue boards, printed paper labels.

> Mary Shelley's second novel, a romance set in fourteenth-century Italy, with its hero modeled upon Byron. Mary Shelley finished *Valperga* in 1820, but had difficulty in getting it published. In the spring of 1821 she sent the manuscript to her father, and asked him to help her see the novel into print; William Godwin then revised the text considerably, and the book was thus postponed until 1823. From the libraries of David Borowitz (sold in 1977) and Gerald E. Slater (sold in 1982). Acquired in 1995.

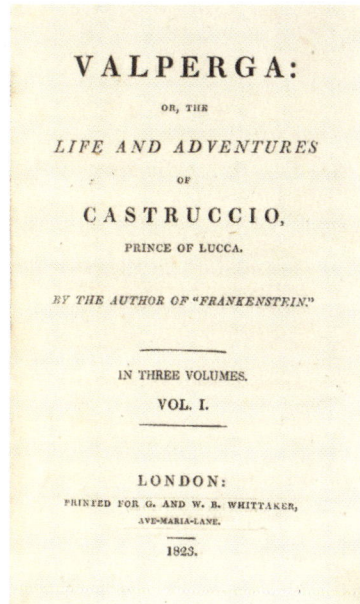

VALPERGA:

OR, THE

LIFE AND ADVENTURES

OF

CASTRUCCIO,

PRINCE OF LUCCA.

BY THE AUTHOR OF "FRANKENSTEIN."

IN THREE VOLUMES.

VOL. I.

LONDON:

PRINTED FOR G. AND W. B. WHITTAKER,
AVE-MARIA-LANE.

1823.

ITEM 174

175. Simon, Mrs. Barbara Anne. Evangelical review of modern genius; or, truth & error contrasted. New York: published and sold by D. A. Borrenstein; sold, also, at John P. Haven's Theological Bookstore; D. Fanshaw, printer, 1823. 12mo, original pale blue boards, printed paper label.

> An unusual book of early American poetry, dedicated to the board of the American Society for Meliorating the Condition of the Jews: "The profits

147

arising from the sale of this edition are, under the direction of the Board, devoted to aid the Hebrew settlement." The author was not herself Jewish, but her name suggests that she may have married a Jew. The first twenty-six pages of this volume are devoted to poetical reviews, from a spiritual point of view, of six major English poets—Walter Scott, Thomas Moore, George Crabbe, Thomas Campbell, the "Poet Laureat" (Robert Southey, in whom she finds "a strange discordant strain"), and Lord Byron. Acquired in 2007.

176. [Anon.] A sketch from public life: a poem, founded upon recent domestic circumstances; with Weep Not for Me! and other poems. London: printed for W. Hone, 1816. 8vo, disbound.

> A parody of Byron's "Sketch from Private Life," in which he had satirized Mrs. Claremont, Lady Byron's companion. He suspected Mrs. Claremont of having broken open his desk to find secrets of his outrageous behavior. A preface here describes this poem as "an antidote to the poison" of Byron's lines. In the poem itself, Byron ("Harold") is characterized as "a base unloved, un-loving, sordid elf." Acquired in 1977.

177. [Stanhope, Leicester Fitzgerald Charter.] "Reminiscences of Lord Byron." An extract from the author's *Greece, in 1823 and 1824* ("new edition," London: 1825). 8vo, bound with seven other titles relating to Byron, mid-nineteenth-century half morocco.

> For the other works, see nos. 150, 154, 156, 161, 162, 169, and 179. This extract is signed by the forger Major Byron on the fly-title ("Geo. Gordon Byron"). The pamphlets in this volume were no doubt acquired in 1851, at an auction of material owned by Major Byron, by Richard Monckton Milnes, poet, patron of the arts, collector, and biographer of Keats. With the bookplate of his son, Robert Crewe-Milnes, 1st Marquis of Crewe, whose crest is stamped in gilt on the front cover. Acquired in 1997.

178. Stevens, Rev. John. Poems. The Battle of Waterloo. Byron's Vision of Judgment, reversed; the victory of Aboukir; and the Portuguese expedition. London: printed for the author; and sold by Rivingtons; Hatchards; Sherwood and Co., and by all the booksellers, 1827. 8vo, original tan printed wrappers.

> A travesty of a Byron poem first published in *The Liberal* in 1822; the rest of the verses in this pamphlet are patriotic, in keeping with the dedication to the Duke of Wellington. The author was the vicar of Swalcliffe (Oxfordshire), and rector of Portingland Magna. Acquired in 1992.

179. [Anon.] To the departed. Stanzas to the memory of Lord Byron. London: J. Hatchard and Son, 1825. 8vo, bound fourth in a volume of eight titles relating to Byron (see no. 177).

> A poetical tribute in twenty-six Spenserian stanzas, praising Byron as the best English poet since Milton; there are also lines on the debt owed by Greece for his support, and sympathetic references to Byron's daughter Ada. This copy is signed on the title page by the forger Major Byron ("Geo. Gordon Byron"). Acquired in 1997.

180. [Todd, Henry John.] A remonstrance addressed to Mr. John Murray, respecting a recent publication. London: printed for F. C. & J. Rivington, 1822. 8vo, disbound.

> One of the first attacks on Byron's *Cain*. The author, a clergyman best known as an editor of the works of Milton, chastises Murray for his long association, as a publisher, with a godless poet. The text is signed "Oxoniensis" at the end. Byron knew of this pamphlet, but claimed not to have seen it; in a letter to Kinnaird he dismisses the author as a clergyman who "wants a living." Acquired in 1992.

181. Trelawny, Edward John. Recollections of the last days of Shelley and Byron. London: Edward Moxon, 1858. 8vo, original green cloth.

> Trelawny was an adventurer and prone to exaggeration, but his reminiscences are of major interest. Acquired in 1971.

182. Trelawny, Edward John. Records of Shelley, Byron, and the author. London: Basil Montagu Pickering, 1878. Two vols., 8vo, original black cloth.

> Second edition. A substantially revised and expanded version of the author's *Recollections* (1858; no. 181). The portrait of Byron has been made rather less sympathetic. Acquired in 1980.

183. [Anon.] What have we got? Or, all our glories; a poetico-political morceau. Fragment I. By *–*–*. London: printed for James Ilbery, 1820. [Bound with:] What have we got? Or, all our glories: a poetico-political morceau. Fragment II. By *–*–*. London: printed for James Ilbery, 1821. 8vo, bound fourth and fifth in a volume containing first editions of Wordsworth's *Peter Bell* (1819; no. 26) and *The Waggoner* (1819; no. 27), and a second edition of Byron's *Beppo* (1818; no. 121).

A verse satire, written, according to the preface to the first "fragment," "in the harmonical, ironical, Byronical, uncanonical manner, so much in vogue." The stanza form is ottava rima, popularized by Byron first in *Beppo*, and later in *Don Juan*. The most remarkable feature here is a poem addressed to Byron, which begins on the half-title of part 2 and is there lithographed in an attempt to make it appear to be written by hand (a device not encountered elsewhere). Acquired in 1979.

184. Wilberforce, Edward, and Edmund Forster Blanchard. Poems. London: Longman, Brown, Green, Longmans, and Roberts, 1857. 8vo, original green cloth.

> An amusing book of verse by two young men. The longer section, containing poems by Wilberforce, begins with a seventeenth canto of Byron's *Don Juan*. He was the twenty-three-year-old grandson of the great philanthropist William Wilberforce. Acquired in 1999.

PERCY BYSSHE SHELLEY (1792–1822)

185. [Shelley, Percy Bysshe.] Zastrozzi, a romance. By P. B. S. London: printed for G. Wilkie and J. Robinson, 1810. 12mo, red morocco, gilt, spine elaborately gilt in compartments with green morocco onlays, by Douglas Cockerell (dated 1903).

> Shelley's first book, a gothic tale in the manner of Ann Radcliffe, written at the age of sixteen while he was at Eton, and published about a year later. With the book label of Chauncey Brewster Tinker. Acquired in 1987.

186. [Shelley, Percy Bysshe.] St. Irvyne; or, the Rosicrucian: a romance. By a gentleman of the University of Oxford. London: printed for J. J. Stockdale, 1811. 12mo, contemporary half calf.

> The second of Shelley's two gothic novels. He thought this sort of fiction would make money, and financed the printing of the book himself, assuming that it was "a thing which almost mechanically sells to circulating libraries." He was wrong, and *St. Irvyne* was little noticed. Acquired in 1980.

187. Shelley, Percy Bysshe. Queen Mab; a philosophical poem: with notes. London: printed by P. B. Shelley, No. 23, Chapel Street, Grosvenor Square, 1813. 8vo, red morocco, by Sangorski & Sutcliffe.

Privately printed in an edition of 250 copies. Shelley gave away many copies of this book, but when he did so he almost always removed the verse dedication to Harriet (either his wife, or Harriet Grove), and cut away the imprints at the foot of the title page and last leaf. This copy is unmutilated. Acquired in 1991.

188. Shelley, Percy Bysshe. Alastor; or, the spirit of solitude: and other poems. London: printed for Baldwin, Cradock, and Joy; and Carpenter and Son; by S. Hamilton (Weybridge, Surrey), 1816. 8vo, contemporary calf. Acquired in 1979.

189. Shelley, Percy Bysshe. Laon and Cythna; or, the revolution of the golden city: a vision of the nineteenth century. In the stanza of Spenser. London: printed for Sherwood, Neely, & Jones; and C. and J. Ollier: by B. M'Millan, 1818. 8vo, original drab boards, printed paper label.

> Second issue, as usual; a few copies are known with an additional leaf preceding the title page and containing a notice for *Laon and Cythna* itself ("in the press"), and a fly-title that precedes the main text and bears a quotation from Pindar. The Britwell copy, sold at Sotheby's on March 30, 1971, for £400 ($960) to Seven Gables Bookshop, on behalf of William E. Stockhausen. Acquired in 1974 at the Stockhausen sale, at Parke-Bernet in New York.

190. Shelley, Percy Bysshe. The revolt of Islam; a poem, in twelve cantos. London: printed for C. and J. Ollier; by B. M'Millan, 1818. 8vo, original blue boards, marbled paper backstrip, printed paper label.

> First edition under this title; the sheets of *Laon and Cythna* with a new title page, and twenty-six canceled leaves to incorporate Shelley's extensive revisions. With the bookplate of H. Buxton Forman on the front pastedown, and a note in his hand stating that this copy belonged to Shelley's close friend Maria Gisborne, to whom one of his most successful poems was addressed ("Letter to Maria Gisborne"). Buxton Forman's note reads as follows: "This is Mrs. Gisborne's copy, bought by Ellis & transferred to me at the sale of the Gisborne Shelleyana at Puttick & Simpson's on the 28th of May 1878. These Shelleyana were left by John Gisborne to a Miss Eliz. Rumble, who was the seller." With the later bookplate of Harry Glemby, and the book label of Jerome Kern. Acquired in 1973.

191. Shelley, Percy Bysshe. Rosalind and Helen, a modern eclogue; with other poems. London: printed for C. and J. Ollier, 1819. 8vo, green morocco, by Riviere.

> The other poems include "Lines Written among the Euganean Hills," "Hymn to Intellectual Beauty," and "Ozymandias." Acquired in 1973.

192. Shelley, Percy Bysshe. The Cenci. A tragedy, in five acts. Italy: printed for C. and J. Ollier (London), 1819. 8vo, green morocco, by Bedford.

> This verse play was printed in Leghorn, in an edition of 250 copies. From the Britwell Court library. A note of acquisition on the front flyleaf, dated August 17, 1878, is in the hand of Wakefield Christie-Miller ("W. C. M."), who owned the collection at that time. He has added his "C & P" ("collated and perfect") and has noted that the book was acquired at A. G. Dew-Smith's sale at Sotheby's for £2 18s. + 6s. commission, for a total of £3 4s. It was subsequently sold at Sotheby's on March 30, 1971. Acquired in 1977.

193. Shelley, Percy Bysshe. Prometheus unbound: a lyrical drama in four acts, with other poems. London: C. and J. Ollier, 1820. 8vo, original gray boards, printed paper label.

> Second issue, as usual, with the contents leaf a cancel, and "miscellaneous" correctly spelled. With the single name "Tighe," in an early hand, on the front flyleaf, no doubt placed there by George William Tighe, who played a major role in Shelley's life during his residence in Italy. In his biography of Shelley (vol. 2, pp. 108–9), Newman Ivy White provides the background:

> The journey to Florence was broken by a one-day stop at Pisa [October 2, 1819], where the Shelleys made an acquaintance destined to be of great value to them and to Claire as long as they remained in Italy. In Ireland many years earlier Mary's mother, Mary Wollstonecraft, had been the much-loved teacher of a young girl who later became Lady Mountcashell. Afterwards Lady Mountcashell had entertained Godwin in Ireland and had ever since been in sporadic correspondence with him and the second Mrs. Godwin. She was a woman of extraordinary mind and appearance. In the early days Godwin had described her as a stern democrat, a republican of unusual understanding and good nature, but rather liable to caricature on account of the combination of these qualities with a handsome countenance and a tall, brawny figure most oddly and carelessly clothed. She had separated from her husband, and when the Shelleys met her had been living for many years in a free-love union with Mr. George William Tighe, the son of an Irish M.P. and a cousin of Mary Tighe, the author of *Psyche*. For eight years "Mr. and Mrs. Mason," as they called themselves, had been living a life of quiet, decent retirement in Italy.

When the Shelleys themselves settled in Pisa, over the course of the year this book was published, Tighe and Lady Mountcashell were their closest friends: "Almost every day for six months the Shelleys and Claire went there for tea, dinner, or an afternoon or morning call. Mrs. Mason's personality, and her garden, very probably contributed something to Shelley's 'The Sensitive Plant'" (p. 180).

The provenance of this copy is confirmed by the fact that it was consigned for sale to Sotheby's on November 10, 1964, by Neri Farina Cini, identified in the auction catalogue as the grandson of the Masons' daughter Nerina, who had married a man named Bartolomeo Cini. It was purchased by Simon Nowell-Smith, who added his book label. Acquired in 2002.

194. Shelley, Percy Bysshe. The Cenci: a tragedy in five acts. London: C. and J. Ollier, 1821. 8vo, later boards.

Second edition, revised. With the nineteenth-century bookplate of Barron Field, Esq., barrister at law of the Inner Temple. Barron Field (1786–1846) as a young man moved in a literary circle that included Leigh Hunt, Charles Lamb, Henry Crabbe Robinson, and William Wordsworth. He emigrated to Australia in 1817. On the front pastedown is the early signature of George Bell, York Street, Covent Garden. Acquired in 1971.

195. [Shelley, Percy Bysshe.] Epipsychidion: verses addressed to the noble and unfortunate lady Emilia V−− now imprisoned in the convent of −−. London: C. and J. Ollier, 1821. 8vo, brown morocco, by Bradstreet.

This copy is inscribed on the half-title, "William Donne Esqre. from his affectionate friend R. C. T." The donor was the poet Richard Chevenix Trench, later archbishop of Dublin. The recipient was William Bodham Donne, a direct descendant of the poet John Donne. The book must have been presented when the two were at Cambridge in the mid-1820s; they were both members of the Apostles, along with Tennyson and Arthur Hallam. Later bookplate of Thomas Jefferson McKee. Acquired in 1979.

196. Shelley, Percy Bysshe. Adonais: an elegy on the death of John Keats, author of Endymion, Hyperion, etc. Pisa: with the types of Didot, 1821. 4to, green morocco.

From the library of Mrs. J. Insley Blair, a portion of which was sold at auction in New York in 2004.

197. Shelley, Percy Bysshe. Hellas: a lyrical drama. London: Charles and James Ollier, 1822. 8vo, late nineteenth-century red morocco, by Maclehose of Glasgow.

> With the book label of George Coats, Belleisle. Acquired in 1996.

198. Shelley, Percy Bysshe. Poetical pieces, by the late Percy Bysshe Shelley; containing Prometheus Unmasked [sic], a Lyrical Drama; with other poems. Hellas; A Lyrical Drama. The Cenci; A Tragedy in Five Acts. Rosalind and Helen; with other poems. London: printed for C. and J. Ollier; and W. Simpkin and R. Marshall, 1823. 8vo, contemporary blue calf, elaborately stamped in blind, with a central panel on each cover of marbled paper with a gilt border, a.e.g.

> A nonce collection, published shortly after Shelley's death, consisting of the unsold sheets of four books originally issued by C. and J. Ollier, bound up with a general title page. Three titles are first editions; *The Cenci* is a second (first London) edition. There are two issues of this collection, this being the first; the second does not contain *Hellas*, as evidently the supply of sheets was used up. This copy is in a striking provincial binding, rather charmingly lettered "Shelly's Poetical Pieces" on the spine. With the book label of Simon Nowell-Smith, and an inserted note in his hand, stating that a bookseller once showed him a very similar binding of 1840, with the binder's ticket of Barrett of Daventry. On a front flyleaf is an earlier inscription, "To Adriana Hogart from her Brother Henry." Acquired in 2002.

199. Shelley, Percy Bysshe. Posthumous poems. London: printed for John and Henry L. Hunt, 1824. 8vo, blue morocco, by Root & Sons.

> This volume was edited by Mary Shelley. Appearing here for the first time are several of Shelley's best-known poems, including "Julian and Maddalo," "The Witch of Atlas," and "The Triumph of Life." After the book appeared, Shelley's father, Sir Timothy Shelley, forbade any further publication of his son's work. Mary Shelley had to wait until after his death to publish the *Poetical Works* (1839; no. 204). With the book label of Hayes Blake Hoyt. Acquired in 1972.

200. [Shelley, Percy Bysshe, contributor.] The keepsake for MDCCCXXIX. Edited by Frederic Mansel Reynolds. London: published for the proprietor by Hurst, Chance and Co., and R. Jennings, n.d. [1828]. 8vo, contem-

porary full red morocco, covers with green morocco onlays outlining a central oval and richly gilt with an overall floral pattern, spine gilt in alternating red and green morocco compartments, inner dentelles gilt, pink silk endpapers, a.e.g.

ITEM 200

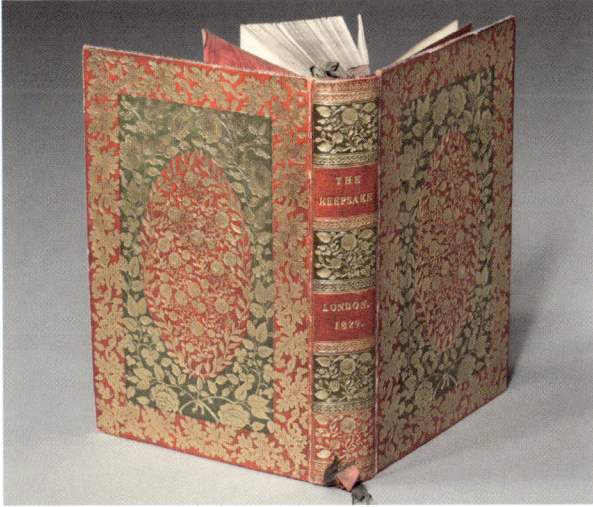

The Keepsake was perhaps the most ambitious of all the literary annuals of the period; inaugurated in 1828 by the novelist W. Harrison Ainsworth, it continued to appear for the next thirty years. In a preface to this second number of *The Keepsake*, the publisher boasts of having spent 11,000 guineas in putting it together. All contributions were original compositions, and the list of authors is indeed impressive. Unpublished writings by Shelley were provided from manuscripts in the possession of Mary Shelley, which included an essay entitled "On Love" and three short poems grouped together as "Fragments." There is also a short story by Mary Shelley herself (described only as "the author of *Frankenstein*"). In addition, there are three stories by Walter Scott, five poems by Wordsworth, four by Coleridge, two by Southey, and one by Moore. Bound in at the front is an engraved presentation leaf bearing a manuscript inscription to the Right Honourable Lady Louisa Stuart, "from her affectionate nephew Evelyn Stuart," dated January 1, 1829. This copy is from the private collection of Michael Papantonio, of Seven Gables Bookshop in New York, with his cost code at the back, dated February 1963, of "ggix" ($33.60); he no doubt kept it because of the spectacular gift binding. Acquired in 1996.

201. Shelley, Percy Bysshe. The revolt of Islam; a poem, in twelve cantos. London: printed for John Brooks 1829. 8vo, original drab boards, printed paper label.

> A reissue of the 1818 sheets (no. 190), with a new title page. With the signature on the title page of Stephen P. Barton. Acquired in 1976.

202. Shelley, Percy Bysshe. The masque of anarchy. A poem. Now first published, with a preface by Leigh Hunt. London: Edward Moxon, 1832. 8vo, original tan boards, printed paper label.

> This copy has an inscription on the front flyleaf from the novelist Mary Russell Mitford to M. W. Blagrave, dated 1833. With the bookplate of H. Buxton Forman, but probably not his copy, as there are no penciled notes in his hand. These bookplates were inserted when Buxton Forman's library was sold at auction in New York in 1920; many specimens left over were placed in other volumes to create false provenance. Acquired in 1976.

203. Shelley, Percy Bysshe. The Shelley papers. Memoir of Percy Bysshe Shelley by T. Medwin, Esq. And original poems and papers by Percy Bysshe Shelley. Now first collected. London: Whittaker, Treacher, & Co., 1833. 8vo, original pink boards, printed paper label.

> Printed here for the first time in book form are poems originally published in *The Athenæum*. This copy is inscribed on the front flyleaf, "Presented to me by Mr. J. C. Francis of the Athenæum. J. H. Ingram." With the later book labels of Dorothy Sturges and "M. C. E." Acquired in 1973.

204. Shelley, Percy Bysshe. The poetical works of Percy Bysshe Shelley. Edited by Mrs. Shelley. London: Edward Moxon, 1839. Four vols., 8vo, original red cloth. Acquired in 1994.

205. Shelley, Percy Bysshe. The poetical works of Percy Bysshe Shelley. Edited by Mrs. Shelley. London: 1840. 8vo, original black cloth.

> Second edition, much altered. When Mary Shelley first printed a collected edition of her late's husband's poems, she dealt rather freely with the text of some of his more controversial works, and various admirers of Shelley raised objections. As she explains in a postcript to the preface here, these defects have been remedied. Added to this edition are two long poems, "Swellfoot the Tyrant" (first privately printed in 1820, but suppressed, and

known in only a few copies) and "Peter Bell the Third," along with a few shorter pieces. Also included is the full text of *Queen Mab,* which had been bowdlerized in the four-volume collection. With the bookplate of Oliver Brett (later Lord Esher). Acquired in 1992.

206. [Shelley, Percy Bysshe.] "We pity the plumage, but forget the dying bird." An address to the people on the death of the Princess Charlotte. By the hermit of Marlow. [Colophon:] London: Compton and Ritchie, printers, n.d. [probably 1843]. 8vo, sewn, as issued.

> An imprint on the verso of the title page reads, "reprinted for Thomas Rodd." Rodd claimed that this was a facsimile of an earlier edition, of which Shelley printed twenty copies in 1816, but no copy of the earlier edition has ever turned up, and it is probable that it never existed. Acquired in 1992.

207. Shelley, Percy Bysshe. The complete poetical works of Percy Bysshe Shelley. The text carefully revised, with notes and a memoir, by William Michael Rossetti. London: E. Moxon, Son, and Co., 1878. Three vols., 8vo, original dark green cloth.

> Second edition as edited by William Michael Rossetti, with an important new preface, and much revised and expanded (from two volumes to three); the first edition had appeared in 1870. Acquired in 2001.

JOHN KEATS (1795–1821)

208. Keats, John. Poems. London: printed for C. and J. Ollier, 1817. 8vo, mid-nineteenth-century half calf.

> Keats's first book, which was not very well received. With the armorial bookplate of Frederick Collins Wilson (1832–1885), a keen amateur actor at Trinity College, Cambridge, whose *Short Poems* was published in 1863. The Gerald E. Slater copy. Acquired in 1982.

209. Keats, John. Endymion: a poetic romance. London: printed for Taylor and Hessey, 1818. 8vo, contemporary calf, rebacked.

> First issue, with the leaf preceding the text containing a single erratum; this was later replaced with a list of five errata. Acquired in 1978.

𝔓𝔬𝔢𝔪𝔰,

BY

JOHN KEATS.

" What more felicity can fall to creature,
" Than to enjoy delight with liberty."

Fate of the Butterfly.—SPENSER.

First Edition

LONDON:

PRINTED FOR

C. & J. OLLIER, 3, WELBECK STREET,

CAVENDISH SQUARE.

1817.

210. Keats, John. Lamia, Isabella, the Eve of St. Agnes, and other poems. London: printed for Taylor and Hessey, 1820. 12mo, red morocco, by Stikeman. Acquired in 1979.

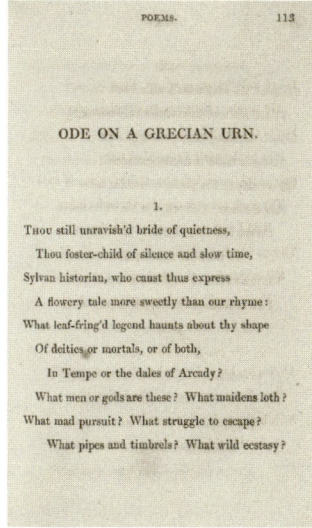

211. Keats, John, Samuel Taylor Coleridge, and Percy Bysshe Shelley. The poetical works of Coleridge, Shelley, and Keats. Complete in one volume. Paris: published by A. and W. Galignani, 1829. 8vo, original gray-green boards, printed paper label.

> First edition. This Galignani printing is the first collected edition of Keats, and a volume of some importance, with a certain number of poems printed in book form for the first time. The short memoirs were written by Cyrus Redding. Acquired in 1987.

212. Keats, John. Life, letters, and literary remains of John Keats. Edited by Richard Monckton Milnes. London: Edward Moxon, 1848. Two vols., 8vo, original violet cloth.

> First edition. An exceedingly important book, in which much by Keats, both in verse and in prose, is printed for the first time. Monckton Milnes, later 1st Baron Houghton and himself a poet of some ability, had access to papers furnished to him by two of Keats's closest friends, Charles Armitage Brown and Joseph Severn. Included here are a great many of the poet's remarkable letters, and Severn's famous portrait. Acquired in 1980.

213. Keats, John. Letters of John Keats to Fanny Brawne written in the years MDCCCXIX and MDCCCXX and now given from the original manuscripts with introduction and notes by Harry Buxton Forman. London: printed for private circulation, 1878. Large 8vo, original light blue-gray cloth.

> This copy is one of fifty printed on large and fine paper. The publication of these letters, arguably the most celebrated love letters in the English language, was a notable literary event, as none of them had ever before appeared in print, and the very name of Fanny Brawne was as yet unknown to the public. Monckton Milnes had left her nameless, and a casual refer-

ence to "Miss Brawn" in his 1876 Aldine edition of Keats's poetry was too fleeting to arouse more than idle curiosity. The letters themselves had long been in the possession of Sir Charles Dilke, the grandson of Keats's great friend Charles Wentworth Dilke. Dilke had purchased the letters at some point, though it is not exactly clear how, or when; he had, however, kept in close touch with surviving members of the Keats circle, especially Keats's sister Fanny (Mrs. Valentin Llanos). In 1833, Fanny Brawne married and became Mrs. Louis Lindon; she died in 1865. In 1876, Dilke was approached by her son Herbert V. Lindon, who asked that the letters be returned to the family. Lindon shortly afterward offered the letters for sale to Monckton Milnes, by then 1st Baron Houghton, but nothing came of the offer, and in the end they were acquired by Buxton Forman for £100. Dilke had always considered the letters too intimately revealing to be fit for the press, and in *The Athenæum* (Feb. 16, 1878) he denounced "the *owners* of these letters," and asserted that "if their publication . . . is the greatest impeachment of a woman's sense of womanly delicacy to be found in the history of literature, Mr. Forman's extraordinary preface is no less notable as a sign of the degradation to which the bookmaker has sunk." This volume in fact prints thirty-seven of the thirty-nine known letters from Keats to Brawne; the originals were widely dispersed at the disastrous US sale of Buxton Forman's library more than forty years later. With the bookplate of Jacobi Barr Lamb. Acquired in 1996.

Appearances in periodicals

214. [Keats, John, contributor.] Annals of the fine arts, for MDCCCXVI [-MDCCCXX]. London: published for the proprietors by Messrs. Sherwood, Neely, and Jones; Boydell and Co.; Arch; Carpenter and Son; T. and G. Underwood; A. Black, etc., 1817–1820. Five vols., 8vo, contemporary half calf, rebacked in cloth.

> A complete run of seventeen numbers of England's first art journal, edited by the architect James Elmes, with the guidance and assistance of Benjamin Haydon, and intended editorially as a Romantic antidote to the grand manner of the Royal Academy. Some of the contributions to this periodical are of exceptional literary interest. In the seventh number (vol. 2) are two original sonnets by Wordsworth, "Upon the Sight of a Beautiful Picture" and "To B. R. Haydon, Esq." In the third volume appear two sonnets by Keats on the Elgin Marbles (a prominent topic throughout); these had first appeared the year before in Leigh Hunt's *Examiner*. In the tenth num-

ber is the first of a series of articles by William Hazlitt, an essay on Joshua Reynolds. Most dramatic of all are two unsigned original poems in vol. 4. In no. 13 is the first printing of Keats's "Ode to the Nightingale" [*sic*] and, in no. 15, "On a Grecian Urn." In addition to a slight rewording of the titles, both texts reveal that certain changes were made for publication in book form. The revisions were most significant in "Ode on a Grecian Urn." For example, the question "What mad pursuit?" in the first stanza, here reads, rather less strikingly, "What love? What dance?" There is also an unfortunate misprint in the second stanza, where the phrase "bid the spring adieu" has been inadvertently repeated from stanza 3, instead of "can those trees be bare." As it stands, the second stanza does not rhyme properly, and makes no sense. This set was found in 1988, after a search of more than twenty years.

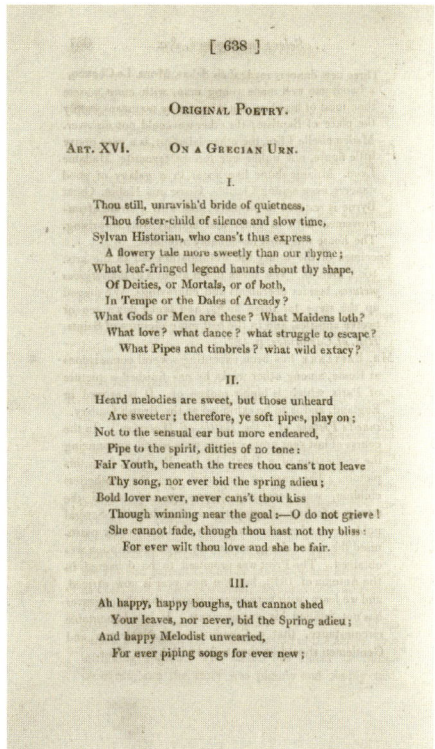

ITEM 214

[638]

ORIGINAL POETRY.

ART. XVI.   ON A GRECIAN URN.

I.

Thou still, unravish'd bride of quietness,
  Thou foster-child of silence and slow time,
Sylvan Historian, who canst thus express
  A flowery tale more sweetly than our rhyme;
What leaf-fringed legend haunts about thy shape,
  Of Deities, or Mortals, or of both,
  In Tempe or the Dales of Arcady?
What Gods or Men are these? What Maidens loth?
  What love? what dance? what struggle to escape?
  What Pipes and timbrels? what wild extacy?

II.

Heard melodies are sweet, but those unheard
  Are sweeter; therefore, ye soft pipes, play on;
Not to the sensual ear but more endeared,
  Pipe to the spirit, ditties of no tone:
Fair Youth, beneath the trees thou canst not leave
  Thy song, nor ever bid the spring adieu;
Bold lover never, never canst thou kiss
  Though winning near the goal:—O do not grieve!
She cannot fade, though thou hast not thy bliss:
  For ever wilt thou love and she be fair.

III.

Ah happy, happy boughs, that cannot shed
  Your leaves, nor never, bid the Spring adieu;
And happy Melodist unwearied,
  For ever piping songs for ever new;

215. [Keats, John, contributor.] The champion: a London weekly journal. London: 1817–1818. Folio and quarto, contemporary half calf.

A volume of sixty-three (of sixty-six) consecutive issues of an important liberal weekly; included are nos. 216–20, 222–25, 227–49, and 251–81. This journal was a major venue for the Romantics, particularly Wordsworth, Lamb, Hazlitt, and Keats. Included in this run are three drama reviews by Keats, the only prose published by him during his lifetime. Also present is a sonnet "from the pen of Mr. Keats," entitled "On the Sea" (August 17, 1817; no. 241), only his seventh poem in a periodical, and the first in anything other than *The Examiner*. From the beginning of this run to December 1817, the editor was Keats's friend John Hamilton Reynolds, whose famous laudatory review of the poet's first book—the earliest long notice of Keats to appear in print—is in the issue for March 9, 1817 (no. 218, a full page, with extensive quotations). Original numbers of the *Champion* are very rare.

161

What is particularly appealing about this run is that it contains all Keats's contributions, as well as the Reynolds review. Given the change in format from folio to quarto at the end of 1817, it is most remarkable to find these numbers bound up in a single volume, and it is doubtful if many other such assemblages survive. Acquired in 1996.

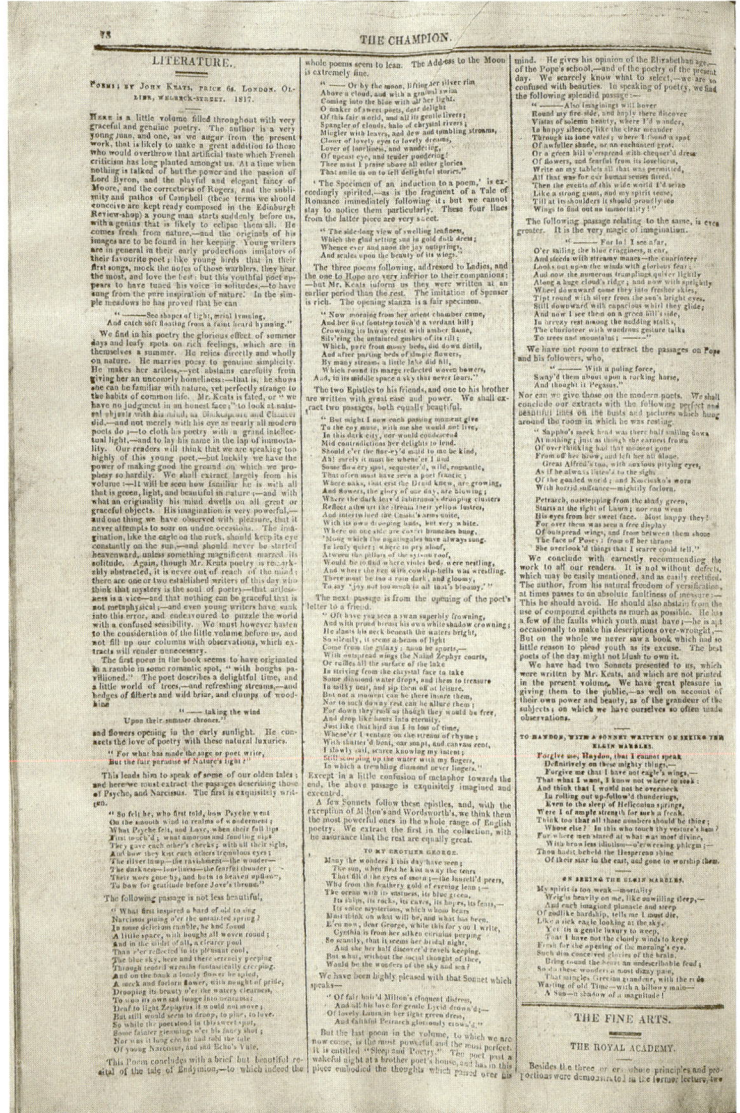

216. [Terrot, Charles Hughes, attributed author.] Common sense: a poem. Edinburgh: printed for David Brown, 1819. 8vo, disbound.

> A remarkable poem by a young Scottish clergyman who went on to become the bishop of Edinburgh. Charles Terrot (1790–1872) was a graduate of Trinity College, Cambridge; he was particularly adept as a mathematician, but he had a taste for verse as well, and won the Seatonian prize in 1816. This new effort is cast in the form of poems like *The Dunciad* and *The Rolliad,* and satirizes the poets and politicians of the day. Included are a good many rather nasty footnotes, beginning on the first page with one on "Mr. John Keates [*sic*], the muse's child of promise, . . . a rising poet of the Cockney school; who, if he had but an ear for rhyme, a little knowledge of grammar, and sufficient intellect to distinguish sense from nonsense, might perhaps do very well." Terrot goes on to deal at length with Byron, Wordsworth ("few poets have been more reviewed, or less read, than Wordsworth"), Coleridge, Southey, Leigh Hunt ("the reputed chief of the Cockney school"), and Shelley ("a young man of talents and liberal education, who has chosen to make war on all the virtues and decencies of life"). This poem is assigned to Terrot in the *DNB,* but the *Oxford DNB* makes no mention of it; whether the omission was deliberate is hard to say. Halkett and Laing cite an entry in the catalogue of the Advocates' Library in Edinburgh, which seems a fairly reliable source. Acquired in 1981.

JOHN CLARE (1793–1864)

217. Clare, John. Poems descriptive of rural life and scenery. London: printed for Taylor and Hessey; and E. Drury (Stamford), 1820. 8vo, original gray boards, printed paper label.

> The author's first book. Acquired in 1972.

218. Clare, John. The village minstrel, and other poems. London: printed for Taylor and Hessey; and E. Drury (Stamford), 1821. Two vols., 12mo, original gray-green boards, printed paper labels.

> Clare's second book. Acquired in 1984.

219. Clare, John. The rural muse, poems. London: Whittaker & Co., 1835. 8vo, original green cloth, printed paper label.

Clare's final book of poetry. He lived on for almost thirty years, but most of this time was spent in a lunatic asylum in Northampton. This copy is inscribed on the front pastedown (later crossed through), "Wm. Chs. Ward Jackson from his uncle E. W. Jackson, 16th May, 1842." On a flyleaf is the signature of W. F. Newton. Acquired in 1997.

THOMAS HOOD (1799–1845)

220. Hood, Thomas. The plea of the midsummer fairies, Hero and Leander, Lycus the centaur, and other poems. London: printed for Longman, Rees, Orme, Brown, and Green, 1827. 8vo, calf, by Riviere.

> With the book labels of the literary journalist Charles Whibley (1859–1930) and Arnold Moon, and the bookplate of Charles Francis Redhead Yorke. Acquired in 1973.

221. Hood, Thomas, Jr., and Frances Freeling Broderip (née Hood). Memorials of Thomas Hood. Collected, arranged, and edited by his daughter. With a preface and notes by his son. Illustrated with copies from his own sketches. London: Edward Moxon & Co., 1860. Two vols., 8vo, original purple cloth.

> The first full-dress biographical account of Hood, arranged by his children. Included are many important letters, details of his publications, uncollected poems, and information on his relationships with other writers of the period, including Dickens. Acquired in 1995.

WALTER SAVAGE LANDOR (1775–1864)

222. Landor, Walter Savage. The poems of Walter Savage Landor. London: printed for T. Cadell, Junr., and W. Davies, 1795. [Bound with:] Moral epistle, respectfully dedicated to Earl Stanhope. London: printed for T. Cadell, Junr., and W. Davies, 1795. Two vols. in one, 8vo, original light blue boards, drab paper backstrip.

> Landor's first two publications, bound together, probably as sometimes issued. According to a letter from Landor's brother Robert to John Forster, cited by Wise, Landor quickly came to regret the first work: "The first of Walter's publications must have appeared almost twenty years ago. A small volume of poems, which was suppressed or withdrawn without any reason as far as I can remember, excepting that he hoped to write better soon." Forster's 1869 biography also cites Landor's own comment: "Before I was twenty years of age I had imprudently sent into the world a volume of which I was soon ashamed." Landor never reprinted any of the poems in this book. His second work, a pamphlet poem, does not bear his name on the title page, but his authorship is revealed in a four-line passage near the end ("it is Landor's fault"). From the collection of Simon Nowell-Smith, who had a particular interest in Landor bibliography. Acquired in 2002.

223. [Landor, Walter Savage.] Gebir; a poem, in seven books. London: sold by Rivingtons, 1798. 8vo, contemporary half calf.

> First edition. Landor's third book, and his first successful poem; this verse narrative was suggested by a story he found in Clara Reeve's *Progress of Romance*. The poem attracted very little notice when it appeared, but was much admired by such early readers as Coleridge and Southey, and some years later, in 1811, Shelley bored his friend Hogg with his absorption in the poem, while the two young men were together at Oxford. This copy is unusual, in that gathering E (pp. 33–40), whose sheets at first appear to be on thick paper, in fact consists of two half sheets pasted together, back to back. The signature had been wrongly imposed, so that the text on the front and back of each half sheet was the same; rather than discard these leaves, the printer resorted to pasting them together. For a full explanation,

see Simon Nowell-Smith's note in *The Library*, 5th ser. 17 (1962), pp. 149–52, where this "freak" copy is fully described. Of particular note is that the half sheets used were in proof state, with numerous errors uncorrected. The Simon Nowell-Smith copy. Acquired in 2002.

224. [Landor, Walter Savage.] Poems from the Arabic and Persian; with notes by the author of Gebir. Warwick: printed by H. Sharpe; and sold by Messrs. Rivington (London), 1800. 4to, sewn, as issued.

> In later years, Landor confessed that these poems were only imitations of "Oriental" verse, and not translations, as the title implies. From the library of H. Bradley Martin. Acquired in 1990.

225. [Landor, Walter Savage.] Poetry by the author of Gebir. London: sold by F. & C. Rivington, 1802. 8vo, original blue-gray wrappers.

> These sheets were first printed in Warwick in 1800, but were not then published; the original text ran to 111 pages, but only the first 64 pages are included here. As far as can be determined, only one copy is known with an 1800 title page, at the British Library. The present copy is Landor's own, with a few manuscript corrections. On p. 12 he has rewritten and then lightly crossed out the first twelve lines of "From the Phocæans," and on pp. 57–58 he has made substantive changes to the Latin poem "De Libertate Ode." This was not the only copy in Landor's possession, as may be surmised from the fact that it is largely unopened; a copy at Harvard has a profusion of manuscript corrections, but is seriously defective, lacking the first ten pages, and with pp. 51–56 mutilated. Acquired in 1993.

226. Landor, Walter Savage. Gebir; a poem: in seven books. Oxford: printed by and for Slatter and Munday; and sold by R. S. Kirby (London), 1803. 8vo, contemporary calf.

> Second edition, revised, with numerous additions and a new preface; first published in 1798 (no. 223). This copy is signed on the front flyleaf by the author's younger brother (by five years), Henry Eyres Landor, who apparently supervised the publication of this new edition. The Simon Nowell-Smith copy. Acquired in 2002.

227. [Landor, Walter Savage.] Gebirus, poema. Oxford: excudunt R. Slatter et J. Munday; veneunt etiam Londini apud R. S. Kirby, 1803. 8vo, contemporary calf.

166

First edition in Latin. This Latin version is, of course, Landor's own; parts of the poem were composed in Latin, and then translated into English for the 1798 edition. Also of importance here are the footnotes, which are sometimes more ample than those accompanying the English text. This copy is signed on the front flyleaf by the author's younger brother, Henry Eyres Landor. With a number of small manuscript corrections in the text, presumably by either Landor himself or his brother. The Simon Nowell-Smith copy. Acquired in 2002.

228. [Landor, Walter Savage.] Simonidea. Bath: printed by W. Meyler; and sold by G. Robinson (London), 1806. 8vo, original light blue boards, drab paper backstrip.

> A small collection of verse, containing twenty-five poems in English and five in Latin. Among the former is the first printed version of one of Landor's most famous poems, untitled here but commonly called "Rose Aylmer." This copy has Landor's initials on the front pastedown, apparently in his own hand. The Simon Nowell-Smith copy. Acquired in 2002.

229. [Landor, Walter Savage.] Count Julian: a tragedy. London: printed for John Murray, by James Moyes, 1812. 8vo, contemporary calf.

> When Landor returned from a trip to Spain, he joined Wordsworth and Southey in denouncing the Convention of Cintra, but the principal result of his expedition was this verse play. Southey tried to arrange for its publication with Longmans, but they refused to print the book, even at the author's expense. Southey then managed to convince John Murray to publish it, and when it appeared he wrote a notice of the play in *The Quarterly Review*. This is arguably the best possible presentation copy of the play, as it is inscribed at the foot of the title page, in the recipient's hand, "Robert

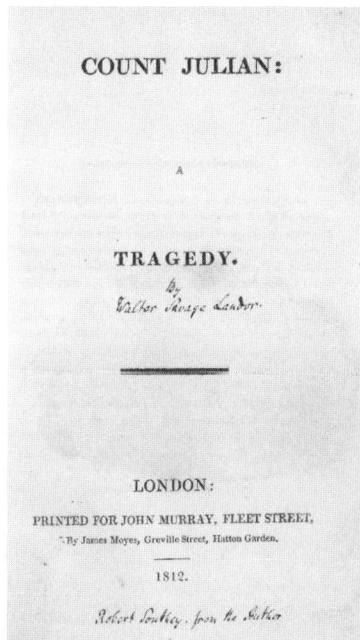

ITEM 229

Southey, from the Author"; Southey has also added Landor's name below the title, and has inserted his woodcut armorial bookplate opposite, on the verso of the half-title. The Simon Nowell-Smith copy. Acquired in 2002.

230. [Landor, Walter Savage.] Letters addressed to Lord Liverpool, and the Parliament, on the preliminaries of peace. By Calvus [pseud.]. London: printed for Henry Colburn; and sold by George Goldie (Edinburgh); and John Cumming (Dublin), 1814. 8vo, wrappers.

These letters urge the British government to deal severely with Napoleon, for whose adventures Landor had a strong antipathy; not long afterward Landor was in Tours, where he claimed to have seen Napoleon on his flight after Waterloo. This copy has a presentation inscription on the title page to the editor of the *Edinburgh Review*, Francis Jeffrey; probably this is in the hand of the publisher. This is one of the rarest Landor first editions; the NUC lists two copies at the Library of Congress, and WorldCat adds copies at the British Library, Aberdeen, the National Library of Ireland, and the Bibliothèque Nationale. Acquired in 1992.

231. Landor, Walter Savage. The Hellenics. . . . Enlarged and completed. London: Edward Moxon, 1847. 8vo, original green cloth.

Many of these poems had appeared in a collected edition of Landor's works the previous year (some of them are from earlier sources); a dozen poems, however, appear here for the first time, and two of them were never printed again during his lifetime. With the armorial bookplate of Lionel George Robinson, and the signatures of Clarence B. Izon (May 1862) and R. E. Gathorne-Hardy (1927). Acquired in 2000.

232. Landor, Walter Savage. Imaginary conversation of King Carlo-Alberto and the Duchess Belgioioso, on the affairs and prospects of Italy. London: Longman, Brown, Green, and Longmans; and all booksellers, n.d. [1848]. 8vo, sewn, as issued. Acquired in 2000.

233. Landor, Walter Savage. Dry sticks, fagoted. Edinburgh: James Nichol; James Nisbet and Co. (London), 1858.

This copy is inscribed on the half-title, "Walter Savage Landor to his friend Edward Capern. January 1, 1858." Capern was a rural postal carrier in Bideford, Devon, who published several volumes of poetry that Landor helped to promote. Capern was also the dedicatee of Landor's *Antony and Octavius*

(1856). Tipped in at the front is a leaf of manuscript poetry (with revisions and deletions) in the hand of Capern; this relates to Landor, and a scandal in which he was involved (the Yescombe affair; see no. 234). With the bookplate of H. Buxton Forman, and the book labels of John A. Spoor and H. Bradley Martin. Acquired in 1990.

234. [Landor, Walter Savage.] Mr. Landor's remarks on a suit preferred against him, at the Summer Assizes in Taunton, 1858, illustrating the appendix to his Hellenics. [London: 1859.] 8vo, four leaves, folded, as issued.

The last of three pamphlets by Landor relating to a libel suit in which he was involved at the age of eighty-three. According to the *Oxford DNB*:

In 1856 he had become acquainted with a clergyman and his wife, Morris and Mary Jane Yescombe. They had taken under their care a young woman called Geraldine Hooper, whom Landor found attractive. He addressed poems to her (as "Erminine") and gave her many gifts: these found their way into Mrs Yescombe's keeping. Eventually, early in 1857, Landor began to suspect that Mrs Yescombe was exploiting Geraldine to enrich herself, and rashly published an attack on her in a pamphlet, "Walter Savage Landor and the Honorable Mrs Yescombe." A libel action was threatened, but John Forster persuaded Landor to sign a retraction. The offence was repeated in three poems included in Landor's next publication, *Dry Sticks, Fagoted* [1858; no. 233]. Mrs Yescombe then did initiate an action for libel, and when it came to court in August 1858 she was awarded £1000 in damages. The newspapers reacted with eloquent denunciations of this libeller and advocate of tyrannicide. By then, though, Landor was no longer in England.

This pamphlet was written by Landor when he was living in Italy, in Fiesole, outside Florence. When the text was first set in type, the London printer included the company device on the title page, but this was removed when it was realized that Landor had repeated some of the statements for which he had been sued. T. J. Wise, in both the bibliography of Landor he published with Stephen Wheeler in 1918 and in the Ashley Catalogue in 1929, was able to describe only a proof copy in his own possession:

The pamphlet is one of the many pieces to be met with in Landor bibliography which are so rare as to be practically impossible of acquisition. No copy in its issued state is at present available, though one was formerly in the possession of Algernon Swinburne. This, the latter asserted, was lost at the time of his removal to The Pines. The present is the finally-corrected proof, and is printed upon thin blue-tinted paper. A greatly reduced facsimile of the title-page is given herewith. As will be seen from a glance at this facsimile the publisher's imprint is in the form of a stereotyped device. But, doubtless as an act of precaution, this device was removed before publication, and the pamphlet appeared without an imprint.

Landor is said to have ordered one hundred copies of this pamphlet. Four of these can now be located, at the British Library, the Bodleian, Harvard, and Yale. As with Wise's proof copy, the final version was printed on flimsy paper with a grayish tint. Acquired in 2013.

235. Landor, Walter Savage. [Heroic idyls, with additional poems.] London: T. Cautley Newby, 1863. 8vo, original orange-brown cloth.

Landor's last book. In 1858, Landor, beset by his legal and financial difficulties, left England to live out the rest of his life in Italy. So long and illustrious had his literary career been, however, that he attracted the universal sympathy of England's younger poets; Browning in particular took it upon himself to look after Landor, and eventually settled him in an apartment in Florence. Here Landor lived until his death in 1864. Swinburne came to Florence expressly to meet him, and dedicated his *Atalanta in Calydon* to him.

Landor had no very regular relationship with any particular English publisher, so that when the manuscript of *Heroic Idyls* was ready for the press, he required someone to represent him in London for the necessary negotiations. For this task he chose a young friend, and the dedicatee of the book itself, Edward Twisleton, who had been introduced to him by Browning ("All my old friends are dead, let their place continue to be supplied by Edward Twisleton"). Twisleton took the manuscript to England, and gave it to the bookseller T. Cautley Newby, a notoriously ungenerous publisher of three-decker novels. In time a set of proofs was sent to Landor, and he seems to have made a number of changes, which were printed up on three inserted leaves, one of them containing thirty-one errata and headed "Correct," and the other two containing additional lines of verse and headed "Insertions." These leaves are found in all copies of the book as published; in the present copy, they seem to have been bound at the front, and then removed. This copy appears to be a set of proofs, sent to Landor for his last corrections. The sheets are bound in a trial binding; eventually the same stamping and lettering were used, but the grain and color of the cloth were changed, from morocco grain to wavy grain, and from orange-brown to crimson. But Landor evidently decided that the book as printed was quite unsatisfactory, and he filled this proof copy with numerous corrections, deletions, and additions, even to the point of clipping away the top of the title page, and changing the title of the book to "Hellenica and Minora." He further indicated his unhappiness with the publisher's handiwork by crossing out Newby's imprint both on the title page and at the end of the text. When Landor finished marking up this copy, he posted it back to Twisleton; the original address panel of the parcel has been preserved; it was pasted, probably by Twisleton himself, onto the front cover (the Florence postmark is still visible).

What happened at this point is not entirely clear; possibly the book simply arrived too late, or perhaps the publisher was not happy about making such extensive additional changes. There is also a remote chance that Landor had in mind a new edition of the book, but the preliminary nature of this copy's binding suggests otherwise, as does the fact that the book sold slowly and was eventually remaindered. At any rate, the changes made by Landor here are quite substantial and extremely interesting. There are more than fifty new lines of verse in his hand, many on his characteristic slips, pasted in. Alterations in spelling and punctuation occur on almost every page, and changes of a word or phrase are frequent; the greater part of these emendations do not appear in the book as published. There are also many notes about changing the order of the poems, and many of the titles have been altered or deleted. This copy was acquired from one of Twisleton's descendants, and has never received the scholarly attention it clearly warrants. Acquired in 1976.

236. Wise, Thomas James. A Landor library. A catalogue of printed books, manuscripts and autograph letters by Walter Savage Landor. London: printed for private circulation only, 1928. 8vo, original purple cloth.

> One of 170 copies printed. This copy is inscribed on the front flyleaf, "For Percy Simpson with most cordial regards from Thos. J. Wise." It belonged subsequently to the collector Simon Nowell-Smith, and bears his penciled bibliographical notes throughout. Acquired in 2002.

LEIGH HUNT (1784–1859)

237. Hunt, Leigh. Juvenilia; or, a collection of poems. Written between the ages of twelve and sixteen, by J. H. L. Hunt, late of the Grammar School of Christ's Hospital. London: printed by J. Whiting, 1801. 8vo, original pale blue boards, drab paper backstrip, printed paper label.

> Leigh Hunt's first book, published by subscription, with the author's father taking an active part in the solicitations. The H. Bradley Martin copy. Acquired in 1990.

238. [Hunt, Leigh.] Critical essays on the performers of the London theatres, including general observations on the practice and genius of the stage. By the author of the theatrical criticisms in the weekly paper called the News. London: printed by and for John Hunt, 1807. 8vo, original gray boards, printed paper label.

> Leigh Hunt's theater criticism attracted a good deal of attention because it was both original and independent; he refused to accept free tickets for plays, or mingle with the performers. With the bookplate of Oliver Brett (later Lord Esher). Acquired in 1982.

239. [Hunt, Leigh.] An attempt to shew the folly and danger of Methodism. In a series of essays, first published in the weekly paper called The Examiner, and now enlarged with a preface and additional notes. By the editor of The Examiner. London: printed for and sold by John Hunt, Examiner Office, 1809. 8vo, blue morocco, by Riviere.

> The Borowitz copy. Acquired in 1978.

240. [Hunt, Leigh.] The reformist's answer to the article, entitled "State of Parties," in the last Edinburgh Review (No. 30). By the editor of The Examiner, in which paper it first appeared. London: printed by and for John Hunt, Examiner Office; and may be had of all the booksellers, 1810. 8vo, disbound.

> One of the rarest Leigh Hunt titles; WorldCat lists six copies, at the National Library of Scotland, the Bodleian, Iowa, Illinois, Ohio University, and Pennsylvania. Acquired in 1992.

241. [Hunt, Leigh.] The reflector, a collection of essays, on miscellaneous subjects of literature and politics; originally published as the commencement of a quarterly magazine, and written by the editor of The Examiner, with the assistance of various other hands. London: printed and published by J. Hunt; and sold by J. Miller; J. Carpenter; and Gale and Curtis, n.d. [1811]. Two vols., 8vo, green morocco, by Riviere.

> A complete set of four quarterly numbers, bound up with general title pages and indexes. Aside from *The Examiner,* which Hunt edited for some fourteen years (beginning in 1808), this is his first periodical. There are, of course, a great many contributions here by Hunt himself, but *The Reflector*

is also of great interest to students of Charles Lamb, who wrote many of the articles, his first serious efforts as an essayist. Acquired in 1990.

242. Hunt, Leigh. The Prince of Wales v. The Examiner. A full report of the trial of John and Leigh Hunt, proprietors of The Examiner, on an information filed ex-officio by the Attorney-General. Decided by Lord Ellenborough, and a special jury, in the King's Bench, Westminster, on Wednesday, the 9th of December, 1812. To which are added, observations on the trial, by the editor of The Examiner. London: printed by and for John Hunt, Examiner Office; and sold by all the booksellers, n.d. [1813]. 8vo, wrappers.

> "This pamphlet was issued . . . shortly after the trial of the Hunts for criminal libel on the Prince Regent, for which they were found guilty and sentenced to two years' imprisonment in separate jails and to pay a fine of £500 each. Hints were given that the fines and imprisonments might be waived if the brothers would promise to 'go and sin no more.' Friends, including Shelley, proffered money to pay the fines. All these generous offers were refused, the imprisonments were undergone, and the fines paid by the Hunts in accordance with the decree."–Luther A. Brewer, *My Leigh Hunt Library* (1922). Acquired in 1992.

243. [Hunt, Leigh.] The feast of the poets, with notes, and other pieces in verse, by the editor of the Examiner. London: printed for James Cawthorn, 1814. 8vo, original gray boards, printed paper label.

> This copy has a manuscript correction, in Hunt's hand, on the last page of text, a sonnet to Thomas Barnes, changing "whisp'ring" to "working." Acquired in 1974.

244. Hunt, Leigh. The feast of the poets, with other pieces in verse. London: printed for Gale and Fenner, 1815. 8vo, original blue boards, dark gray paper backstrip, printed paper label.

> Second edition, "amended and enlarged"; first published the year before (no. 243). This second edition contains important additions and alterations. Hunt's new four-page preface speaks at some length about his opinion of Wordsworth, which had changed for the better. The Simon Nowell-Smith copy. Acquired in 2002.

245. Hunt, Leigh. The story of Rimini, a poem. London: printed by T. Davison; for J. Murray; W. Blackwood (Edinburgh); and Cumming (Dublin), 1816. 8vo, original gray boards, printed paper label.

This poem, inspired by the story of Paolo and Francesca in Dante's *Inferno*, is dedicated to Byron. Acquired in 1987.

246. Hunt, Leigh. Foliage; or poems original and translated. London: printed for C. and J. Ollier, 1818. 8vo, original light blue boards, printed paper label.

Included in this volume are poems addressed to Keats, Shelley, Byron, Lamb, Moore, and other poets of the day; there is also an interesting preface on the modern school of poetry. This copy is signed on the front flyleaf by Mary Peacock, Thomas Love Peacock's daughter; she later married the novelist George Meredith. Acquired in 1974.

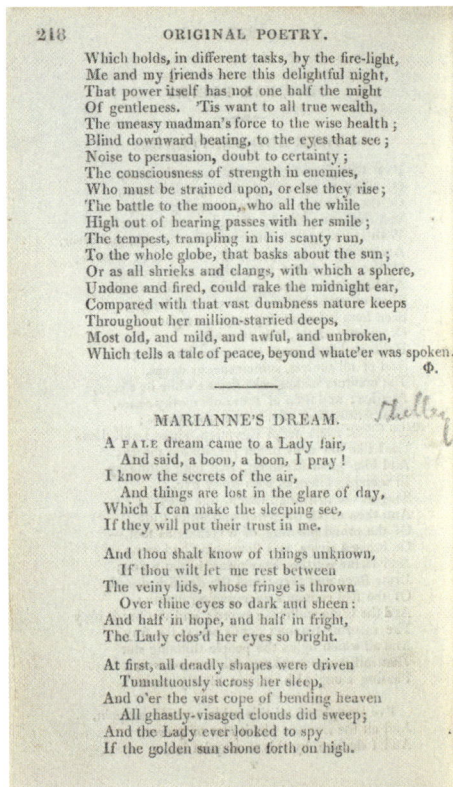

ITEM 247

247. [Hunt, Leigh.] The literary pocket-book; or, companion for the lover of nature and art. 1819. (To be continued annually.) London: printed for C. and J. Ollier; sold also by G. and W. B. Whittaker; W. Whiteley; Munday and Slatter (Oxford); and W. Newby (Cambridge), n.d. [1818]. 12mo, green morocco.

> The first in a series of pocket diaries issued annually by Hunt over a period of five years. A substantial portion of the book is essentially blank, to be used for "appointments and other memoranda." Of great interest, however, is a section near the end (pp. 217–26), entitled "Original Poetry," which includes seven poems, all signed with single Greek capital letters. Two of these poems are by Keats ("The Human Seasons" and "Sonnet to Ailsa Rock"), one is by Shelley ("Marianne's Dream"), two are by Bryan Waller Procter ("Hymn to Diana" and "Sonnet Descriptive of a Painting by Nicolas Poussin"), and two are by Leigh Hunt himself ("Power and Gentleness" and "The Summer of 1818"). All issues of this annual are of the greatest rarity. This copy turned up as part of a large, finely bound set of Leigh Hunt first editions; the other four years were never found, despite an assiduous search. Acquired in 1990.

248. Hunt, Leigh. Hero and Leander, and Bacchus and Ariadne. London: printed for C. and J. Ollier, 1819. 8vo, original gray wrappers, printed paper side label.

> The Simon Nowell-Smith copy. Acquired in 2002.

249. Hunt, Leigh. The months: descriptive of the successive beauties of the year. London: C. & J. Ollier, 1821. 12mo, original drab boards, printed paper label.

> A series of nature essays, written in the tradition of Gilbert White's *Natural History of Selborne*. These sketches were originally published in *The Literary Pocket-Book*, and are here reprinted "with considerable additions." Included are poetical quotations from Hunt's contemporaries; along with passages from Wordsworth and Coleridge there are substantial excerpts from Shelley and Keats (whose last book had appeared in 1820). Acquired in 1980.

250. [Hunt, Leigh, editor.] The liberal. Verse and prose from the south. London: printed by and for John Hunt, 1822–1823. Two vols., 8vo, half brown morocco (original tan printed front wrappers bound in).

A complete run of four numbers. The idea for this magazine was suggested to Hunt by Byron, through Shelley. The three had hopes of making a great success, but when sales proved only moderate, Byron began to lose interest, and to think of the project merely as a repository for that part of his work that was too scandalous for his publisher Murray. The four numbers include Byron's "Vision of Judgment" and "Heaven and Earth"; Shelley's "Song, Written for an Indian Air," "May-Day Night," and "Lines to a Critic"; and three articles by Hazlitt. With the bookplate of George Merryweather. Acquired in 1978.

251. Hunt, Leigh. Ultra-crepidarius: a satire on William Gifford. London: printed for John Hunt, 1823. 8vo, calf, by Riviere.

> Gifford, as editor of *The Quarterly Review*, was seen by many contemporaries as the worst sort of reactionary; in his preface, Hunt speaks of Gifford's "unfeeling attack" on Keats, and his "unchristian hatred" of Shelley. Acquired in 1979.

252. [Hunt, Leigh.] The literary examiner: consisting of the Indicator, a review of books, and miscellaneous pieces in prose and verse. London: printed for H. L. Hunt, 1823. 8vo, green morocco, by Riviere.

> A complete run of twenty-six weekly numbers, bound up with a general title page and a leaf of contents at the end. This periodical was established after *The Liberal* had failed; technically it was edited by Leigh Hunt's brother. This volume came from the same uniformly bound set of first editions as *The Literary Pocket-Book* (no. 247). Acquired in 1990.

253. Hunt, Leigh. Bacchus in Tuscany, a dithyrambic poem. From the Italian of Francesco Redi, with notes original and select. London: printed for John and H. L. Hunt, 1825. 8vo, original light blue boards, gray paper backstrip, printed paper label. Acquired in 2012.

254. Hunt, Leigh. The companion. London: printed for Hunt and Clarke, 1828. 8vo, blue morocco, by Riviere.

> A complete run of twenty-nine weekly numbers, bound up with a general title page and table of contents. Bound in to face the title page is a one-page autograph letter from Leigh Hunt to the Anglo-Indian poet David Lester Richardson (1801–1865), dated January 10, 1829. Richardson seems to have been one of Hunt's contributors; here he is asked to "make a memorandum

for me about the Gipsies, in case you can find anything respecting them, in the country from which they are generally supposed to have issued." Hunt and Richardson must have been on close terms; Hunt speaks of having sent some verses, and adds a light request that Richardson "make my compliments to Serendib, and the memory of Sinbad." At the end, Hunt complains of the quality of his ink, but notes that the addition of a little wine has brought about an improvement. The Borowitz copy. Acquired in 1978.

255. [Hunt, Leigh.] Christianism: or belief and unbelief reconciled; being exercises and meditations. [London: 1832.] 8vo, calf, by Root.

One of seventy-five copies printed for private circulation. This copy is inscribed on the title page, "To Mrs. Dashwood, with the cordial respects of Leigh Hunt." Tipped in at the front is a watercolor by Thornton Hunt, Leigh Hunt's eldest son, also inscribed to Mrs. Dashwood and illustrating the motto on the title page: "Mercy and truth have met together; righteousness and peace have kissed each other" (Ps. 85:10). Thornton Hunt was intended by his father to become a painter. Acquired in 1973.

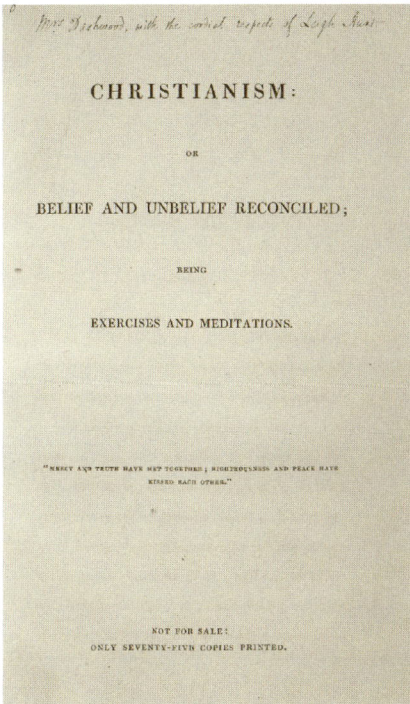

ITEM 255

CHRISTIANISM:

OR

BELIEF AND UNBELIEF RECONCILED;

BEING

EXERCISES AND MEDITATIONS.

"MERCY AND TRUTH HAVE MET TOGETHER; RIGHTEOUSNESS AND PEACE HAVE
KISSED EACH OTHER."

NOT FOR SALE:
ONLY SEVENTY-FIVE COPIES PRINTED.

See the Motto.

With Thornton Leigh Hunts' respects to Mrs. Dashwort.

ITEM 255

256. [Hunt, Leigh.] Sir Ralph Esher: or, adventures of a gentleman of the court of Charles II. London: Henry Colburn and Richard Bentley, 1832. Three vols., 12mo, contemporary half calf, binder's tickets of H. T. Cook of Warwick.

Leigh Hunt's only novel, involving an historical reconstruction of English court life during the Restoration. The sheets of these three volumes were printed in 1830, and a few copies are known with title pages so dated. This set is inscribed on the title page of vol. 1, "To Chandos Leigh Esqre. with the author's grateful regards." The recipient was the only child of James Henry Leigh (1765–1823), a nephew of James Brydges, 3rd Duke of Chandos, and the man after whom Leigh Hunt himself had been named (his full name, which he did not use, was James Henry Leigh Hunt). Hunt's father, Isaac Hunt, was born in Barbados about 1742, but he had been sent as a boy to be educated in Philadelphia, where he became a lawyer and political pamphleteer. At the outbreak of the Revolution he remained an outspoken Loyalist, and was soon forced to flee to England. There he became a clergyman, and he was eventually employed as a tutor in the household of the Duke of Chandos, whence he selected a name for his first son, who was born in 1784.

Chandos Leigh, seven years younger, developed an abiding interest in literature and the arts. His early involvement in the theatrical world brought him the friendship of Richard Brinsley Sheridan and Edmund Kean, and his political bias led to his introduction into the Holland House set, where he came to know Byron and Hobhouse. In 1823 he inherited from his father the Stoneleigh Abbey estate, with property in several counties providing an income of some £90,000 a year. At this point Chandos Leigh, who was also a distant cousin of Jane Austen, retired to a life in the country, and his involvement with his literary contemporaries largely came to an end. He is known, however, to have provided Leigh Hunt with some sort of financial assistance, though the details are obscure. Hunt, in his *Autobiography*, gives a glowing account of Chandos Leigh, and compares him to Henry Fielding's beloved Squire Allworthy. On the front pastedowns here are his armorial bookplates, printed in gold on white glazed paper and inscribed "Leigh" (he was by this time Baron Leigh). The inscription on the first title page, "by Leigh Hunt," is probably in his hand. Acquired in 2006.

257. Hunt, Leigh. A legend of Florence. A play. In five acts. London: Edward Moxon, 1840. 8vo, original gray wrappers, printed paper side label. Acquired in 1983.

258. Hunt, Leigh, editor. The dramatic works of Wycherley, Congreve, Vanbrugh, and Farquhar. With biographical and critical notices. London: Edward Moxon, 1840. 8vo, original dark blue cloth.

> Hunt's essay on these four Restoration dramatists runs to just over one hundred pages. With the bookplate of Sir George Ralph Fetherston, Bart. (1784–1853). Acquired in 1990.

259. Hunt, Leigh. The palfrey; a love-story of old times. London: How and Parsons, 1842. 8vo, original pink printed wrappers.

> Most copies were bound in cloth. The Simon Nowell-Smith copy. Acquired in 1989.

260. Hunt, Leigh. The poetical works of Leigh Hunt. Containing many pieces now first collected. London: Edward Moxon, 1844. 12mo, contemporary black morocco.

> This copy, in an elaborate gift binding of the period, is inscribed on the front flyleaf, "To Charles Gavan Duffy, with the best compliments of Leigh Hunt." The recipient was an Irish journalist and poet who is chiefly known as the founder, in 1842, of *The Nation*, a progressive journal that did much to encourage the development of Irish letters. In 1855, Duffy emigrated to Australia. With the book label of Payson Grier Gates (1894–1955). Acquired in 2001.

261. Hunt, Leigh. Stories from the Italian poets: with lives of the writers. London: Chapman and Hall, 1845. Two vols., 8vo, original dark blue cloth. Acquired in 2004.

262. Hunt, Leigh. Men, women, and books; a selection of sketches, essays, and critical memoirs, from his uncollected prose writings. London: Smith, Elder and Co., 1847. Two vols., 8vo, original rose cloth.

> With the signature on a flyleaf of H. P. Clinton, and the bookplate of Frank Fletcher. Acquired in 1973.

263. Hunt, Leigh. The autobiography of Leigh Hunt; with reminiscences of friends and contemporaries. London: Smith, Elder and Co., 1850. Three vols., 8vo, original dark yellow cloth.

> One of the finest English literary autobiographies. Acquired in 1972.

264. Hunt, Leigh, editor. Leigh Hunt's journal; a miscellany for the cultivation of the memorable, the progressive, and the beautiful. London: Publishing Office; Stewart & Murray, printers, 1850–1851. Four parts in one vol., 8vo, green morocco, by Riviere.

> A complete run of seventeen weekly numbers, in four parts. Leigh Hunt's last periodical, which was not a financial success, despite an impressive array of contributors assembled from Hunt's friends and acquaintances; these include Carlyle, Landor, William Allingham, and R. H. Horne. As usual, the greatest number of pieces are by Hunt himself. This volume came from the same uniformly bound set of first editions as *The Literary Pocket-Book* (no. 247). Acquired in 1990.

265. Hunt, Leigh. Table-talk. To which are added imaginary conversations of Pope and Swift. London: Smith, Elder and Co., 1851. 8vo, original blue cloth.

This copy is inscribed by Hunt on the half-title to his daughter and her husband, "To Charles and Jacintha Cheltnam, with father's love." Acquired in 1994.

266. Hunt, Leigh. Stories in verse. . . . Now first collected. With illustrations. London: Geo. Routledge & Co., 1855. 8vo, original red cloth.

This is an exceptionally interesting presentation copy, inscribed on the half-title, "To Robert Bell, with Leigh Hunt's kindest regards"; at the front is the additional bookplate of the novelist Anthony Trollope (initialed "R.B."). Robert Bell (1800–1867) was a prominent journalist, miscellaneous writer, and editor of the *Annotated Edition of the British Poets* (24 vols., 1854–57). He was an intimate of Thackeray, and a frequent contributor to *The Cornhill*. He was friendly as well with Leigh Hunt; ten of his letters to Hunt were partly published in Luther A. Brewer's *My Leigh Hunt Library: The Holograph Letters* (pp. 289–93). Bell also became a close friend and literary associate of Trollope; he recruited him on behalf of the Royal Literary Fund and proposed him for membership in the Garrick Club (Thackeray was the seconder). In 1867, Trollope asked Bell to be the subeditor of *St. Paul's Magazine*, but the ill health that would soon lead to his death forced him to resign. Trollope later wrote a memorial tribute to Bell, and worked to obtain a pension for his widow. When she was subsequently forced to put her husband's library up at auction, Trollope went to the executors, had the auction arrangements canceled, and bought the entire library at a price above market value. "We all know," he said, "the difference in value between buying and selling books." The present volume is one of the few titles that can definitely be traced to Trollope's magnanimous gesture. Acquired in 1992.

Huntiana

267. Dubost, Antoine. Hunt and Hope. An appeal to the public . . . against the calumnies of the editor of the Examiner. London: printed for the author by Compton, and to be had of all the principal booksellers, n.d. [1810]. 8vo, disbound.

A vitriolic attack on Leigh Hunt and *The Examiner*, by a French painter. Dubost was involved in a dispute with Thomas Hope over the sale of a painting that Dubost had fraudulently represented as his own work. *The*

Examiner ran two pieces on this affair, both strongly critical of the Frenchman; in fact they were not by Leigh Hunt himself, but by his brother Robert. Acquired in 1992.

268. [Hunt, Leigh: trial.] Report of the proceedings on an information filed ex officio, by His Majesty's Attorney General, against John Hunt, and Leigh Hunt, proprietors of The Examiner, for publishing an article on military punishment, which originally appeared in Drakard's Stamford News: tried in the Court of King's Bench at Westminster, on Friday, February 22, 1811, before the Right Honourable Lord Ellenborough, Chief Justice, &c. and a special jury. Stamford: printed and published by and for John Drakard, and sold by all the booksellers in town and country, 1811. 8vo, disbound.

> The best account of the third trial (and third acquittal) of Leigh Hunt and his brother for articles published in *The Examiner*; this one, on flogging, had been written for a Stamford periodical by John Scott, one time editor of *The London Magazine*. After the trial, Shelley, then a student at Oxford, introduced himself to Hunt by sending him a letter of congratulation on his acquittal. With the signature on the title page of Thomas Frankland Lewis, a prominent politician who first became an MP in 1812. Acquired in 1998.

269. [Hunt, Leigh: trial.] The King v. John and Leigh Hunt. A report of the trial "The King v. John and Leigh Hunt," for a libel on the Prince Regent; before Lord Ellenborough and a special jury, at the sittings in the Court of King's Bench, Westminster, on Wednesday, December 9, 1812. Taken in short hand by an eminent barrister. London: printed and sold by M. Jones, 1812. 8vo, disbound.

> Leigh Hunt soon published his own version of this trial, with annotations (no. 242). Acquired in 1992.

JOHN ANSTER (1793–1867)

270. Anster, John. Xeniola. Poems, including translations from Schiller and De La Motte Fouqué. Dublin: Milliken and Son; Longman, Rees, Orme, and Co. (London), 1837. 8vo, original dark gray-green cloth, printed paper label.

> The author's principal book of original verse, incorporating a number of youthful poems that had first appeared in 1815, in *Ode to Fancy, and Other Poems*; the earlier volume was suppressed. John Anster was an Irish professor of law with a taste for literature; he is described as having been a man of great wit and social charm. He had a particular interest in German poetry, and in 1835 produced a translation of Goethe's *Faust*, advertised here on the verso of the half-title. This copy is inscribed, "To the College of St. Columba. From the author." Acquired in 1989.

JOANNA BAILLIE (1762–1851)

271. Baillie, Joanna. Ahalya Baee: a poem. London: printed for private circulation, 1849. 8vo, original gray-green cloth.

> Joanna Baillie was a Scot by birth but lived most of her life in London. In the course of a long literary career she was best known for her verse plays. This poem, which concerns a legend about a wise and good sovereign in India, was her last publication. It was written and printed when she was in her mideighties; the *DNB* wrongly describes the poem as having been published posthumously, but the error has now been corrected in the *Oxford DNB*. On the title page is the signature of James Burnet. Acquired in 1981.

RICHARD HARRIS BARHAM (1788–1845)

272. [Barham, Richard Harris.] Verses spoken at St. Paul's School, on the public celebrations, May the 1st, 1807, and April the 30th, 1807. London: printed by C. Spilsbury, 1807. 12mo, brown morocco, by Zaehnsdorf.

> The author's first publication, privately printed when he was eighteen. Barham went on, with some diffidence, to a literary career. In 1840 he began publication of his long humorous narratives in verse, *The Ingoldsby Legends*. These poems, widely read and often reprinted, raised him to the front rank of English comic writers. Of this early pamphlet, three copies

have been located, at the Bodleian, Harvard (Barham's own copy), and St. Norbert College, Wisconsin. With the bookplate of Charles Plumptre Johnson (1889), a collector of Dickens and Thackeray. Acquired in 1988.

BERNARD BARTON (1784–1849)

273. [Barton, Bernard.] Mr. John Rogers and his opponents. Remarks upon remarks. The poetical regulator. Ipswich: n.d. [1813]. 4to, two leaves, folded.

The author's second publication, preceded only by his *Metrical Effusions*, published in Woodbridge, in Suffolk, in 1812; this poem is dated at the end, Woodbridge, June 29, 1813, and signed with the initials "B. B." The poem is a humorous squib in rhymed couplets, having to do with a squabble among the local churchwardens. The dispute seems to have arisen from the fact that one of the churchwardens ("my friend Goodwyn"), along with some of his colleagues, had entered into a contract for the construction of new pews, at a cost of £83, without consulting the parish at large. John Rogers, and others, "felt somewhat disgusted," and an exchange of statements followed ("Remarks" and "Remarks on Remarks"), presumably published in the local press. Bernard Barton had by this time settled in Woodbridge, where he worked as a clerk in a bank; Barton himself was a Quaker, but he appears to have been well aware of the foibles of the established church.

No other copy of this poem has been located. This one was acquired from the estate of Claude Cox, a bookseller who for many years had a shop in Ipswich, where this leaflet was printed. Cox had a particular interest in East Anglian printing, and he seems to have reported his discovery of this imprint to the bibliographer J. R. de J. Jackson, a specialist in English Romantic verse, and the reviser of many of the author entries for the period 1800–1835 in the most recent edition of the *CBEL* (1999), whence the poem's appearance in his revised list of Barton's publications. Acquired in 2006.

274. [Barton, Bernard.] The convict's appeal. London: printed and sold by Darton, Harvey, and Darton, 1818. 8vo, original tan wrappers.

A complaint in verse against the severity of the legal code, asking for "a milder system of punishment." This poem, first published in the *The Sheffield Iris*, is here dedicated to James Montgomery (by "B. B."). Barton is now chiefly remembered as a close friend of Charles Lamb and Edward FitzGerald. Four other copies are located, at the British Library, North Carolina, Swarthmore, and the State Library of New South Wales. This copy is inscribed on the front wrapper, "Miss Mathew, from the author." Acquired in 1994.

275. [Barton, Bernard.] Poems, by an amateur. London: printed for the author by J. M'Creery, 1818. 4to, original boards, printed paper label.

> The author's fifth publication, privately printed by subscription; the four-page list of subscribers includes the names of William Wordsworth, Robert Southey, and Thomas Moore. Included is a poem addressed to Wordsworth, and another, "Madame Lavalette," which was widely thought at the time to be by Byron (as Barton says in his preface). The book is nicely produced, in a large format, on thick paper; in the preface to his *Poems* (1820), Barton says that 150 copies were printed. Acquired in 1990.

276. Barton, Bernard. Verses on the death of Percy Bysshe Shelley. London: printed for Baldwin, Cradock, and Joy, 1822. 8vo, half green morocco.

> An attempt by Barton to reconcile Shelley's talent with his rejection of Christian belief. In a two-page preface, Barton speaks of having been sent a copy of *An Elegy on the Death of Percy Bysshe Shelley* by the author, John Chalk Claris, a poet and journalist who used the pseudonym "Arthur Brooke." Barton found the unqualified praise in this poem disturbing: "A poem of this sort, sent directly to the writer of the following few pages, by its author,—seemed to render silence on his part criminal: were it only for the sake of a few whom such praise may have a tendency fatally to mislead." Acquired in 2012.

277. Barton, Bernard. Sea-weeds; gathered at Aldborough, Suffolk: in the autumn of 1846. Woodbridge: Edw. Pite, printer, 1846. 8vo, disbound.

> "Printed for private circulation." This fifteen-page pamphlet begins with a dedicatory poem to Sir Robert Peel. The title poem is described as "brief records of thought, and feeling, by the sea-side." At the end is a two-page poem, "A Post-Script: To the Memory of Crabbe." The only copy located is in the British Library. The present copy is inscribed by Barton on the title page, "Martha Jefferys from her fr. B. B." Acquired in 2004.

278. Barton, Bernard. A memorial of Joseph John Gurney. London: Charles Gilpin, 1847. Sm. 4to, original brown cloth.

> A poem in honor of one of the best-known philanthropists of the period; like Barton, Gurney was a Quaker. Acquired in 1983.

279. Barton, Bernard. Selections from the poems and letters of Bernard Barton. Edited by his daughter. London: Hall, Virtue, and Co., 1849. 8vo, original light blue-gray cloth.

This posthumous collection is notable for containing a memoir of Barton by Edward FitzGerald (signed "E. F. G."), his first appearance in print, at the age of forty. FitzGerald later married Barton's daughter Lucy, who assembled this volume. With a list of subscribers. Acquired in 1976.

NATHANIEL THOMAS HAYNES BAYLY (1797–1839)

280. Bayly, Nathaniel Thomas Haynes. Mournful recollections. Oxford: J. Vincent, 1820. 8vo, wrappers.

> An early pamphlet of verse by a student at St. Mary Hall, Oxford, who went on to become the most successful songwriter of the Regency. The only copy located is in the British Library. Acquired in 1992.

281. Bayly, Nathaniel Thomas Haynes. Weeds of witchery. London: published by Ackermann and Co., 1837. 8vo, original purple cloth.

> Each of these twelve poems is accompanied by a fine etched plate, unsigned, but very much in the manner of George Cruikshank and sometimes attributed to him. Acquired in 1999.

ROBERT BLOOMFIELD (1766–1823)

282. Bloomfield, Robert. The banks of Wye; a poem. In four books. London: printed for the author; Vernor, Hood, and Sharpe; and Longman, Hurst, Rees, Orme, and Brown, 1811. 8vo, original gray boards, printed paper label.

> Bloomfield came from a modest background, and was trained in his youth as a shoemaker. In 1800 he published *The Farmer's Boy*, which is said to have sold twenty-six thousand copies in under three years, and he quickly became one of the most popular poets of the early nineteenth century. The Simon Nowell-Smith copy. Acquired in 2002.

283. Bloomfield, Robert. May Day with the muses. London: printed for the author; and for Baldwin, Cradock, and Joy, 1822. 12mo, original gray boards, printed paper label.

> With eight wood-engraved illustrations by Thomas Bewick. On the front flyleaf is the contemporary signature of John Nelson. Acquired in 1984.

ALEXANDER BOSWELL (1775–1822)

284. Boswell, Alexander. Clan-Alpin's vow: a fragment. Edinburgh: printed by George Ramsay and Company, 1811. 8vo, contemporary olive green morocco.

> A privately printed historical poem by James Boswell's son. With the book label of John Whitefourd Mackenzie, who edited texts for the Bannatyne Club and the Maitland Club, and was undoubtedly known to the author. On the back pastedown is the bookplate of J. Dawson Brodie. Acquired in 1989.

CAROLINE ANNE BOWLES, LATER SOUTHEY (1786–1854)

285. [Bowles, Caroline Anne.] Ellen Fitzarthur: a metrical tale, in five cantos. London: printed for Longman, Hurst, Rees, Orme, and Brown, 1820. 8vo, contemporary half calf.

> The author's first book. Caroline Anne Bowles sent the manuscript of this poem to Robert Southey, knowing that he had helped the poet Henry Kirke White. Southey recommended it to John Murray, but Murray declined. Bowles and Southey maintained a correspondence for almost twenty years, and in 1839 they married, shortly after the death of Southey's wife. Within months, however, Southey became senile, and his new wife led an unhappy life as his carer until his death in 1843; she was badly treated by his family. On the front flyleaf is the early signature of Louisa Rigge. Acquired in 1973.

BOWRING, JOHN (1792–1872)

286. Bowring, John. Hymns. London: printed for the author, sold by Rowland Hunter; and C. Fox and Co., 1825. 12mo, original black boards, printed paper label.

> Bowring's reputation rests largely on his skills as a linguist and a translator. He made accessible to English readers for the first time the poetry of many other countries, particularly of Eastern Europe, including Russia, Poland, Hungary, Bohemia, and Czechoslovakia. Bowring also achieved fame as a writer of hymns, and this little volume contains some of his best-known efforts. One of them, "In the Cross of Christ I Glory," is still part of the standard English hymnal. This copy is inscribed by Bowring on the front flyleaf, "To a kind father, from a grateful son, Aug. 31, 1825." With the later

signature of the poet John Drinkwater (1920), along with his penciled note and book label. Also present is a book label of Mary C. Young and Mary Young Moore, and the stamp of the library of St. Joseph's Seminary, Dunwoodie (NY). Acquired in 1976.

287. [Bowring, John.] [Caption title:] Many minds in one body. [London: 1826.] 8vo, two leaves, folded, as issued.

> The authorship, date, and occasion of the poem are indicated by a contemporary inscription at the top of the first page: "The Committee of the British and Foreign Unitarian Association meeting in Walbrook Buildings, 1826. Written by Sir John Bowring." This four-page poem is essentially a tribute, in light verse, to the members of the committee (including Bowring himself); the same hand has identified all the members, whose names are omitted in the text and indicated only by dashes. No other copy of this poem has been located. Acquired in 1994.

HENRY BOYD (1748/9–1832)

288. Boyd, Henry. A translation of the Inferno of Dante Alighieri, in English verse. With historical notes, and the life of Dante. To which is added, a specimen of a new translation of the Orlando Furioso of Ariosto. London: printed by C. Dilly, 1785. Two vols., 8vo, original pale blue boards, drab paper backstrips.

> First London edition; there was a Dublin edition at more or less the same time. The second English translation of Dante, preceded only by a version of the *Inferno* by Charles Rogers, printed in 1782. Dante was as yet little known in England. Boyd's versification follows the conventions of the eighteenth century and reveals an imperfect grasp of the original; his notes, however, show intelligence and a good education (at Trinity College, Dublin). He published a complete version of the *Divine Comedy* in 1802, but Dante remained largely unfamiliar to English readers until Coleridge discovered Henry Francis Cary's translation in 1814. With the pink book labels of the Broughton Baptist Library. This is the earliest book in the Wachs Collection. Acquired in 1977.

HARTLEY COLERIDGE (1796–1849)

289. Coleridge, Hartley. Poems. Vol. I [all published]. Leeds: published by F. E. Bingley; and Baldwin and Cradock (London), 1833. 8vo, contemporary calf.

The first book by Coleridge's eldest son, and the only book of poems he published in his lifetime. On the front pastedown is a prize label, presenting this copy in 1834 to Charles Kingsley, then a precocious schoolboy of fourteen, but later to become a major Victorian novelist. The prize was given at the Helleston Grammar School in Cornwall, of which Hartley Coleridge's younger brother Derwent was then headmaster. With Kingsley's later bookplate on the verso of the front flyleaf. Acquired in 1978.

290. Coleridge, Hartley. Poems. . . . With a memoir of his life by his brother. London: Edward Moxon, 1851. Two vols., 8vo, original green cloth.

The second volume consists entirely of new material; the biographical memoir is by Derwent Coleridge, and runs to 215 pages. On each title page is the signature of Susan Oates, Sidmouth, dated 1851. With the later bookplates of William Edward Oates (1897) and Robert Washington Oates. Acquired in 1992.

JOSIAH CONDER (1789–1855)

291. [Conder, Josiah, and others.] The associate minstrels. London: printed by George Ellerton, for Thomas Conder (Bucklersbury), 1810. 8vo, contemporary calf.

The author's first book. Josiah Conder was a young bookseller who had begun to contribute poetry to the periodicals. He later became a friend and correspondent of both Robert Southey and James Montgomery. This anthology includes poems by Conder himself; his father; his future wife, Joan Elizabeth Turner; Jacob Strutt; and, most notably, by the Taylors of Ongar, who wrote some of the most popular children's books of the period; there are ten poems by Ann Taylor, nine by Jane, and one by Isaac. This copy bears the early name stamps of Lt. Col. Pepper, and is inscribed "Ballygrath House" on the first page of the text. Acquired in 1987.

ITEM 291

190

292. Conder, Josiah. The star in the east; with other poems. London: printed for Taylor and Hessey, 1824. 12mo, contemporary maroon straight-grained morocco.

> This copy is inscribed on a flyleaf, "To Mr. J. Allam, presented Feby. 6th 1825 as a tribute of unfeigned affection, M. C. Allam." Acquired in 1994.

GEORGE CROLY (1780–1860)

293. [Croly, George.] Paris in 1815. A poem. London: John Murray, 1817. 8vo, original drab wrappers.

> The author's first publication, a poem much influenced by Byron's *Childe Harold*. This copy is signed on the front wrapper by Matthew Arnold. Presumably Arnold purchased the poem as a young man. Acquired in 1974. Another copy of this poem in the collection is bound with Henry Hart Milman's *Fazio, a Tragedy* (1815; no. 390).

294. Croly, George. The angel of the world; an Arabian tale. Sebastian; a Spanish tale: with other poems. London: John Warren, 1820. 8vo, contemporary half dark green morocco.

> The author's first substantial book of verse. Croly was born and raised in Dublin, where he was ordained as a clergyman; he had ultra-Protestant views. In 1810 he moved to London, and became involved in the literary world. Many of his poems show the influence of Byron, but his staunch Tory political leanings earned him an unkind reference in *Don Juan*. A penciled note on a front flyleaf indicates that this copy was from the library of William Beckford, which passed to his son-in-law, the 10th Duke of Hamilton; the books were sold at Sotheby's in 1882–83. The binding, with its pink boards and square morocco corners, is typical of many of Beckford's books. In view of the first poem in this volume, this is a particularly appropriate provenance, as Beckford's most famous book, the gothic novel *Vathek*, was itself "an Arabian tale" (this was, in fact, its full title when it was first published in English in 1787). Acquired in 2008.

GEORGE DARLEY (1795–1846)

295. [Darley, George, editor.] Ayton, Richard. Essays and sketches of character. By the late Richard Ayton, Esq. With a memoir of his life. London: printed for Taylor and Hessey, 1825. 8vo, original tan boards, printed paper label.

Richard Ayton wrote a number of unsuccessful plays; he also accompanied William Daniell on his voyage around Great Britain, and wrote some of the text for what became one of the most famous of all English colorplate books. The present volume is a posthumous collection of his essays, compiled, along with a fourteen-page memoir, by George Darley. Acquired in 1994.

296. [Darley, George.] The labours of idleness; or, seven nights' entertainments. By Guy Penseval [pseud.]. London: printed for John Taylor, 1826. 8vo, contemporary half calf.

> The author's second original book, a collection of stories. Darley was one of the most interesting minor poets of the early nineteenth century. His works brought him little public acclaim, but his ability was recognized by such contemporaries as Lamb, Tennyson, and Carlyle. He suffered from a severe speech impediment, which tormented him and made him shun society. Darley's first book, *The Errors of Ecstasie* (1822) never turned up, nor did his *Nepenthe*, privately printed in 1835. With the early armorial bookplate of Gen. Honble. Robert Taylor (1760–1839), an Irish soldier and politician. Acquired in 1991.

297. Darley, George. Sylvia; or, the May Queen. A lyrical drama. London: published for John Taylor, by James Duncan; and sold by J. A. Hessey, and John Hatchard and Son, 1827. 8vo, original gray boards, printed paper label.

> The poet's most important book, an ambitious attempt to revive the form of Elizabethan drama; the result was much admired by both Coleridge and Elizabeth Barrett Browning. This copy is inscribed on the half-title, "To Mr. M. Reimbach with John Clare's best respects and kindest remembrances. July 16, 1829." Clare was, of course, himself a major poet, and a good friend of Darley. A letter from 1827 survives from Clare to the publisher John Taylor, in which he says, "Darley's play I make no doubt is a good one and I shall feel anxious for its publication and happy at his success for I esteem him both as an author, a poet and a friend." With the later signature on the front pastedown, "Samuel Loveman, Oct. 15, 1915, Cleveland Ohio" (Loveman subsequently became a disheveled bookseller in New York, and had a predilection for forging inscriptions, but this is not one of them). Acquired in 1978.

298. Darley, George. Familiar astronomy. London: printed for John Taylor, 1830. 12mo, original green cloth.

> The last of the poet's school texts; in 1826 and 1827 he had published three mathematical schoolbooks, on geometry, algebra, and trigonometry. Darley's book on astronomy is not a conventional treatise. The text is arranged in the form of family conversations, extending over a period of twelve evenings; a fair amount of poetry is interspersed, from Shakespeare, Milton, Pope, Byron, and other sources (occasionally unnamed). Acquired in 2000.

299. Darley, George. Thomas à Becket. A dramatic chronicle. In five acts. London: Edward Moxon, 1840. 8vo, half blue morocco, by Zaehnsdorf.

> The first of the author's two historical dramas in verse, the last works published in his lifetime. This copy is inscribed by Darley on the title page, "Alfred Tennyson, Esq., from the author." Tennyson was later to write a verse play on the same subject, and was much influenced by Darley's effort. Acquired in 2003.

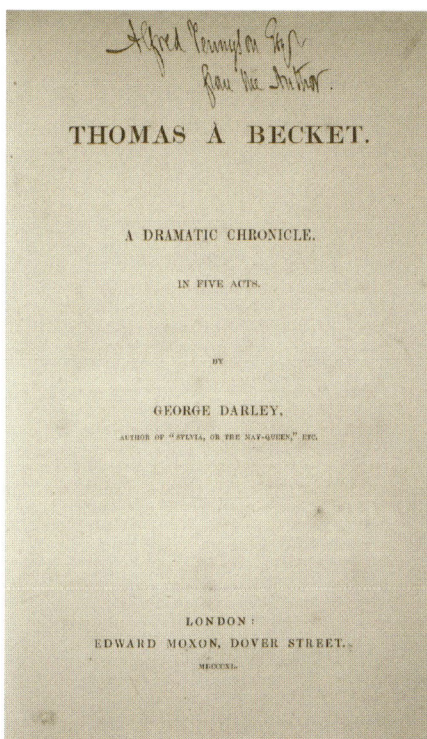

300. Darley, George. Ethelstan; or, the battle of Brunanburh. A dramatic chronicle. In five acts. London: Edward Moxon, 1841. 8vo, boards, cloth spine.

> This copy is inscribed on the title page, "Rev. T[homas] Worsley, with the author's regards." With the book label of Ian Jack. Acquired in 1998.

ITEM 299

301. Darley, George. Poems of the late George Darley. A memorial volume printed for private circulation. Copies may be obtained from A. Holden,

Church Street, Liverpool. [Colophon:] London: printed by Perry, Gardner and Co., n.d. [1889]. 8vo, original dark green cloth.

> An important collection, with many poems first printed here, and a biographical memoir. The volume was compiled and edited by the poet's relations Canon and the Hon. Mrs. Livingstone. Acquired in 1985.

THOMAS DOUBLEDAY (1790–1870)

302. [Doubleday, Thomas.] Sixty-five sonnets; with prefatory remarks on the accordance of the sonnet with the powers of the English language: also, a few miscellaneous poems. London: printed for Baldwin, Cradock, and Joy, 1818. [Bound with:] Doubleday, Thomas. Dioclesian. A dramatic poem. London: Hurst, Chance, and Co., 1829. Two vols. in one, 12mo and 8vo, later nineteenth-century calf.

> The first and fourth publications, both very rare, of a native of Newcastle who went on to become active in the areas of social reform and political economy, and the author of numerous songs and poems having to do with angling. These copies belonged to a friend of Doubleday named G. H. Gilchrist, who has provided at the front a special title page, which reads: "Sonnets and Dioclesian, by T. Doubleday, with autograph notes by the author. 1850." Gilchrist has also signed the first title page. Toward the end, Doubleday's long preface to his collection of sonnets reveals that some of the poems are by another hand: "He would scarcely, perhaps, have been induced to obtrude himself upon the world, had he not been seconded by the assistance of a friend, whose contributions are of merit sufficient to distinguish them from his own." At the head of the first poem, Gilchrist has added the following note: "These sonnets were the joint production of Thomas Doubleday and William Greene. The initials 'T. D.' and 'W. G.' were written by Mr. Doubleday, in my house, to show their respective claims."

> Doubleday's markings in fact show that Greene was the author of twenty-seven of the sixty-five sonnets, as well as five of the miscellaneous pieces at the end. Nothing more has as yet been discovered of Greene; as far as can be determined, his participation in this book has hitherto remained unknown. Also included are several further manuscript annotations, by both Gilchrist and Doubleday, providing bits of information about the subjects and dates of composition. Of particular importance are three pages of inserted notes in Doubleday's hand at the end, containing remarks on three of the poems. The first note reads: "Sonnet LIV. This was, I believe,

SONNETS.

I.

THEY know not least, who have most need, of rest,
 That last, kind refuge from o'erwhelming woes;
 Thee I invoke then, Sleep, thou friend of those
By ill on ill, and wrong on wrong oppress'd,
The happiness that sometime I possess'd,
 Though now bereft me by the craft of foes,
 Return in pitying visions of repose,
And bid me for a time again be bless'd;
The while thou mak'st their waking conscience see
 Crimes that the noise and glare of day can hide;
Yes, when that Judge impartial giveth thee
 O'er his eternal balance to preside,
 Repel th' o'erweenings of injurious pride,
And what thou tak'st from them restore to me.

B 2

the first sonnet that I ever penned. I fear I have written few better, and I hope not many worse," and the second: "Sonnet XLI. This sonnet had an odd origin. A friend asserted that it was not possible to write anything original on 'The Moon!' I bet a wager that I should succeed in doing so, &' this sonnet won me five shillings—more than it is worth." The third and longest goes on to remark:

Page 120. Epistle to——. These lines were addressed to my old and worthy friend Robert Roxby, and were written when I was about nineteen years old. I cannot read them without emotion. A more single hearted man, or a more social, never lived. He then lodged in a court called Mackford's Buildings, and had not long before published his "Lay of the Reedwater Minstrel," an odd but by no means unpoetical ballad poem of which some stanzas were contributed by me. He now lies in the church yard of St. Paul Westgate Hill, a place where we often used to walk and where some of the verses were composed. "Requiescat in pace." Such is human life.

Roxby's poem was published anonymously in Newcastle in 1809, and then reprinted, with his authorship revealed, in 1832. Roxby was more than twenty years older than Doubleday, and died in 1846; Doubleday's participation in his poem appears not to have been previously recognized.

To the second work here, a verse play, Doubleday has appended the following manuscript comment:

Dioclesian is in my humble opinion the least bad poem I have written, and it was by far the least fortunate. By Babington [another verse play, published in 1825] I got a drop of fame to cool my parched tongue, and a trifle of money—more than many poets get, but this Dioclesian was under a black spell from the beginning. First it made a quarrel between that worthy and clever man old Mr. Blackwood and me. When he saw it he refused to publish it having promised to do so; but for this he pleaded a tender conscience. He fancied me too compassionate to a persecutor of religion, which at one time Dioclesian was, and so stood upon orthodoxy. This I got over; relying at all events that he would let the work have fair play in his Magazine. I never, however, could get it noticed. My fiery nature rebelled, and we parted. The Reform Bill completed the separation. But this was not all. No sooner was the poem published than the bookseller became bankrupt; so that it literally dropped dead born and unnoticed from the press, save a few kind words for it by Allan Cunningham [the dedicatee] in one of the weekly literary journals. Such is the history of this production, which has not been read, I dare say, by twenty people, but which cost me more labour than all my verses put together.

This remarkable volume was acquired in 2000.

GEORGE DYER (1755–1841)

303. Dyer, George. Poems. By G. Dyer, B.A. late of Emanuel College, Cambridge. London: printed for J. Johnson, 1792. 4to, boards, vellum spine.

The author's first publication in verse, preceded only by a prose pamphlet on a theological subject, which was printed in 1789. Dyer is now best remembered for his slovenly eccentricities, and for his close friendship with Charles Lamb, who found him endlessly amusing. Of particular interest here is an ode entitled "On Liberty," which includes several stanzas on women writers of the period, including Mary Wollstonecraft, Helen Maria Williams, Laetitia Barbauld, Charlotte Smith, Catharine Macaulay, and Mary Hays; Dyer's attitude toward these women is positive and sympathetic.

This collection was printed by the publisher Joseph Johnson in the same quarto format he used for the earliest poems of Wordsworth, and for two early titles by Coleridge. There are two manuscript corrections in the preliminaries, and three in the text proper, all no doubt in Dyer's hand. The Simon Nowell-Smith copy. Acquired in 2002.

304. Dyer, George. The poet's fate, a poetical dialogue. London: printed for G. G. and J. Robinson, J. Johnson, and J. Debrett, 1797. 8vo, wrappers.

A long literary poem, with ample footnotes. Samuel Johnson is the subject of several verses on the lack of adequate government pensions for writers, and the note on him begins as follows: "A man to be admired for his talents, rather than his principles; as a moralist, he appears a less exalted character." Of particular interest is a reference to the Pantisocrats, which is followed by a long note about "two very ingenious modern poets," Coleridge and Southey. The note continues: "In connection with these names, I cannot forbear mentioning those of three young men, who have given early proofs, that they can strike the true chords of poesy; W. Wordsworth, author of Descriptive Sketches in Verse, taken during a pedestrian tour in the Italian, Grison, Swiss, and Savoyard Alps; W. Lloyd, author of a volume of very elegant sonnets; and Charles Lamb, author of some tender sonnets in Coleridge's Poems, of a fine poem in Charles Lloyd's Poems, and of sonnets in the Monthly Magazine." This copy has two manuscript corrections in an early hand, presumably that of Dyer himself. Acquired in 2004.

305. Dyer, George. Poems. London: printed for the author; and sold by Longman and Rees, 1801. 8vo, original pale blue boards, drab paper backstrip, printed paper label.

> Second issue. Following the table of contents is a leaf with an "Advertisement," in which Dyer explains that he has canceled a long introductory essay on the nature of lyric poetry ("not only written, but actually printed off"); at least two copies survive with this essay preserved, and with the title page dated 1800. This is Dyer's first substantial book of poetry. Only one poem from his slim quarto of 1792 has been included here, "Monody on the Death of Robert Robinson," a substantially revised version of "Monody on the Death of a Friend"; Robinson was a dissenting minister from Cambridge. Also present are forty odes, interspersed with a variety of other pieces, including "The Madman" ("collected by the author from several characters seen in different madhouses"); "On Visiting the Tomb of David Hume," a Latin poem addressed to the classical scholar Gilbert Wakefield (with a facing English translation by Thomas Busby); and, at the end, several poems on literary themes. On the title page is the signature of Maria Eleanora Giffard, of Nerquis, Flintshire, dated 1807 (see also no. 413). The Simon Nowell-Smith copy. Acquired in 2002.

306. Dyer, George. To a lady, requesting some verses on the birth of her sister's first-born child. [Colophon:] London: Barnard and Farley, n.d. [1815?]. 8vo, two leaves, folded.

> A privately printed occasional poem in an invented early English dialect. Three copies are recorded, at the Bodleian, the National Library of Scotland, and the University of London; the last of these is dated 1815 in an early hand. Acquired in 1975.

EBENEZER ELLIOTT (1781–1849)

307. [Elliott, Ebenezer.] The vernal walk, a poem. Cambridge: printed by and for B. Flower; and sold by Crosby and Letterman (London), 1801. 8vo, half calf.

> The author's first book, written when he was seventeen and published when he was twenty. Elliott came from a working-class family in Yorkshire; his father was an extreme radical in politics and an ultra-Calvinist in religion. Elliott married a woman with a small fortune, which he dissipated in a succession of business speculations; in 1821 he managed to set up

a small company in the iron trade in Sheffield, and thereafter he prospered. Elliott was much interested in political and economic reform, and in 1831 he produced *Corn-Law Rhymes*, the book for which he is now chiefly remembered. Three copies of this early poem have been located, at the British Library, Yale, and Wellesley College. Acquired in 2000.

308. Elliott, Ebenezer. Love: a poem, in three parts. To which is added, The Giaour, a satirical poem. London: published by Charles Stocking, 1823. 8vo, half blue morocco, by Riviere (original wrappers bound in at the end).

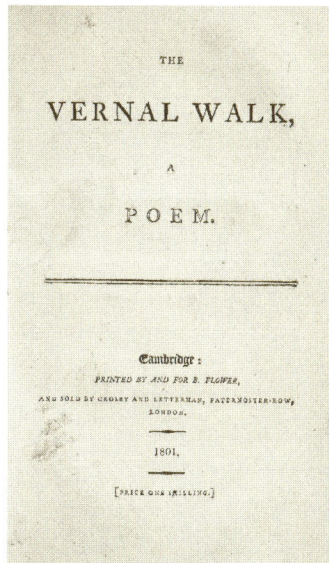

THE

VERNAL WALK,

A

POEM.

Cambridge:
PRINTED BY AND FOR B. FLOWER,
AND SOLD BY CROSBY AND LETTERMAN, PATERNOSTER-ROW,
LONDON.

1801.

[PRICE ONE SHILLING.]

ITEM 307

The first poem is philosophical; an introductory note refers to Malthus on population. The second piece is a long attack on Byron, whose own *Giaour* had been published ten years earlier. This copy is inscribed on the front flyleaf, "To James Montgomery Esq. from the author." The recipient was an older poet whom Elliott much admired, and to whom he had dedicated one of his earlier poems. With the bookplate of Oliver Nowell Chadwyck-Healey. Acquired in 1981.

REGINALD HEBER (1783–1826)

309. Heber, Reginald. Europe: lines on the present war. London: printed for J. Hatchard, 1809. 8vo, original drab printed wrappers.

Heber's first publication, aside from a prize poem and a prize essay (both printed in Oxford). He went on to become bishop of Calcutta, and England's foremost writer of hymns. Acquired in 1980.

310. Heber, Reginald. Poems and translations. London: printed for Longman, Hurst, Rees, Orme, and Brown, 1812. 12mo, original gray boards, printed paper label.

The author's second book. On the title page is the inscription "M. A. T., Whitby," dated 1817. With the bookplate of Mary Elizabeth Hudson. Acquired in 1973.

311. Heber, Reginald. Hymns, written and adapted to the weekly church service of the year. London: John Murray, 1827. 8vo, original light blue boards, drab paper backstrip, printed paper label.

> First edition. This volume was edited shortly after Heber's death by his widow. Included are some of the most famous hymns in the English language, such as "Hark! the Herald Angels Sing," and "Holy, Holy, Holy, Lord God Almighty." Acquired in 1974.

FELICIA DOROTHEA HEMANS, NÉE BROWNE (1793–1835)

312. Browne, Felicia Dorothea. England and Spain; or, valour and patriotism. London: printed by J. M'Creery, for T. Cadell and W. Davies, 1808. 4to, disbound.

> Felicia Hemans published her first book of poems in Liverpool, in 1808, at the age of fifteen; it excited a good deal of interest in the literary circles of London. Shelley is known to have tried to strike up a correspondence with the young girl, but this effort was circumvented by her mother, who was suspicious of Shelley's intentions. This quarto pamphlet poem appeared shortly afterward; the only copies located are at the British Library, the University of California at Davis, the Sutro Library, and Columbia. Felicia Hemans went on to become an enormously popular poet, particularly in the United States. Her most famous poem, "Casabianca," begins, "The boy stood on the burning deck." Acquired in 1974.

313. [Hemans, Felicia.] Modern Greece. A poem. London: John Murray, 1817. 8vo, bound second in a volume with Henry Hart Milman's *Fazio, a Tragedy* (1815; no. 390).

> Byron, who had admired some of the author's earlier verse, criticized this poem for its stance on the issue of the Elgin Marbles. The controversial subject may explain the fact that this poem was published anonymously. Acquired in 1981.

WILLIAM HENRY IRELAND (1777–1835)

314. Ireland, William Henry. Ballads in imitation of the antient. London: printed for T. N. Longman and O. Rees, by Biggs and Cottle (Bristol), 1801. 8vo, original pink boards, drab paper backstrip, printed paper label.

Ireland's first book of original poetry, published some five years after the first appearance of his notorious Shakespeare forgeries, which he had produced, much to his father's astonishment, at the age of nineteen. The verses here show his taste for the antique, which was to some extent a result of his youthful fascination with Chatterton. This book was printed in Bristol; the binding is the same as the one Biggs and Cottle used for *Lyrical Ballads* in 1798. From the collection of Halsted Vander Poel. Acquired in 2004.

315. [Ireland, William Henry.] The sailor-boy. A poem. In four cantos. Illustrative of the navy of Great Britain. By H. C. Esq. Author of "The Fisher-Boy." London: printed for Vernor, Hood, and Sharpe, 1809. 8vo, contemporary calf.

> A sentimental novel in verse. At this point in his career, Ireland lived by his wits, pouring forth a bewildering variety of satirical and sentimental poems, and gothic novels, often issued under pseudonyms. This narrative is the second of three titles published under the initials "H. C."; the first is cited here on the title page, and *The Cottage-Girl* followed in 1810. Acquired in 2012.

JOHN KENYON (1784–1856)

316. [Kenyon, John.] Rhymed plea for tolerance. In two dialogues. With a prefatory dialogue. London: Edward Moxon, 1833. 8vo, original gray boards, printed paper label.

> The author's first book. Kenyon was the son of a rich Jamaica planter. After being educated at Cambridge, he began to make the acquaintance of a wide circle of men of letters, including Coleridge, Wordsworth, Southey, and Lamb. Around 1838, Kenyon became a close friend of his cousin Elizabeth Barrett, and virtually her only link to the outside world; six or seven years later he introduced her to Robert Browning. He was the dedicatee of *Aurora Leigh* (1857; no. 469). This copy is inscribed on the front flyleaf, "From the author." Acquired in 1973.

317. Kenyon, John. Rhymed plea for tolerance. In two dialogues. With a prefatory dialogue. London: Edward Moxon, 1839. 8vo, original dark green cloth.

> Second edition, revised and enlarged. This is the ideal presentation copy, inscribed by Kenyon on the half-title, "To E. B. Barrett from her affectionate

friend and cousin the Author." With the label of "The Browning Collections," sold at auction in 1913. With the additional bookplate of P. H. Hood. The Simon Nowell-Smith copy, acquired in 1978, and not part of the dispersal of his books by Rota in 2002.

318. Kenyon, John. A day at Tivoli: with other verses. London: Longman, Brown, Green, and Longmans, 1849. 8vo, original rose cloth.

> Kenyon's third and last book of poems. This copy is inscribed on the half-title, "To his friend the Revd. J. Eagles, from the Author." The recipient was John Eagles (1783–1855), nominally a clergyman, but better known as an art critic, poet, and journalist. Acquired in 1991.

ROBERT EYRES LANDOR (1781–1869)

319. [Landor, Robert Eyres, attributed author.] Guy's porridge pot: a poem, in twenty-four books. The first part. London: printed for the author, and sold by all the booksellers, 1808. 8vo, original drab wrappers.

> A satire on Dr. Samuel Parr and other scholars. Apparently the first published poem of Walter Savage Landor's younger brother, but the authorship remains uncertain. The Simon Nowell-Smith copy. Acquired in 2002.

320. [Landor, Robert Eyres.] The fawn of Sertorius. London: printed for Longman, Brown, Green, and Longmans, 1846. Two vols., 12mo, original claret cloth.

> An historical novel, set in Rome in the first century BC; the book was at first ascribed to the author's older brother. With "Raffalovich Bequest" bookplates. Acquired in 1993.

CHARLES LLOYD (1775–1839)

321. Lloyd, Charles. Poems on various subjects. Carlisle: printed by F. Jollie, for J. Richardson (Penrith); and sold by C. Law (London); T. Pearson (Birmingham), 1795. 8vo, original pale blue boards, drab paper backstrip.

> The author's first book, published when he was twenty. In 1796, Lloyd met Coleridge in Birmingham, and the two soon became close friends; before long they were sharing lodgings in Bristol, an arrangement cut short by Lloyd's emotional instability. Lloyd also formed a close attachment to Charles Lamb, and in 1798 they collaborated on *Blank Verse* (no. 323). In later years he settled near Wordsworth in Ambleside, but his days

in the Lake District were clouded by fits of madness, as chronicled by his friend De Quincey; he died despondent in Paris in 1839. This copy has a contemporary oval printed book label of Deborah Birkbeck (1756–1821), of Settle, in Yorkshire; she was a Quaker. From the collections of Louis H. Silver (sold at auction in 1965), and Simon Nowell-Smith. Acquired in 2002.

322. Lloyd, Charles. Poems on the death of Priscilla Farmer, by her grandson. Bristol: printed by N. Biggs, and sold by James Phillips (London), 1796. Folio, half calf.

> Lloyd's second publication. Of particular interest is the introductory sonnet by Coleridge, as well as a three-page poem entitled "The Grandam," which is headed "The following beautiful fragment was written by Charles Lamb of the India-House." Lloyd had just been introduced to Lamb by Coleridge. Acquired in 1997.

323. Lloyd, Charles, and Charles Lamb. Blank verse. London: printed by T. Bensley; for John and Arthur Arch, 1798. 8vo, citron morocco, by Riviere.

> A slim volume containing thirteen poems by Lloyd and seven by Lamb. The most interesting of the first group is a long tribute to Mary Wollstonecraft, though in an introductory note Lloyd takes pains to note that "I avow a complete dissent from Mrs. Godwin with regard to almost all her moral speculations." This is the first book to contain any considerable body of verse by Lamb. With the bookplate of Myrtle A. Crummer. Acquired in 1997.

324. Lloyd, Charles. Edmund Oliver. Bristol: printed by Bulgin and Rosser, for Joseph Cottle; sold in London by Messrs. Lee and Hurst, 1798. Two vols., 12mo, red morocco, by the Club Bindery.

> An unusual epistolary novel. "*Edmund Oliver* is a book of very considerable Coleridge interest. Coleridge enlisted in the dragoons under the assumed name of Private Silas Tomkyn Comberbach. After leaving the army he related to Lloyd his experiences. These experiences, disguised in the thinnest manner possible, the latter made use of as incidents in his novel. Coleridge resented the impertinence and his friendship for Lloyd cooled."–T. J. Wise. With the book label of Robert Hoe and the bookplate of A. Edward Newton. Acquired in 1972.

325. Lloyd, Charles. A letter to the Anti-Jacobin reviewers. Birmingham: printed by James Belcher; sold by J. and A. Arch (London), 1799. 8vo, disbound.

A rare pamphlet in which Lloyd replies to a hostile review of *Edmund Oliver*. At the end is an interesting appendix, which includes remarks on Charles Lamb. Acquired in 1985.

326. Lloyd, Charles, translator. The tragedies of Vittorio Alfieri; translated from the Italian. London: printed for Longman, Hurst, Rees, Orme, and Brown, 1815. Three vols., 12mo, contemporary half calf.

This set is inscribed on each half-title, "Susan Lloyd, from the translator"; there are additional signatures on each flyleaf of Anne Lloyd. Lloyd came from a family of fifteen children; presumably these are two of his sisters. Acquired in 1990.

327. Lloyd, Charles. Poems. London: Longman, Hurst, Rees, Orme, and Brown, and C. and H. Baldwyn; and Beilby and Knotts (Birmingham), 1823. 8vo, original gray boards, printed paper label.

Lloyd's last book, a slim volume of meditative verse; the opening poem, "Address to a Virginia Creeper," contains references to Coleridge, Southey, and Leigh Hunt. The Simon Nowell-Smith copy. Acquired in 2002.

HENRY LUTTRELL (1765–1851)

328. [Luttrell, Henry.] Crockford-House, a rhapsody. In two cantos. A rhymer in Rome. London: John Murray, 1827. 8vo, original light blue boards, drab paper backstrip, printed paper label.

A poetical satire on London's gambling houses and playing for high stakes. Luttrell had a reputation as one of the great wits of the early nineteenth century. He was friendly with Byron, Moore, Rogers, and other writers of the day, but he himself never published a great deal; this was his last book. Acquired in 1983.

HENRY FRANCIS LYTE (1793–1847)

329. Lyte, Rev. Henry Francis. The spirit of the Psalms, or the Psalms of David adapted to Christian worship. Brixham: printed by W. King; Rivington, Hatchard, Seely, and Nisbet (London), 1834. 16mo, contemporary red morocco.

Rev. Lyte achieved lasting fame as a writer of hymns. His two most famous poems are "Abide with Me" and "Pleasant Are Thy Courts Above"; the latter was first printed in this volume, which went through many editions. For twenty-five years Lyte was in charge of the parish of Lower Brixham, in Devonshire, near where this small volume was printed. The Simon Nowell-Smith copy. Acquired in 2002.

JOHN MITFORD (1781–1859)

330. Mitford, John. Miscellaneous poems. London: John Russell Smith, 1858. 8vo, original brown cloth.

> The author's last book, published a year before his death. Mitford lived a life of some variety. As a clergyman he held a number of country livings, while at the same time maintaining a permanent residence in London, where he was the neighbor and close friend of Samuel Rogers. Mitford was also a great collector of books, manuscripts, coins, drawings, and prints, and for many years he was the editor of *The Gentleman's Magazine*. This copy is signed by the author on the front flyleaf (dated 1858); beneath his signature Mitford has added, "With the author's kind regards." With the contemporary signature of Elizabeth Sandby, presumably the recipient, on the same leaf. Acquired in 1981.

JAMES MONTGOMERY (1771–1854)

331. [Montgomery, James.] Prison amusements, and other trifles: principally written during nine months of confinement in the Castle of York. By Paul Positive [pseud.]. London: printed for J. Johnson, 1797. 8vo, original light blue boards, drab paper backstrip, printed paper label.

> The author's first book of poems, preceded only by a prose pamphlet published in 1793. Montgomery did in fact write this book while he was in prison; his incarceration was the result of two prosecutions for libel in curred during the course of his work as a printer. He went on to become one of the most widely read poets of the early nineteenth century. With "William Brydon's" on the title page in a contemporary hand. Acquired in 1981.

332. Montgomery, James. Greenland, and other poems. London: printed by Strahan and Spottiswoode; for Longman, Hurst, Rees, Orme, and Brown, 1819. 8vo, original gray boards, printed paper label.

> The H. Bradley Martin copy. Acquired in 1990.

333. Montgomery, James. A poet's portfolio; or, minor poems: in three books. London: printed for Longman, Rees, Orme, Brown, Green, & Longman, 1835. 8vo, original gray boards, printed paper label.

> The author's last book of verse, though he lived another twenty years. Acquired in 2007.

333a. Montgomery, James. Consecration hymns, by James Montgomery, Esq. (Presented for the use of the New Episcopal Chapel, Lisson Grove.) 1837. N.p. [London]: J. Poulter, typog., (1837). 4to, two leaves, folded.

> Two hymns, the second in two parts, composed for the consecration of a London chapel. Montgomery produced hymns for a number of such occasions over the course of his long career. This particular example appears to be unrecorded; an attractive feature is the fact that the border of the first leaf has been stamped to resemble a piece of lace. Acquired in 2005.

JOHN MOULTRIE (1799–1874)

334. [Moultrie, John.] My brother's grave: from "The Poetry of the College Magazine." Windsor: published by Knight and Dredge, 1820. 8vo, disbound.

> First separate edition. A sentimental poem, highly regarded at the time, written for *The Etonian* in October 1820, when the author was twenty. Moultrie had entered Eton College seven years after Shelley; he went on to a moderately successful career as a poet, often writing in the manner of Wordsworth. No other copy of this eight-page pamphlet has been located. Acquired in 1994.

BRYAN WALLER PROCTER (1787–1874)

335. [Procter, Bryan Waller.] A Sicilian story, with Diego de Montilla, and other poems. By Barry Cornwall [pseud.]. London: C. and J. Ollier, 1820. 12mo, contemporary calf.

> The author's second book. Procter, a man of some means, was one of the best-loved literary figures of his day. His early friends included Leigh Hunt and Charles Lamb, both of whom had a great influence on his verse; he also knew Shelley, and helped guarantee, along with Thomas Lovell Beddoes and Thomas Kelsall, the expense of printing his *Posthumous Poems* (1824). In later years he was particularly generous toward such younger writers as Browning and Swinburne. Procter's early books were

all published under the pseudonym "Barry Cornwall." With the armorial bookplate of the writer Chandos Leigh, who must have known Procter. Acquired in 1992.

EDWARD QUILLINAN (1791–1851)

336. [Quillinan, Edward.] The retort courteous. Edinburgh: printed for and sold by John Robertson, 1821. 8vo, disbound.

> Edward Quillinan is now perhaps best remembered as Wordsworth's son-in-law. Wordsworth had great misgivings about the marriage of his beloved daughter Dorothy, but the match turned out to be very successful. Quillinan spent his early years in the army, but he had a fancy for satirical verse. In 1814, when he was twenty-three, he published *Dunluce Castle*, the first of several more serious poems to be printed by Egerton Brydges at the Lee Priory Press. For some reason this work later attracted the notice of Thomas Hamilton, a reviewer (under the name "Morgan O'Doherty") for the prestigious *Blackwood's Magazine*, who in 1819 ridiculed it in a piece called "Poems by a Heavy Dragoon." Quillinan deferred his rejoinder for two years, but in the end he published the present poem, a satirical attack in the manner of Byron's *English Bards*; Quillinan's chief targets here are John Gibson Lockhart and John Wilson, whom he erroneously assumed were responsible for the review in *Blackwood's*. Acquired in 1992.

337. Quillinan, Edward. The King: the lay of "a Papist." [London: 1829.] 12mo, contemporary black morocco.

> A poem expressing Ireland's debt to George IV for his support of Catholic Emancipation (though the king had sometimes opposed this reform). This little book was privately printed; two other copies have been located, one at the Bodleian, and the other at Huntington (with a note that only thirty copies were printed). The Simon Nowell-Smith copy. Acquired in 2002.

338. Quillinan, Edward, translator. The Lusiad of Luis de Camoens. Books I to V. . . . With notes by John Adamson. London: Edward Moxon, 1853. 8vo, original purple cloth.

> This translation was published two years after Quillinan's death by his close friend John Adamson, an antiquary and Portuguese scholar, who himself died two years later. This copy is inscribed on the half-title, "P. H. Howard Esq. from John Adamson." Acquired in 1997.

DOROTHY QUILLINAN, NÉE WORDSWORTH (1771–1855)

339. [Quillinan, Dorothy, née Wordsworth.] Journal of a few months' residence in Portugal, and glimpses of the south of Spain. London: Edward Moxon, 1847. Two vols., 8vo, original green cloth.

> The only book by Wordsworth's daughter Dora; it is dedicated to her parents. The trip described here was undertaken because of Dora's delicate health; she died shortly after her account was published. "A charming book."–*DNB*. Acquired in 1993.

JOHN HAMILTON REYNOLDS (1796–1852)

340. Reynolds, John Hamilton. Safie. An eastern tale. London: printed for James Cawthorn; and John Martin, 1814. 8vo, contemporary calf.

> The author's second book, an Oriental tale very much in the manner of Byron, to whom the poem is dedicated: "This tale is inscribed, with every sentiment of gratitude and respect, to the Right Honourable Lord Byron." As might be expected, Reynolds sent a copy to Byron (though he did not know him personally), as Byron mentions in a journal entry for February 20, 1814: "Answered–or, rather, acknowledged–the receipt of young Reynolds's Poem, Safie. The lad is clever, but much of his thoughts are borrowed,– whence, the Reviewers may find out. I hate discouraging a young one; and I think,–though wild, and more oriental than he would be, had he seen the scenes where he placed his tale,–that he has much talent, and, certainly, fire enough." On the same day, Byron wrote a long letter to Reynolds, thanking him for his "pleasing present," and offering some slightly sententious advice on profiting from experience, along with rather more amusing hints on how to deal with criticism. This copy has a most intriguing inscription on the title page (slightly cropped at the top by the binder): "L. B. A Gift. 1814." It has not yet been established whether this inscription is in the author's hand; if it is, then this appears to be the very copy that Reynolds sent to Byron. Byron's books were dispersed at auction in April 1816, upon his departure from England (see no. 146). This poem is not mentioned in the catalogue of this sale, but it could no doubt have been included in one of the mixed lots, such as lot 11: "Shee's Commemoration of Reynolds, 1814. Lord Thurlow's Poems, 1813, and 10 more." Acquired in 1998.

341. [Reynolds, John Hamilton.] An ode. London: printed for John Martin, 1815. 8vo, disbound.

An early poem written in a febrile manner, in which a fallen monarch, regretting his past crimes, is confronted by a vision of Terror, Remorse, and other abstractions. The only other recorded copies of this pamphlet are at Harvard and Keats House, and neither of these appears to have the final leaf of advertisements. Listed here are six other titles published by the bookseller John Martin, the first two of which are *Safie* and *The Eden of Imagination*, both by Reynolds and printed in 1814. The poem has been correctly identified on the title page in an early hand as "by J. H. Reynolds." Within, possibly in the same hand, are a fair number of penciled notes, citing parallels with Robert Southey's *Curse of Kehama* (1810), Leigh Hunt (the word "pranksome"), and Walter Scott's *Marmion* (the final word, "Lost"); one passage is marked as "exquisite," and another "a suitable subject for a picture." This copy came from the same volume as Thomas Moore's poem on the death of Sheridan (no. 95), which may have belonged to Thomasine Leigh, a young woman much involved with Reynolds and his friends James Rice and Benjamin Bailey (see also no. 95); unfortunately the volume was disassembled in 2011 by a provincial English bookseller, and the contents scattered.

342. [Reynolds, John Hamilton.] The naiad: a tale. With other poems. London: printed by T. Miller; for Taylor and Hessey, 1816. 8vo, original blue wrappers.

This slim volume was published anonymously in the summer of 1816, a few months before Reynolds first met Keats; it is dedicated to Benjamin Haydon. Acquired in 2013.

343. [Reynolds, John Hamilton.] Peter Bell. A lyrical ballad. London: printed for Taylor and Hessey, 1819. 8vo, disbound.

A parody of Wordsworth's poem of the same name (no. 26). In fact, Reynolds must have seen Wordsworth's text in manuscript, as his parody was printed first. Reynolds is probably now best remembered for having been one of Keats's best friends. A final leaf of advertisements here includes a notice for *Endymion* as "just published." Acquired in 1977.

344. [Reynolds, John Hamilton.] Benjamin the waggoner, a ryghte merrie and conceitede tale in verse. A fragment. London: printed for Baldwin, Cradock, and Joy, 1819. 8vo, disbound.

Another parody of a Wordsworth poem with the same title (no. 27). More than half this pamphlet is taken up with notes and introductory material, much of it exceedingly funny, ridiculing Wordsworth's style, his choice of homely subjects, and his excessive sensitivity to nature. Acquired in 1977.

WILLIAM SOTHEBY (1757–1833)

345. Sotheby, William. Oberon, a poem, from the German of Wieland. London: printed for Cadell and Davies; Edwards; Faulder; and Hatchard, 1798. Two vols., 8vo, contemporary calf.

> The author's second book, preceded by a collection of poems printed in Bath in 1790, and reprinted in London in 1794. Sotheby was born and raised in a wealthy family, and decided at an early age to pursue a literary career. He entertained all the best-known men of letters of his day, and benevolently interested himself in the struggles of young writers. In time he became very friendly with Scott, Wordsworth, Coleridge, Southey, Byron, and Moore. With the contemporary signature on each title page of Sophia Dunbar, of Burgie. Acquired in 1980.

346. Sotheby, William. Oberon, a poem. From the German of Wieland. London: printed by W. Bulmer and Co.; for T. Cadell and W. Davies, 1805. Two vols., 8vo, original light blue boards, cream paper backstrips, labeled and numbered in manuscript.

> Second edition, revised, with some stanzas rewritten and others omitted, though these changes are not anywhere mentioned. Of particular importance are the twelve newly added plates, engraved after designs by Henry Fuseli, one of the best English artists of the period. With the armorial bookplates of the Earl of Annesley. The Simon Nowell-Smith copy. Acquired in 2002.

347. Sotheby, William. A song of triumph. London: printed for John Murray, by W. Bulmer and Co., 1814. 4to, original gray wrappers.

> A poem on the defeat of Napoleon. This copy is inscribed, "from the Author" on the title page. Acquired in 1994.

348. Sotheby, William. Poems. London: printed by William Nicol, 1825. 8vo, original drab wrappers, printed paper label.

> This copy is inscribed on the title page, "To Andrew Knight Esqre. from the author." With the recent book label of Douglas Ewing. Acquired in 1993.

349. Sotheby, William. The first book of the Iliad; the parting of Hector and Andromache; and the shield of Achilles. Specimens of a new version of Homer. London: John Murray, 1830. 8vo, contemporary half calf.

> Sotheby's last literary project was his translation of the works of Homer. The present fifty-two-page specimen was well received, and the full text of the *Iliad* duly appeared the following year, in two volumes. Sotheby went on to complete the *Odyssey*, but did not live to see its publication in 1834. From the library of Chandos Leigh, with his large, glazed armorial bookplate. Acquired in 1992.

EDWARD HOVELL-THURLOW, 2ND BARON THURLOW (1781–1829)

350. Thurlow, Edward Hovell-, 2nd Baron Thurlow. Verses on several occasions. . . . The first volume [all published]. London: printed by William Bulmer and Co., Shakspeare [*sic*] Press, 1812. 8vo, contemporary red straight-grained morocco, covers very elaborately decorated in gilt and blind, spine gilt, broad inner dentelles gilt, yellow silk endpapers, a.e.g.

> The author's first collection of verse. The poems included here were also separately published in 1812, but those printings were anonymous; another version of this book appeared in 1813, but was retitled *Poems on Several Occasions.* Lord Thurlow appears to have anticipated printing a second volume, but there was nothing further in this format. He was a gentleman-poet who contributed frequently to the periodicals of the day. Byron once wrote a parody of one of his poems, and Moore reviewed one of his books harshly. Only one other copy of this book has been located, at the Bodleian. The present copy is in a highly ornate binding of the period. Acquired in 2001.

351. Thurlow, Edward Hovell-, 2nd Baron Thurlow. Poems on several occasions. London: printed by William Bulmer and Co., Shakspeare [*sic*] Press, for Messrs. White, Cochrane, and Co., 1813. [With:] An appendix to poems on several occasions; being a continuation of The Sylva. London: printed by William Bulmer and Co., Shakspeare Press, for Messrs. White, Cochrane, and Co., 1813. Two vols., 8vo, contemporary black straight-grained morocco.

> Second edition, "considerably enlarged," of the first title; first edition of the appendix. The first half of the first volume, comprising the dedicatory and other poems prefixed to the author's edition of Sidney's *Defence of Poesy*, and

the two cantos of the unfinished "Hermilda," had first been privately printed in 1812, also by Bulmer, as *Verses on Several Occasions* (no. 350), and then reprinted for public distribution, under the present title, earlier in 1813. This expanded edition adds sixty-two further poems, grouped under the general title "Sylva" (pp. 109–240). The *Appendix*, printed separately, adds seventy-two more poems, rather eccentrically numbered both 1–72, and 63–134. Lord Thurlow printed these volumes at his own considerable expense, despite a financial crisis and the derision of some of his contemporaries. Byron, dining with Rogers and Moore, is recorded as having opened the "Sylva" to a poem addressed to Rogers (1, p. 162), "but when he tried to recite it, he could not get beyond the first line . . . without bursting into laughter, which infected the company."—Jerome J. McGann, ed., *Byron* (1980–93), vol. 3, p. 426. These two volumes belonged to Thurlow himself, as is indicated by a note on a front flyleaf of the first volume: "Lord Thurloe's own copy, purchased at a sale of part of His Lordship's books in 1816" (though Thurlow did not die until 1829). They were subsequently in the celebrated library of the preeminent collector Richard Heber, and bear his note: "Sale by Evans–Jan. 1817, 2 Vols. 15.6." Also present are the later armorial bookplates and acquisition note of Frances Mary Richardson Currer (1785–1861), England's first great female book collector: "Mr. Heber's sale, Pt. 4, 1834. 2 vols. 8s." The linking of Heber and Currer is particularly appealing; it has always been said that Heber considered marrying Currer to obtain her library. Acquired in 2006.

352. Thurlow, Edward Hovell-, 2nd Baron Thurlow. Select poems. Chiswick: printed by C. Whittingham, 1821. 8vo, original light blue-green boards, binder's ticket of Backwell, bookbinder, of Brighton.

Second edition, though not so designated; a prior edition had been printed in Brussels in 1816. The new edition was privately printed. Acquired in 1981.

MARY TIGHE (1772–1810)

353. [Tighe, Mary.] Psyche; or, the legend of love. London: printed for James Carpenter by C. Whittingham 1805. Sm. square 8vo, contemporary red straight-grained morocco, covers elaborately decorated in gilt, spine gilt, pink silk flyleaves and pastedowns bordered in gilt, a.e.g.

The author's first book, privately printed in an edition reported to have been one hundred copies. This long poem in Spenserian stanzas, based on the story of Cupid and Psyche in Apuleius, was much admired by such Romantic poets as Leigh Hunt, Thomas Moore, and Felicia Hemans. It has long been recognized that Keats was a particularly avid reader of Mary Tighe's verses, and many parallel passages have been pointed out. This copy is neatly inscribed on the title page in a minuscule hand, "Caroline Hamilton from her most affectionate and grateful M. Tighe. Sept. 2, 1805." In a very pretty binding of the period. Acquired in 1995.

CORNELIUS WEBBE, OR WEBB (1789–1858)

354. [Webbe, Cornelius.] The posthumous papers, facetious and fanciful, of a person lately about town. London: William Sams, 1828. 8vo, original pale blue boards, drab paper backstrip, printed paper label.

> A collection of stories, sketches, and essays by a writer now chiefly remembered because John Gibson Lockhart once lumped him together with John Keats, in an article in *Blackwood's Edinburgh Magazine* (1817), as coming from the "Cockney school" of English poetry. On the front pastedown is the early signature of J. P. Holloway. Acquired in 1992.

355. Webbe, Cornelius. Lyric leaves. London: Thomas Griffiths, 1832. 12mo, original rose boards.

> The author's final volume of poetry. This copy is inscribed by the author on the front flyleaf, "Sir J. F. K., with the author's sincere respects." The recipient was Sir John Foley Kealy, a manufacturer of agricultural implements. From the library of H. Buxton Forman, with his bookplate, and a few penciled notes, including his initials, dated May 1, 1876, and the comment, "Look to 18, 81, &c sonnets." Acquired in 1973.

CHARLES JEREMIAH WELLS (1800–1879)

356. [Wells, Charles Jeremiah.] Stories after nature. London: T. and J. Allman; and C. and J. Ollier, 1822. 12mo, original blue boards, drab paper backstrip, printed paper label.

> Wells was educated at Cowden Clarke's school at Edmonton, where he came to know Keats (and was a classmate of Keats's younger brother Tom). When he came to London, Wells became a part of the literary circle that included Keats, Leigh Hunt, and Hazlitt; with Hazlitt he was particularly friendly. He was also on good terms with Keats until their acquaintance was dissolved by a cruel practical joke played by Wells upon the then invalid Tom Keats (involving the invention of a series of love letters). Keats speaks

of this episode with bitter resentment. Wells published only two books, of which this is the first, a striking collection of tales in the Renaissance Italian manner. With the signature of Samuel Loveman, of Cleveland, Ohio, dated 1919 (see also no. 297). Acquired in 1977.

357. [Wells, Charles Jeremiah.] Joseph and his brethren, a scriptural drama; in two acts. By H. L. Howard [pseud.]. London: printed for G. and W. B. Whittaker, 1824. 8vo, nineteenth-century green morocco, by Mansell.

The author's second and last book, and a minor masterpiece of the Romantic period. This ambitious verse drama was essentially ignored when it was published, though Hazlitt pronounced it "not only original but aboriginal." The text was rediscovered by the Pre-Raphaelites, however, and in 1876 Buxton Forman prepared a new edition, with an introduction by Swinburne, who had been attracted to Wells's work by an appreciative notice Rossetti in Gilchrist's *Life of Blake*. Rossetti compared the play to Blake's work: "One grand poem, on the same footing as his own . . . may be found in Wells's scriptural drama *Joseph and His Brethren*." The Simon Nowell-Smith copy. Acquired in 2002.

358. Wells, Charles Jeremiah. Joseph and his brethren: a dramatic poem. . . . With an introduction by Algernon Charles Swinburne. London: Chatto and Windus, 1876. 8vo, original dark blue cloth.

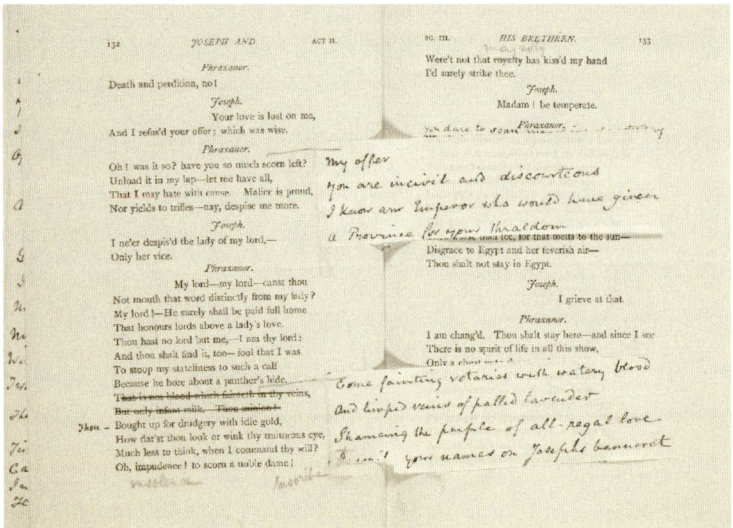

ITEM 358

214

Second edition, substantially revised, and seen through the press by Buxton Forman; first published in 1824 (no. 357). This extraordinary copy belonged to Wells himself, and reveals that he spent the remaining three years of his life making further alterations to the text. On the half-title is a presentation inscription from the author to his editor H. Buxton Forman. For some reason, Wells seems to have changed his mind about this gift, and to have pasted this leaf down onto the front flyleaf, obscuring what he had written; the flyleaf has later been partly peeled back, to reveal the inscription. On the verso of the half-title Wells has subsequently written, "R. H. Horne Esq. with the affection of the author." He has also added two lines to the quotation from Milton. As far as can be determined, this volume remained in Horne's possession until his death in 1884, when many of his literary effects were acquired by Buxton Forman. On the title page Wells has crossed out "Joseph and His Brethren," and has altered the title in blue pencil to "Sephenath Phaanech." On the verso he has added: "Sephenath Phaanech. The first and second edition of this work were published under the title of Joseph and his Brethren. The text being nearly doubled since the first edition and the principal characters so much develop'd the historical title instituted by Pharaoh has been adopted to this third edition." Wells has made a vast number of manuscript additions, deletions, and corrections throughout the text of his verse play; these range from the change of a single word, to the addition of an entire scene. The alterations are either in ink, neatly written, or in blue pencil; on balance the blue-pencil changes seem to have been done at a slightly later date. Many of the additions have been made on separate slips, sometimes neatly tipped in at one end, and sometimes pasted down to obscure the lines being replaced. Some of the more extensive additions are on separate leaves, inserted as required. In general, the revisions are more extensive in the later stages of the verse drama. Of greatest importance is the presence at the end of an entirely new scene ("Scene IV"), consisting of twenty-eight pages in manuscript. This scene was selected by Buxton Forman as a contribution to vol. 1 of *Literary Anecdotes of the Nineteenth Century* (1895), compiled by W. R. Nicoll and T. J. Wise. This was the last book added to the Wachs Collection, in 2012.

JEREMIAH HOLMES WIFFEN (1792–1836)

359. [Wiffen, Jeremiah Holmes, with James Baldwin Brown and Thomas Raffles.] Poems by three friends. London: printed for Thomas Underwood, and Adam Black (Edinburgh), by W. Heseltine, 1813. 8vo, contemporary calf.

Wiffen's first book, published when he was twenty-one, as a collaboration with two young friends. Raffles was a first cousin of Sir Thomas Stamford Raffles, whose name is inextricably involved with British colonial affairs in the East Indies. Included in this volume is a dedicatory poem to Thomas Campbell, and a long poem addressed to Walter Scott; no authorship is anywhere indicated, but the three friends revealed their names in a reprint of 1815. On the front flyleaf is the contemporary signature of John Beal. Acquired in 1995.

360. [Wiffen, Jeremiah Holmes.] Verses written in the portico of the Temple of Liberty at Woburn Abbey, on placing before it the statues of Locke and Erskine, in the summer of 1835. London: printed by James Moyes, 1836. 4to, original gray wrappers, printed paper side label.

One of only fifty copies printed for private distribution (as noted on the verso of the title page). Wiffen was the brother-in-law of Alaric Watts, and an acquaintance of Wordsworth and Southey; as a poet he is best remembered as the translator of the works of Tasso. In 1821 he was appointed librarian to John Russell, 6th Duke of Bedford, at Woburn Abbey. Acquired in 1994.

CHARLES WOLFE (1791–1823)

361. Wolfe, Charles. The burial of Sir John Moore; with other poems. By the late Rev. Charles Wolfe. Preceded by a biographical memoir. London: printed for Thomas Wilson, 1825. 12mo, original gray printed wrappers.

This slender collection contains the first printing outside of a newspaper or periodical of Wolfe's best-known poem. "The Burial of Sir John Moore" was first published in a Newry newspaper in 1817. In 1822, Byron drew attention to this elegy, and was subsequently credited with having written the lines himself. Byron denied authorship of the poem, with regret, but Thomas Medwin later hinted (1824) that the stanzas were really by his hero, which brought forth friends to justify Wolfe's title and establish his reputation. Acquired in 2011.

362. Wolfe, Charles. Remains of the late Rev. Charles Wolfe, A.B., curate of Donoughmore, diocese of Armagh, with a brief memoir of his life. By the Rev. John A. Russell, M.A., chaplain to His Excellency the Lord Lieutenant of Ireland, and curate of St. Werburgh's, Dublin. Dublin:

printed for A. and W. Watson; and Hamilton, Adams and Co. (London), 1825. Two vols., 12mo, contemporary half calf.

> The principal source for the life and writings of an Irish clergyman who died of consumption in 1823, at the age of thirty-one. Acquired in 1996.

FRANCIS WRANGHAM (1769–1842)

363. Wrangham, Francis. Poems. London: sold by J. Mawman, (1795). 8vo, red morocco, by Riviere.

> The author's first book, preceded only by two prize poems. Wrangham was a classical scholar, poet, and book collector, whose numerous publications during his lifetime were for the most part issued privately in small editions. This early collection is notable for containing contributions by both Wordsworth and Coleridge. From Wordsworth there is a translation of a French poem by Wrangham on the birth of love. Coleridge has translated one of Wrangham's Latin poems and then, in a footnote, added a twelve-line poem of his own. Wrangham and Wordsworth seem to have become friends at Cambridge, and by the mid-1790s they were very close. Both were sympathetic toward the French Revolution, and in Wrangham's case these sympathies appear to have cost him a Cambridge fellowship. His disappointment may explain why this book seems not to have been published at the time it was printed, but to have been held back in sheets for some years; in all probability the title page, with the date in parentheses, was printed around 1803, and the book first circulated at that time. It is clear, however, from a three-page "Advertisement," that the sheets were printed in 1795. Tipped in is an interesting one-page autograph letter, dated July 27, 1819, to the publisher Henry Colburn, in which Wrangham speaks of possible contributions to Colburn's magazines. With the book label of Hannah D. Rabinowitz. Acquired in 1975.

OTHER POETRY, MAJOR AND MINOR, OF THE EARLY NINETEENTH CENTURY

JAMES BIRD (1788–1839)

364. Bird, James. Machin; or, the discovery of Madeira. A poem. In four cantos. London: John Warren, 1821. 8vo, original gray wrappers, printed paper side label.

> A long narrative poem, printed in Yarmouth. James Bird, the son of a Suffolk farmer, was first apprenticed as a miller; he later owned a stationer's shop in Yoxford, which he maintained until his death. Laid into this copy is a fine two-page autograph letter from Bird, dated Sept. 9, 1819, to his first publisher, Robert Baldwin, of Baldwin and Cradock, who had issued Bird's first book, a poem called *The Vale of Slaughden*, earlier that year. Part of the letter is about his new venture: "I am making progress in a new poem, founded on the discovery of Madeira, an interesting subject, for the Muse, even were the poet to confine himself to bare historical facts." Bird concludes with a reference to a much more famous writer, whose masterpiece had just begun its appearance: "'Don Juan' possesses many poetical beauties, but its gross immorality will soon consign it to 'Oblivion's dreary shelf,' leaving it there among the cobwebs." How wrong he was! This letter was once in the collection of the well-known Norfolk antiquary Dawson Turner, and bears his note at the top. Acquired in 1999.

JAMES BISSET (1762?–1832)

365. Bisset, James. The origin, rise, and progress of Leamington Spa; a poetic effusion. Leamington: printed by E. Heathcote; and sold by Baldwin and Cradock (London), 1828. 12mo, original tan printed wrappers.

> A charming piece of local advertising for what had become a popular resort not far from Birmingham, written and published by a sixty-six-year-old manager of a picture gallery. The verse is conventional, but the pamphlet is greatly enhanced by the presence at the end of an advertising section, most of which consists of reproductions of engraved calling cards, submitted by local merchants; included are trade cards for tea dealers, barbers, bootmakers, upholsterers, wine merchants, piano dealers, and others. Three copies of this poem are recorded, at the British Library, Birmingham, and the National Library of Scotland. Acquired in 1987 (my gift to Dr. Wachs for his fiftieth birthday).

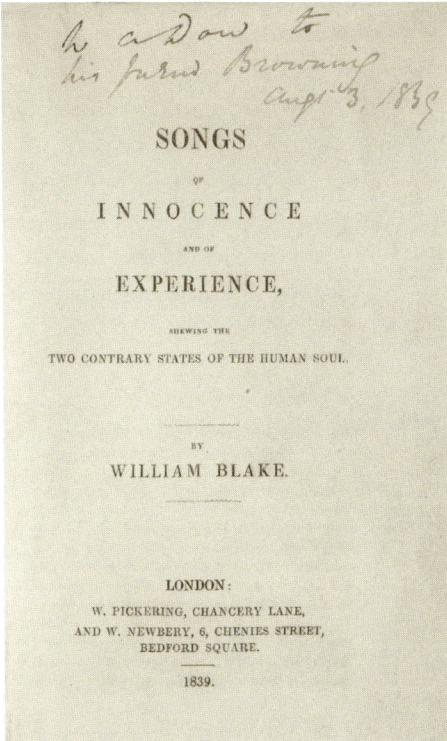

> SONGS
>
> OF
>
> INNOCENCE
>
> AND OF
>
> EXPERIENCE,
>
> SHEWING THE
>
> TWO CONTRARY STATES OF THE HUMAN SOUL.
>
> BY
>
> WILLIAM BLAKE.
>
> LONDON:
>
> W. PICKERING, CHANCERY LANE,
> AND W. NEWBERY, 6, CHENIES STREET,
> BEDFORD SQUARE.
>
> 1839.

WILLIAM BLAKE (1757–1827)

366. Blake, William. Songs of innocence and of experience, shewing the two contrary states of the human soul. London: W. Pickering, and W. Newbery, 1839. 8vo, original purple cloth.

First letterpress edition; preceded only by the unobtainable illuminated edition of 1789. This volume was edited and seen through the press by James John Garth Wilkinson, a Swedenborgian whose mystical temperament attracted him to Blake's verse, which was as yet little known. This was Robert Browning's copy; it is inscribed on the title page, "W. A. Dow to his friend Browning, August 3, 1839." William Alexander Dow (1807–1848) was a lawyer who had been introduced to Browning by the actor and theater manager William Charles Macready; a lasting friendship ensued. Browning was twenty-seven when he was given this book. The *NCBEL* classifies Blake as a late eighteenth-century poet. Acquired in 1992.

WALTER BLUNT (1802–1868)

367. [Blunt, Walter, editor.] Poetry of the College Magazine. Windsor: printed by Knight and Son, 1819. 8vo, contemporary full red morocco, covers elaborately decorated in gilt and blind, with central panels and wide borders in gilt, spine and inner dentelles gilt, a.e.g.

> A privately printed collection of poems by a group of students at Eton. This copy, in a highly decorative binding of the period, is inscribed on a front flyleaf, "Robert Crawfurd, the gift of his friend John Wilder, Eton Coll., 1820"; the recipient's armorial bookplate is on the front pastedown. John Wilder was a student at Eton, and contributed a poem called "Pity" to this collection (p. 87); either he, or his friend, has identified in pencil all the authors and a great many of the allusions in the poems themselves. The first poem, a ballad called "The Bride of the Cave," is by Coleridge's nephew (and later his literary executor), Henry Nelson Coleridge. The most prolific contributor was John Moultrie, whose later poetry was much admired by Tennyson. The editor of this volume, William Blunt, also contributed a poem. Other contributors include Howard, Neech, Lukin, Angelo, and the Hon. F. C. Curzon. Acquired in 2003.

HANS BUSK (1772–1862)

368. Busk, Hans. Fugitive pieces in verse. London: printed by W. M. Thiselton, 1814. 8vo, contemporary green straight-grained morocco.

> The author's first book. This is the dedication copy, inscribed on a front flyleaf in the year of publication, "to Maria Busk, a tribute of esteem from the author"; the recipient was the author's wife, as is revealed by an effusive three-page printed dedication. That this was a special copy is indicated not only by the ornate presentation binding, but by the fact that the engraved title page and seven unsigned plates are all present in three states, plain, sepia, and hand-colored. Acquired in 1996.

GEORGE CRABBE (1754–1832)

369. Crabbe, George. Tales of the hall. London: John Murray, 1819. Two vols., 8vo, original gray boards, printed paper labels.

> The author's last book. Crabbe was one of the few important poets of the eighteenth century to publish anything of significance after 1800.

His verse is commonly styled "pre-Romantic," and there is no question that he was a major influence on Wordsworth. This set bears the inscription "Cumbusmore," in an early hand, on the title page of each volume. Acquired in 1978.

JOHN WILSON CROKER (1780–1857)

370. [Croker, John Wilson.] The battles of Talavera. A poem. Dublin: printed by N. Kelly, 1809. 8vo, disbound.

> An enormously popular patriotic poem, written in the manner of Scott's *Marmion*, in celebration of Wellington's victories in the Peninsular War. The poem was quickly reprinted in London by John Murray, and by the end of 1810 had reached an eighth edition. This original Dublin printing is rare; three copies are recorded, at the National Library of Ireland, the New York Public Library, and McMaster. Croker is now best known for one of the most famous book reviews in the annals of English letters, a nasty attack on Keats's *Endymion* and the "Cockney school" of English poetry, published in *The Quarterly Review* in 1818. Acquired in 1974.

GEORGE DANIEL (1789–1864)

371. [Daniel, George.] Suppressed evidence; or, r–l intriguing: being the history of a courtship, marriage and separation, exemplified in the fate of the Princess of––. Together with a particular account of those characters which immediately led to it, and the private transactions of the secret committee in a certain delicate investigation. Comprising the hitherto unknown mysteries of "My Own Memoirs." By P–– P––, Poet Laureat, author of "R––l Stripes,"–(suppressed.) London: published by E. Wilson; printed by G. Hazard, 1813. 8vo, disbound.

> One of a series of five poems in the tradition of "Peter Pindar" (John Wolcot), satirizing the marital scandals of the Prince of Wales; the text contains a reference to Byron, whom Daniel much admired. Daniel later became a close friend of Charles Lamb. He is now chiefly remembered as one of the great book collectors of the mid-nineteenth century; his library had splendid holdings of Elizabethan literature, including Shakespeare, and early English theatrical history. Acquired in 1992.

JOHN HOOKHAM FRERE (1769–1846)

372. [Frere, John Hookham.] Prospectus and specimen of an intended national work, by William and Robert Whistlecraft, of Stow-Market, in Suffolk, harness and collar-makers. Intended to comprise the most interesting particulars relating to King Arthur and his Round Table. London: John Murray, 1817. [With:] Cantos III and IV. London: John Murray, 1818. Two vols. in one, 8vo, disbound.

> Frere was by profession a diplomat, but he had a sparkling wit, and a facility for writing humorous verse. When Murray published the first two cantos of this poem, he sent a copy to Byron in Italy. Byron read it in Venice, and was sufficiently impressed that he set about immediately to write an imitation; the result was *Beppo*. One of the most important features of Frere's poem is his revival of ottava rima; this stanza form proved highly congenial to Byron, and he went on to use it again in *Don Juan*. Acquired in 1977.

JOHN GALT (1779–1839)

373. Galt, John. Poems. London: Cochrane and M'Crone, 1833. 8vo, original rose moiré cloth, morocco label.

> A late collection of verse by one of the leading Scottish novelists of the early nineteenth century. This copy is inscribed on the title page, "To Mr. D'Israeli with the best respects of the author John Galt." Isaac D'Israeli, a prominent man of letters and the father of Benjamin Disraeli, was eleven years Galt's senior and also reaching the end of a successful literary career. Acquired in 1986.

GEORGE GOODWIN (FL. 1798)

374. Goodwin, George. Rising Castle, with other poems. Lynn: printed for the author by W. Turner; and sold by all the booksellers in Lynn; Messrs. Robinson (London); Stevenson and Matchett (Norwich); and Gedge (Bury), 1798. 8vo, contemporary black calf, gilt, spine decorated in red and gilt.

> A collection of poems by a nineteen-year-old who published no other book. Most of the verse appears to be in the manner of Gray, with hints of early Wordsworth. This is the dedication copy; on the front pastedown is the armorial bookplate of the dedicatee, Richard Howard, of Ashtead Hall, Surrey. The binding is attractive and unusual, and clearly provincial. With the later bookplate of Harry Lawrence. Acquired in 1987.

WILLIAM HAZLITT (1778–1830)

375. Hazlitt, William, editor. Select British poets, or new elegant extracts from Chaucer to the present time, with critical remarks. . . . Embellished with seven ornamental portraits, after a design by T. Stothard, R.A. London: published by Wm. C. Hall, and sold by all booksellers, 1824. Large 8vo, contemporary red embossed morocco, a.e.g.

> Hazlitt may have begun to compile this anthology as early as 1818; he was certainly at work on it in 1821, as both Keats and Shelley, who died in 1821 and 1822, are included in the section "Living Poets." That Charles Lamb helped in the production of this book is known from a passage in a letter from Mary Shelley to Leigh Hunt (September 9, 1823). As soon as the volume was published, it was discovered that many copyrights of writers in the "Living Poets" section had been infringed, and the book was immediately withdrawn from circulation. At some point the text was entirely reset; the contents of the new edition were the same, except that the "Living Poets" section was omitted. A substantial number of copies of the suppressed edition were sent to the United States, where copyright was less strictly enforced; the binding of this copy is clearly American. With the signature of Gilbert D. Collins on the title page, and the signature of John Milton (?) Collins on the front flyleaf. Acquired in 1980.

ELIZABETH HITCHENER (1782?–1822)

376. Hitchener, Elizabeth. The Weald of Sussex, a poem. London: printed for Black, Young, and Young, 1822. 8vo, original drab boards, printed paper label.

> The author's major book of verse; besides this topographical poem she also published two slim volumes of poetical enigmas and other parlor games. Elizabeth Hitchener's fame derives from her association with Shelley. A correspondence between the two sprang up in 1811, when Shelley was nineteen and Hitchener was twenty-nine; at a later date she resided in Shelley's household, but he soon found her presence irksome. He subsequently described her as "the Brown Demon" and "an artful, superficial, ugly, hermaphroditical beast of a woman." The Simon Nowell-Smith copy. Acquired in 2002.

JOHN CAM HOBHOUSE, 1ST BARON BROUGHTON
(1786–1869)

377. Hobhouse, John Cam. Imitations and translations from the ancient and modern classics, together with original poems never before published. London: printed for Longman, Hurst, Rees, and Orme, 1809. 8vo, contemporary half dark blue straight-grained morocco and pink boards.

> The author's first book. Included in this volume are nine poems by the author's close friend Lord Byron, all signed with the initials "L. B." Byron's authorship is confirmed by Hobhouse in his preface. Acquired in 1985.

378. [Hobhouse, John Cam.] The wonders of a week at Bath; in a doggerel address to the Hon. T. S——, from F. T——, Esq. of that city. London: printed for James Cathorn; and sold by the booksellers at Bath, 1811. 8vo, contemporary calf.

> The author's second book, published the year after Hobhouse and Byron completed their famous tour of the Mediterranean (the origin of *Childe Harold*). Hobhouse's authorship of this volume, once a matter of conjecture, has been confirmed by references in Byron's correspondence. Acquired in 1992.

379. [Hobhouse, John Cam, Baron Broughton.] A cotemporary [*sic*] narrative of events connected with the separation of Lord and Lady Byron; also an account of the destruction of Lord Byron's memoirs, by the late Lord Broughton. London: John Murray, 1870. 8vo, cloth.

> This is a proof copy of the first edition; an altered version, with a new title, was privately printed by John Murray later the same year (see no. 380). In 1830, Thomas Moore published his edition of Byron's letters and journals, to which he added notices of the poet's life. Moore's biographical account elicited several replies, the most important of which were an answer in a pamphlet by Lady Byron herself, and a defense of Lady Byron's position by the poet Thomas Campbell, which appeared in *The New Monthly Magazine*. Hobhouse, as Byron's most intimate friend, felt called upon to compose some sort of vindication of the poet's character, and of his actions in leaving his wife and country, but his friends dissuaded him from engaging Lady Byron in open debate.
>
> The controversies surrounding Byron's life lay relatively dormant over

the next forty years, but in 1870 the American novelist Harriet Beecher Stowe, who had become close friends with the elderly Lady Byron, reopened the whole matter, and in particular raised the specific charge that Byron had committed incest with his half sister, and that a child had been born of the union. Byron's life once more became a subject of intense public speculation.

Hobhouse himself had died the year before, but his literary executors felt that his contribution to Byron's biography should now appear in print. The present set of proof sheets, with a small number of corrections, indicate that Murray was to publish the book. Apparently there were second thoughts once more, and Hobhouse's account was only issued privately, in a relatively small number of copies. In fact the book as distributed bore a somewhat different title, and certain passages were suppressed. The final version contains a two-page preface; in the proof copy the preface runs to eight pages, and contains a very interesting three-page appraisal of Byron's character, excerpted from a manuscript work on Italy. The body of the text also underwent some alteration; it runs to 242 pages in proof, but only 239 pages in the private printing. Acquired in 1978.

380. Hobhouse, John Cam, Lord Broughton. Contemporary account of the separation of Lord and Lady Byron; also of the destruction of Lord Byron's memoirs. London: privately printed, 1870. 8vo, half dark blue morocco, by Zaehnsdorf. Acquired in 1990.

FREDERICK HOWARD, 5TH EARL OF CARLISLE (1748–1825)

381. Howard, Frederick, 5th Earl of Carlisle. Poems. London: printed by William Bulmer and Co., 1807. 8vo, contemporary red morocco, by Charles Hering.

"A new edition, with additions"; essentially a new book, however, as the three editions printed in 1773 were all seventeen-page quarto pamphlets, containing only four of the twenty-two pieces here. The Earl of Carlisle was Byron's guardian, and a liberal patron of the arts, with a taste for poetry. This copy was presumably one of the author's own, as the binding bears in gilt his coat of arms and the Garter surmounted by a coronet. Acquired in 2001.

JOHN KEBLE (1792–1866)

382. [Keble, John.] The Christian year: thoughts in verse for the Sundays and holydays throughout the year. Oxford: printed by W. Baxter, for J. Parker; and C. and J. Rivington (London), 1827. Two vols., 8vo, original boards, covered at an early date in plain light brown muslin cloth.

> This collection, the first book by the acknowledged founder of the Oxford Movement, went on to become the most popular work of poetry of the nineteenth century; according to the *Oxford DNB*, by the time the book's copyright expired in 1873, 158 editions had been published, in a total of 379,000 copies. This first edition is inscribed on the front flyleaf of the first volume, "Thos. & Eliz. Keble, June 22, 1827, with J. K.'s best love." The recipients were Keble's brother and his wife, to both of whom he was exceedingly close. Laid into this copy is an autograph letter, on a large oblong slip, from the Oxford publisher, Parker, to Rev. W. J. Copelan, dated Nov. 30, (1865), which reads as follows: "Dear Sir, I think this memorandum should be considered strictly private as I have not Mr. Keble's permission to give it to you. Practically there is no harm in giving out publicly that more than 200,000 have been sold, and that the annual sale is as large now (1865) as ever it was –but the details are only for your own satisfaction." On the verso, Parker has very neatly compiled a list of the print run for each edition, beginning with the first (500 copies), and ending with the eighty-fourth (1,000 copies), for a total of 210,000. This copy turned up in Swindon, in Wiltshire. Keble was born and raised in the village of Coln St. Aldwyn, Gloucestershire, where his father was the vicar; Coln St. Aldwyn is about twenty miles from Swindon. Acquired in 2001.

383. [Keble, John.] Ode for the Encænia at Oxford, June 11, 1834, in honour of His Grace, Arthur, Duke of Wellington, Chancellor of the University. Oxford: 1834. 8vo, folded, as issued.

> This ode was published anonymously, but was included in the author's *Miscellaneous Poems* in 1869. WorldCat and Copac together list four copies, at the British Library, the Bodleian, Yale, and North Carolina. Acquired in 1986.

THOMAS W. KELLY (FL. 1824)

384. Kelly, Thomas W. Myrtle leaves; a collection of poems, chiefly amatory. London: printed for Sherwood, Jones, and Co.; C. S. Arnold; Steuart and Panton; C. Baldwin; and W. T. Andrews, 1824. 8vo, contemporary calf.

The author's first book. Four further volumes of verse, published between 1836 and 1862, are assigned to Kelly, but whether these books are by the same person is not entirely clear. This is the dedication copy, inscribed on the half-title, "To Chandos Leigh Esq. With the Author's most Respectful Compliments." In the printed dedication, Kelly describes himself as "a young bard, aspiring far beyond his merits." For the dedicatee, see no. 386. Acquired in 1972.

WILLIAM KENNEDY (1799–1871)

385. Kennedy, William. Fitful fancies. Edinburgh: published by Oliver & Boyd; and Geo. B. Whittaker (London), 1827. 8vo, contemporary maroon morocco.

> The author's first book. Kennedy went on to achieve some success as a poet, but is now chiefly remembered for his residence in Texas, where he was the British consul from 1841 to 1847. This is the dedication copy. The printed dedication is to the prominent statesman (and later prime minister) Robert Peel; on a front flyleaf Peel has inscribed the book to his wife, Julia. Acquired in 1991.

CHANDOS LEIGH (1791–1850)

386. Leigh, Chandos. Trifles light as air. London: printed by G. Sidney; for F. Benedict, 1813. 8vo, contemporary black morocco.

> The author's second book, published privately, according to the preliminary "Advertisement," when he was twenty-two. Chandos Leigh was a schoolmate of Byron at Harrow; as a young man he was friendly with Sheridan, Hobhouse, Byron, and other liberals who gathered at Holland House. His poems were never widely known, but are said to have been prized by the scholarly few. The last poem in this small collection is addressed to Byron, after the publication of Childe Harold. Curiously, the small number of copies located all seem to have thirty-one pages, as opposed to forty pages in this copy; this discrepancy has not as yet been investigated. This copy is inscribed on a front flyleaf, "with the author's best regards." Acquired in 1978.

DAVID MALCOLM (FL. 1801–14)

387. [Malcolm, David.] The sorrow of love, a poem, in three books. Edinburgh: printed by Mundell & Son, 1801. 12mo, contemporary calf.

Apparently the author's only book; a much expanded version was published in 1814, bearing the author's name. This copy is inscribed on the flyleaf facing the half-title, "To Her Royal Highness the Princess of Wales with most respectful compliments from the Author." The significance of the inscription is revealed at the beginning of the poem itself. In the prose "argument" the poem is "inscribed to the Princess of Wales"; ll. 6–7 of the poem read, "O lovely Caroline! accept the lay, / And round the groves thy favoring smiles display." This, then, is the dedication copy. Acquired in 1983.

THOMAS MEDWIN (1788–1869)

388. Medwin, Thomas. Prometheus Bound, a tragedy, from the Greek of Aeschylus. Siena: printed by Onorato Porri, 1827. 8vo, disbound.

Thomas Medwin was a boyhood friend and schoolmate of Shelley; their mothers were first cousins. The relationship lapsed for a time, but was eventually revived; in 1821, in Pisa, Shelley introduced Medwin to Byron as his cousin. Medwin remained in Italy, for the most part, and in 1824 he married an heiress, whose fortune he proceeded to squander over the next five years. It was during this period that he published this translation of Aeschylus in Siena; in 1832 it was reprinted by William Pickering in London. The original Italian printing is very rare; the only other copies located are at the British Library and the New York Public Library (Pforzheimer). This copy is inscribed on the title page, "Paris, 23 May 1828 to L. Goldsmid from T. Medwin." Acquired in 1986.

WILLIAM HENRY MERLE (1791–1878)

389. Merle, William Henry. Odds and ends. In verse and prose. . . . Illustrated by George Cruikshank from designs by the author. London: printed for Longman, Rees, Orme, Brown, and Green, 1831. 8vo, original gray boards, printed paper label.

The author's second book; he had already published a poem called *Costança* in 1828, and went on to write three three-decker novels. This copy is inscribed by the author on the title page to Miss Mariann Cockburn. With the bookplate and bibliographical label of Albert M. Cohn, the greatest of all Cruikshank collectors. Cohn has written on the label, "The first G. Ck. item ever purchased by me." Acquired in 1978.

HENRY HART MILMAN (1791–1868)

390. Milman, Henry Hart. Fazio, a tragedy. Oxford: printed by Samuel Collingwood; sold by J. Parker; and J. Murray (London). 1815. 8vo, bound with three other poems, contemporary calf.

> The author's first book, preceded only by two prize poems. As a poet, Milman belonged to the school of Byron and Moore; his verse proved very popular. He went on to become a clergyman of some prominence, and the dean of St. Paul's. This volume also contains a third edition of *The Field of Waterloo* (1815), by Walter Scott; a first edition of *Modern Greece* (1817), by Felicia Hemans (no. 313); and a first edition of *Paris in 1815* (1817), by George Croly (no. 293). With the contemporary bookplate of Edward Knight, Jun., and his signature on each title page. Acquired in 1981.

391. Milman, Henry Hart. Belshazzar: a dramatic poem. London: John Murray, 1822. 8vo, contemporary half blue morocco.

> The *DNB* calls this poem "far from contemptible." Acquired in 1981.

MARY RUSSELL MITFORD (1787–1855)

392. Mitford, Mary Russell. Dramatic scenes, sonnets, and other poems. London: Geo. B. Whittaker, 1827. 8vo, original purple cloth.

> Mary Mitford is now best remembered for her fiction; a series of tales published under the collective title *Our Village* (five vols., 1824–32) was among the first books to depict life in small English towns in an accurate way. Acquired in 1976.

DAVID MACBETH MOIR (1798–1851)

393. [Moir, David Macbeth.] Domestic verses. By Δ. Not published. Edinburgh: 1843. 8vo, original limp purple cloth.

> Moir was a physician by profession, but he had an abiding interest in literature and was a regular contributor to some of the major periodicals of his day, especially *Blackwood's Magazine* (using the same upper-case Greek letter delta as his signature). Copies of this slim, privately printed collection ("not published") were sent to such writers as Wordsworth, Tennyson, and Dickens, and their responses persuaded Moir to allow the poems to be regularly published by William Blackwood and Sons later the same year,

as part of a much larger volume. Of this original printing, four copies are located, at the British Library, the National Library of Scotland, Arizona, and Cornell. Acquired in 1999.

WILLIAM THOMAS MONCRIEFF (1794–1857)

394. Moncrieff, William Thomas. Poems. London: printed (for private circulation only,) at the author's private press, Saville House, Lambeth, 1829. 8vo, early Victorian dark green morocco.

> Moncrieff was for many years a highly successful dramatist and theatrical impresario; he is credited with more than 170 plays, of which his adaptations from Dickens and Pierce Egan were enormously popular. His later years were spent at the Charterhouse, and he died there in 1857. Nothing more has been discovered printed at Moncrieff's private press. This copy is inscribed on the title page, "To R. Tucker Esqre. with the author's best acknowledgements." Bound in at the front is a nine-page manuscript poem, in twenty-five four-line stanzas, addressed to "R. Tucker, Manciple, Charter House," and dated "Charter House, Goose Day, 1845." The poem may be in a secretarial hand, as it is very neatly copied out, but it is signed by Moncrieff at the end. It is a humorous poem of praise, offered to Tucker in his role as the Charterhouse steward. Acquired in 2004.

AMELIA OPIE (1769–1853)

395. Opie, Amelia. Lays for the dead. London: Longman, Rees, Orme, Brown, Green, and Longman, 1834. 12mo, original gray boards, printed paper label.

> Amelia Opie's last book, a rather lugubrious collection of poems on themes relating to death; the book was printed in Norwich. Opie lived another twenty years, but published nothing further. In her youth she had been a conspicuous member of literary society, and she was friendly with Godwin, Wordsworth, Scott, Byron, Sheridan, and many others; she is chiefly remembered now as a novelist, though she did publish several other collections of verse. In the early 1820s she became a Quaker, and this soon put a stop to her novel-writing. This copy is inscribed by the author on the front flyleaf to Archibald Hope Cullen, a Scottish advocate. Acquired in 1979.

THOMAS LOVE PEACOCK (1785–1866)

396. Peacock, Thomas Love. Palmyra, and other poems. London: printed by T. Bensley, for W. J. and J. Richardson, 1806. 8vo, contemporary dark blue morocco.

Peacock's second book of verse, preceded only by the very rare, privately printed *Monks of St. Mark* (1804). Peacock is now best remembered for his brilliant series of humorous intellectual novels, whose characters were modeled on some of his more famous contemporaries, including Shelley, Byron, and Coleridge. No attempt was made to include his fiction in the collection. With the signature of Eliza de St. Croix on the front pastedown, and the signature of Eleanor Noel on the front flyleaf. Acquired in 1979.

397. [Peacock, Thomas Love.] Sir Proteus: a satirical ballad: by P. M. O'Donovan, Esq. [pseud.]. London: printed for T. Hookham, Junr. and E. T. Hookham, 1814. 8vo, original blue printed boards.

A very rare literary satire. The chief target is Robert Southey, though Wordsworth, Coleridge, Scott, and others also crop up in the numerous footnotes that embellish the text. The dedication is to Byron. This copy is inscribed on the front flyleaf in Peacock's hand, "From the author," and is signed by the recipient just above, "T. Jefferson Hogg. 1814." Hogg was, of course, at this time Shelley's closest friend; the volume surfaced among a substantial group of Hogg family books sold over the course of several auctions in 1984. Shelley and Peacock were introduced in 1812 by the publisher of this volume, Thomas Hookham; from 1814 to 1818 the two were on very intimate terms. Acquired in 1985.

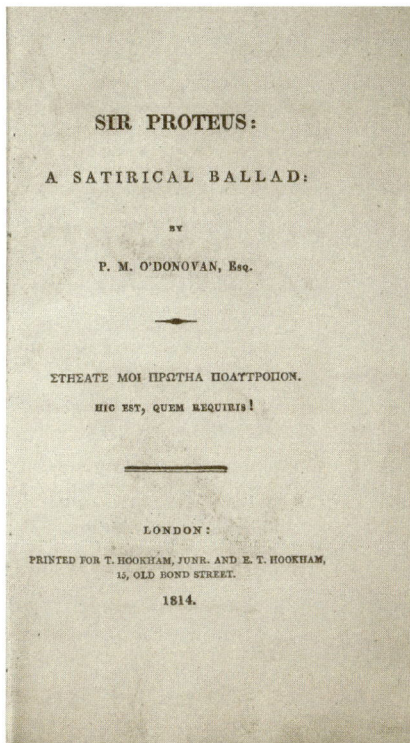

SIR PROTEUS:

A SATIRICAL BALLAD;

BY

P. M. O'DONOVAN, Esq.

ΣΤΗΣΑΤΕ ΜΟΙ ΠΡΩΤΗΑ ΠΟΛΥΤΡΟΠΟΝ.

HIC EST, QUEM REQUIRIS!

LONDON:

PRINTED FOR T. HOOKHAM, JUNR. AND E. T. HOOKHAM,
15, OLD BOND STREET.

1814.

ITEM 397

398. [Peacock, Thomas Love.] Rhododaphne: or the Thessalian spell. A poem. London: printed for T. Hookham, Jun.; and Baldwin, Cradock and Joy, 1818. 8vo, contemporary calf.

> Shelley's influence on Peacock can be clearly traced in this poem. Shelley wrote an enthusiastic review of the book in *The Examiner* just before his final departure for Italy. With the bookplate of Eric S. Quayle. Acquired in 2000.

399. [Peacock, Thomas Love.] Paper money lyrics, and other poems. London: printed by C. and W. Reynell, 1837. 8vo, original black glazed wrappers., black paper side label.

> "Only 100 copies printed: not for sale." A series of humorous poems on economic subjects, mostly "written in the winter of 1825–6, during the prevalence of an influenza to which the beautiful fabric of paper-credit is periodically subject."–Preface. Peacock's literary career had by this time more or less come to an end, though he lived for another thirty years, and was much involved in the official affairs of the East India Company. The Simon Nowell-Smith copy. Acquired in 2002.

JAMES ROBINSON PLANCHÉ (1796–1880)

400. Planché, James Robinson. William with the ring. A romance in rhyme. London: Tinsley Brothers, 1873. 8vo, original blue cloth.

> An historical narrative in verse, set in the fourteenth century during the reign of Edward III. Planché published this poem when he was seventy-seven, and nearing the end of a long career as a prolific and successful dramatist; he also had a considerable reputation as an antiquary and a scholarly student of heraldry and costume. The genesis of this poem is explained in a preliminary note: "The principal incidents in this Romance formed, originally, the plot of an Opera I wrote for Mr. Felix Mendelssohn Bartholdy, but which, from circumstances I have recently narrated in my 'Recollections,' was not composed by him." This copy is inscribed on the half-title, "Lady Molesworth with the author's kind regards, 16 Decr. 1872." Acquired in 2004.

JOHN WILLIAM POLIDORI (1795–1821)

401. Polidori, John William. Ximenes, The Wreath, and other poems. London: Longman, Hurst, Rees, Orme, and Brown, 1819. 8vo, contemporary half calf.

Polidori is best remembered for having served for a time as Byron's secretary-physician, beginning in 1816; the relationship did not last long. In 1821, Polidori committed suicide, evidently because of a gambling debt. One of his sisters later married Gabriele Rossetti, and was the mother of Dante Gabriel and Christina. Polidori's best-known book is a short piece of fiction, also published in 1819, called *The Vampyre*; this was written at the celebrated gathering at the Villa Diodati, near Geneva, where Mary Shelley began to write *Frankenstein*. The title of this book of verse made it essential for the collection. With the bookplate of Edward Owen Vaughan Lloyd, of Rhagatt (1857–1914). Acquired in 1981.

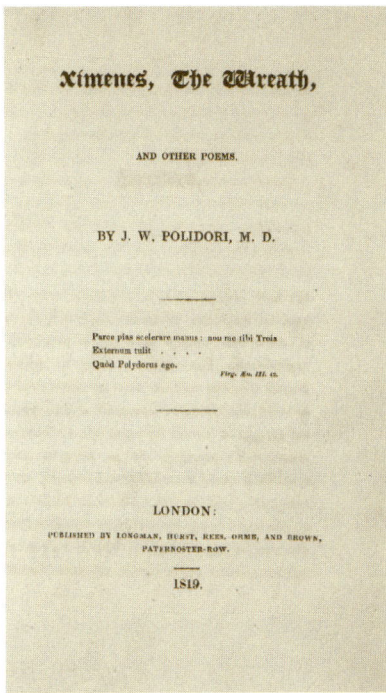

Ximenes, The Wreath,

AND OTHER POEMS.

BY J. W. POLIDORI, M. D.

Parce pias scelerare manus : nou me illi Troia
Externum tulit . . . . .
Quôd Polydorus ego.
Virg. Æn. III. et.

LONDON:

PUBLISHED BY LONGMAN, HURST, REES, ORME, AND BROWN,
PATERNOSTER-ROW.

1819.

ITEM 401

RICHARD POLWHELE (1760–1838)

402. [Polwhele, Richard.] The fair Isabel of Cotehele, a Cornish romance, in six cantos. By the author of Loyal Attachment, and translator of Theocritus. London: printed for J. Cawthorn, by Michell and Co. (Truro), 1815. 12mo, contemporary half calf, binder's ticket of J. Gill, binder, Penryn.

> Polwhele was born in Cornwall. During a long and fruitful literary career he was by turns a poet, topographical writer, and theologian, and numbered among his friends such diverse figures as Cowper, Cobbett, Gibbon, and Walter Scott (the dedicatee of this long poem). This copy is inscribed on the title page, "Mr. Liddy, from his friend the author." With the bookplate of Davies Gilbert. Acquired in 1981.

CYRUS REDDING (1785-1870)

403. Redding, Cyrus. Gabrielle, a tale of the Swiss mountains. London: John Ebers and Co., 1829. 8vo, original dark green cloth, printed paper label.

> The title poem, which occupies the first fifty-one pages of this volume, is a narrative involving mountaineering in the area around Mont Blanc. The first among the shorter pieces is a nine-page poem entitled "Stanzas on the Death of Byron." Cyrus Redding was born in Cornwall, but settled in London as a young man and became an industrious and successful journalist. This copy is inscribed on the title page, "H. Meestun, Esqr., with the author's kindest regards. Bath, Jany., 1834." Acquired in 2005.

THOMAS CLIO RICKMAN (1761-1834)

404. Rickman, Thomas Clio. Poetical scraps. London: printed for the author; and sold also by Mr. Symonds; Mr. Fisher (Brighton); Mr. Lee (Lewes); Mr. Claris (Canterbury); Mr. Flower (Cambridge); Mr. Watts (Gosport); Messrs. Gore and Son (Liverpool); Mr. Cowdroy (Manchester); Mr. Rackham (Bury St. Edmunds); and all booksellers, 1803. Two vols., 8vo, original blue boards, drab paper backstrips, printed paper labels.

> The major collection of poetry by a radical bookseller and intimate friend of Thomas Paine; Paine wrote his *Rights of Man* at Rickman's house. There are twenty-six pages of subscribers in vol. 1, including both Paine and Thomas Jefferson; also listed are Shelley's father, Timothy Shelley, and his future father-in-law William Godwin. With the signature on the title page of Charlotte M. Ogle, dated 1804. Acquired in 1994.

MARY ROBINSON (1758-1800)

405. Robinson, Mary. Lyrical tales. London: printed for T. N. Longman and O. Rees, by Biggs and Co. (Bristol), 1800. 8vo, original marbled boards, pale green paper backstrip.

> The author's last book, published the year of her death. Mary Robinson's life was a tangled tale. She was the daughter of a whaling captain, and received a passable, if eccentric, education. In 1774 she married a libertine, and began to write verse; in 1776 she met Garrick and Sheridan, and became a successful actress. In 1779 she appeared as Perdita in *The Winter's Tale*, and attracted the notice of the seventeen-year-old Prince of Wales (later

George IV), who persuaded her to become his mistress in exchange for a bond of £20,000, to be paid when the young prince came of age. After a year the prince lost interest, and his father, through Lord North, settled Mrs. Robinson's claim for £5,000 ("an enormous sum, but I wish to get my son out of this shameful scrape"). In her later years she supported herself by writing novels, and came under the influence of William Godwin and Mary Wollstonecraft; she also was admired by Coleridge, who called her "a woman of undoubted genius" and showed her a very early version of "Kubla Khan." This copy has the signature on the front pastedown, dated April 1805, of Eliza Rose (see no. 85). The Simon Nowell-Smith copy. Acquired in 2002.

THOMAS ROMNEY ROBINSON ((1792–1882)

406. Robinson, Thomas Romney. Juvenile poems. . . . To which is prefixed a short account of the author, by a member of the Belfast Literary Society. Belfast: printed by J. Smyth and D. Lyons, 1806. 8vo, contemporary calf.

An exceptional example of literary precocity; these poems were written when the author was between the ages of seven and thirteen, and published when he was fourteen. Robinson later became a well-known astronomer and mathematical physicist. There is a long list of subscribers, containing almost 1,500 names (including "Miss Edgeworth," four copies). Acquired in 1972.

WALTER SCOTT (1771–1832)

407. [Scott, Walter, translator.] Bürger, Gottfried Augustus. The chase, and William and Helen: two ballads, from the German. Edinburgh: printed by Mundell and Son, for Manners and Miller; and sold by T. Cadell, Jun. and W. Davies (London), 1796. 4to, nineteenth-century green morocco.

Scott's first book, preceded only by a very rare legal pamphlet in Latin (1792), and two briefs for the Court of Session, also extremely rare. This copy has an appealing inscription by Scott on the title page: "George Chalmers Esq. from his sincere friend and obedt. servant, the Translator." Chalmers was one of the first to encourage Scott's literary efforts; he was an older man, but, like Scott, a lawyer, antiquary, and enthusiast of literature. Acquired in 1988.

408. Scott, Walter. The vision of Don Roderick, and other poems. Edinburgh printed for and sold by John Ballantyne and Co.; Longman and Co., William Miller, White and Co., and Gale and Co. (London), 1811. 8vo, original light blue boards, printed paper label.

> Second edition. To this edition were added nine shorter poems, not previously published in book form; the first edition, published earlier the same year, was a quarto. With the signature of William Boyd on the title page. Acquired in 1972.

409. Scott, Walter. Halidon Hill; a dramatic sketch, from Scottish history. Edinburgh: printed for Archibald Constable and Co.; and Hurst, Robinson, and Co. (London), 1822. 8vo, original drab printed wrappers. Acquired in 1975.

RICHARD SHARP (1759–1835)

410. [Sharp, Richard.] Epistles in verse. London: John Murray, 1828. 8vo, contemporary plum morocco.

> The author's only book of poems. Sharp was a wealthy businessman; his remarkable ability to speak in society gave him the nickname "Conversation" Sharp, and he is said to have been the model for Conversation Kenge in *Bleak House*. He had many friends. In his early years he knew Johnson and Burke; he later became a close friend of Samuel Rogers and, in time, of most of the better-known Romantic poets, including Wordsworth, Byron, and Moore. Sharp also had an abiding interest in political economy, and was on intimate terms with James Mill and David Ricardo. This copy is inscribed on the verso of the half-title, "Lady King from her old friend the author." Acquired in 1979.

CHARLES DOYNE SILLERY (1807–1837)

411. Sillery, Charles Doyne. Vallery; or, the citadel of the lake; a poem. Edinburgh: printed for the author; and sold by Oliver & Boyd; Simpkin & Marshall (London); Robertson & Atkinson (Glasgow); and W. Curry, Jun. & Co. (Dublin), 1829. Two vols., 12mo, contemporary red morocco.

> The author's first book. Sillery was Irish by birth. As a young man he served as a midshipman on a trip to China and India; upon his re-

turn he settled in Edinburgh, where he published a number of other volumes of poetry. This is the dedication copy, inscribed by the author at the front of the first volume, "To His Excellency Baron Vander Capellen, . . . these volumes are dedicated and presented, with every feeling of sincere esteem and respect, by his Excellency's most obedient humble servant the author." There is a two-page printed dedication to Baron Vander Capellen, whom Sillery seems to have met on his voyage home from India. Acquired in 1989.

CHARLES SNART (FL. 1801–15)

412. [Snart, Charles, editor and contributor.] Selection of poems. London: printed for Longman, Hurst, Rees and Orme, by M. Hage (Newark), 1808. Two vols., 8vo, original pale blue boards, white paper backstrips, printed paper labels.

> An unusual provincial anthology, printed in Newark, with many original poems by the editor, Charles Snart. Included are verses by such major writers as Robert Southey, Samuel Rogers, and Coleridge ("The Sigh," 2, p. 394). A fair number of the contributions are taken from manuscript sources. Charles Snart published a book on angling in 1801; two further poetry anthologies appeared in 1807–8 and 1813–15. This copy is from the celebrated Mount Bellew library, an Irish collection dispersed in the 1930s. The books are noted for their fine original condition: "It would hardly be possible to over-state the perfection of Bellew condition or the excitement of those Bellew days, with parcels from Dublin trickling in and immaculate treasures slowly encumbering my table."–Michael Sadleir, *XIX Century Fiction.* With the book label of John Sparrow. Acquired in 1992.

JOHN TAAFFE (CA. 1787–1837)

413. Taaffe, John. Padilla: a tale of Palestine. London: printed for J. M. Richardson, 1816. 8vo, original blue-gray boards, printed paper label.

> The author's first book, published when he was about thirty; it is a long narrative poem in rhymed couplets, set in Palestine and Spain in the late eleventh and early twelfth centuries, at the time of the Crusades. John Taaffe was born in Ireland to a prominent Catholic family; he was educated at Stonyhurst and Ulverstone, where he was encouraged to write poetry. An unfortunate love affair with a woman in Edinburgh forced him into exile,

and in 1812 he began his travels, which took him to Spain, Portugal, and North Africa. In 1815 he settled in Italy, and he stayed there until his death in 1837; in his adopted country he was widely known as "Count" Taaffe. In November 1820, he met the Shelleys in Pisa, and became a frequent visitor. At first Shelley was quite taken with Taaffe, but it was not long before he considered him an amiable bore. Taaffe left his mark, however, on one occasion, when he persuaded Shelley to tone down a passage on reviewers in the preface to *Adonais*. Taaffe had a high opinion of his own literary abilities, and undertook a translation of Dante's *Divine Comedy*, to which he added an elaborate commentary. Shelley and his friends used to laugh at the translation, but they had some respect for the annotations. Shelley at one point recommended Taaffe's translation to the bookseller Charles Ollier, but Ollier was not tempted. Somewhat later, Byron, who also came to know Taaffe well, badgered John Murray into publishing the first portion of the commentary (1822); no further instalments were printed. On March 24, 1822, Taaffe was a member of Byron's customary riding party, along with Shelley, Trelawny, Count Gamba, and Captain Hay, followed at a short distance by Mary Shelley and Countess Guiccioli in a carriage. As they all approached the city gates of Pisa a drunken Italian dragoon brushed up against Taaffe in what the latter, in his usual pompous fashion, took to be an insolent manner. A fracas ensued, in which Shelley was knocked off his horse, Captain Hay was cut on the nose, Countess Guiccioli was stricken with hysteria, and the dragoon was almost killed by one of Byron's servants. In the confused aftermath of this ridiculous affair Taaffe made equivocal statements to the authorities, playing down his own role; Byron and others began to refer to him as "False-taaffe." In the end he was forgiven, and largely forgotten. With signatures on the front pastedown and the title page of Eliza Giffard, of Nerquis, Flintshire (see also no. 305). Acquired in 2006.

THOMAS NOON TALFOURD (1795–1854)

414. [Talfourd, Thomas Noon.] The Castilian. An historical tragedy. In five acts. London: Edward Moxon, 1853. 8vo, original purple cloth.

Talfourd is now chiefly remembered as a close friend of Charles Lamb, whose executor he was; he was also friendly with such major literary figures as Wordsworth, Coleridge, Hazlitt, and Godwin. This copy is inscribed by the author on the half-title to Mr. Serjeant Shee, a member of Parliament. Acquired in 1977.

WILLIAM SIDNEY WALKER (1795–1846)

415. Walker, William Sidney. Gustavus Vasa, and other poems. London: printed for Longman, Hurst, Rees, Orme, and Brown, 1813. 8vo, contemporary red morocco.

> The author's first book, published when he was seventeen and a student at Eton. In his preface Walker says that the idea for the title poem, an epic based upon the life of the king of Sweden, was formed when he was only eleven, and that the first two parts (of four), had been completed by 1810. Walker was a precocious, disheveled, and deeply eccentric young man, who became a lifelong friend of the poet Praed. Acquired in 2003.

JOHN WILSON (1785–1854)

416. Wilson, John. The magic mirror. Addressed to Walter Scott, Esq. Edinburgh: printed by James Ballantyne and Co., 1812. 4to, wrappers.

> Privately printed, as indicated by the phrase "Author's copy" on the title page. This interesting Romantic poem was first published in *The Edinburgh Annual Register* for 1810. Included are references to Coleridge and Wordsworth, both of whom Wilson knew; a footnote to the fourth stanza indicates that Wilson has borrowed an image from an unpublished Coleridge poem. Wilson went on to fame and notoriety as one of the editors of *Blackwood's Magazine*; he wrote under the pseudonym "Christopher North," and is now chiefly remembered for a devastating review of Keats. Acquired in 1994.

THE

IMPROVISATORE,

IN THREE FYTTES,

WITH

Other Poems.

BY

THOMAS LOVELL BEDDOES.

I have sung
With an unskilful, but a willing voice.
Webster's Appius and Virginia.

OXFORD:

PRINTED FOR J. VINCENT, NEAR BRASENNOSE COLLEGE;
AND G. AND W. B. WHITTAKER, AVE MARIA LANE,
LONDON.

1821.

ITEM 417

The Mid-Nineteenth Century

♃ MAJOR POETS

THOMAS LOVELL BEDDOES (1803–1849)

417. Beddoes, Thomas Lovell. The improvisatore, in three fyttes, with other poems. Oxford: printed for J. Vincent; and G. and W. B. Whittaker (London), 1821. 8vo, contemporary black straight-grained morocco.

> The author's first book; he was the son of a prominent physician. "Of this jejune production he speedily became so much ashamed that he endeavoured to suppress it, and with such measure of success that very few copies of it are now known to exist."—*DNB*. Wise calls this "a book of very considerable rarity." This copy is signed on the front pastedown by Maria Edgeworth, the author's aunt, and herself a major novelist of the period. Inserted is a clipping of a poem called "The Comet," dated July 5, 1819, possibly from *The Morning Post*, and the author's first appearance in print. With the book labels of Michael Sadleir and H. Bradley Martin. Acquired in 1990; no other copy has ever been seen on the market.

418. [Beddoes, Thomas Lovell.] Death's jest-book: or the fool's tragedy. London: William Pickering, 1850. 8vo, original purple cloth, printed paper label.

> A verse-play set in thirteenth-century Silesia. Beddoes began this work in 1825, and finished a first version in 1829. By that time, however, he had become caught up in the political upheavals in Europe, and he spent the next twenty years going from one country to another, polishing the manuscript, which he carried about with him. His last years were marked by eccentricity and ill health; when he died in 1849, the manuscript passed to his lifelong friend Thomas Forbes Kelsall, who arranged to have it published anonymously. On the front pastedown is an inscription from Edward Ricketts to R. M. Phillimore, dated 1850. The Simon Nowell-Smith copy. Acquired in 2002.

WINTHROP MACKWORTH PRAED (1802–1839)

419. Praed, Winthrop Mackworth. The poetical works of Winthrop Mackworth Praed. Now first collected, by Rufus W. Griswold. New York:

Henry G. Langley, 1844. Large 12mo, original green cloth.

The first collection of the poetry of one of the most talented nineteenth-century writers of light verse. The book was published posthumously, some five years after the author's death at the early age of thirty-seven; there were no collected works printed in England until the two-volume edition of 1864, compiled by Praed's closest friend, Derwent Coleridge. The Simon Nowell-Smith copy. Acquired in 2002.

TENNYSON, ALFRED, LORD (1809–1892)

420. [Tennyson, Alfred, Charles Tennyson, and Frederick Tennyson.] Poems, by two brothers. London: printed for W. Simpkin and R. Marshall; and J. and J. Jackson (Louth), 1827. 8vo, red morocco, by Bedford.

Tennyson's first appearance in print. About half the poems are his, chiefly written between the ages of fifteen and seventeen. The rest are, for the most part, by his older brother, Charles, though his other brother, Frederick, also contributed three or four poems (despite the wording on the title page). The authorship of the various poems is to some extent sorted out in an edition published by Hallam Tennyson in 1893, though uncertainties remain. The book was printed by provincial booksellers in Louth, Lincolnshire, where Tennyson had gone to school as a boy. The brothers received an advance of £20, in cash and books. There were only two reviews, both perfunctory, and sales were negligible, but the boys were excited and pleased by their debut. Tennyson himself used to refer to the book as "early rot," but he once admitted, as he reread it, that "some of it is better than I thought it was." Surprisingly, the volume was issued in two forms, on ordinary paper for 5 s., and on large paper for 7 s. Despite the poor sales, the book is not uncommon in either format, as a substantial remainder of both was discovered, in about 1870, in the printing office in Louth. This copy is on large paper, and is undoubtedly from that remainder. Acquired in 1974.

421. Tennyson, Alfred. Poems, chiefly lyrical. London: Effingham Wilson, 1830. 12mo, original pink boards, printed paper label.

Tennyson's second book, and the first to bear his name. As originally planned, the book was to have included poems by Arthur Hallam, but Hallam decided to issue his own volume privately, to Tennyson's disappointment. With the early signature of John Bowes on the title page. Acquired in 1975.

422. Tennyson, Alfred. Poems. London: Edward Moxon, 1833. 8vo, original blue boards, drab paper spine, printed paper label.

Moxon printed 450 copies of this book. He seems to have used several styles of paper-board binding; Wise's copy was in drab boards, and Hallam himself mentions in a letter having seen the book in Moxon's window, "resplendent in lilac covers." This proved for many years a difficult title to find in acceptable condition, but in the end one turned up in a beautifully preserved original binding, with an interesting provenance. This copy belonged to Lady Emmeline Charlotte Elizabeth Stuart-Wortley, and is signed by her both on the front cover and front flyleaf (the latter inscription dated Newmarket, April 1833). Lady Emmeline was herself a prolific poet; her first book, also entitled *Poems*, appeared the same year as the present volume, and there were many others to follow. She also edited several numbers of *The Keepsake*, the most popular literary annual of the period; in 1837 she persuaded Tennyson to contribute his poem "St. Agnes' Eve." Tennyson did not much care for the annuals. When Monckton Milnes later asked him for a poem Tennyson replied: "Three summers back, provoked by the incivility of editors, I swore an oath that I would never again have to do with their vapid books, and I broke it in the sweet face of Heaven when I wrote for Lady What's-her-name Wortley. But then her sister wrote to Brookfield and said that she (Lady W.) was beautiful, so I could not help it." The slightly unusual wallet-style slipcase for this copy was provided by Riviere in 1892 for Louis Samuel Montagu, the eldest son of Sir Samuel Montagu, 1st Baron Swaythling, a prominent banker and philanthropist, and long a pillar of conservative Judaism in England. Louis Montagu succeeded to his father's title in 1911. Acquired in 1996.

423. Tennyson, Alfred. The lover's tale. London: Edward Moxon, 1833. 8vo, contemporary calf, rebacked.

One of the great rarities of nineteenth-century English literature. Tennyson wrote this poem in 1828, when he was nineteen. In 1832 the text was set in type, along with the thirty other pieces that eventually formed his *Poems* of 1833; at the last minute, however, Tennyson decided that the poem was in need of substantial revision, and it was therefore held back for publication at some future date. Before the type was distributed, a few copies were printed at Tennyson's expense. Wise quotes a letter from Arthur Hallam to a friend in Italy saying that six copies only were produced, which Tennyson had sent to Hallam for circulation to friends; the original of this letter appears to have vanished, and it now seems probable that a few further copies were retained by Tennyson himself. The total printing, in any case, can have been no more than ten or twelve copies at most. In the Ashley Catalogue, Wise characterizes the rarity of this book as follows:

With the exception of *Timbuctoo The Lover's Tale* of 1833 is the earliest in order of date of the series of Tennyson "Trial-Books" and privately printed volumes. Possibly it is the most attractive, from the point of view of the collector. Unquestionably it is one of the three most valuable, the two ranking with it in this respect being *The True and the False* and *The Birth of Arthur* [separately printed prepublication versions of two Arthurian poems]. Probably, with the exception of Shelley's *Necessity of Atheism, Œdipus Tyrannus,* and *Original Poems by Victor and Cazire,* these are the most interesting and valuable First Editions in English Nineteenth Century Literature. Certainly *The Lover's Tale* is the most widely known; and few books, either ancient or modern, have been hunted for so keenly, or advertised for so persistently, as this tiny octavo of sixty pages.

In fact, seven other copies are now known: (1) Wise's own copy, now in the British Library; originally given by Hallam to Rev. W. H. Thompson. This copy has later autograph corrections in Tennyson's hand (added in 1835). (2) Texas. This copy is inscribed by Hallam to Adelaide Kemble, and is bound with *Poems Chiefly Lyrical.* (3) Huntington. This copy was the one given to W. E. Gladstone. It eventually came into the hands of the collector William Harris Arnold, at whose sale in 1924 it fetched $6,900 (to Rosenbach). (4) Virginia. This copy surfaced in the 1920s on the Isle of Wight, and passed to the California collector Templeton Crocker. (5) New York Public Library. This copy belonged originally to D. M. Heath. In time it came into Wise's possession, and was sold via Maggs to Jerome Kern, at whose sale in 1929 it was purchased by Owen D. Young (for $4,500); Young's books later became part of the Berg Collection. (6) Harvard. This copy surfaced in 1955 at a Parke-Bernet sale in New York, where it was catalogued as the property of "an English owner." The name of the original recipient has been erased from the title page; the book fetched $425. (7) Private collection. This copy was given by Tennyson to John Forster, who passed it on to Robert Browning; it first came up at auction in 1870, where it was purchased by Basil Montagu Pickering, whose library was dispersed in 1879. The next owner was Frederick Locker-Lampson (the Rowfant Library), whence it passed in 1905 to John A. Spoor, whose books were sold at auction in 1939; it subsequently belonged to Walter P. Chrysler, Jr., whose collection was sold in 1952. The book appeared once more in 2011, at a Bonham's & Butterfield auction in San Francisco. The present copy, now the eighth known, was

THE

LOVER'S TALE.

BY

ALFRED TENNYSON.

LONDON:

EDWARD MOXON, 64, NEW BOND STREET.

MDCCCXXXIII.

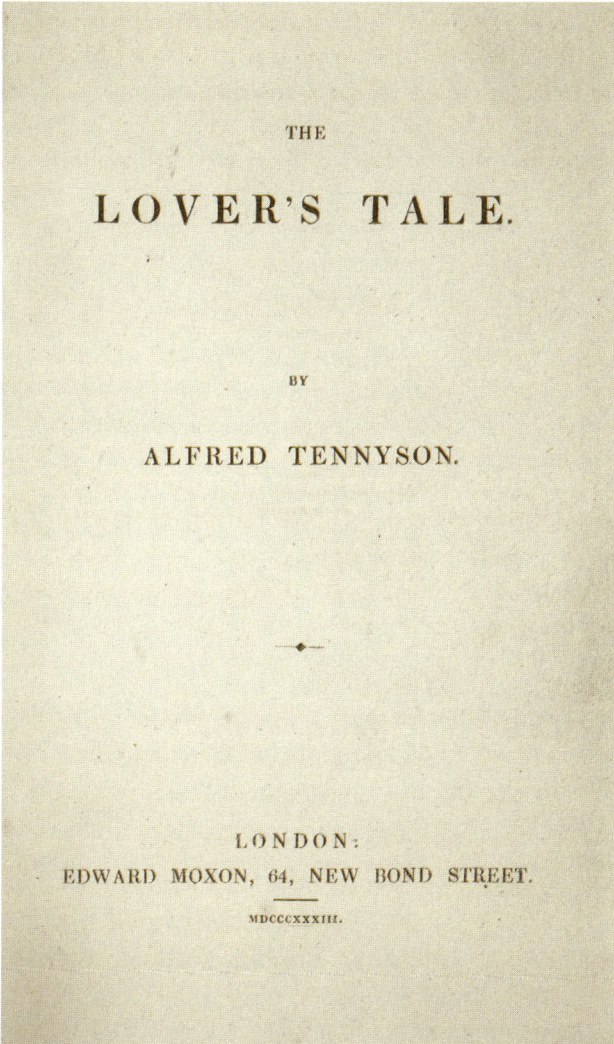

acquired in 1998 from descendants of Arthur Hallam's sister Julia Hallam, who married Sir John Lennard of Wickham Court, Kent, and lived until 1888; the book later belonged to her daughter Eleanor Lennard (d. 1933) and her granddaughter Lady Lennard. The family possesses no further copies, and it is therefore probable that this is Arthur Hallam's own copy, though there are no markings in it of any kind.

424. Tennyson, Alfred. Poems. London: Edward Moxon, 1842. Two vols., 8vo, contemporary full red morocco, gilt, spines gilt, a.e.g., by Hayday.

A major collection, breaking a silence of ten years, published on May 14, in an edition of eight hundred copies. By September, five hundred had been sold, which Moxon considered a very good result, as the book trade was at the time in the doldrums. This copy belonged to Tennyson's sister Mary, and is signed by her three times, once at the front of each volume, and a third time on the pastedown at the back of vol. 2, to which she had apparently turned by mistake. Mary was a year younger than her brother, and closer to him than any of her sisters. His sister Cecilia was engaged to Edmund Lushington in October, and Tennyson inscribed a copy to her, perhaps to acknowledge the forthcoming event. That copy, in a quite different binding of green morocco, was later in the collections of A. Edward Newton (sold in 1941 for $240), and Walter P. Chrysler, Jr. (sold in 1952 for $250); on March 3, 2004, it resurfaced in the library of Halsted B. Vander Poel, sold at Christie's London (lot 212, for £4,200 hammer). Mary Tennyson's set is in an appropriate "gift" binding by James Hayday, who began in the trade as early as 1829, and carried on for another thirty years or more; in 1842 he was very active. Later nineteenth-century ownership stamp of M. T. Ker (a family connection, as Mary Tennyson later married Alan Ker). Acquired in 1971.

425. Tennyson, Alfred. Poems. London: Edward Moxon, 1845. Two vols., 8vo, original dark green cloth, printed paper labels.

Third edition. "This edition is a reprint of the two preceding editions of 1842 and 1843, but again several slight verbal variations are to be found in it."—T. J. Wise. Acquired in 2012.

426. Tennyson, Alfred. The princess; a medley. London: Edward Moxon, 1847. 8vo, original dark green cloth.

On the verso of the front flyleaf is the signature of Elizabeth Ann Worship, dated January 1, 1848. With the bookplate of David Kennedy, and the later book labels of Michael Sadleir and Simon Nowell-Smith. Acquired in 2002.

427. [Tennyson, Alfred.] In memoriam. London: Edward Moxon, 1850. 8vo, original purple cloth.

A collection of poems in memory of Tennyson's close friend Arthur Hallam, who had died prematurely in 1833, at the age of twenty-two. This copy is signed on the half-title by Franklin Lushington, and dated June 1, 1850, the first day of publication. The name of Lady Reid, dated May 1856, may also be in Lushington's hand. Franklin Lushington, and his brothers Edmund and Henry, were among Tennyson's best friends. Portions of this book, in fact, deal with the marriage of Edmund to the poet's younger sister Cecilia (see especially the "marriage lay" on pp. 203–10). Acquired in 1975.

428. Tennyson, Alfred. Ode on the death of the Duke of Wellington. London: Edward Moxon, 1852. 8vo, original light blue printed wrappers.

With the signature of S. Wissenden on the front wrapper. Acquired in 1993.

429. Tennyson, Alfred. Maud, and other poems. London: Edward Moxon, 1855. 8vo, original green cloth.

The first book appearance of "The Charge of the Light Brigade." With the signature of V. [?] J. Vaillant on the title page; on the front pastedown has been added, "Vendu £1 le 7 Avril 1879 par Puttick & Simpson." Acquired in 1971.

430. [Tennyson, Alfred.] The charge of the Light Brigade. N.p. [London]: 1855. 4to, two leaves, folded; mounted on a larger sheet.

The first separate edition. The "charge" took place during the Crimean War, on October 25, 1854, and was reported in *The Times* on November 13 and 14. Tennyson wrote his poem on December 2, and sent it to John Forster, who printed it in *The Examiner* on December 9. Tennyson was not satisfied with the text, however, and before the publication of *Maud* in July, he revised the poem considerably. Shortly afterward he decided that these revisions had in fact weakened the poem, and he rewrote it further. As a patriotic gesture he had a thousand copies of this final text printed as a leaflet, to be sent to the Crimea for distribution "among the brave soldiers before Sebastopol." This last version represents the text as it is printed today. It contains fifty-five lines, with one extra stanza, as opposed to the forty-six-line text in *Maud*. The most notable addition is the famous phrase "Someone had blundered" (which Tennyson had dropped from the version printed in *Maud*). In August, Tennyson wrote to John Forster, "I wish to send out about 1000 slips, and I don't at all want the S. P. G. [Society for the Propagation of the Gospel] or anyone to send out the version last printed; it would, I believe, quite disappoint the soldiers."

This leaflet has always been very difficult to acquire. The only copies located by WorldCat and Copac are two at Harvard (one inscribed to

THE

CHARGE OF THE LIGHT BRIGADE.

HALF a league, half a league,
  Half a league onward,
All in the valley of Death
  Rode the six hundred.
" Forward, the Light Brigade !
" Charge for the guns !" he said :
Into the valley of Death
  Rode the six hundred.

" Forward, the Light Brigade !"
Was there a man dismay'd ?
Not tho' the soldier knew
  Some one had blunder'd :
Their's not to make reply,
Their's not to reason why,
Their's but to do and die,
Into the valley of Death
  Rode the six hundred.

My Father Col: Adolphus Burton C.B. was in the Charge of Heavy Brigade at Balaclava. GWB

Ruskin), one at the Morgan Library, and one at the British Library. Wise himself, an enthusiastic collector of Tennyson, never managed to acquire an example, though he does note the presence of the copy in the British Museum. Two copies appeared at auction in 1919, and one of them was apparently acquired by the Saint Louis collector William K. Bixby. That copy, with a presentation inscription in Tennyson's hand, later turned up in the New York sale of Roderick Terry's books in 1934, where it fetched $990. It subsequently passed to Frank J. Hogan, and when his collection was sold at Parke-Bernet in 1945, the price was $1,100, evidently to the New York bookseller James F. Drake. In 1957, Drake sold this copy for $1,125 to Marjorie Wiggins Prescott, whose collection was dispersed at Christie's, again in New York, in 1981. The buyer this time was an art dealer, hitherto unknown to the book trade, and appropriately named Wilder, who unexpectedly purchased a fair number of Prescott lots, often at rather high prices; for this one he paid $19,800. Wilder soon tired of his acquisitions, and in 1984 they were resold, this time at Parke-Bernet; at this sale the price of Tennyson's poem fell to $9,000, plus the 10% buyer's premium. Shortly afterward, another copy, in rather poor condition, surfaced in the trade. The whereabouts of these two copies has not been determined. The present copy appears to have been one of those sent to the theater of war, as it is endorsed in pencil at the bottom of the mount, beneath the first page, as follows: "My father Col. Adolphus Burton C. B. was in the Charge of the Heavy Brigade at Balaclava. G. D. B." It surfaced in Boston at Goodspeed's, where it was purchased by the bookseller Theodore Hofmann; the autograph department at Goodspeed's offered it as a lagniappe along with a Tennyson letter of little consequence, having failed to recognize its value. Acquired in 1976.

431. Tennyson, Alfred. Idylls of the king. London: Edward Moxon & Co., 1859. 8vo, original green cloth.

This copy is inscribed by Tennyson on the title page to Charlotte Schreiber (August 12, 1859). The recipient, a daughter of the Earl of Lindsey, was born in 1812. In 1833 she married Sir Josiah John Guest, by whom she had ten children before his death in 1852; during this period she lived in Wales, and became an accomplished Welsh scholar, noted for her important edition of the *Mabinogion*, and other ancient Welsh texts. Her second marriage, in 1855, was to Charles Schreiber. She was later involved with a private press at Canford Manor, the home of her son Sir Ivor Bertie Guest; the two most important products of this press were poems by Tennyson, *The Victim* and *The Window*, printed from manuscripts he gave to his friends in 1867 (see below, nos. 436 and 437). In her later years Lady Charlotte Schreiber was a great collector of china, playing cards, and fans. With her bookplate; an old inserted note says that this copy turned up in a lot of books at a house sale at Canford Manor. Acquired in 1994.

432. [Tennyson, Alfred.] Dedication. [London: 1862.] 8vo, two leaves, folded.

A separate printing of the dedicatory verses to the memory of Prince Albert, written for inclusion in the fourth edition of *Idylls of the King* (July 1862). Wise says that "a few copies only were struck off separately for the benefit of those readers who possessed the original edition of 1859." This statement makes little sense, as the print run of the first edition was forty thousand copies, and the second and third editions also were published without a dedication. A clue to the true nature of this leaflet is contained in a letter of February 1862 from Sir Charles Phipps, asking Tennyson on the queen's behalf for "several copies of the dedication printed separately." The final version of the poem was sent to Moxon in mid-May, and this "dedication printed separately" is presumably an offprint from proofs of the book then in production. Six copies are located, at the British Library (Wise's copy), Harvard (two copies), North Carolina, Texas, and Yale (inscribed by Tennyson to Caroline Gordon). Acquired in 1999.

433. Tennyson, Alfred. The ode by Alfred Tennyson on the opening of the Exhibition. 1862. [Coventry: Charles Newsome, ribbon manufacturer, 1862.] Silk ribbon, mechanically woven in color, 15 x 3½ in., mounted and displayed in a contemporary wood frame.

The first separate edition, and possibly the first printing of any kind, of a poem written by Tennyson in his capacity as Poet Laureate for the opening of the International Exhibition held at the Crystal Palace in 1862. Tennyson began writing this poem late in 1861, but found it difficult because the words were to be set to music by William Sterndale Bennett, and sung by a choir of thousands. Traditionally the first printing of the poem is identified as the one that accompanied the full score, published just prior to the opening of the exhibition, on April 12, 1862; a copy in the British Library bears advertisements on the last page, dated February 20, 1862, for Bennett's musical compositions. The text was also included in the official program for the opening, which took place on May 1. In addition, there was a newspaper printing, with inaccuracies, in *The Times* on April 24. T. J. Wise later used this poem for one of his forgeries, an eight-page pam-

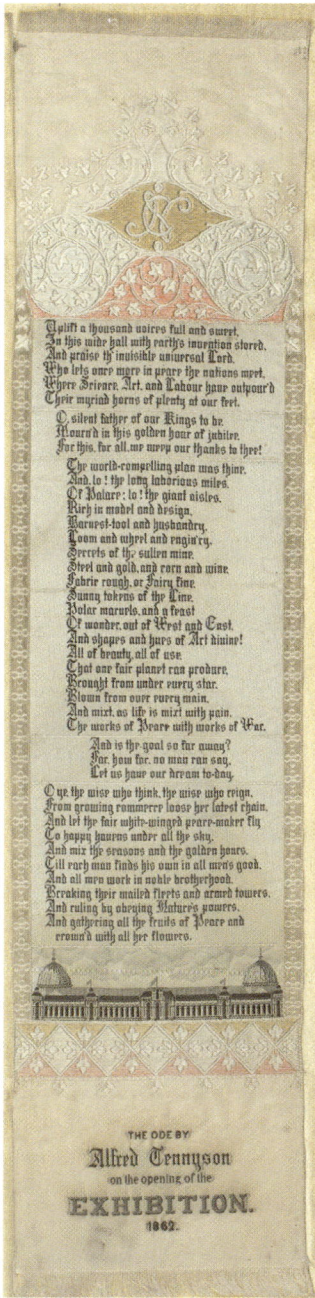

phlet produced at some point after 1889; he claimed that this printing, to which he gave priority, had been done in an edition of one thousand copies, most of which "must have been wasted at the time." This handsome silk ribbon was also intended for the exhibition. The designer was Edwin Rollason, then aged twenty-seven, and it was produced by Charles Newsome, a ribbon manufacturer of Coventry, whose monogram ("C. N.") appears in white and gold at the top; below the forty-one-line poem, in decorative colored borders, is a picture of the Crystal Palace, and the poem's title. The *Art Journal* report of the 1862 Exhibition includes a mention of this firm: "We can do scant justice, by engravings, to the ribbons of Coventry, yet no report of the Exhibition would be complete without some examples of one of the most important manufactures of our Country. . . . The specimens shown by the principal manufacturers: Messrs. Ratcliffe, Mr. C. Newsome, Messrs. J. & J. Cash . . . will safely bear comparison with those of St. Etienne." This appearance of Tennyson's poem has not hitherto been noticed; it is not mentioned in the edition published by Christopher Ricks in 1987 (vol. 2, pp. 622–25). Acquired in 2003.

ITEM 433

434. Tennyson, Alfred. [Enoch Arden.] Idylls of the hearth. London: Edward Moxon &' Co., 1864. 8vo, contemporary limp black morocco.

A proof copy of the first edition, with the title subsequently rejected in favor of *Enoch Arden*. This is apparently one of nine such sets of page proofs, each numbered in Roman numerals at the top of the title page; this copy is numbered "II," and another, sold in 1929 at the Jerome Kern sale in an identical binding, is numbered "IV." Some of the proof copies were used by Tennyson himself for significant revisions. This one was evidently an in-house set, and contains markings on four pages only, not in Tennyson's hand; these are essentially a reader's queries about punctuation, spacing, and other typographical matters. There are, in any case, important textual differences between the proof copies and the book as finally published. In "The Voyage," for example, one stanza was rewritten, and the order of two other stanzas reversed. In addition, "A Welcome to Alexandra," which occupies pp. 164–65 of the book as published, is not present in the proofs at all, and was presumably a last-minute insertion (extending the book to 178 pages, as opposed to 175 pages here). There had been a kind of tug-of-war between Tennyson and his wife, Emily, over the title of this book. Surviving correspondence indicates that Emily, who took a tenacious interest in such matters, wanted it to be called "Enoch Arden &' Other Poems," whereas Tennyson himself suggested, among other alternatives, "Idylls, Chiefly of Seventy Years Ago." Clearly the proof copies were produced before the matter had been settled. The first proof copy to surface appeared in 1889, and its discovery immediately suggested to Wise and Buxton Forman the possibility of a fabrication. Title pages reading "Idylls of the Hearth" were printed up, and inserted in ordinary copies of *Enoch Arden*, thereby creating "examples of the book, with the original titlepage uncancelled . . . no doubt copies that were handed to friends or entrusted to reviewers." That these purported "first issues" are forgeries is made amply clear by the fact that they are all rebound in morocco, to conceal the cancellation; in addition, none bears a presentation inscription, which Tennyson would have provided for copies "handed to friends." The proof copies are, however, entirely genuine, and self-evidently very rare. The slightly unusual slipcase for this example was provided by Riviere in 1892 for Louis Samuel Montagu (for another Tennyson title from his library, similarly housed, see no. 422). Acquired in 1996.

435. Tennyson, Alfred. Moxon's miniature poets. A selection from the works of Alfred Tennyson, D.C.L., Poet Laureate. London: Edward Moxon &' Co., n.d. [1865]. Eight parts, square 8vo, original mauve printed wrappers.

A complete set of eight parts; the half-title, general title page, and table of contents are bound at the end of the last part, along with an engraved portrait. Each part contains thirty-two pages of text, and was sold for sixpence. Most copies of this book were issued in decorated cloth, either for 5s., plain, or 6s., with gilt edges; there was also an issue bound in full morocco, for 10s. 6d. Of the parts issue, Wise, who apparently did not himself own a set, observes: "Copies of the book in this, the more desirable, condition are of considerable and increasing scarcity." With the contemporary signature of William Douglas on the front wrapper of part 3. Acquired in 1985; no other set has ever been seen for sale.

436. Tennyson, Alfred. The victim. Canford Manor: 1867. Folio, original limp red "French morocco" boards, a.e.g.

> The Canford Manor Press was the joint undertaking of five English aristocrats, Sir Ivor Bertie Guest (later Lord Wimborne); his mother, Lady Charlotte Schreiber (formerly Lady Charlotte Guest; see no. 431); and Sir Ivor's three sisters, Enid, Constance, and Blanche. Work began in 1861 on a very old press that had stood in the schoolroom at Canford Manor, in Dorset, for many years. Early efforts were not of great textual interest, but in 1867 an approach was made to Tennyson, a family friend, to furnish some verses for the amateur printers, and he responded by sending several original manuscripts. It is not known precisely how many copies of this book were produced, but the number must have been very small; the print run is sometimes described as twenty-five copies. Some were bound in unlettered gray paper boards; this copy, in a more elaborate binding, has Sir Ivor Bertie Guests's monogram in gilt on the back cover. With the bookplate of Lady Charlotte Schreiber, the later bookplate of John A. Spoor, and the book label of Walter Chrysler, Jr. Acquired in 1985.

437. Tennyson, Alfred. The window. Or the loves of the wrens. Canford Manor: 1867. Folio, original limp red "French morocco" boards, a.e.g.

> The second of two Tennyson poems first printed by the Canford Manor Press (see no. 436). A very revised version was published in 1870, as set to music by Sir Arthur Sullivan. There was also a pirated edition, falsely dated 1867 (for 1870), produced by Richard Herne Shepherd. As with *The Victim*, the print run is sometimes stated to have been twenty-five copies. This one does not have Lady Charlotte Schreiber's bookplate, but may have been hers as well; it is contained in a case with the preceding poem.

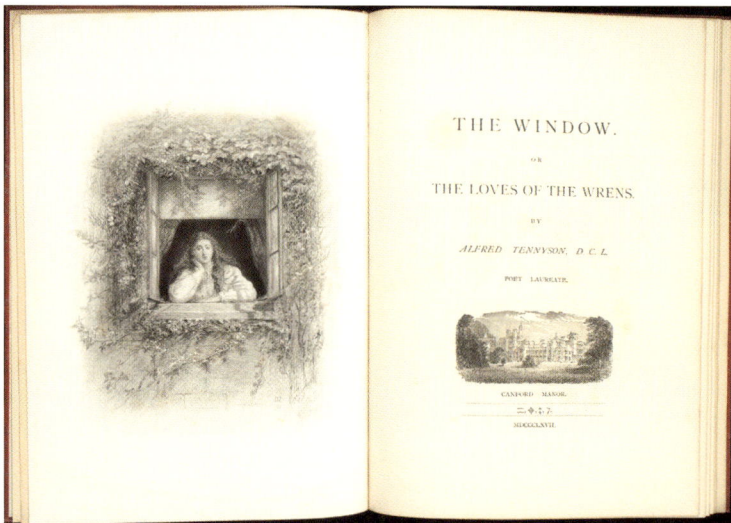

Tipped in are three lines of verse in Tennyson's hand, not from this poem, but probably from the manuscripts he submitted to the amateur printers. There is also a proof of a plate by Millais, inserted as a frontispiece (a Pre-Raphaelite young woman looking out a window). With the bookplates of Frederick Locker and John A. Spoor. Acquired in 1985.

438. Tennyson, Alfred. The holy grail: and other poems. London: Strahan and Co., 1870. 8vo, original bright green cloth.

This copy is inscribed by the author on the title page, "W. Allingham from A. Tennyson, Jan. 12th, '70, Farringford." William Allingham, a younger Irish poet, was a close friend and admirer of Tennyson for some fifty years. On a flyleaf at the back of this volume is a list of fifteen page numbers; these correspond to several brief remarks or queries in the text, and appear to be in Allingham's hand. Below the list, in the same hand, is the comment, "T. is a landscape poet of the first order." The Simon Nowell-Smith copy. Acquired in 2002.

439. [Tennyson, Alfred.] To the Queen. [London: 1873.] 4to, two leaves, folded.

A private printing of a poem written in Tennyson's capacity as Poet Laureate, and first regularly published as an epilogue to a new edition of *Idylls of the King*, which appeared as vols. 5 and 6 in the so-called Library Edition

254

of his collected works (1872–73). Two separate printings are recorded. One, described by Wise as "now of extreme rarity," is in an octavo format, and has a proper title page at the front, and a leaf at the end blank save for a printer's imprint. Wise quotes records to the effect that fifty copies only were printed. The present printing has no title page or final leaf, and is a quarto, with all edges gilt; in addition it is signed by Tennyson himself at the end. How many copies were printed is hard to say, but there can have been only a handful. There is no indication of provenance in this copy, but it is said to have come from the papers of the Hallam family. Acquired in 1996.

440. [Tennyson, Alfred.] A welcome. [London: 1874.] 4to, two leaves, folded.

A great Tennyson rarity, privately printed for use at court. This poem was written to mark the arrival in England of the new wife of Queen Victoria's second son, the Duke of Edinburgh. The duke's marriage to the Grand Duchess Maria Alexandrovna, daughter of Tsar Alexander II of Russia, took place at the Winter Palace in Saint Petersburg on January 23, 1874; the marriage did not prove to be a happy one. There appear to be four separate printings of this poem, presumably in the following order: (1) as here, with a short title below a large rectangular type ornament, and the incorrect spelling "Alexandrowna" in the text. The present copy is signed by Tennyson at the end. WorldCat records two other copies, one at Brigham Young (part of the Victorian collection purchased from David Magee) and one at North Carolina (formerly in the collection of the bookseller Harry Pratley). Neither of these copies is signed. (2) As the preceding, but with the duchess's name added to the title, and Tennyson identified as the author; a colophon gives Henry S. King as the publisher. The only copy recorded is at Huntington; it is not signed. (3) As (2), but with the correct spelling, "Alexandrovna." Of this version two copies can be traced, one at the British Library (the Ashley copy) and one at British Columbia (the Colbeck copy); both of these are signed by Tennyson. (4) An eight-page octavo printing, with a proper title page and the imprint of Henry S. King & Co.

T. J. Wise fastened upon this poem as an opportunity for skulduggery, and forged an octavo "first edition" of it, probably about 1897, in which he had the gall to change one of Tennyson's words in the second stanza (from "palms" to "plains"). In his bibliography he relegates version (3) to the status of a "second private edition," though he concedes: "The number of copies printed has not been recorded, but so far as rarity goes the quarto is more uncommon even than the octavo, only some two or three examples now being traceable." In the Ashley catalogue Wise notes the existence of quarto copies with "Alexandrowna"; this variant he describes as "an early (probably authorised) reprint." His forgery, he asserts, was limited to forty copies. Acquired in 2010.

441. Tennyson, Alfred. A welcome to Her Royal Highness Marie Alexandrovna, Duchess of Edinburgh. [Colophon:] London: Henry S. King & Co., n.d. [1874]. 4to, two leaves, folded.

Probably the third printing, as described above (no. 440). With the book label of Howard Lehman Goodhart (1884–1951), a noted collector, many of whose books went to Bryn Mawr. Acquired in 1996.

442. Tennyson, Alfred. Harold: a drama. London: Henry S. King & Co., 1877. 8vo, contemporary full green morocco, gilt, spine and inner dentelles gilt, silk endpapers, a.e.g. (rebacked, original spine laid down).

This is the dedication copy, inscribed by the author on the title page as follows: "Lord Lytton from A. Tennyson, Jany. 16th / 77. Poeta poetae [from poet to poet]." The recipient was Edward Robert Bulwer Lytton, 1st Earl of Lytton (1831–1891), described on the printed leaf of dedication as Viceroy and Governor-General of India, a post he had just assumed. Lord Lytton was, as Tennyson's inscription indicates, a poet of considerable ability and reputation; his earliest works, published under the pseudonym "Owen Meredith," are in the manner of Browning. In his printed dedication Tennyson explains that his verse drama was in part inspired by a novel on the same subject by Lord Lytton's father, Edward Bulwer Lytton. That work was *Harold, or the Last of the Saxon Kings* (1848); as Tennyson points out, the novel was dedicated to Tennyson's uncle. Acquired in 1991.

443. Tennyson, Alfred. The lover's tale. London: C. Kegan Paul & Co., 1879. 8vo, original green cloth.

The first published edition, much revised. Tennyson wrote this poem when he was very young, and had it set in type in 1833, for inclusion in his *Poems* of that year; but when only the first two parts had been printed, he thought better of the whole matter, and withdrew the poem from that book. A few "trial" copies were printed (see above, no. 423), and many years later the text was, in Tennyson's words, "mercilessly pirated" by Richard Herne Shepherd (see below, no. 457). This copy is inscribed on the half-title, "Mary Brotherton from A. Tennyson." Mary Brotherton was a friend and neighbor of Tennyson on the Isle of Wight. She wrote several novels and at least two books of poetry; a copy of one of her novels in the Robert Lee Wolff collection (now at Texas) was inscribed to Tennyson's older brother in 1859, indicating that her relationship with the family was a long one. With the later bookplate of Geoffrey Harmsworth. Acquired in 1994 .

444. Tennyson, Alfred. Becket: a dramatic poem. London: Macmillan and Co., 1884. Sm. 8vo, original plain light brown wrappers.

This is a proof copy of the first edition, which was published later the same year. Tennyson had completed this verse play in 1879, when he showed it to Henry Irving, the most celebrated actor of his day; Irving admired the play, but judged it too long, and too expensive to produce. *Becket* was then set aside for five years, and not printed until 1884. At some point (ca. 1895), T. J. Wise produced a "trial" edition, dated 1879, with a significant number of textual variants, as described in full in his Tennyson bibliography; this has now been conclusively exposed as a forgery. The present proof copy is genuine and reveals that there were a number of interesting last-minute changes, most notably in the title, where Tennyson decided to omit the phrase "a dramatic poem." There is also a slight change in the dedication to Earl Selborne, in which the phrase "you have assured me" was altered to "for so you have assured me." The following leaf contains a list of "dramatis personae," in which the three female characters, Eleanor de Aquitaine, Rosamund de Clifford, and Margery, have been inadvertently omitted; these were added to the published version. There are other technical changes as well. In acts 1 and 2, for example, the phrase "Scene I" was originally set on a separate line; in the published edition it has been moved to precede the first stage direction, as was done in acts 3–5. Small corrections occur in the stage directions throughout, changing, for example, "enter" to "re-enter" wherever appropriate (e.g., on pp. 115, 139, 175, and 198). There is a more significant change in the stage direction on p. 210, where "Strikes off the Archbishop's mitre" was expanded to include "and wounds him in the forehead." This proof copy contains only a single proofreader's mark, on p. 127, where the second *z* in the word "buzz" is noted as having been set in the wrong font ("w. f."); the correction was made in the published edition. And, finally, the last leaf here is blank; in the book as issued it contains an advertisement for a seven-volume collected edition of Tennyson's works. No other proof copy of *Becket* has been located. Acquired in 2010.

445. Tennyson, Alfred. The cup and the falcon. London: Macmillan and Co., 1884. 8vo, original bright green cloth.

This copy is inscribed on the half-title, "Helen Allingham from Tennyson, Jan. 27th, 1885." The recipient was the wife of the Irish poet William Allingham (see no. 438). The Simon Nowell-Smith copy. Acquired in 2002.

446. Tennyson, Alfred. Tiresias and other poems. London: Macmillan and Co., 1885. 8vo, original green cloth.

This copy is inscribed on the title page: "W. Allingham from Tennyson." For the recipient, see no. 438. Acquired in 1971.

447. Tennyson, Alfred. Locksley Hall sixty years after etc. London and New York: Macmillan and Co., 1886. 8vo, original green cloth.

This copy is inscribed by Tennyson on the half-title, "Martin [?] Brown d. d. A. T." The recipient has not been identified. The abbreviation "d. d." is no doubt for the Latin phrase "donum dedit." Acquired in 1990.

448. Tennyson, Alfred. Demeter and other poems. London and New York: Macmillan and Co., 1889. 8vo, original green cloth.

This copy is inscribed on the half-title: "Mary Brotherton from Tennyson." Beneath this inscription Tennyson has written: "Errata. Poems to M. Boyle p. 1 for 'One' Cuckoo read Our. Romney's Remorse p. 150 9th line from top for 'More than all' (a stupid misprint) read Than all &c." For the recipient, see above, no. 443. Later bookplate of Geoffrey Harmsworth (Sotheby's, June 19, 1930, lot 661). Acquired in 1994.

449. Tennyson, Alfred. The foresters: Robin Hood and Maid Marian. London and New York: Macmillan and Co., 1892. 8vo, original green cloth.

Tennyson finished his verse play for the American theater manager Daly in 1891; an American printing may have preceded this London one by a few days. This is the last book published in Tennyson's lifetime; he died later in the year, having looked over proofs for *The Death of Œnone*. This copy is inscribed by Tennyson on the half-title, "Mary Brotherton from Tennyson, May 15th, 1892." For the recipient, see above, no. 443. Acquired in 1993.

450. Tennyson, Alfred. The death of Œnone, Akbar's dream, and other poems. . . . with five steel portraits of the author. London and New York: Macmillan and Co., 1892. Large 8vo, original white cloth.

Tennyson's last book, published shortly after his death. This is one of five hundred numbered copies on large paper; the copies on ordinary paper did not have the five fine portraits present here. Acquired in 1999.

451. Tennyson, Alfred. Becket. . . . As arranged for the stage by Henry Irving. For stage use only. 1893. [Verso of title page:] London: C. Whittingham and Co., Chiswick Press. Large 8vo, full dark olive green morocco, gilt, spine and inner dentelles gilt, gilt decorated endpapers, a.e.g., by Zaehnsdorf.

> A hitherto unrecorded variant of the very rare acting edition of Tennyson's verse play. The basis for this text was first published in 1884. Shortly after Tennyson's death, the play was modified by the celebrated actor Henry Irving, for performance on the stage. In 1893 a trade edition of the acting version was published by Macmillan, running to sixty-two pages. This was, however, preceded by a privately printed text "for stage use only," consisting of seventy pages. The print run of this latter version must have been very small. The incomparable collection at the Tennyson Research Centre, City Library, Lincoln, has two copies of the seventy-page printing, but both are in wrappers, without a proper title page, and are printed on one side of the page only; similar copies of this prompt book are at Folger and Harvard. The present copy is more elegantly produced, on fine paper, with a half-title and title page; on the front cover is printed in gilt "Lyceum," the name of the theater where the play was first performed. There is no sign here of previous ownership, nor has another copy so printed been located. Acquired in 1987.

452. [Tennyson, Alfred, Charles Tennyson, and Frederick Tennyson.] Poems by two brothers. London and New York: Macmillan and Co., 1893. Large 8vo, original white cloth, gray printed dust wrapper.

> Second edition. No. 163 of three hundred copies on large paper. A type-facsimile reprint of the first edition of 1827, published by Hallam Tennyson, with a preface, shortly after his father's death. Included here are four additional poems, which were part of the original manuscript but were for some reason omitted from the first edition. At the end are six leaves of the original manuscript in photographic facsimile; these plates were not included in the trade edition. Acquired in 1983.

453. [Anon.] Arthur: or the hididdle-diddles of the king; an original traves-
tie, in three acts, written expressly for the private dramatic performance,
January 18, 1860. By our own poet laureate. [Colophon:] London: Bod-
dington, printer, (1860). 8vo, original dark blue printed wrappers.

> A very rare burlesque in verse of Tennyson's *Idylls of the King*, which had
> just been published; the only copy located is at North Carolina. In a pre-
> liminary note, dated "London, Christmas, 1859," the anonymous author
> reveals that his humor is meant to be kind: "The author's idea of a trav-
> estie is that it represents the single step which proverbially separates the
> sublime from the ridiculous, and consequently presupposes sublimity in
> the original. In no other spirit has he ventured to select as the basis of the
> following burlesque 'The Idylls of the King,' a work whose transcendent
> merit it would be presumptuous for him to criticise." The effect is a bit like
> Tennyson turned into Gilbert and Sullivan. Acquired in 1999.

454. Dabbs, George H. R. Poems. Newport, Isle of Wight: printed by W.
R. Yelf, 1872. Sm. 8vo, original green cloth.

> "Printed for private circulation only." Dabbs lived on the Isle of Wight, and
> there came to be Tennyson's friend and physician; he attended the poet on
> his deathbed. This copy is inscribed by the author on the title page, "Miss
> Weld. With kind regards. 15th June, 1872." The recipient was Agnes Weld,
> Tennyson's sister-in-law. On the front flyleaves is a sixty-line manuscript
> poem on the death of Julia Margaret Cameron, also a friend and neighbor
> of Tennyson, and now famous as a pioneer in photography. The poem is
> signed with the author's initials and dated March 1879; it was apparently
> written into this copy shortly after Cameron's death. Acquired in 1988.

455. Irving, Walter. Tennyson. Edinburgh: Maclachlan and Stewart; Simp-
kin, Marshall, & Co. (London), 1873. 8vo, sewn, as issued.

> A vituperative attack on Tennyson's *Idylls of the King* (first published in
> 1859). The following is typical: "Mr. Tennyson's verse does not lack for
> sound. There is so much shrilling, bellowing, roaring, and howling con-
> tinually going on, that any one may easily be led to believe the poet had
> spent the greater part of his life in the neighbourhood of a menagerie. The
> *Idylls of the King* is a great failure." This copy is signed on the title page
> by the poet Siegfried Sassoon, who has added "rare"; his monogram book
> label is on the verso. Acquired in 1992.

456. Mann, Robert James. Tennyson's "Maud" vindicated: an explanatory essay. London: Jarrold & Sons, n.d. [1856]. 8vo, original dark blue cloth.

The first critical study devoted entirely to Tennyson. Robert James Mann (1817–1886) was trained as a physician, but retired from practice at an early age, for reasons of health, and devoted himself to writing a long series of textbooks on various aspects of science and medicine. Mann was for a time a neighbor of Tennyson on the Isle of Wight, and the two engaged in conversations about Tennyson's experimental poem. Tennyson is known to have read the proofs of this little book, and there is no doubt that he made substantial contributions to it, including the introduction of the term "monodrama," which was here used for the first time. The book was printed in Norwich; most copies appear to have been bound in pink printed wrappers. Acquired in 2004.

457. Shepherd, Richard Herne. Translations from Charles Baudelaire. With a few original poems. London: John Camden Hotten, 1869. 8vo, original bright green cloth.

Second issue; the first issue is made up of the same sheets, but stops at p. 87. The first appearance in English of anything by Baudelaire, whose influence on Swinburne and his contemporaries was great. Richard Herne Shepherd (1841–1895) was an industrious literary editor and bibliographer with an occasional tendency to produce piracies of literary texts. This is a truly remarkable presentation copy, inscribed in Shepherd's hand (though not signed) on the front endpaper as follows: "From the meanest of living singers to the noblest. A peace offering and act of homage. Aug. 5, 1875." The recipient was undoubtedly Tennyson, and the explanation is clear. In 1870, Shepherd produced a pirated edition of Tennyson's *Lover's Tale*, in an edition of fifty copies, "for private circulation." This volume he was persuaded to suppress, and the matter was dropped (though Wise later created a forgery of it). In 1875, Shepherd issued another "private" edition, with additional poems, and again without Tennyson's authorization. This time, in July, Tennyson instituted a lawsuit against him, and a final injunction against the book was served on Shepherd on August 5–the date of the inscription. It cannot be doubted that Shepherd sent this volume to Tennyson as a "peace offering," just after receiving the injunction. In fact, Tennyson declined to collect the £100 legal costs awarded to him by the court, "since he heard that Mr. Shepherd was very poor and that his aged mother depended upon him for her livelihood." Acquired in 1978.

261

458. [Tennyson, Hallam.] Materials for a life of A. T. Collected for my children. [London: 1895.] Four vols., 8vo, original plain stiff blue wrappers.

A precursor, privately printed, of Hallam Tennyson's *Alfred, Lord Tennyson: A Memoir by His Son*, first published by Macmillan in two volumes in 1897. As is well known, the biography of Tennyson by his devoted eldest son was long planned and carefully orchestrated. Work seems to have begun even before the poet's death on October 6, 1892, and within a fortnight of the funeral at Westminster Abbey the project became Hallam's abiding concern. A huge archive of letters and reminiscences was assembled, and carefully sorted and mounted, with connecting narrative, in ten massive folio volumes now preserved at the Tennyson Research Centre in Lincoln. Out of this matter, Hallam generated the present set of four volumes, always referred to by Tennysonians as "Materials." Thirty-two copies are known to have been printed, of which fifteen are in the Tennyson collection at Lincoln, and at least a dozen more can be located in various institutions. The text here is of critical scholarly importance for two reasons. First, of the more than forty thousand letters assembled for possible use, more than three quarters were destroyed, including all those from Emily Selwood, written prior to their marriage; these, of course, are not preserved in the folio archive, but excerpts are printed in this set. Secondly, "Materials" contains a great deal of text from letters and diaries later omitted from the published *Memoir* (e.g., the early letters from Emily Selwood). Acquired in 1999.

ELIZABETH BARRETT BROWNING (1806–1861)

459. Barrett, Elizabeth B. The battle of Marathon. A poem. London: printed for W. Lindsell, 1820. 8vo, nineteenth-century half rose calf and marbled boards.

The poet's first book, privately printed in an edition of fifty copies; of these only fifteen copies are known to survive, of which this is the only one in private hands. It is inscribed by the author on the verso of the title page, "For her dearest Grandmamma with Elizabeth's love, Baker Street 67, March 19th, 1820." On the title page is the signature of Elizabeth Barrett's maternal grandmother, Arabella Graham Clarke. A copy inscribed on March 6 to her paternal grandmother, Elizabeth Moulton, is in the Morgan Library. T. J. Wise's copy, now in the British Library and one of only two to survive in its original state, bears a slightly later presentation inscription to a Miss

Arabella Graham Clarke

THE

11783

BATTLE OF MARATHON.

A POEM.

—————————————————" Behold
What care employs me now, my vows I pay
To the sweet Muses, teachers of my youth !"
                                        AKENSIDE.

" Ancient of days! August Athena! Where,
Where are thy men of might, thy grand in soul?
Gone—glimmering through the dream of things that were,
First in the race that led to glory's goal,
They won, and past away."   BYRON.

BY E. B. BARRETT.

for her dearest Grandmama with Rorabella's love. Baker Street by March 19th 1820.

London:

PRINTED FOR W. LINDSELL, **87,** WIMPOLE-
STREET, CAVENDISH-SQUARE.

1820.

T. Whingates. That copy has 27 small manuscript corrections, essentially
to punctuation and spelling, most of which can also be found in a copy
at the Newberry Library. The present copy has all but 6 of these, but also
contains an additional 24 corrections of a similar nature. A copy acquired
at the Prescott sale in 1981 by Armstrong Browning Library at Baylor has 22
of the 27 corrections, and 18 others. From the library of H. Bradley Martin.
Acquired in 2001.

263

460. [Barrett, Elizabeth B.] An essay on mind, with other poems. London: James Duncan, 1826. 12mo, original blue-gray boards, printed paper label.

The author's first published book, issued when she was twenty; her husband-to-be was as yet only fourteen. With the bookplate of William Harris Arnold, whose collection was sold at the Anderson Galleries, in 1924. Acquired in 1975.

461. Barrett, Elizabeth B. The seraphim, and other poems. London: Saunders and Otley, 1838. 12mo, original claret cloth.

The author's fourth book. This copy is inscribed on a front flyleaf, "Frederick Robertson—from his affectionate friend H. D. [?]" The recipient was Frederick William Robertson (1816–1853), one of the most influential English clergymen of his day; the presenter, if the last initial is *D* and not *O*, was Helen Denys, whom he married in 1841. With the bookplate of Frank Fletcher. Acquired in 1993.

462. Barrett, Elizabeth B. Poems. London: Edward Moxon, 1844. Two vols., 8vo, original gray-green cloth.

This copy is inscribed on the verso of the flyleaf facing the first title page, "With the author's love to Miss Biddulph, London, August, 1844." The recipient was one of five daughters—there were also four sons—of a country gentleman whose Herefordshire estate was adjacent to Hope End, the home of Elizabeth Barrett's family from 1809 until they moved by stages to Wimpole Street in London. In fact, Elizabeth Barrett seems not to have much cared for the Biddulph girls; in her diary she calls them "cold, formal and commonplace." She was rather generous with presentation copies of these two volumes; no fewer than twenty-nine examples are recorded, the earliest of which are dated, as here, August 1844. The Simon Nowell-Smith copy. Acquired in 2002.

463. Barrett, Elizabeth B. A drama of exile: and other poems. New York: Henry G. Langley, 1845. Two vols., 12mo, original dark brown cloth.

First American edition; first published in London in 1844 as *Poems* (no. 462). Included here is an important six-page "preface to the American edition," in which the author discusses her poetry. Acquired in 2005.

464. [Browning, Elizabeth Barrett.] Sonnets. By E. B. B. Reading: [Not for publication.], 1847 [ca. 1893]. 8vo, full brown morocco, by Riviere.

A fabricated first edition, and the most famous and most important of Thomas J. Wise's forgeries. Wise's usual method was to take a well-known literary text—in this case "Sonnets from the Portuguese"—and concoct a private and necessarily rare printing purporting to have preceded the regularly published first edition; the sonnets in question had originally appeared in the author's two-volume *Poems* of 1850 (no. 465). This forty-seven-page pamphlet was first revealed as a forgery and attributed to Wise in 1934 by John Carter and Graham Pollard. Their research indicated that the paper was composed of chemical wood with a trace of rag, which could not have been manufactured before 1874, and was unlikely before 1883. In addition, the text is printed in a typeface called Clay's Long Primer No. 3, of which certain letters were not cut until 1880. The true date of printing, based upon remarks in a letter from Wise to Edmund Gosse, was probably about June 21, 1893. The H. Bradley Martin copy. With the book label of James O. Edwards. Acquired in 2008.

465. Browning, Elizabeth Barrett. Poems. . . . New edition. London: Chapman & Hall, 1850. Two vols., 8vo, original blue cloth.

> Second edition, with major additions. Vol. 2 contains the first appearance of "Sonnets from the Portuguese," the love poems for which the author will always be best remembered. Acquired in 2005.

466. Browning, Elizabeth Barrett. Poems. London: Chapman & Hall, 1853. Two vols., 8vo, original slate green cloth.

> Third edition. This edition incorporates further changes, as indicated by a brief postscript: "In the present edition the author has done her best to remedy the oversights and defects of that former revision, which her absence from England rendered less complete than it should have been." Acquired in 1994.

467. Browning, Elizabeth Barrett and Robert. [Wrapper title:] Two poems. London: Chapman & Hall, 1854. 8vo, original cream printed wrappers.

> This pamphlet, more than any other, seems to have suggested to Wise the basic format for many of his forgeries. Acquired in 1994.

468. Browning, Elizabeth Barrett. Poems. London: Chapman & Hall, 1856. Three vols., 8vo, original green cloth.

> Fourth edition. This was the last lifetime edition. There are revisions to twenty poems, as well as to the whole of "Casa Guidi's Windows"; in addition,

three new poems and three translations have been added, and the order of "Sonnets from the Portuguese" has been slightly altered. Acquired in 1980.

469. Browning, Elizabeth Barrett. Aurora Leigh. London: Chapman and Hall, 1857. 8vo, original green cloth.

Despite the date on the title page, the book was published on November 15, 1856. This copy has an unusual inscription on the title page: "Mary Sophia Knight. From Mr. Kenyon. November 19th, 1856." John Kenyon was the son of a wealthy Jamaica sugar planter; as a young man he was friendly with most of the major literary figures of the period, including Wordsworth, Coleridge, Southey, and Lamb. About 1840 he met Robert Browning at a dinner party, and this was the beginning of a long and close friendship that lasted the rest of Kenyon's life. It was Kenyon who in 1846 first introduced Browning to a distant cousin, Elizabeth Barrett, thus beginning the most famous romance in English literary history. In later years the Brownings lived at Kenyon's house when they were in England; this book is, in fact, dedicated to Kenyon, the manuscript having been finished while the Brownings were staying with him. What is surprising about the inscription is the fact that Kenyon was at this time terminally ill, and he died on December 3, 1856, just over two weeks after the book was presented. The recipient has not been identified. This copy also has the bookplate of Edmund Gosse (1849–1928), poet, miscellaneous writer, and bibliophile, who, when he was young, knew Browning well; a letter to Gosse from Alexandra Orr is laid in. With the later bookplates of Ruth Swetland Kane and Frank Fletcher. Acquired in 1975.

470. Browning, Elizabeth Barrett, and Richard Hengist Horne. Psyche apocalypté: a lyrical drama. Projected by Elizabeth Barrett Browning and R. H. Horne. Reprinted from the St. James's Magazine and United Empire Review for February, 1876. London and Aylesbury: printed by Hazell, Watson, and Viney, for private circulation, 1876. 8vo, sewn, as issued.

Elizabeth Barrett Browning and Richard Hengist Horne had planned to write a verse play together, but the project was never completed. Horne prepared the interesting notes and letters that had passed between them for magazine publication in 1876. This pamphlet is an offprint of that article; according to Wise, sixty-five copies were printed. This is Horne's own copy, later in the collection of H. Buxton Forman, who acquired Horne's papers; there are a few penciled corrections in Horne's hand. Of additional interest is a list, also in Horne's hand, of those to whom copies were to be sent, including Disraeli, Swinburne, Meredith, and other familiar names; also laid in are two contemporary reviews, clipped out by Horne, one of them with his annotations. Acquired in 1975.

ROBERT BROWNING (1812–1889)

471. Browning, Robert. Paracelsus. London: published by Efingham Wilson, 1835. 8vo, original gray boards, printed paper label.

> Browning's second book, preceded only by *Pauline*, which had appeared two years earlier. This is a particularly fine copy in original condition, acquired at the Arthur A. Houghton sale in 1979.

472. Browning, Robert. Strafford: an historical tragedy. London: printed for Longman, Rees, Orme, Brown, Green, & Longman, 1837. 8vo, red morocco, by Riviere; original drab wrappers, with a printed paper side label, bound in.

> Browning's third book, a verse play written at the suggestion of the famous actor and theater manager William Charles Macready; the play was produced at Covent Garden in May 1837, but ran for only five nights. Acquired in 1994.

473. Browning, Robert. Sordello. London: Edward Moxon, 1840. 8vo, original violet cloth, printed paper label.

> Browning's fourth book. Acquired in 1973.

474. Browning, Robert. Bells and pomegranates. No. I.–Pippa passes. London: Edward Moxon, 1841. [With:] No. II.–King Victor and King Charles. London: Edward Moxon, 1842. [With:] No. III.–Dramatic lyrics. London: Edward Moxon, 1842. [With:] No. IV.–The return of the Druses. A tragedy. In five acts. London: Edward Moxon, 1843. [With:] No. V.–A blot in the 'scutcheon. A tragedy, in three acts. London: Edward Moxon, 1843. [With:] No. VI.–Colombe's birthday. A play, in five acts. London: Edward Moxon, 1844. [With:] No. VII. Dramatic romances & lyrics. London: Edward Moxon, 1845. [With:] No. VIII and last. Luria; and A soul's tragedy. London: Edward Moxon, 1846. Together eight parts in one volume, 8vo, original black cloth.

The sheets of all eight numbers, originally issued in tan printed wrappers, were bound up and offered for sale as a single volume. This copy is unusual, in that part 5 is a first edition; this part was apparently underprinted, and is almost always found as a second edition in the collection issued in cloth. Part 3 contains "The Pied Piper of Hamelin," as well as several of Browning's finest dramatic monologues, including "My Last Duchess." Acquired in 1975.

475. Browning, Robert. Christmas-eve and Easter-day. A poem. London: Chapman and Hall, 1850. 8vo, original dark green cloth.

Copies of this book are normally bound in brown cloth. John Carter, in his *Binding Variants* (pp. 97–98) reports having seen only two copies of this green cloth binding. With the signature on the front flyleaf of Jessie Turner, dated Christmas, 1865. Acquired in 1980.

476. [Browning, Robert, contributor.] Letters of Percy Bysshe Shelley. With an introductory essay, by Robert Browning. London: Edward Moxon, 1852. 8vo, original purple cloth.

Browning's introductory essay, which runs to forty-four pages, proved a major embarrassment, because upon publication it was discovered that Moxon had been deceived, and that all but one of these letters had been forged by Major Byron (for details, see no. 144). The book was immediately withdrawn. With the book label of John Bell Sedgwick. Acquired in 1994.

477. Browning, Robert. Men and women. London: Chapman and Hall, 1855. Two vols., 8vo, original green cloth.

This set is signed on the front flyleaf of each volume by E. L. Lushington. Edmund Law Lushington (1811–1893) entered Trinity College, Cambridge, in 1828; he was two years younger than Tennyson, but the two became friends and, along with Arthur Hallam, were members of the noted club of twelve called the Apostles. In 1842 he married Tennyson's sister Cecilia; the marriage was celebrated by Tennyson in the epilogue to "In Memoriam." Lushington was a capable classical scholar, but published little. The Borowitz copy. Acquired in 1978.

478. Browning, Robert. The ring and the book. London: Smith, Elder and Co., 1868–1869. Four vols., 8vo, original dark green cloth.

This set is inscribed on the first title page, "Mrs. Grant Duff with RB's best regards. Dec. 1, '68." The recipient was the wife of Sir Mountstuart Elphinstone Grant Duff (1829–1906), a statesman and man of letters celebrated for his refinement and high social style. Fifteen other presentation copies of this title are known (about the average number for Browning's books), of which at least five others were inscribed on the same day as this one, including the set presented to Matthew Arnold (now in the Berg collection at the New York Public Library). Vol. 4 has an additional inscription reading simply, "From the author"; this looks to be in Browning's hand as well. Acquired in 1992.

479. Browning, Robert. Fifine at the fair. London: Smith, Elder and Co., 1872. 8vo, original red-brown cloth.

This copy is inscribed on the half-title, "To Bryan Waller Procter with all the old admiration, and ever, as the years go by, some new affectionateness of R. B. June 4, '72." Procter, most of whose popular verse had been published under the pseudonym "Barry Cornwall," was eighty-five years old when this book was published. He had been extremely generous and helpful to the young Browning at the beginning of his literary career, and the two men, despite the disparity in age, became close friends. Procter died in 1874. With the later bookplate of John A. Spoor (sold in his sale at Parke-Bernet, April 26, 1939). Acquired in 1988.

480. Browning, Robert. Pacchiarotto and how he worked in distemper: with other poems. London: Smith, Elder, & Co., 1876. 8vo, original lilac cloth.

This copy is inscribed on a front flyleaf, "Fanny Haworth from her old and affectionate friend R. B. July 18, '76." Euphrasia Fanny Haworth (1801–1883) was an artist and writer who first met Browning in 1835 at the home of the actor William Charles Macready; she had already published, in 1827, a collection of stories called *The Pine Tree Dell, and Other Tales*. She and Browning became lifelong friends and correspondents. Fanny Haworth makes an appearance as Eyebright in *Sordello*, and years later she painted a well-known portrait of Pen Browning. Acquired in 1981.

481. Browning, Robert. The Agamemnon of Æschylus. Transcribed by Robert Browning. London: Smith, Elder, & Co., 1877. 8vo, original green cloth.

This copy is inscribed on the half-title, "Thomas Linton Esq. in grateful remembrance of the visit, Nov. 20, '77, from his cordially ever Robert Browning, Nov. 22, '77." Nothing has been discovered about the recipient, or the occasion of his visit. The Simon Nowell-Smith copy. Acquired in 2002.

482. Browning, Robert. Dramatic idyls. London: Smith, Elder, & Co., 1879. 8vo, original brown cloth.

> This book and the next were added to the collection at a very early stage; we soon decided that there needed to be something special about copies of common titles of this sort to make them worthy of inclusion. The two were never replaced, however, for sentimental reasons. Acquired in 1971.

483. Browning, Robert. Dramatic idyls. Second series. London: Smith, Elder, & Co., 1880. 8vo, original dark brown cloth. Acquired in 1971.

484. Browning, Robert. Parleyings with certain people of importance in their day: to wit: Bernard de Mandeville, Daniel Bartoli, Christopher Smart, George Bubb Doddington, Francis Furini, Gerard de Lairesse, and Charles Avison. Introduced by a dialogue between Apollo and the Fates; concluded by another between John Fust and his friends. London: Smith, Elder, & Co., 1887. 8vo, original light brown cloth.

> This copy is inscribed on the half-title, "Alfred Domett, with all affectionate regards from his old friend RB, Jan. 28, '87." This is one of sixteen presentation copies noted by Kelley and Coley in *The Browning Collections* (no. C446, unlocated), of which at least five others were inscribed on the same day; the copy presented to Tennyson was inscribed a day later. Alfred Domett (1811–1887) was a close family friend of Browning. In 1842 he emigrated to New Zealand, where he was employed in the civil service, and eventually became premier. Browning's poem "Waring," first published in *Dramatic Lyrics* in 1842, was inspired by his friend's departure. Upon his retirement in 1871, Domett returned to England, and over the next five years he published two volumes of undistinguished verse. Acquired in 2006.

ARTHUR HUGH CLOUGH (1819–1861)

485. Clough, Arthur Hugh, and Thomas Burbidge. Ambarvalia. London: Chapman and Hall; Francis Macpherson (Oxford), 1849. 8vo, original dark brown cloth.

> The second of two collections of verse published by Clough during his lifetime; his poems in this collaborative volume occupy the first sixty-four pages. Thomas Burbidge is now largely forgotten, except for his participation in this book. This copy has the ownership inscription of J. J. Hooper

of Oriel College, Oxford; no doubt he knew Clough, who was a tutor there until 1848. Acquired in 1977.

486. Clough, Arthur Hugh. Poems. . . . With a memoir. Cambridge and London: Macmillan and Co., 1862. 8vo, original dark green cloth, front cover decorated in black and gilt.

> The first collection of Clough's poetry, edited by Francis T. Palgrave, who wrote the introductory memoir. This copy is inscribed on the half-title, "T. Woolner from F. T. Palgrave, July, 1862." The recipient, Thomas Woolner, was one of the most distinguished Pre-Raphaelite artists, and an interesting poet in his own right. What makes this inscription particularly appealing is that Woolner had designed the vignette illustration for the title page of Palgrave's *Golden Treasury*, the celebrated anthology of English poetry first published the year before. "Perhaps the most beautiful work he ever wrought is not a sculpture at all, but the vignette of the flute-player on the title page of Palgrave's 'Golden Treasury,' a gem of grace and charm."– Richard Garnett, in the *DNB*. Acquired in 1999.

MATTHEW ARNOLD (1822–1888)

487. [Arnold, Matthew.] Alaric at Rome. A prize poem, recited in Rugby School, June XII, MDCCCXL. Rugby: Combe and Crossley, 1840. 8vo, original pink printed wrappers.

> Matthew Arnold's first publication. This prize poem is a slightly unusual example of the genre in that it was printed anonymously, and not intended for general circulation. The text was first identified as Arnold's by Edmund Gosse in 1888. Arnold himself replied to a query from Gosse on February 19, 1888, just two months before his death: "Yes, 'Alaric at Rome' is my Rugby prize poem, and I think it is better than my Oxford one, 'Cromwell'; only you will see that I had been very much reading 'Childe Harold.'" T. J. Wise quickly recognized the value of this publication: "*Alaric at Rome* holds a high place in the rank of modern poetical rarities. To Mr. Edmund Gosse belongs the credit of unearthing the first recovered copy, and of identifying its author. Some ten examples in all have now been brought to light. Mr. Buxton Forman's copy sold for $900 in March, 1920." In fact the number of surviving copies is difficult to determine, because in 1893 Wise issued a close facsimile of the pamphlet; from some copies he removed the prefatory matter, and these he passed off as originals. They deceived collectors

until the forgery was exposed by an examination of the typeface employed, which proved to be identical to the hybrid font (Clay's Long Primer No. 3) used in the notorious forgery by Wise of Elizabeth Barrett Browning's *Reading Sonnets* (no. 464). The NUC, WorldCat, and Copac together list sixteen copies, but some of these, including the copies at Huntington and Texas, and one of the two copies at the British Library, are not genuine. Proper examples of the original are now very rare on the market; prior to this one, the last to appear at auction was in the Houghton sale, rebound without wrappers, in 1979 (£3,400).

ITEM 487

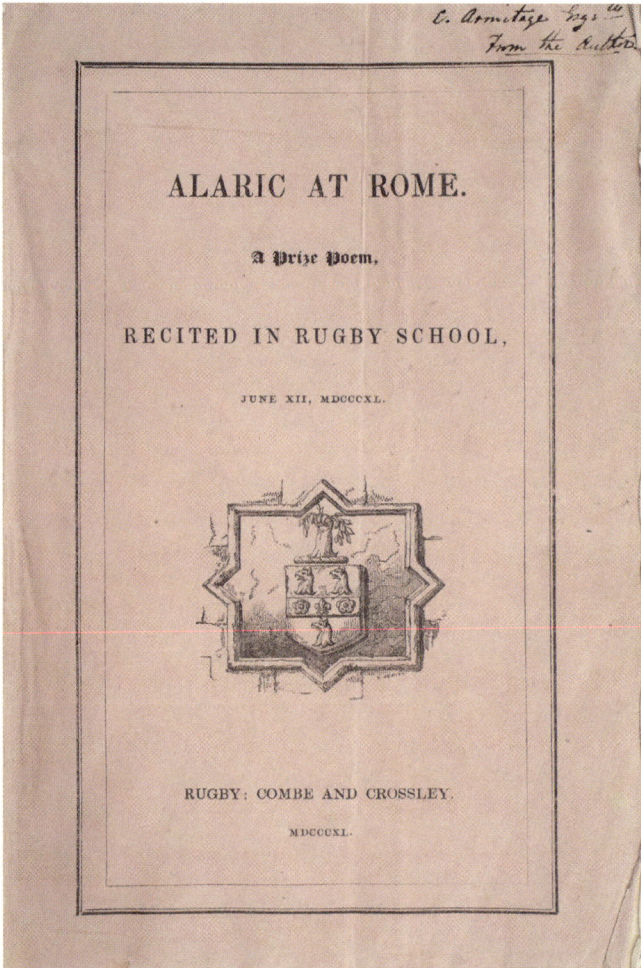

This is no doubt the most desirable surviving copy of Arnold's literary debut, as it is inscribed by him on the front wrapper, "E. Armitage Esqr. from the Author." The recipient, Edward Armitage, was a fellow pupil at Rugby. The only other copy known to bear an inscription by Arnold ("Miss Ward, 1840") is at the Morgan Library. Included with the present copy is correspondence to show that it was first acquired in 1905 by the New Jersey collector Dr. J. B. Clemens, from Dodd, Mead & Co., New York. Dr. Clemens asked the booksellers to verify the authenticity of the presentation inscription, and received two letters in reply from a member of the firm, Luther S. Livingston, guaranteeing Arnold's handwriting and enclosing a transcript of a letter from an unnamed bookseller in London:

In reply to yours of the 15th instant referring to the inscription . . . I have much pleasure in saying that there is no doubt whatever about the genuineness thereof. I do not precisely know who the Armitage was, further than that he was a scholar at Rugby, at or about the time of presentation. In proof of this there is in existence (in the possession of Mr. T. J. Wise) a very interesting document—the Master of Rugby's Report of the said Armitage's studentship, &c. at Rugby—signed "T. Arnold." Mr. Wise has also a presentation copy of Tennyson's Poems (2 vol. edn.) with the name of Armitage & from the same source as the "Alaric." Mr. Wise no doubt will be perfectly willing to confirm the above, if necessary. He wished very much to buy the "Alaric" as his has no cover & is not quite (tho' very near) as large, & it of course has no presentation inscription! Should Mr. Wise find a purchaser for <u>his</u> copy he will no doubt be still in the market for this very remarkable copy, & should your customer decline, perhaps you can, between you, negotiate the matter.

Whether or not the Ashley Library copy is genuine is open to question; Wise never secured a copy in wrappers. The Clemens library was dispersed at Parke-Bernet in New York, in 1945, where this copy was sold for $400. It was acquired at the sale, or shortly afterward, by Halsted Billings Vander Poel (1911–2003), a collector whose taste for rare books was shaped by Chauncey Brewster Tinker at Yale, whence he had graduated in 1935. We made several attempts in the 1990s to persuade Mr. Vander Poel to part with his *Alaric at Rome*; he was friendly, but evasive. In the end it was necessary to wait for the sale of his library at Christie's London in 2004.

488. Arnold, Matthew. Cromwell: a prize poem, recited in the Theatre, Oxford; June 28, 1843. Oxford: printed and published by J. Vincent, 1843. 8vo, original tan printed wrappers.

Arnold's second publication. Acquired in 1979.

489. [Arnold, Matthew.] The strayed reveller, and other poems. By A. London: B. Fellowes, 1849. 8vo, original green cloth.

> Arnold's first collection of poems, printed in an edition of five hundred copies. This one is inscribed on the front flyleaf, "From the author." The inscription is not in Arnold's hand, and no doubt originated with the publisher. Also on the same flyleaf is the signature of Archer Gurney (1820–1887), dated August 1854. Gurney was a Church of England clergyman who wrote many hymns and published a number of verse plays and other collections of poetry. Acquired in 1975.

490. [Arnold, Matthew.] Empedocles on Etna, and other poems. By A. London: B. Fellowes, 1852. 8vo, original gray-green cloth.

> Arnold's second book of poems. With the bookplate of Humphry and Mary Ward (the novelist). The H. Bradley Martin copy. Acquired in 1990.

491. Arnold, Matthew. Poems. . . . Second series. London: Longman, Brown, Green, and Longmans, 1855. 8vo, original green cloth.

> This copy is inscribed by the publishers, "From the author" on the front flyleaf; in fact this is the copy Arnold asked to have sent to his brother Walter Arnold, who has signed the title page. With the book label of John Sparrow. Acquired in 1992.

492. Arnold, Matthew. Merope. A tragedy. London: Longman, Brown, Green, Longmans & Roberts, 1858. 8vo, original dark green cloth.

> This copy is inscribed by Arnold on the half-title, "With the author's most affectionate regards, Dec. 1857." The recipient was Arnold's father-in-law, Sir William Wightman, whose penciled initials are just above the inscription; on the front flyleaf is the signature (1883) of Alice E. F. Benson, Arnold's niece (the daughter of one of his wife's sisters). Arnold first met his future wife, Frances Lucy ("Flu") Wightman, at a party. As a young man at Oxford he was both frivolous and flamboyant, and he kept the serious side of his nature well hidden. He fell in love with Wightman, but her parents were opposed to any notion of marriage to someone without prospects of a lucrative career; they took their daughter to the Continent, and told Arnold to stay away. He followed, however, and in time became an acceptable suitor, particularly after his appointment as Inspector of Schools; the couple wed in 1851, and the marriage proved a happy one. Arnold and his wife lived with the Wightmans for seven years. He traveled frequently with his

father-in-law in the course of his duties as a judge, and acted on occasion as his marshal. The two men became very close, and maintained excellent relations until Sir William's death in 1863. Acquired in 1999.

493. Arnold, Matthew. The popular education of France: with notices of that of Holland and Switzerland. London: Longman, Green, Longman, and Roberts, 1861. 8vo, original green cloth.

> Inscribed on the half-title, "With the Author's regards." The inscription is in Arnold's hand. Acquired in 1977.

494. Arnold, Matthew. On translating Homer. Three lectures given at Oxford. London: Longman, Green, Longman, and Roberts, 1861. 8vo, original dark green cloth.

> The first of Arnold's two books severely criticizing the unrhymed metrical translations of F. W. Newman (Cardinal Newman's brother). This copy is inscribed by Arnold on the half-title, "With the Author's affectionate regards, Jan. 31st, 1861." The recipient has not been identified, but was undoubtedly a member of his wife's family, possibly his father-in-law, Sir William Wightman (see above, no. 492); on the front flyleaf is the signature of Arnold's niece Alice E. F. Benson and the date 1883. Acquired in 1999.

495. Arnold, Matthew. On translating Homer: last words. A lecture given at Oxford. London: Longman, Green, Longman, and Roberts, 1862. 8vo, original green cloth.

> This copy is inscribed by Arnold on a front flyleaf: "J. M. F. from M. A. March, 1862." The recipient was Jane Martha Forster, née Arnold. "Of the girls, Jane, the oldest child and Matthew's famous sister, the beloved 'K,' was intelligent and well educated; a strong partisan of liberalism, she was the wife of William Forster, a Quaker manufacturer who played a prominent part as a liberal member of Parliament and was associated with Matthew as a proponent of popular education."–Lionel Trilling, *Matthew Arnold* (1939). Acquired in 1985.

496. Arnold, Matthew. Essays in criticism. London: and Cambridge: Macmillan and Co., 1865. 8vo, original red-brown cloth.

> This key title was somewhat flimsily produced, and it is difficult to find in acceptable state. This copy has the book label of Michael Sadleir, whose eye for condition was keen. Acquired in 1975.

497. Arnold, Matthew. Culture and anarchy: an essay in political and social criticism. London: Smith, Elder and Co., 1869. 8vo, original brown beveled cloth.

> Matthew Arnold's most important prose work, a plea for high culture in a society he viewed as materialistic and self-satisfied. This is another title difficult to find in acceptable condition; the text block is rather heavy for a book of this size, and the inner hinges have a tendency to break. This fine copy has an inscription on the blank flyleaf facing the title page from Wordsworth Donisthorpe to his cousin Mary Flower Donisthorpe, dated August 9, 1871. Wordsworth Donisthorpe (1847–1913) was an anarchist, inventor, pioneer of cinematography, and chess enthusiast (cofounder of the British Chess Association in 1885). Acquired in 2000.

498. Arnold, Matthew. Friendship's garland: being the conversations, letters, and opinions of the late Arminius, Baron von Thunder-Ten-Tronkh. Collected and edited, with a dedicatory letter to Adolescens Leo, Esq., of "The Daily Telegraph." London: Smith, Elder and Co., 1871. 8vo, original white cloth.

> A curious book, humorous in form, but seriously intended to advocate a scientific method of dealing with political and public affairs. The baron's name is from Voltaire's *Candide*. This is an evocative presentation copy, inscribed on the title page in Arnold's hand, "Thos. Hughes, from his old schoolfellow." The recipient is famous for his *Tom Brown's Schooldays*, first published in 1857. This was set at Rugby School, where Arnold's father, Dr. Thomas Arnold, was headmaster, and perhaps the most widely known English schoolmaster of the nineteenth century. Arnold and Hughes were in fact "schoolfellows" at both Rugby and Oxford. With the later bookplate of the Arthur Hughes Memorial Section of the library of the Beccles Working-Men's Co-operative Association; Arthur Hughes was the son of Thomas Hughes. Acquired in 1983.

499. Arnold, Matthew. Poems. . . . New and complete edition. London: Macmillan and Co., 1877. Two vols., 8vo, original bright green cloth.

> Second collected edition, preceded by the smaller-format collected edition of 1869; after eight years only one new poem was added, as Arnold had largely abandoned the writing of poetry. This set is inscribed by Arnold on the first half-title, "To Georgina Wightman, with every affectionate wish for her birthday of 1877, M. A." The recipient was his wife's unmarried

youngest sister, who was a devoted aunt to Arnold's children; beneath the inscription is the signature of Arnold's niece Alice E. F. Benson, dated 1883. Acquired in 1999.

500. Arnold, Matthew. Selected poems. London: Macmillan and Co., 1878. 8vo, original blue cloth.

One of 250 copies printed on large paper. With the bookplate of E. H. Firth, of Winchester. Acquired in 1982.

501. Arnold, Matthew. Selected poems. London: Macmillan and Co., 1878. Sm. 8vo, original dark blue cloth.

A copy on ordinary paper, issued as a volume in the Golden Treasury series. This copy is inscribed by Arnold on the front flyleaf, "F. E. Nicholls, from M. A." The recipient was probably a Miss Nicholls, who was a friend of Arnold's sister Susy. Acquired in 1999.

502. Arnold, Matthew, editor. Wordsworth, William. Poems of Wordsworth: chosen and edited by Matthew Arnold. London: Macmillan and Co., 1880. Sm. 8vo, original dark blue cloth.

A reprint, with additions, of a book first published in 1879. This selection of Wordsworth's poetry, with a long and important preface by Arnold, was published as a volume in the Golden Treasury series. This copy is inscribed by Arnold on the front flyleaf, "To Georgina, with every affectionate wish for March the 7th, 1880. M. A." The recipient was Georgina Wightman (see no. 499); the occasion of this gift was almost certainly her birthday. Below the inscription is the signature of Arnold's niece Alice E. F. Benson, dated 1883. Acquired in 1999.

503. Arnold, Matthew, editor. Byron, George Gordon, Lord. Poetry of Byron: chosen and arranged by Matthew Arnold. London: Macmillan and Co., 1881. Sm. 8vo, original dark blue cloth.

Published as a volume in the Golden Treasury series. This copy is inscribed by Arnold on the fly-title to the preface, "With every good wish, M. A." The recipient was no doubt Alice E. F. Benson, Arnold's niece, who has added her signature, dated 1883, below the inscription. Acquired in 1999.

504. Arnold, Matthew. Discourses in America. London: Macmillan and Co., 1885. 8vo, original dark green cloth.

This copy has a special engraved leaf tipped in at the front, reading, "From the Author." The recipient was John Edwin Eddison (1842–1929), a distinguished professor of medicine at the University of Leeds, who has signed and dated (June 1885) the verso of the half-title. Laid in is a three-page letter from Arnold, addressed to Dr. Eddison on May 29, 1885, and reading in part: "You were to have the American discourses, were you not? They will be out in a few days, and you shall have them." The rest of the letter refers to the possibility of a farewell banquet for the American writer James Russell Lowell, who had been serving as ambassador in London ("You could not come to a worse person than me to promote a 'banquet'; I hate the thing so cordially"). Acquired in 1984.

505. Arnold, Matthew. Essays in criticism. Second series. London and New York: Macmillan and Co., 1888. 8vo, original dark blue cloth.

This collection of nine essays was the last ever assembled by Arnold, who died shortly before its publication; included are chapters on Milton, Gray, Keats, Wordsworth, Byron, Shelley, and Tolstoy. This copy is inscribed (but not signed) by Matthew Arnold's wife, "To dear Tiny in loving remembrance, November, 1888." The recipient was almost certainly one of Matthew Arnold's nieces, probably a daughter of his wife's sister Mary Henrietta Benson. Acquired in 1999.

EDWARD FITZGERALD (1809–1883)

506. [FitzGerald, Edward.] Euphranor: a dialogue on youth. London: William Pickering, 1851. 8vo, original green cloth.

FitzGerald's first book, preceded only by a long memoir contributed to a collected edition of the poems and letters of his friend Bernard Barton (no. 279). "A philosophical dialogue about education in which he argued for a balance between academic and athletic pursuits."—*Oxford DNB*. With the book label of Willis Vickery. Acquired in 1981.

507. [FitzGerald, Edward, editor.] Polonius: a collection of wise saws and modern instances. London: William Pickering, 1852. Sq. 8vo, original light green cloth.

FitzGerald's second book, a collection of aphorisms from a variety of sources. This copy is inscribed on the front pastedown, "Gerald FitzGerald from the compiler Edward FitzGerald." The recipient was presumably a relative,

278

but he has not been identified. Facing the title page is a manuscript note in Edward FitzGerald's hand, signed with initials: "The part of Hamlet was omitted from Polonius: I mean, Michel de Montaigne, of whom I have added a few commentaries. A little collection of aphorisms from him (Paris 1783) is one of the few books of the sort I have found readable." FitzGerald has also added a French quotation from Montaigne at the foot of p. 136. Acquired in 1991.

508. FitzGerald, Edward. Six dramas of Calderon. Freely translated by Edward FitzGerald. London: William Pickering, 1853. 8vo, original rose cloth.

With the signature on the front flyleaf of G. E. Woodberry, dated 1884. Acquired in 1974.

509. [FitzGerald, Edward.] Euphranor. A dialogue on youth. London: John W. Parker and Son, 1855. Sm. 8vo, sewn, as issued.

Second edition, much revised and enlarged. Included for the first time is a reference to Tennyson on p. 72, and the ballad "Our Yorkshire Jen." This copy was formerly the property of the great-granddaughter of FitzGerald's housekeeper at Little Grange. Acquired in 1984.

510. [FitzGerald, Edward.] Rubáiyát of Omar Khayyám, the astronomer-poet of Persia. Translated into English verse. London: Bernard Quaritch, 1859. 4to, original tan printed wrappers.

This famous poem was published anonymously in an edition of 250 copies; it did not sell well at first, and some copies were remaindered and others destroyed. FitzGerald was not publicly identified as the author until his name appeared in a Quaritch advertisement in 1875; he was upset at the disclosure. As in most copies, there is a manuscript correction by FitzGerald on p. 4. This remained for many years a frustrating gap in the collection. Copies came on the market with some frequency, but were always either too expensive or not in good condition. This one was finally acquired from the library of Mrs. J. Insley Blair, sold at Sotheby's New York on December 3, 2004.

511. [FitzGerald, Edward.] The mighty magician. [Bungay: 1865.] 8vo, original gray wrappers.

Two further plays translated from the Spanish of Calderón; the second, with its own fly-title, is "Such Stuff as Dreams Are Made Of." FitzGerald wrote in a letter that he had one hundred copies of this book printed, for distribution to friends; it was issued without a proper title page. H. Buxton Forman's copy, with his bookplate, and his penciled initials and date of acquisition. Acquired in 1987.

512. [FitzGerald, Edward.] The two generals. N.p.: n.d. [1868?]. 4to, blue morocco, by Roger de Coverly.

Two original poems, one on Lucius Aemilius Paullus, the other on Sir Charles Napier. They were issued by FitzGerald for circulation to a small number of friends; according to the British Library Catalogue, the print run was twenty-five. The date of printing of this six-page quarto is uncertain. This copy has the bookplate of the poet and essayist Edmund Gosse. On the front flyleaf, Gosse has written, "I think that this is the rarest of all FitzGerald's issues." Tipped in is a three-page letter to Gosse dated May 21, 1893, from W. Aldis Wright, who edited various volumes of FitzGerald's literary remains between 1889 and 1903; the letter discusses in detail the date and origin of these two poems. Acquired in 1975.

513. [FitzGerald, Edward.] Agamemnon. A tragedy, taken from Aeschylus. N.p.: n.d. [1869]. 8vo, original bright blue wrappers.

Privately printed in a small number of copies. This copy contains ten autograph alterations by FitzGerald, ranging from a change in punctuation to the revision of a full line to the deletion of an entire paragraph. Acquired in 1984.

514. [FitzGerald, Edward.] Salámán and Absál. An allegory. From the Persian of Jámi. Ipswich: Cowell's Steam Printing Works, 1871. 4to, original tan wrappers.

Second edition, greatly revised, and privately printed in a small number of copies; first printed in 1856. This copy was formerly the property of the great-granddaughter of FitzGerald's housekeeper at Little Grange (see also no. 509). Acquired in 1984.

515. [FitzGerald, Edward.] Readings in Crabbe's 'Tales of the Hall.' [Guildford: 1879.] 8vo, original dark green pebbled cloth.

Privately printed in a small edition. The text consists of lines from Crabbe's poem, interspersed with FitzGerald's prose commentary. This copy is inscribed by FitzGerald to Mary Crabbe, the poet's granddaughter. With the later signature of John Drinkwater, poet and bibliophile. Acquired in 1975.

516. [FitzGerald, Edward.] The downfall and death of King Œdipus. A drama in two parts. Chiefly taken from the Œdipus Tyrannus and Colonæus of Sophocles. The interact choruses are from Potter. [Guildford: 1880–81.] 8vo, original dark blue wrappers.

> FitzGerald's last publication (aside from revisions). This book was printed in two stages. Part 1 appeared in February 1880; the second part, containing a preface addressed to Charles Eliot Norton and signed with the pseudonym "Littlegrange" was printed in February of the following year. The print run for both parts was fifty copies. Tipped in at the front is an autograph letter from FitzGerald to a Mr. S[palding?]. Acquired in 1975.

517. [FitzGerald, Edward.] Euphranor, a May-day conversation at Cambridge. "'Tis forty years since." [Guildford: 1882.] 8vo, original pale green wrappers, dark green cloth spine.

Third edition, privately printed in an edition of fifty copies. This is a revised version of an essay first published in 1851 (no. 506), and reprinted, in an enlarged version, in 1855 (no. 509). This copy is inscribed by FitzGerald on the front flyleaf, "Charles Keene, from his friend Little Grange." Little Grange was the name of FitzGerald's house in Woodbridge. Of particular interest are the manuscript changes made by FitzGerald on half a dozen pages, the most important of which are alterations on p. 10, where he has deleted seven lines, and added a new version at the top of the page. With Keene's bookplate. Laid in is a letter from Charles Ganz of the Cockerel Press to the poet Siegfried Sassoon. Acquired in 1977.

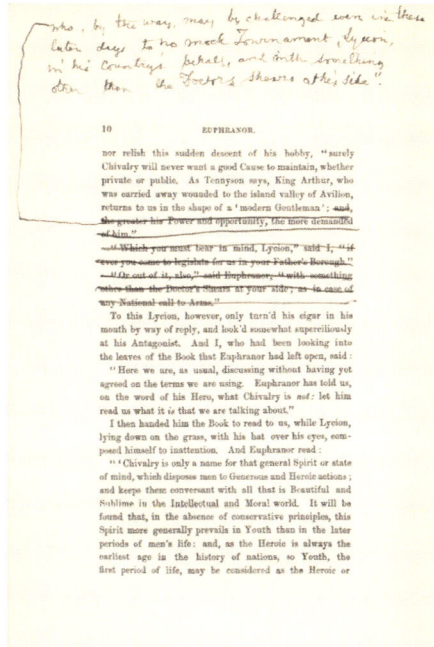

ITEM 517

518. [FitzGerald, Edward.] Readings in Crabbe. "Tales of the Hall." London: Bernard Quaritch, 1882. 8vo, original blue cloth (a bit rubbed).

> A reissue of the edition of 1879 (no. 515), with a new preface. Surviving

records indicate that fifty-six copies of the preface were printed, and that FitzGerald sent about forty of these to Quaritch. Laid into this copy is a one-page autograph letter of Crabbe, dated January 8, 1829. With the book label of Willis Vickery. Acquired in 1981.

COVENTRY PATMORE (1823–1896)

519. Patmore, Coventry. Poems. London: Edward Moxon, 1844. Sm. 8vo, polished calf, by Root.

> The author's first book. Siegfried Sassoon's copy, with his monogram book label. Acquired in 2007.

520. [Patmore, Coventry.] The angel in the house: the betrothal. London: John W. Parker and Son, 1854. [Bound with:] The espousals. London: John W. Parker and Son, 1856. Two vols. in one, sm. 8vo, contemporary black morocco, gilt, with the name of Julia Margaret Cameron stamped in gilt on the front cover, edges gilt and gauffered.

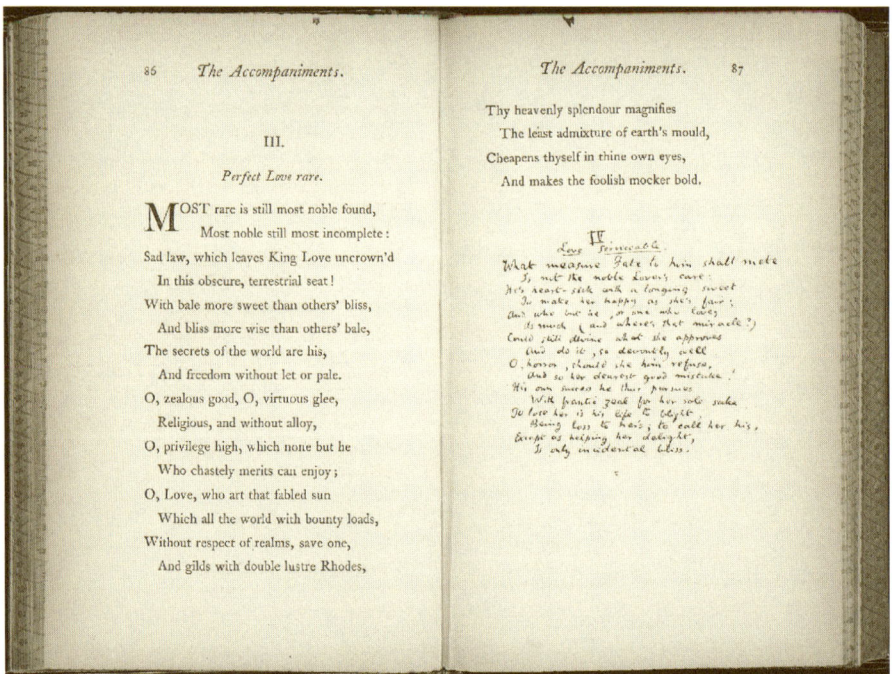

ITEM 520

This is a remarkable copy of Patmore's most famous book, inscribed by him on the first title page to Julia Margaret Cameron, a close friend of Tennyson and one of the most famous Victorian photographers. In addition, Patmore has made important manuscript additions and revisions throughout the text. In the first part, he has added a four-line stanza on p. 33, eight lines on p. 35, eight lines on p. 59, sixteen lines on p. 87, five lines on pp. 104–5, four lines on p. 114, twelve lines on p. 120, and four lines on p. 176. In the second part, he has added sixteen lines ("The Kites") on p. 12, four lines on p. 114, four lines on p. 128, four lines on p. 142, thirty-two lines ("Love-Charm") on p. 152, four lines on p. 159, and eight lines on p. 168. No correspondence survives between Patmore and Julia Cameron, but he must have come to know her when he became a member of Tennyson's circle in the 1850s. Patmore constantly revised his poem over the years. Many of the insertions in this copy can be found in the final version, published in 1878, usually reworked and repositioned, but other lines, both printed and manuscript, were omitted. With the book label of Arthur A. Houghton, and acquired at his sale at Christie's London in 1980.

521. Patmore, Coventry. Faithful for ever. London: John W. Parker and Son, 1860. 8vo, original purple cloth.

This copy is signed on the title page by Emily Patmore, the author's wife, and his "angel in the house." One five-page passage has been crossed out in pencil, possibly as an expression of Patmore's dissatisfaction with it. Acquired in 1977.

522. [Patmore, Coventry.] Odes. [Not published.] [London: 1868.] 8vo, original pale blue printed wrappers.

The metrical experiments that characterize these nine poems shaped the course of Patmore's later career, and exerted a significant influence on a number of major writers, especially Gerard Manley Hopkins. Only 250 copies of this small book were printed, and of these Patmore seems to have destroyed about a hundred. This copy is inscribed on the preliminary printed presentation leaf ("From the Author"), "To Denis Florence MacCarthy, Esq. C. Patmore, March 31, 1870." Laid in is the front portion of the original mailing envelope; the recipient was an Irish poet of some note. Acquired in 1984.

523. Patmore, Coventry. The unknown Eros. I–XLVI. London: George Bell and Sons, 1878. Sm. 4to, original purple cloth, printed paper label.

The second issue of the first edition, greatly expanded and revised; a shorter version had appeared anonymously the year before. H. Buxton Forman's copy, with his bookplate, initials, and the following note, dated March 13, 1879: "For this edition it would seem that the sheets of the 1st edition are used with cancels for the bulk of the book, pp. 1–126. The fly-title is the same; but the title and contents are new, as also pp. 127 to 210. The object seems to have been to get rid of Ode XXXI, '1877,' of the 1st ed. and the two miscellaneous poems, and to add more Odes. (Patmore's real motive in this manipulation was to avoid reviews. He smuggled the new Odes into the edition and thus escaped the notices of a new Work)." With the book label of Joseph L. Lilienthal. Acquired in 1986.

524. Patmore, Coventry. Amelia. N.p. [London]: 1878. 4to, original white printed wrappers.

A privately published twelve-page quarto. There is no statement of limitation here, but the press run is commonly said to have been twenty-five copies; the poem was reprinted later the same year as the first piece in a regularly published collection. Laid into this copy is a two-page letter from John Louis Garvin (signed "Garve") to "my dear Molly," dated March 23, 1921, which reads in part: "Within the covers I have kept the book intact just as I got it and as Coventry Patmore left it when he did 25 for the private pleasure of his own fastidious eye and for a very few friends. This was one of half a dozen or so that he never gave away." Garvin (1868–1947) was the influential editor of *The Observer*, and a friend of Patmore's later years. Acquired in 2008.

525. Patmore, Coventry. Amelia, Tamerton church-tower, etc. With prefatory study on English metrical law. London: George Bell and Sons, 1878. 8vo, original purple cloth, printed paper label.

H. Buxton Forman's copy, with his bookplate, initials, and penciled notes; he has annotated the table of contents with dates of composition. With the book label of Joseph L. Lilienthal. Acquired in 1986.

526. Patmore, Coventry. Florilegium amantis. Edited by Richard Garnett. London: George Bell & Sons, n.d. [1879]. Sm. 8vo, original gray-purple cloth, printed paper label.

A selection of Patmore's poetry, as chosen by his friend Richard Garnett, poet, essayist, and writer on Shelley. This copy is inscribed on the front flyleaf to the editor's wife, "Mrs. Garnett, with the kind regards of Coventry Patmore. March 30, 1879." Inserted is an important one-page letter from Patmore that clearly accompanied the book, and includes the following: "Will you ask your husband to insert, in all his copies, the word which I have inserted in yours, p. 71? It's [*sic*] accidental omission ruins one of the best passages in the best poem in the book." The poem in question is "The Day after Tomorrow." Acquired in 1983.

527. Patmore, Coventry. The unknown Eros. London: George Bell and Sons, n.d. [1879]. 8vo, original quarter roan and maroon cloth.

The revised text of a series of poems first published in 1877–78, regularly issued as part of a four-volume collected edition of Patmore's poems, but here bound as a separate book. This copy is inscribed on the half-title from Patmore to H. Buxton Forman; the inscription is dated November 1, 1888. With Buxton Forman's penciled note, dated the same day: "Mr. Patmore tells me that of this rearranged edition only 50 copies were printed as a separate book, and that none were sold apart from the 4 volume edition of his poems." With the book label of Joseph L. Lilienthal. Acquired in 1986.

528. Patmore, Marianne Caroline and Coventry, translators. Saint Bernard on the love of God. London: Burns and Oates, 1884. 8vo, original dark blue cloth, printed paper label.

Second edition; first published in 1881. The first part of the translation here is by Patmore's second wife (of three), who was a Catholic convert from a wealthy Gloucestershire family, and something of a nun in residence; when she died, he finished the text. This copy is inscribed on the half-title from Patmore to H. Buxton Forman, who has added the following note: "Of the first edition, C. P. says, about 500 out of 750 were burnt at Kegan Paul's." Acquired in 1986.

529. Patmore, Coventry. The rod, the root, and the flower. London: George Bell and Sons, 1895. Sm. 8vo, original olive green cloth, printed paper label.

The poet's last book, published a year before his death; the text is a collection of aphorisms and short essays. This copy is inscribed by Patmore on the front flyleaf to H. Buxton Forman. Acquired in 1986.

DANTE GABRIEL ROSSETTI (1828–1882)

530. Rossetti, Dante Gabriel. Sir Hugh the Heron. A legendary tale, in four parts. By Gabriel Rossetti, Junior. London: G. Polidori's Private Press, 15 Park Village East, Regent's Park, 1843. (For private circulation only.) 4to, turquoise morocco, by Macdonald (New York), original plain green wrappers bound in.

> Rossetti's first book, written for the most part when he was twelve, but not completed for another two years, when it was printed by his grandfather, Gaetano Polidori, on his small private press. Rossetti appears to have modeled his poem on the romances of Walter Scott; he later described this juvenile effort as "absurd trash." How many copies of this twenty-four-page quarto were printed is not known. Whatever the number, many of them ended up in the hands of his brother, William Michael Rossetti, who records that "he once got me to destroy a rather considerable stock of copies which remained." In June 1889, William Michael Rossetti replied to a request for a copy from T. J. Wise, saying that he no longer had one to dispose of; about ten days later he wrote again to Wise that in fact three further copies had turned up, in stitched sheets without wrappers. The earliest distributed copies were bound in either pink or green plain wrappers. In this copy the title of the poem has been written in pencil on the front wrapper, in a slightly juvenile hand (Rossetti's?). With the leather book label on the front silk endpaper of Judge Willis Vickery, whose collection was sold at auction in 1933. Later armorial bookplate on the verso of this leaf of Jean S. Arthur (1915–1963) and A. Watson Armour III (1908–1991), a socially prominent Chicago couple. This copy, surprisingly, turned up in Germany, where it was acquired in 2007.

531. [Rossetti, Dante Gabriel.] Hand and soul. [Colophon:] London: Strangeways and Walder, printers, n.d. [1869]. 12mo, original buff printed wrappers, neatly sewn into limp green cloth, with manuscript material, and laid into nineteenth-century flexible calf wallet-style wrappers.

> A privately printed edition of a story that had first appeared in *The Germ* in 1850; according to Wise, the print run was one hundred copies. The text was set in type for a projected edition of Rossetti's poems, but was excluded from that book in 1870. This copy was sent by William Michael Rossetti to an admirer of his family, Louisa Summerbell. Bound in are five interesting letters he wrote between 1896 and 1906, in which he discusses at length both Dante Gabriel and Christina, the publication of their works, various

biographies that had appeared, and more. The second letter mentions sending this copy as a souvenir. Acquired in 1987.

532. Rossetti, Dante Gabriel. Poems. London: F. S. Ellis, 1870. 8vo, blue morocco, by Riviere.

A 260-page proof copy, privately printed, of Rossetti's major book of verse, which was regularly published later the same year. Rossetti spent a considerable amount of time assembling this volume, and in the course of 1869–70 printed up so-called trial books, which he showed to friends. Of the first of these, undated but printed in 1869, there are two issues, the first with 199 pages and the other with 231 pages. This second version includes eight new poems. "Troy Town" and "Eden Bower" were very recent compositions, and the other six poems, according to his brother, must have been recovered from Dante Gabriel's wife's coffin, exhumed in October 1869. As finally published, the book had 282 pages, and contained one further poem ("The Stream's Secret"); in addition, the order of the contents was rearranged. From the library of Jerome Kern, sold at auction in 1929. Acquired in 1996.

533. Rossetti, Dante Gabriel. Poems. London: F. S. Ellis, 1870. 8vo, original white linen cloth.

This is one of twenty-five large-paper copies printed for private circulation on special Whatman's handmade paper; the binding, though clearly original, is somewhat different from that described by Wise (blue paper boards, with a white spine). With the book label of the British artist George Abraham Crawley (1864–1926). Acquired in 1978.

534. Rossetti, Dante Gabriel. The poems. . . . With illustrations from his own pictures and designs. Edited with an introduction and notes by W. M. Rossetti. London: Ellis & Elvey, 1904. Two vols., 4to, original vellum.

An important collected edition, the first to be illustrated with Rossetti's own pictures; many poems are included for the first time. This set is one of thirty numbered copies on large paper, with the plates on Japan vellum. Acquired in 1971.

535. Rossetti, Dante Gabriel. The ballad of Jan van Hunks. London: printed for private circulation only, 1912. 8vo, original light brown printed wrappers.

Rossetti completed this poem just before he died and gave the manuscript to Theodore Watts-Dunton, who lived at The Pines with Swinburne. Watts-Dunton kept the manuscript as one of his treasured possessions until the summer of 1909, shortly after Swinburne's death, when he sold it to T. J. Wise. This pamphlet, however, was published by Watts-Dunton in an edition of thirty copies. Acquired in 1980.

Rossettiana

536. Caine, T. Hall. Recollections of Dante Gabriel Rossetti. London: Elliot Stock, 1882. 8vo, original dark green cloth.

The first biography of Rossetti, written by a young man who went on to become a successful novelist. Hall Caine (1853–1931) had formed a close friendship with Rossetti; from 1881 until the poet's death in 1882, he lived at Rossetti's house and worked as his secretary. Acquired in 1981.

CHRISTINA GEORGINA ROSSETTI (1830–1894)

537. Rossetti, Christina. Verses. . . . Dedicated to her mother. London: privately printed at G. Polidori's, No. 15, Park Village East, Regent's Park, 1847. Sm. 8vo, green morocco, by Riviere.

Christina Rossetti's first book; she wrote the poems between the ages of twelve and sixteen. Most surviving copies of this little book come from a family cache preserved in sheets, in the possession of William Michael Rossetti; this may well have been one of them. Tipped in is an autograph letter,

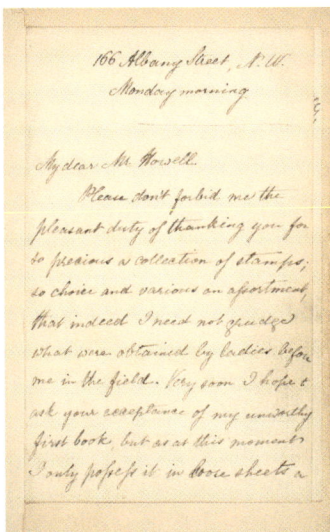

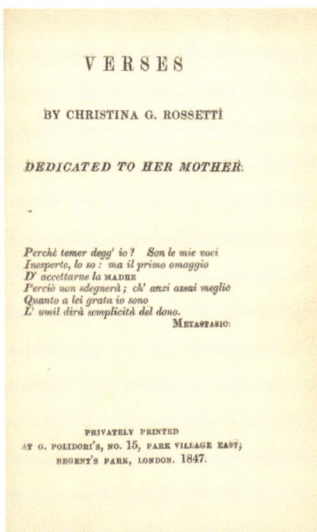

ITEM
537

written by the author in the mid-1860s to a somewhat disreputable art "agent" named Charles Augustus Howell, who had attached himself to the Rossetti family. The letter begins, "Please don't forbid me the pleasant duty of thanking you for so precious a collection of stamps." Acquired in 1972.

538. Rossetti, Christina. The prince's progress: and other poems. London: Macmillan and Co., 1866. Sm. 8vo, original green cloth.

The wood-engraved frontispiece and title page were both designed by Dante Gabriel Rossetti and executed by W. J. Linton. Acquired in 1993.

539. Rossetti, Christina. Sing-song. A nursery rhyme book. . . . With one hundred and twenty illustrations by Arthur Hughes. Engraved by the brothers Dalziel. London: George Routledge and Sons, 1872. Sq. 12mo, original green cloth.

One of the most successful of all Victorian books of poetry for children. This copy is inscribed by the author on the front flyleaf, "Holman Stephens with C. G. R.'s love." The recipient was the three-year-old son of the Pre-Raphaelite painter and art critic Frederic George Stephens. Tipped in is a two-page letter dated December 28, 1871, which reads: "My dear Holly, Please thank your Papa for his kind note,–and thank you very much for the portrait which in a way brings your little face before me though it shows me no pink or blue or yellow. My love to your Mamma." Inserted with the letter is an autograph poem, also written for the recipient: "Common Holly bears a berry / To make the Xmas Robins merry:– / Golden Holly bears a rose, / Unfolding at October's close / To cheer an old Friend's eyes and nose." Also tipped in at the end is a one-page fragment of a manuscript by Christina Rossetti; the subject is Saint Mark; the leaf is possibly from one of the devotional books she wrote toward the end of her life. From the library of Jerome Kern, sold at auction in New York in 1929. Acquired in 1976.

540. Rossetti, Christina. A pageant and other poems. London: Macmillan and Co., 1881. 8vo, original dark blue cloth.

This copy has the bookplate of the artist and poet William Bell Scott. Scott's meeting with Dante Gabriel Rossetti in 1847 led to his being accepted as a Pre-Raphaelite, though Swinburne later described Scott's relationship with the Rossettis as "parasitical." By the time he acquired this volume, Scott was seventy; he appears not to have read a word of it, as the volume is entirely unopened. The Simon Nowell-Smith copy. Acquired in 2002.

WILLIAM EDMONSTOUNE AYTOUN (1813–1865)

541. [Aytoun, William Edmonstoune.] Poland, Homer, and other poems. London: Longman, Rees, Orme, Brown, Green, & Longman; and Adam Black (Edinburgh), 1832. Sm. 8vo, contemporary half calf.

> The author's first book, published when he was twenty-one. Among the "other poems" here is a long "lament" for Shelley. Aytoun published little more in the way of verse until the 1840s, when he embarked on a poetical career that made him one of Scotland's most popular writers; he acquired a reputation for both humorous poetry and Scottish ballads. From the library of the Society of Writers to the Signet. Acquired in 1980.

542. [Aytoun, William Edmonstoune.] Firmilian: or the student of Badajoz. A spasmodic tragedy. By T. Percy Jones [pseud.]. Edinburgh and London: William Blackwood and Sons, 1854. 8vo, original red and black marbled moiré cloth.

> A parody of the so-called Spasmodic School of poetry, as practiced by such writers as Philip James Bailey (especially in *Festus*), Richard Hengist Horne, Sydney Dobell, and Alexander Smith. The spoof was so successful that it was taken by some as a serious poem, but in the end it achieved its purpose of exposing to ridicule the excesses of some of Aytoun's contemporaries. This copy is signed by Aytoun on the half-title, using his pseudonym, "T. Percy Jones," and dated Kirkwall, 1854. Evidently Aytoun gave away several copies on this occasion, as the unidentified recipient of this one has copied a twelve-line dedicatory poem onto the back flyleaf, with an explanation: "The following sonnet was written by the author at Kirkwall on the night of Monday 11th Sept. 1854 on the copy of the tragedy belonging to David Balfour of Balfour." Acquired in 1981.

PHILIP JAMES BAILEY (1816–1902)

543. Bailey, Philip James. Festus. A poem. London: William Pickering, 1839. 8vo, Victorian maroon morocco.

> The author's first book, an interminable but exceedingly popular reworking of the Faust legend. Acquired in 1976.

544. Bailey, Philip James. The age; a colloquial satire. London: Chapman and Hall, 1858. 8vo, original blue cloth.

> Bailey's fourth book, a three-way conversation in verse involving the author, a critic, and a friend. This copy is inscribed on the title page from the author to his son. Acquired in 1976.

WILLIAM BARNES (1801–1886)

545. Barnes, William. Orra: a Lapland tale. Dorchester: printed by J. Criswick, 1822. 8vo, half rose morocco, original drab wrappers bound in.

> The author's second publication; preceded by his *Poetical Pieces* of 1820, also printed in Dorchester. Barnes's first two books are both very rare. Of the first no copy is located in either WorldCat or Copac. Of this second work the only copy located is in the British Library. The text of this narrative poem is embellished with a number of small wood engravings. These are in fact by Barnes himself, who had recently learned to make such illustrations, at the age of about twenty; preserved at the end is an integral leaf of advertisements, in which Barnes speaks of "having taught himself the arts of copper & wood engraving, and drawing," and offers his services as an illustrator, with "likenesses taken in pencil, at from 7s 6d to 10s 6d each; and correct drawings made of antiquities, architecture, curiosities, &c." This leaf does not seem to have been preserved in the British Library copy. Bound into the present copy is a charming trade card, in which a young man (presumably this is a self-portrait) is seated with his elbow on a headstone inscribed "W. Barnes, engraver, Dorchester"; this must be very rare indeed. Also bound in is a fine three-page letter, dated Dorchester, August 18, 1846, from Barnes to Charles Tomlinson (1808–1897), a writer on science and chess, who had just sent Barnes one of his own books. In this letter Barnes speaks of his first volume of poetry in the Dorset dialect (1844), and of his new collection of poems:
>
> I wish I could believe myself half as worthy of your very encouraging praise, as I am deserving of much more than your corrective criticism. I am only unexpectedly happy to find that my rustic verse has recommended itself to cultivated minds, as it was first written for the poet's corner of a provincial newspaper, to engage the attention of our West Saxon farmers' sons and dairymaids. Inasmuch as my poems are on subjects of rural life, they may put a reader in mind of Burns's, though I never wrote any of them with him before me as a model. You will most likely wonder to hear me say that I have followed, in some of them, and in more of a small volume of English

poems which I have just published, a principle or two which I fancy I have discovered in Homer.

> The Simon Nowell-Smith copy. Acquired in 2002.

546. Barnes, William. A few words on the advantages of a more common adoption of the mathematics as a branch of education or subject of study. London: Whittaker and Co.; Clark (Dorchester); Thomas (Weymouth); Shipp (Blandford); Abraham (Wimborne); Sydenham (Poole); Toll (Sherborne); Tucker (Bridport); and all other booksellers, 1834. 12mo, original green printed wrappers.

> One of a number of pamphlets published by Barnes in his capacity as a schoolmaster. Acquired in 1972.

547. Barnes, William. A mathematical investigation of the principle of hanging doors, gates, swing bridges, and other heavy bodies swinging on vertical axes. Dorchester: printed and published by Simonds and Sydenham, 1835. 8vo, original light green wrappers.

> A pamphlet published by Barnes as a promotion for his new school for boys in Durngate, in Dorchester; the last two pages are devoted to an interesting prospectus for the school. This copy has a couple of manuscript corrections to the prospectus, probably by Barnes himself. Acquired in 1972.

548. Barnes, William. Poems, partly of rural life, (in national English). London: J. R. Smith, 1846. 8vo, original rose cloth, printed paper label. Acquired in 1983.

549. Barnes, William. Reading by the Rev. William Barnes, from his Poems in the Dorset Dialect, at Mrs. Charles Tennant's, 2, Richmond Terrace, Whitehall. Friday, June 24th, 1870. [London: J. Russell Smith, 1870.] 8vo, disbound.

> The only copy located is at Princeton. Acquired in 1984.

WILLIAM COX BENNETT (1820–1895)

550. [Bennett, William Cox.] Songs, ballads, &c. Greenwich: printed by Henry S. Richardson, 1845. Sm. 8vo, contemporary half calf.

The author's second book, privately printed; preceded by *My Sonnets*, also privately printed and issued anonymously in Greenwich in 1843. Bennett, the son of a watchmaker, was born and raised in Greenwich, where he took an active interest in political reform. This copy is inscribed on the title page, "T. N. Talfourd, Esqre, with the profound admiration of the writer"; it is also signed by Bennett below the title. The recipient was a poet and judge, and a good friend of Lamb, Coleridge, and Dickens. With the bookplate of the collector Frederick William Cosens (1819–1889), whose library was sold at auction in 1890. Acquired in 1988.

551. Bennett, William Cox. Poems. London: Chapman and Hall, 1850. 8vo, original blue cloth

This copy is inscribed on the title page to Tennyson, "with the profoundest admiration and respect of the author." On p. 221 of the book itself is a laudatory sonnet addressed to Tennyson. Acquired in 1974.

552. Bennett, William Cox. Queen Eleanor's vengeance. And other poems. London: Chapman and Hall, 1857. 8vo, original dark green cloth.

This copy is inscribed by the author on the title page to Edward Robert Bulwer Lytton, who, as "Owen Meredith," became one of the most popular English poets in the second half of the nineteenth century. The recipient evidently did not read much of the book, as it is unopened, save for a few pages at the beginning and end. Acquired in 1980.

553. [Bennett, William Cox.] Prometheus the fire-giver. An attempted restoration of the lost first part of the Promethean trilogy of Æschylus. London: Chatto and Windus, 1877. 8vo, original maroon cloth.

This copy is inscribed on the title page, "Robert Potts Esq. M. A. with all the good wishes from the author W. C. Bennett." The recipient was a mathematician at Cambridge. Acquired in 1983.

EDWARD HENRY BICKERSTETH (1825–1906)

554. [Bickersteth, Edward Henry, wrongly attributed author.] Poems and songs by E. H. B. London: William Pickering, 1848. 8vo, original orange cloth.

Bickersteth was a distinguished Anglican clergyman who served as vicar of Christ Church, Hampstead, for thirty years before being named bishop of Exeter by Gladstone. Aside from his various religious publications, he wrote a great many hymns, and was the author of *Yesterday, To-day, and For Ever* (1866), an imitation of Milton that became enormously popular among religious readers. He did not, however, publish as a young man this substantial volume of sentimental verse, despite the fact that it is attributed to him without comment in the NUC, WorldCat, and Copac, as well as in all editions of the *CBEL*. The poems themselves indicate clearly that the book was written by a woman; included are such verses as "A Mother to a Sleeping Child" and "A Mother to Her Son on His Birthday." The author's sex is confirmed by a presentation inscription in this copy, "To Wm. Waller with the kind regards of the son of the authoress. Kensington, January 3, 1889." To their credit, neither the *DNB* nor the *Oxford DNB* assigns this title to Bickersteth. The true author awaits identification. Acquired in 1986.

Almost thirty years after the preceding paragraph was written, this book was included in an exhibition of selections from the Wachs Collection held at the Special Collections Research Center in the University of Chicago Library (September–December 2015); at the same time, details of this event, along with transcriptions of all the exhibition labels, were posted on the library's website. By a stroke of good fortune the label for *Poems and Songs*, which was similar to the entry above, came to the attention of Angela Phippen, in Sydney, Australia, who immediately got in touch with the library to say that she could identify the author with some certainty. It turns out that Phippen had for some time been engaged in research on the life of the stained-glass artist George Hedgeland, who had been active in England in the 1850s, before emigrating to Australia. During the course of her investigations she had come across a newspaper reference to a window that Hedgeland had designed for a church in Upper Tooting, in southeast London, and that was dedicated in 1856 to Elizabeth Henry Butterworth, the wife of the noted publisher of law books Henry Butterworth (1786–1860). Curiosity led Phippen to an obituary of Butterworth printed in *The Gentleman's Magazine* in February 1861, which includes the following: "Mrs. Butterworth possessed a refined and cultivated intellect, and was a pleasing poetess; a volume of her 'Poems and Songs' published by Pickering, anonymously, in 1848, was noticed with approval at the time in these pages." Now at last, through the miracle of cyberspace, the true identity of "E. H. B." has been recovered.

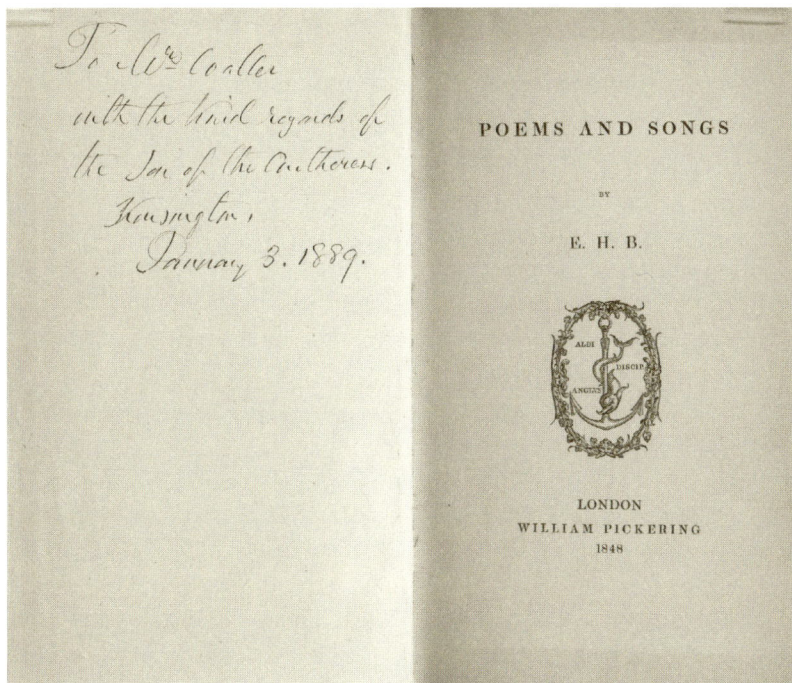

POEMS AND SONGS

BY

E. H. B.

LONDON
WILLIAM PICKERING
1848

ITEM 554

JOHN STUART BLACKIE (1809–1895)

555. Blackie, John Stuart. Musa Burschicosa: a book of songs for students and university men. Edinburgh: Edmonston and Douglas, 1869. 8vo, original dark blue cloth.

> Blackie was professor of Greek at Edinburgh University; he was noted for his genial eccentricity and determinedly Scottish manner. Acquired in 2001.

SAMUEL LAMAN BLANCHARD (1804–1845)

556. Blanchard, Samuel Laman. Lyric offerings. London: William Harrison Ainsworth, 1828. 12mo, original pink boards, printed paper label.

> The author's first book, dedicated to Charles Lamb. Blanchard went on to become a prolific writer of popular literature, especially for periodicals. In later life he became a close friend of Charles Dickens, Robert Browning,

and Leigh Hunt. This early work shows the influence of Wordsworth. It is also one of a relatively small number of titles published by Ainsworth, who was soon to become a novelist of great popularity. Laman Blanchard's wife, Ann Elizabeth Gates, died in 1844. This led to a period of depression, brought on by the pressures of work and concern for his four children; the following year he committed suicide. Acquired in 1977.

THOMAS EDWARD BROWN (1830–1897)

557. [Brown, Thomas Edward.] Christmas rose. Cockermouth: printed at the office of I. Evening, 1873. 8vo, original marbled wrappers.

The author's second book of verse, privately printed. T. E. Brown is the best known of all Manx poets, but despite his extensive use of dialect, he was not at all an untutored bard, but a very sophisticated and well-educated poet, who used the sights and sounds of his native island as a source of literary inspiration. Brown was the fifth son of a Manx vicar. He entered

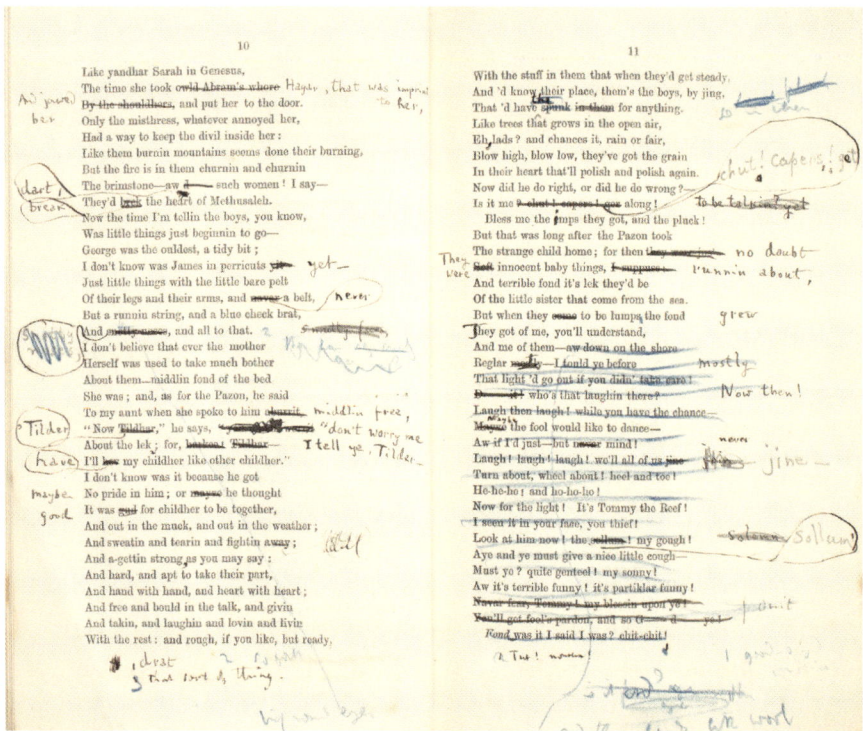

ITEM 557

Christ Church, Oxford, in 1849, and took a double first in classics and history in 1853; for his achievements he was awarded a fellowship at Oriel the following year, at a time when this position was the highest distinction that Oxford could confer. He later became the vice-principal of King William's College in the Isle of Man, and in 1861 he began a two-year term as the headmaster of the Crypt School in Gloucester, where W. E. Henley was one of his students. He subsequently took up a post at Clifton (Bristol), where he remained for some thirty years, but during his vacations he renewed his acquaintance with the old salts of the Manx harbors, and in the early 1870s began to transform this experience into poetry. His first of several books of rather racy narrative verse, *Betsy Lee*, was privately printed in Cockermouth, in Cumberland, in 1872; the present volume followed shortly afterward. Brown's "yarns," which recall to some extent the tales of Crabbe, rise far above the level of traditional dialect verse, and were much admired by such readers as George Eliot and Robert Browning. In time they were brought to a general readership by Macmillan, but for London publication the text had to be much revised. Brown's poetry in its original form had a certain Rabelaisian quality, with the potential to shock a Victorian reader, and Brown accepted the fact that some modification, at least temporarily, was necessary for wider distribution: "These omissions were intended to pacify one of Macmillan's partners, and also to avert the anger of the Methodists in this island. But I wish them restored." For a brief appreciation of Brown, and a short bibliography of his works, see Simon Nowell-Smith's "Some Uncollected Authors XXXIII," *The Book Collector* vol. 11, no. 3 (Autumn 1962), pp. 338–44. This remarkable copy of *Christmas Rose* is from Nowell-Smith's own collection. It has been heavily marked up by Brown for publication by Macmillan in 1881, with his revisions and deletions on every page, hundreds in all, along with further blue-penciling by the publisher. Acquired in 2002.

558. [Brown, Thomas Edward.] The doctor. By the author of "Betsy Lee." Douglas (Isle of Man): James Brown & Son, "The Isle of Man Times" Office, 1876. Sm. 8vo, original green stiff glazed printed wrappers.

The author's third major poem. It was eventually published in London in 1887 by Swan Sonnenschein, who did not require the same sort of revisions that Brown had been forced to make for Macmillan. These original Manx printings of Brown's verse are very rare; of this one, five copies are recorded, at the British Library, the Bodleian, Brown, Illinois, and the Turnbull Library in New Zealand. The Simon Nowell-Smith copy. Acquired in 2002.

559. [Brown, Thomas Edward.] Captain Tom and Captain Hugh: a Manx story in verse. Reprinted from "The Isle of Man Times." By the author of "Betsy Lee," "The Doctor," &c. &c. Douglas (Isle of Man): James Brown and Son, printers & lithographers, n.d. [1878]. Sm. 8vo, original green stiff glazed printed wrappers.

> The author's fourth major poem. When it was reprinted in 1881 by Macmillan, some 150 of the poem's 1,250 lines were deleted. Three other copies of this Manx printing have been located, at the Bodleian, Illinois, and New York University. Tipped to the front pastedown of this copy is a charming two-page letter in dialect verse, addressed to "Masthar Hutchinson" and dated at the end May 2, 1896. In it, Brown playfully describes the alterations in his verse that Macmillan had required. The Simon Nowell-Smith copy. Acquired in 2002.

560. [Brown, Thomas Edward.] Old John. Douglas (Isle of Man): J. Brown & Son, n.d. [1881?]. 8vo, original limp blue pebbled cloth.

> This poem was written on December 29, 1880, and first printed in *The Isle of Man Times* on January 8, 1881. Of this fourteen-page separate printing, no other copy has been located. This one is inscribed by the author on the title page, "S. T. Irwin d. d. TEB. Oct. 27 / 89." The Simon Nowell-Smith copy. Acquired in 2002.

SYDNEY DOBELL (1824–1874)

561. [Dobell, Sydney.] The Roman. A dramatic poem. By Sydney Yendys [pseud.]. London: Richard Bentley, 1850. 8vo, original blue cloth.

> A poem about Italy during the Revolution of 1848–49. "Inspired by the stirring events of the time, this dramatic poem, from its intrinsic merit and its accord with a popular enthusiasm, had a rapid and decided success, and while establishing his reputation enlarged the circle of the author's friends, among whom were numbered Tennyson and Carlyle, artists like Holman Hunt and Rossetti, and prominent patriots like Mazzini and Kossuth."–*DNB*. The Simon Nowell-Smith copy. Acquired in 2002.

562. [Dobell, Sydney.] Balder. Part the first [all published]. London: Smith, Elder, and Co.; Smith, Taylor, and Co. (Bombay), 1854. 8vo, original green cloth.

The poet's second book, and his most ambitious poem. From the library of John Sparrow, with his book label. Acquired in 1993.

563. Dobell, Sydney. England in time of war. London: Smith, Elder & Co., 1856. 8vo, original dark green cloth.

Dobell's third book of poems; included are verses on the Crimean War, whence the book's title. This copy is inscribed on the title page, "To Willie and Nelly from their loving brother the Author." From the library of John Sparrow, with his book label. Acquired in 1993.

SEBASTIAN EVANS (1830–1909)

564. Evans, Sebastian. In the studio: a decade of poems. London: Macmillan and Co., 1875. 8vo, original green cloth.

Evans was both a poet and an artist; he had an enthusiasm for wood-carving, engraving, and bookbinding. His social charm led him to an acquaintance with such prominent figures as Thackeray, Darwin, Matthew Arnold, and Ruskin; he became an intimate friend of Edward Burne-Jones. This volume is signed by Evans on p. 180. On the half-title is the signature of E. A. Lawrence, dated June 22, 1875. The Simon Nowell-Smith copy. Acquired in 1985.

565. Evans, Sebastian. John Baptist Spagnolo of Mantua Carmelite to John Crestoni of Piacenza Carmelite then going away for a time to Monte Calestano. Englished with an introduction by Sebastian Evans. Twenty-five copies privately printed as New-Year gifts, 1884. [London: 1833.] 4to, sewn, as issued.

A translation in rhymed couplets. This copy is inscribed by Evans on the title page to the poet and critic Austin Dobson. On the verso is a manuscript sonnet by Evans ("L'Envoy"), signed with his initials. Acquired in 1993.

JULIAN HENRY CHARLES FANE (1827–1870)

566. Fane, Julian Henry Charles, translator. Poems by Heinrich Heine translated by Julian Fane. Not published. Vienna: from the Imperial Court and Government Printing-Office, 1854. 8vo, contemporary purple straight-grained morocco.

Julian Fane began his study of German poetry while serving as an attaché in Vienna from 1851 to 1853. This privately printed gathering of selections from Heine is the principal result of that effort. This copy is inscribed by Fane on the title page, "Lady Evelyn Stanhope from the translator." The recipient was the daughter of the Earl of Chesterfield. There are several corrections in the text in Fane's hand. Acquired in 2005.

567. Fane, Julian Henry Charles. Julian Fane, ad matrem. 1849–1857. Not published. [London: 1857.] 8vo, original red cloth.

> A privately printed collection of nine poems addressed by the author to his mother, the Countess of Westmoreland. The Simon Nowell-Smith copy. Acquired in 2002.

DORA GREENWELL (1821–1882)

568. Greenwell, Dora. Poems. London: William Pickering, 1848. 8vo, original green cloth.

> The author's first book. Dora Greenwell later became a close friend of Christina Rossetti, and was much involved in such social causes as the education of women, and the struggle for universal suffrage. This copy is inscribed by the author on the front flyleaf, "To E. M. 'Je langer, Je lieber.' page 165." The recipient was Elizabeth Mewburn, one of Greenwell's closest friends. The reference here is to a footnote in the text: "The pansy, called in German, *je langer je lieber*, 'the longer the more dear.'" Acquired in 2005.

569. Greenwell, Dora. Stories that might be true: with other poems. London: William Pickering, 1850. 8vo, original green cloth.

> The author's second book. This copy is inscribed by the author on the front flyleaf to "E. M.," with a sixteen-line manuscript poem, dated December 25, 1850. The recipient was Elizabeth Mewburn (see no. 568); the printed poems include "To E. M. on Her Birthday," dated June 23, 1849. Laid in is the folded galley proof of a poem called "A Dialogue," as printed in *The Durham Advertiser*. Acquired in 2005.

THOMAS GORDON HAKE (1809–1895)

570. Hake, Thomas Gordon. Parables and tales. . . . With illustrations by Arthur Hughes. London: Chapman and Hall, 1872. 8vo, original dark green cloth.

Hake was a physician by training. He published a couple of volumes of poetry when he was young, and then stopped writing for more than twenty-five years, not taking up the pen again until he was in his sixties. At this point his verse caught the attention of Rossetti, and he became involved with the Pre-Raphaelites. This book was published at about the same time that Hake was looking after Rossetti while he was going through a crisis of laudanum addiction. Rossetti reciprocated by providing the design with which the cloth covers are decorated in gilt (though this was apparently not used in all copies). This copy is inscribed on the half-title, "Thomas Bayne Esq. with the author's kind regards." The recipient wrote critical and biographical notices of various Pre-Raphaelites. From the library of John Sparrow, with his book label. Acquired in 1994.

ROBERT STEPHEN HAWKER (1803–1875)

571. Hawker, Robert Stephen. Reeds shaken with the wind. London: James Burns, 1843. 12mo, original green cloth.

For a good account of Hawker of Morwenstow, as he is commonly called, see Simon Nowell-Smith (Cecil Woolf [pseud.]), "Some Uncollected Authors XXXIX," *The Book Collector*, vol. 14, nos. 1–2 (Spring and Summer 1965), where he is described as an "engaging 19th-century parson-poet, mystic, antiquary, and eccentric." Many of Hawker's early books of poetry, of which this one is fairly typical, were printed in small numbers, and are now rare. Nowell-Smith describes the binding as maroon cloth, though he mentions the present variant in green cloth from a bibliography in a collected edition of Hawker's poetry published in 1899, where this book, and its sequel, are described as "tiny volumes . . . of great interest and rarity." Acquired in 1987.

572. [Hawker, Robert Stephen.] Reeds shaken with the wind, the second cluster, by the Vicar of Morwenstow, Cornwall. Derby: Henry Mozley and Sons; and James Burns (London), 1844. 12mo, original dark green cloth.

A companion volume to the preceding collection, and of comparable rarity. With the book label of the poet John Drinkwater. Later bookplate of the Brother Julian, F. S. C., Collection, Manhattan College, donated by Mr. Christian A. Zabriskie, New York City. Acquired in 1992.

RICHARD HENGIST HORNE (1802–1884)

573. [Horne, Richard Hengist, editor.] The poems of Geoffrey Chaucer, modernized. London: Whittaker & Co., 1841. 8vo, original dark green cloth.

> The notion of providing a modern version of Chaucer was proposed by Wordsworth, who contributed two of the tales; there are also three by Leigh Hunt, one by Elizabeth Barrett Browning, and others by Robert Bell, Richard Monckton Milnes, and Dr. Leonard Schmitz, as well as Horne himself (three tales). Horne's introduction occupies more than a hundred pages. For his friendship and collaboration with EBB, see no. 470. Acquired in 1973.

574. Horne, Richard Hengist. Orion: an epic poem in three books. London: J. Miller, 1843. 8vo, original green figured cloth.

> One of the oddest poems of the nineteenth century, and the work by which Horne is chiefly remembered. Though Horne was forty when he wrote this poem and had already printed a number of books, he could not find a publisher for his "epic" and was forced to pay for its production himself. Out of frustration, and to attract attention, he priced copies at a farthing, and undertook to sell them himself; this device proved successful, and no fewer than three "farthing" editions were called for within a matter of weeks. The author was thereafter known as "Farthing" Horne, though later editions were priced more conventionally. Edgar Allan Poe was a particular admirer of these verses. Acquired in 1992.

575. Horne, Richard Hengist. Ballad romances. London: John Russell Smith, n.d. [1846]. Sm. 8vo, original dark slate blue cloth.

> Second issue; the slightly more common first issue has a Charles Ollier imprint, and a dated title page (though the sheets are the same). Acquired in 1993.

576. Horne, Richard Hengist. The great peace-maker: a sub-marine dialogue. . . . With a preface by the author of "Our Living Poets," etc. London: Sampson Low, Marston, Low, & Searle, 1872. 8vo, original dark blue cloth.

> First published edition, to which has been added a seven-page preface by H. Buxton Forman; a private printing had appeared in 1871. "A striking poem . . . on the laying of the submarine cable between Dover and Calais."–DNB. This copy is inscribed on the title page, "W. C. Bonaparte Wyse, with R. H. Horne's regards, 1875"; the recipient himself published several collections of verse. Acquired in 2003.

577. Horne, Richard Hengist. Cosmo de' Medici: an historical tragedy; and other poems. London: George Rivers, 1875. 8vo, original dark blue cloth.

> The title piece, a verse play, had originally been published in 1837, but the text here has been extensively altered; the other twenty-four poems in the book are all new. This copy bears an inscription by Horne on the title page, dated 1877, to Mrs. R[ose] M[ary] Crawshay (1828–1907), who was in her day a prominent feminist. Tipped in is a four-page letter from Horne, written in 1878, suggesting that Crawshay read a poem in the book on the subject of euthanasia, as she had published something on the same subject in 1872. Horne has also made two manuscript changes in the text, one to alter a spelling, and the other to rewrite a line of verse. Acquired in 1977.

578. Horne, Richard Hengist. Laura Dibalzo: or the patriot martyrs. A tragedy. London: Newman & Co., 1880. 8vo, original dark blue cloth.

> A verse drama. This copy is initialed by the author on the title page; tipped in is a two-page letter from Horne to Sir Charles Gavan Duffy, the prominent Irish nationalist. Horne tells Duffy that he had also sent a copy of his book to Benjamin Disraeli, "a week or two after he had doubled my pension." Duffy had helped Horne in 1856 to secure a post on a commission for water and sewerage: "I hope it is not too late for me to make a similar reference to what you did with regard to me in Australia, a good many years ago, as I am equally sure I never rendered you the slightest service of any kind." Acquired in 1991.

JEAN INGELOW (1820–1897)

579. Ingelow, Jean. A story of doom: and other poems. London: Longmans, Green, and Co., 1867. 8vo, original green cloth.

> A major book by one of the most popular female poets of the second half of the nineteenth century. Inscribed on the half-title: "Mrs. Stephen Paul [?] from Miss Ingelow. June 7th, 1867." The Simon Nowell-Smith copy. Acquired in 1980.

WILLIAM JOHNSON, LATER CORY (1823–1892)

580. [Cory, William Johnson.] Ionica. London: Smith, Elder and Co., 1858. [Bound with:] Ionica II. N.p. [Cambridge]: 1877. Two vols. in one, 8vo, maroon morocco, by Riviere.

The author's first book, bound up with, as often, a privately printed second part. William Johnson was for many years a schoolmaster at Eton. In 1872 he suddenly resigned, possibly because he had shown himself to be dangerously fond of some of the boys. It was at this point that he adopted the new surname of Cory. In 1878 he retired for reasons of health to Madeira, where he married a young woman of twenty. He once described the first part of *Ionica* as follows: "This booklet was made up in a fortnight spent in solitude at Pangbourne on the Thames, August 1858, and was published secretly at the cost of £40 paid in advance." The poem was for a time neglected, but came to be recognized as a small masterpiece of Victorian lyric poetry. The sequel is eccentric in that it is largely printed without punctuation, and without capital letters at the beginning of lines. Acquired in 1977.

581. [Cory, William Johnson.] Eton reform. London: Longman, Green, Longman, and Roberts, 1861. [Bound with:] Eton reform. II. London: Longman, Green, Longman, and Roberts, 1861. Two vols. in one, 8vo, half blue morocco, by Roger de Coverly.

A defense of Eton against criticism by Matthew James Higgins and Sir J. T. Coleridge, some of it published in *The Cornhill Magazine*: "You go to a great school not so much for knowledge, as for arts and habits." Part 2 is inscribed on the title page, "Dalmeny, Eton, 1861." From the library of Lord Rosebery, with his Durdans book label. Acquired in 1987.

EBENEZER JONES (1820–1860)

582. Jones, Ebenezer. Studies of sensation and event; poems. London: Charles Fox, 1843. Large 8vo, olive green morocco, by Larkins.

A large-paper copy, 8½ in. high, of the first and most important book by a self-taught young Welshman. The poetry here is much influenced by Shelley, and is an extraordinary mixture of the highly original and the utterly ludicrous. Unhappily, Jones's faults were more obvious than his genius, and his work met an indifferent reception, which left him in despair; he published little else before his death in 1860, at the age of forty. Ten years later, Rossetti wrote a note about Jones in *Notes and Queries* that commented upon his "vivid disorderly power"; this led to his rediscovery by the Pre-Raphaelites, and a reprint of the present volume in 1879. "There can be no question of Jones's genius."–*DNB*. From the library of John Sparrow, with his book label. Acquired in 1993.

ERNEST CHARLES JONES (1819-1869)

583. Jones, Ernest Charles. Infantine effusions. Hamburg: printed by F. H. Nestler, 1830. 8vo, contemporary green morocco.

> The author's first book, published when he was eleven; a prefatory note states that the poems were written between the ages of eight and ten. The longest piece here is a translation of canto 1 of Voltaire's *Henriade*; the first poem, "Rodriguo," is an imitation of Byron ("a celebrated author"). Jones went on to become one of England's most prominent political radicals. In 1846 he met Karl Marx and Friedrich Engels, by whom he was much influenced. This juvenile production is rare. WorldCat locates copies at Stanford and Harvard, along with one in the Netherlands and two in Germany; there appear to be no copies at all in the United Kingdom. Acquired in 1991.

ITEM 583

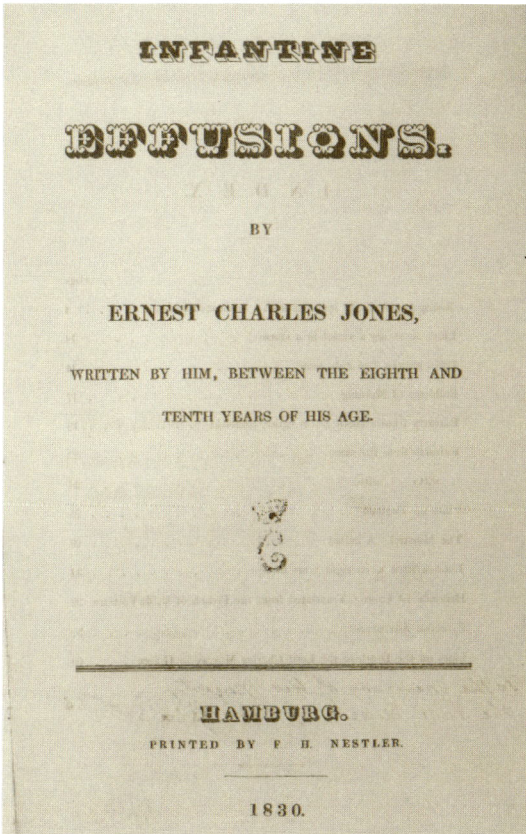

INFANTINE

EFFUSIONS.

BY

ERNEST CHARLES JONES,

WRITTEN BY HIM, BETWEEN THE EIGHTH AND
TENTH YEARS OF HIS AGE.

HAMBURG.
PRINTED BY F. H. NESTLER.

1830.

584. Jones, Ernest Charles. The battle-day: and other poems. London and New York: G. Routledge & Co., 1855. 8vo, original blue cloth.

> The author's first important collection of poems, on Chartist themes. Walter Savage Landor wrote Jones a letter of congratulations: "It is noble; Byron would have envied, Scott would have applauded." This is, in fact, Landor's copy, and has his signature on the front flyleaf. Acquired in 1992.

FRANCES ANNE KEMBLE, LATER BUTLER (1809–1893)

585. Kemble, Frances Anne (later Butler). Journal by Frances Anne Butler. London: John Murray, 1835. Two vols., 12mo, original gray boards, printed paper labels.

> The first of Fanny Kemble's celebrated journals describing her life in the United States. A highly successful London actress, she first came to America in 1832, and stayed for four years. In 1834 she married Pierce M. Butler, who owned a plantation in Georgia; a disastrous stay there in 1838–39 is described in a later diary. The present account concerns life on the Eastern Seaboard, and is a classic of its kind; there is, of course, much theatrical material. For an amusing glimpse of the author in her old age, see below, no. 669 (n). This set is inscribed, "Belmore" on each front cover. Acquired in 1992.

586. Kemble, Frances Anne (later Butler). Poems. London: Henry Washbourne; Oliver & Boyd (Edinburgh); Machen & Co. (Dublin), 1844. 12mo, original purple cloth.

> First London edition; first printed in Philadelphia earlier the same year. With the signature of William Honyman on the title page. Acquired in 1992.

LETITIA ELIZABETH LANDON (1802–1838)

587. Landon, Letitia Elizabeth. The golden violet, with its tales of romance and chivalry: and other poems. London: printed for Longman, Rees, Orme, Brown, and Green, 1827. 8vo, original blue boards, drab paper backstrip, printed paper label.

> The author's fourth book. As "L. E. L.," Letitia Elizabeth Landon became enormously popular, and she earned substantial sums from her pen. The price of fame was gossip and rumor, and she was slandered in the gutter press. She managed nonetheless to become an integral part of the London literary scene, though some considered her common. An engagement to

John Forster was broken off, and in 1838 she married the governor of Cape Coast Castle in South Africa. Shortly after her arrival there, she died from taking prussic acid, but whether this was suicide, or something more sinister, was never determined. The details of Landon's career show up in some detail in Elizabeth Barrett Browning's *Aurora Leigh* (no. 469). Inscribed on the front flyleaf, "Eliza Berry, from G. J. B." With the book label of Simon Nowell-Smith. Acquired in 1982.

CHARLES MACKAY (1814–1889)

588. Mackay, Charles. Songs and poems. London: Cochrane and M'Crone, 1834. Sm. 8vo, contemporary blue calf.

> The author's first book, published when he was twenty. Mackay went on to become a prominent poet and journalist. This copy is inscribed on the front flyleaf, "Rosa Mackay, from her affectionate Charles. Febr. 13th, 1834." The recipient was the author's wife, whom he had just married. Acquired in 1990.

THEODORE MARTIN (1816–1909)

589. Martin, Theodore, translator. King René's daughter: a Danish lyrical drama by Henrik Hertz. London: Wm. S. Orr and Co., 1850. Sq. 8vo, original brown cloth.

> A verse translation of a very popular Danish play. Martin says in a short preface that the part of the blind Iolanthe "seemed to be peculiarly adapted to the genius of Miss Helen Faucit." Faucit was a popular actress with whom Martin was infatuated, and he pursued her from place to place until 1851, when they were married. This copy is inscribed on the half-title, "To M. Marcellin de Fresne with the kind regards of the Translator. 19 October, '53." Tipped in at the front of this copy is a four-page autograph letter written on the same day from Helen Faucit, now Mrs. Martin, to M. de Fresne, transmitting the book: "I am sure you will find pleasure in the perusal of this little book, especially when I tell you that Iolanthe is now one of my very favorite characters." Acquired in 2003.

590. Martin, Theodore, translator. The odes of Horace translated into English verse: with a life and notes. London: John W. Parker and Son, 1860. 8vo, original brown cloth.

This copy is inscribed on a front flyleaf, "To Arthur Helps, Esq. with the kind regards of Theodore Martin." The recipient was a historian of note, who also published several novels. He was one of Martin's best friends; as an adviser to Queen Victoria, he recommended Martin to write the biography of the Prince Consort (in 1866), which duly appeared in five volumes, from 1870 to 1875. Acquired in 1981.

591. Martin, Sir Theodore, translator. The works of Horace: translated into English verse, with a life and notes. Edinburgh and London: William Blackwood and Sons, 1881. Two vols., 8vo, original maroon cloth.

This set is inscribed on the first half-title from the author to the poet and essayist Austin Dobson (Jan. 11, 1888); the recipient's bookplate is on the front pastedown of the first volume. Acquired in 2002.

GERALD MASSEY (1828–1907)

592. Massey, Gerald. Craigcrook Castle. London: David Bogue, 1856. 8vo, original green cloth.

Second edition, "revised"; first printed earlier the same year. Massey came from a Scottish working-class background and had little formal education. He went to London at an early age, and established himself as a successful poet. He worked for a time for the publisher John Chapman, and there he met George Eliot, whose *Felix Holt: The Radical* is to some extent based upon his career. This copy is inscribed on the title page, "W. B. Johnstone, Esq., with Gerald Massey's kind regards." The recipient was a prominent Scottish painter and writer on art. Massey has also made manuscript revisions on nine pages of text, changing words, and deleting or transposing whole lines. From the collection of Michael Sadleir, with his book label. Acquired in 1994.

593. Massey, Gerald. A tale of eternity and other poems. London: Strahan & Co., 1870. Large 8vo, original green cloth.

A privately printed issue, on large paper, with a dedication to Lady Marian Alford, Massey's patron; the published edition was in a much smaller format. Acquired in 1973.

RICHARD MONCKTON MILNES, 1ST BARON HOUGHTON (1809-1885)

594. Milnes, Richard Monckton. Memorials of a tour in some parts of Greece: chiefly poetical. London: Edward Moxon, 1834. 8vo, original gray boards, printed paper label.

> The author's first book of poetry, preceded only by a Cambridge prize essay. The verses are interspersed with prose passages that describe his trip, made in his midtwenties, in some detail; he was accompanied by Christopher Wordsworth. Milnes in his university days was a conspicuous member of the literary club of twelve known as the Apostles, whose members included Tennyson and Arthur Hallam. He is now perhaps best remembered for having edited the literary remains of Keats (no. 212). This copy is inscribed by Milnes on the front pastedown to Viscount Galway, his uncle. Acquired in 1986.

595. Milnes, Richard Monckton. Palm leaves. London: Edward Moxon, 1844. 8vo, original purple cloth, printed paper label.

> This volume of poetry was the result of the author's tour in Egypt and the Levant in the winter of 1842–43. Acquired in 1976.

596. Milnes, Richard Monckton. The earl and the duchess, a dialogue, translated and adapted from De Musset's Proverbe, "Il faut q'une porte soit ouverte ou fermée," expressly for representation at Nuneham, in July, 1850; and dedicated to Frances, Countess of Waldegrave. N.p. [London]: 1851. 8vo, original pink printed wrappers.

> A humorous dialogue composed for a private theatrical performance at the Palladian country house of George Granville Harcourt, in Oxfordshire. Monckton Milnes visited Nuneham in his customary round of country houses following the season of 1850, and he and Lady Waldegrave played the two roles. James Pope-Hennessy mentions this privately printed pamphlet in his biography of Monckton Milnes (1, p. 302), but there was no example to be found in any obvious institution until a small batch surfaced in 2004; there are now copies located in the British Library, Harvard, and Yale. Acquired in 2005.

ROBERT MONTGOMERY (1807–1855)

597. Montgomery, Robert. Ellesmere Lake; the Pistyll Rhaiadr; and the Vale of Clwyd: poems. London: printed for Simpkin and Marshall; and J. Seacome (Chester), 1836. Sm. 8vo, original purple watered silk cloth.

A young clergyman with a facility for verse and a slight resemblance to Byron, Montgomery enjoyed an alarming success. Such poems as his *Omnipresence of the Deity* (1828) proved so enormously popular—by 1858 some twenty-eight editions had appeared—that serious critics were soon obliged to take a stand against his fame; a famous essay by Macaulay in *The Edinburgh Review* (1830) set the tone for much that followed, to the extent that the entry in the *DNB*, written more than sixty years later, defines him merely as a "poetaster," with "an unfortunate facility in florid versification." This small collection of three topographical poems was published in aid of a campaign to raise funds for a new church in Oswestry. Acquired in 1997.

EDWARD MOXON (1801–1858)

598. Moxon, Edward. Sonnets. London: 1830. 8vo, original dark blue cloth.

At the age of nine, Moxon was apprenticed to a bookseller in Wakefield, an arrangement that in time led him into publishing. When still in his twenties he got to know Charles Lamb, and the two became close friends; in 1833 he married Lamb's adopted daughter. Moxon began his career as a publisher in 1830 with Lamb's *Album Verses*; he soon secured the support of many writers of established reputation, chief among them Wordsworth and Tennyson. Moxon also printed several small volumes of his own verse, of which this is the third. This copy is inscribed on the half-title, "To S. T. Coleridge, Esq. with the Author's best respects." Acquired in 1981.

JOHN MASON NEALE (1818–1866)

599. Neale, John Mason, translator. Mediæval hymns and sequences. London: Joseph Masters, 1851. 16mo, original dark blue cloth.

Neale was a prolific contributor to the most popular of all English hymnals, *Hymns Ancient and Modern*; he was also responsible for some of the best-known Christmas carols, notably "Good King Wenceslaus." The Simon Nowell-Smith copy. Acquired in 2002.

FRANCIS WILLIAM NEWMAN (1805–1897)

600. Newman, Francis William. The Gospel of Paul of Tarsus, and of his opponent, James the Just, from our current New Testament. Nottingham: Stevenson, Bailey and Smith, 1893. 8vo, original purple limp cloth.

> A late work by the younger brother of Cardinal Newman. Francis Newman is listed by the *NCBEL* as a poet, but he was better known for his linguistic, political, and religious writings. This slim volume is signed by the author on the front endpaper, with the note, "My private copy with some small corrections." In fact there are quite a few manuscript changes, some of them rather substantial. Acquired in 1981.

CAROLINE ELIZABETH NORTON (1808–1877)

601. [Norton, Caroline.] The sorrows of Rosalie. A tale. With other poems. London: John Ebers and Co., 1829. Sm. 8vo, original blue boards, drab paper backstrip, printed paper label.

> The author's first book. Caroline Norton was the granddaughter of Richard Brinsley Sheridan; as a young woman she was celebrated for her beauty and wit. A disastrous early marriage ended in scandal and a contentious divorce, as a result of which Norton began to write on a variety of women's issues, including the right of a mother to the custody of her children. Her intelligent essays had a significant impact on subsequent parliamentary legislation. These early verses, rather in the manner of Byron, were an immediate success. The original binding of this copy is in a remarkable state of preservation. With the bookplate of Hansard Watt. Acquired in 1990.

FRANCIS TURNER PALGRAVE (1824–1897)

602. Palgrave, Francis Turner. Idyls and songs. 1848–1854. London: John W. Parker and Son, 1854. 8vo, original blue and black marbled cloth.

> The author's second book, preceded only by a tale in verse called *Preciosa* (1852). Tipped in at the front is a four-page letter from Palgrave, sending this copy to Charles George Milnes Gaskell (1842–1919), whose bookplate appears on the front pastedown; the recipient is perhaps now best remembered as a lifelong friend and correspondent of the American historian Henry Adams. The letter, which can be dated 1861, refers to this volume as "my long suppressed little poems," and mentions a second copy being

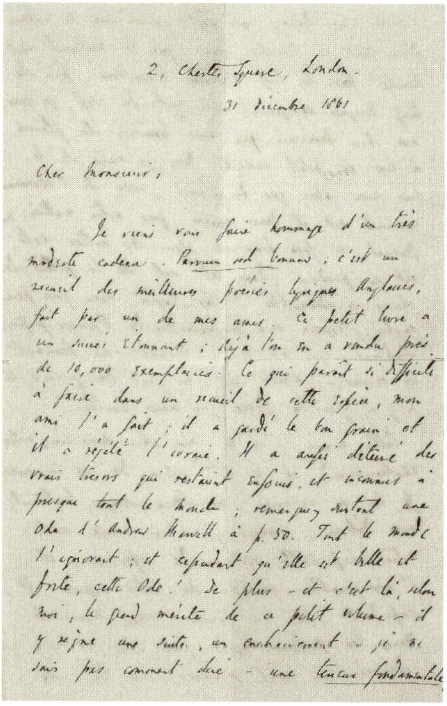

2, Chester Square, London.
31 décembre 1861

Cher Monsieur,

Je viens vous faire hommage d'un très modeste cadeau. Parmi nos lunes(?); c'est un recueil des meilleures poésies lyriques Anglaises, fait par un de mes amis. Ce petit livre a un succès étonnant; déjà l'on en a vendu près de 10,000 exemplaires. Ce qui paraît si difficile à faire dans un recueil de cette espèce, mon ami l'a fait; il a gardé le bon grain et il a rejeté l'ivraie. Il a aussi déterré des vrais trésors qui restaient enfouis, et inconnus à presque tout le monde; remarquez surtout une Ode d'Andrew Marvell à p. 50. Tout le monde l'ignorait; et cependant qu'elle est belle et forte, cette Ode! De plus – et c'est là, selon moi, le grand mérite de ce petit volume – il y règne une suite, un enchaînement – je ne sais pas comment dire – une teneur fondamentale

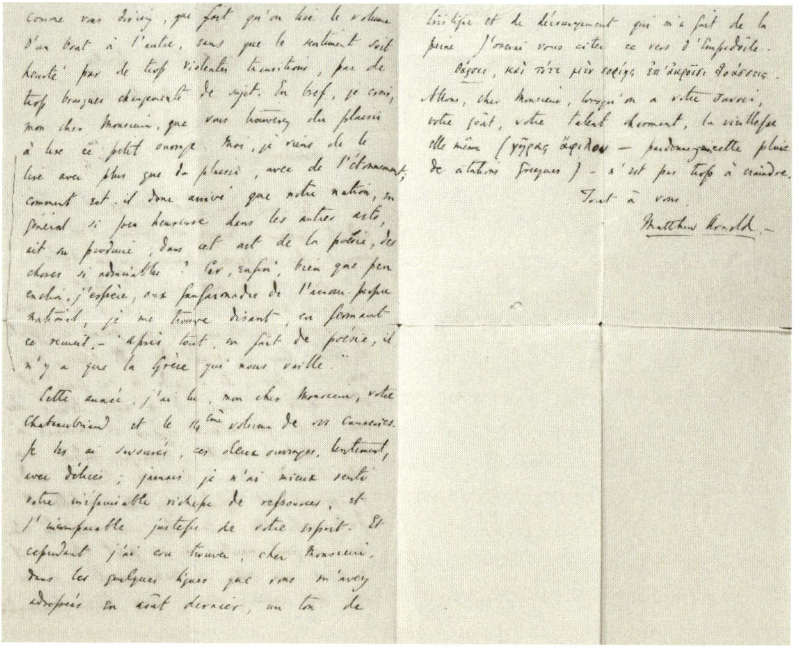

comme vous diriez, qui fait qu'on lise le volume d'un bout à l'autre, sans que le sentiment soit heurté par de trop violentes transitions, par de trop brusques changements de sujet. En bref, je crois, mon cher Monsieur, que vous trouverez du plaisir à lire ce petit ouvrage. Moi, je viens de le lire avec plus que du plaisir, avec de l'étonnement; comment est-il donc arrivé que notre nation, en général si peu heureuse dans les autres arts, ait su produire, dans cet art de la poésie, des choses si admirables? Car, enfin, bien que peu enclin, j'espère, aux fanfaronnades de l'amour-propre national, je me trouve disant, en fermant ce recueil, – "Après tout, en fait de poésie, il n'y a que la Grèce qui nous vaille."

Cette année, j'ai lu, mon cher Monsieur, votre Chateaubriand et le 14ème volume de vos Causeries. Je les ai savourés, ces deux ouvrages, lentement, avec délices; jamais je n'ai mieux senti votre inépuisable richesse de ressources, et l'incomparable justesse de votre esprit. Et cependant j'ai cru trouver, cher Monsieur, dans les quelques lignes que vous m'avez adressées en août dernier, un ton de tristesse et de découragement qui m'a fait de la peine. J'oserai vous citer ce vers d'Empédocle.

θάρσει, καὶ τότε μὲν σοφίης ἐπ' ἄκροισι θοάζεις.

Allons, cher Monsieur, lorsqu'on a votre savoir, votre goût, votre talent charmant, la vieillesse elle même (γῆρας ἄφιλον – pardonnez-moi cette pluie de citations Grecques) – n'est pas trop à craindre.

Tout à vous.

Matthew Arnold.

sent "as your Father collects scarce books." Palgrave also speaks of sending a fragment of the manuscript of Tennyson's *Princess*, "to decorate a portrait of him, if you have one." Palgrave and Tennyson were, of course, very close friends. Palgrave married Milnes Gaskell's sister in 1862. With two small corrections in the text, presumably in Palgrave's hand. With the book label of Simon Nowell-Smith. Acquired in 1979.

603. Palgrave, Francis Turner, editor. The golden treasury of the best songs and lyrical poems in the English language selected and arranged with notes. Cambridge: Macmillan and Co., 1861. 8vo, original green cloth.

> The most famous of all English anthologies of poetry. This copy is inscribed on the half-title from England's foremost literary critic, Matthew Arnold, to his French counterpart, Charles-Augustin Sainte-Beuve ("souvenir affectueux," dated January 1, 1861). Tipped in at the front is a splendid three-page letter in French from Arnold to Sainte-Beuve, sending the book ("un très modeste cadeau–parvum sed bonum"), and commenting upon it at length. Arnold names Palgrave as his friend and praises his efforts, particularly his ability to find poems of great quality not widely known, such as an ode by Andrew Marvell. Arnold goes on to express his astonishment at the poetical abilities of the English nation, comparable, in his opinion, only to those of ancient Greece. In his conclusion Arnold speaks warmly of Sainte-Beuve's most recent books, but expresses some concern over the tone of sadness and discouragement that he found in his friend's last letter; he suggests that Sainte-Beuve have a look at his poem "Empedocles." This volume was once owned by the Arnold critic and bibliographer Thomas Burnett Smart, before being offered for sale in 1913 by the bookseller Herbert E. Gorfin (known for his association with T. J. Wise), and then resurfacing at a Hodgson's auction in London in 1945. The H. Bradley Martin copy. Acquired in 1990.

604. [Palgrave, Francis Turner.] The visions of England. N.p. [London]: fifty copies printed for Francis T. Palgrave, Feb: 1880. [Bound with, as issued:] The visions of England. Second part. N.p. [London]: fifty copies printed for Francis T. Palgrave, April: 1881. Together two parts in one volume, 8vo, original half red morocco and marbled boards.

> These two collections of poems were regularly published by Macmillan as a single volume, with additions, in 1881. The title page to the first part of this private printing is within a red border; the poems are printed on one side of the sheet only. Acquired in 2007.

605. Palgrave, Francis Turner. Amenophis and other poems sacred and secular. London and New York: Macmillan and Co., 1892. 8vo, original dark blue cloth, printed paper dust wrapper.

> Palgrave's last substantial book of verse, published five years before his death. The dust wrapper, on quite thin paper, is printed on the spine only; its survival in fine state is very unusual. This is the only proper publisher's dust wrapper in the collection. Acquired in 2001.

JOSEPH NOËL PATON (1821–1901)

606. [Paton, Joseph Noël.] Poems by a painter. Edinburgh and London: William Blackwood and Sons, 1861. 8vo, original white cloth, decorated in gilt.

> The first book of verse by an artist associated with and strongly influenced by the Pre-Raphaelites. Paton's title had in fact already been used by another Pre-Raphaelite, William Bell Scott, in 1854. On the verso of the front flyleaf of this copy is an inscription from the author to the American man of letters James Lorimer Graham, dated Jan. 29, 1867: "You ask me to write some lines in this volume of aimless and vapid verse. But rather than add more of the same kind, let me inscribe this page with some stanzas from one of the noblest poems of one of the truest thinkers and sweetest singers that the world has known: your own Longfellow." Paton goes on to transcribe eight lines of "Life is real! Life is earnest!" Acquired in 1987.

JOHN CRITCHLEY PRINCE (1808–1866)

607. Prince, John Critchley. Hours with the muses. Manchester: J. B. Rogerson, 1861 [i.e., 1841]. 12mo, original brown cloth.

> A working-class poet's first book, which attracted a good deal of attention and was quickly reprinted in London. This original edition has an interesting eleven-page list of subscribers, including Charles Dickens, who took two copies. Acquired in 2000.

608. Prince, John Critchley. The poetic rosary. Ashton-under-Lyne: printed for the author, and sold by him; Simpkin and Marshall (London); Geo. Hatton (Manchester), 1850. 8vo, original light blue cloth.

> Prince's third book, dedicated to Dickens, from whom he no doubt expected a handout; for the most part Prince distributed his later books

by sending them himself to friends and strangers, with begging letters. Acquired in 1990.

609. Prince, John Critchley. Autumn leaves: original poems. Hyde: printed by G. Booth, and sold by the author, n.d. [1856]. 12mo, original claret cloth.

> With the signature on the front flyleaf of Lillie Travis, dated March 2, 1868. Acquired in 1980.

610. Prince, John Critchley. The poetical works of John Critchley Prince. Edited by R. A. Douglas Lithgow, LL.D. Manchester: Abel Heywood & Son; Simpkin, Marshall, & Co. (London), 1880. Two vols., 8vo, original dark brown cloth. Acquired in 1992.

ADELAIDE ANNE PROCTER (1825–1864)

611. Procter, Adelaide Anne, editor. The Victoria Regia: a volume of original contributions in poetry and prose. London: printed and published by Emily Faithfull and Co., Victoria Press, (for the employment of women), 1861. 8vo, original green cloth.

> This volume contains contributions from a remarkable array of major writers, including Tennyson, Matthew Arnold, Thackeray, and Trollope (a short story). "The Victoria Press was a venture in mid-Victorian feminism, and designed to show that printing and its allied trades offered new opportunities for the remunerative employment of women and girls, which would not conflict with existing wage-conditions or rouse social or trade prejudices."– Michael Sadleir, *Trollope: A Bibliography* (1928), p. 214. Acquired in 1976.

WILLIAM BELL SCOTT (1811–1890)

612. Scott, William Bell. Hades; or, the transit: and the Progress of Mind. Two poems. London: published by Henry Renshaw, 1838. 8vo, original red cloth.

> The author's first book. Scott was a painter who later became closely involved with the Pre-Raphaelites. As a poet he was much influenced by Shelley. This slim volume contains two engraved plates that bear a striking resemblance to the work of Blake. On the title page of this copy the word "juvenile" has been added in manuscript above the phrase "Two Poems," possibly by the author himself. Acquired in 2001.

613. Scott, William Bell. Hades; or, the transit: and the Progress of Mind. Two poems. London: printed by J. Last, 1838. 8vo, original red cloth.

> A variant issue of the preceding, with the printer's name only in the imprint. This copy is inscribed on the half-title, "Mr. John Forbes, with the author's compliments." Acquired in 1983.

614. Scott, William Bell. The year of the world; a philosophical poem on "redemption from the fall." Edinburgh: William Tait; Simpkin and Marshall (London), 1846. 8vo, original pink boards, brown figured cloth spine.

> Scott's second book, and his only long poem. This copy is inscribed on the half-title, "Thomas Wyse Esquire, M.P. &c. with the author's respects, Gov. School of Design, Newcastle, June, 1846." The recipient was a noted Irish politician and diplomat. The Simon Nowell-Smith copy. Acquired in 2002.

615. Scott, William Bell. Poems. London: Smith, Elder, & Co., 1854. Sm. 8vo, original green cloth, printed paper label.

> This copy is inscribed on the front pastedown, "Miss Greenwell with the author's most kind remembrances. W. B. Scott." The recipient was Dora Greenwell (1821–1882), a poet and essayist then at the beginning of a successful literary career. Acquired in 2005.

616. Scott, William Bell. A poet's harvest home: being one hundred short poems. London: Elliot Stock, 1882. Sm. 8vo, original vellum, printed in red.

> The author's last book, with a touching dedication to Dante Gabriel Rossetti. This copy is inscribed on the front flyleaf, "Rafe Leycester Esquire with kindest regards of the author." Acquired in 1987.

EDWARD GEORGE GEOFFREY SMITH STANLEY, 14TH EARL OF DERBY (1799–1869)

617. [Stanley, Edward George Geoffrey Smith, 14th Earl of Derby, translator.] Translations of poems, ancient and modern. Not published. London: printed for Hatchard & Co., 1862. Sq. 8vo, original violet-blue cloth.

> This privately printed collection is the most important literary publication by a major Victorian statesman. Stanley is best remembered for reviving, with Disraeli, the Conservative Party, after the fall of Peel; he was three times prime minister. Included are translations of book 1 of the *Iliad* (com-

pleted and fully published in 1864), thirteen odes of Horace, and one poem by Catullus, along with poems from French, Italian, and German (Schiller). This copy is inscribed on the front flyleaf, "Richd. C. Trench from the author (Lord Derby). March 23, '63." The recipient, Richard Chenevix Trench, an accomplished poet and philologist, was one of the leading clergymen of his day; he became archbishop of Dublin a few months after receiving this volume. Acquired in 1996.

THOMAS TOD STODDART (1810–1880)

618. [Stoddart, Thomas Tod.] Periods of the mind; or irregular sonnets on truth. N.p.: n.d. [ca. 1860?]. Sm. 8vo, four leaves, folded.

> An unrecorded leaflet of twelve contemplative poems. The authorship is revealed in a letter tipped to the front, addressed by the Oxford don Charles Appleton to the office of *The Academy*, a literary and scholarly periodical that Appleton had founded in 1869: "The enclosed is the work of Thomas Tod Stoddart one of the earliest of the 'spasmodic' poets. Perhaps you may remember his <u>magnum opus</u> 'The Deathwake or Lunacy; a Necromaunt in three Chimaeras.' If you care to say 10 lines for the <u>Academy</u>, do so." Stoddart's *Death-Wake*, printed in Edinburgh in 1831, was long forgotten, until in 1905 Andrew Lang first drew attention to it in his *Adventures among Books*: "It is full of the new note, the new melody which young Tennyson was beginning to waken. It anticipates Beddoes, it coincides with Gautier, and *Les Chimères* of Gérard [de Nerval], it answers the accents, then unheard in England, of Poe." The poems in this pamphlet appear to have been written in the same vein, but are clearly later; the printing looks mid-Victorian. Acquired in 1992.

HENRY SEPTIMUS SUTTON (1825–1901)

619. Sutton, Henry Septimus. Rose's diary. N.p. [Glasgow]: David M. Main, n.d. [1886?]. 8vo, contemporary light blue morocco.

> First separate edition. A sequence of poems in memory of a young woman who died in 1850. They were first published as an appendix to a volume of meditations called *Quinquinergia* (1854), where the woman is identified as Rose Fryer. Together, the poems are in effect an imaginary poetical diary, month by month, of the last year of Fryer's life. A comparison with the text of the 1854 version indicates that some of the poems were heavily revised for this new edition. Henry Sutton was a professional journalist, and an

317

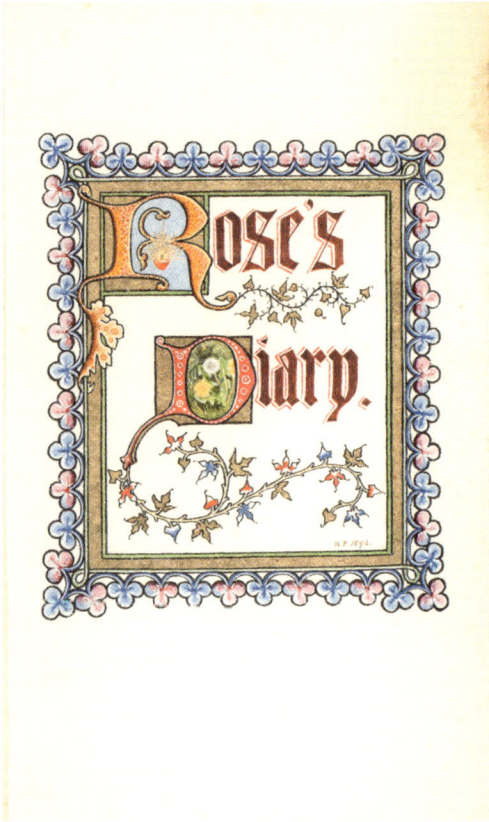

early friend of the poets Philip James Bailey (they both came from Nottingham) and Coventry Patmore. A more important influence was Ralph Waldo Emerson, who reciprocated Sutton's admiration; they met in 1847 and began a lifelong friendship. Sutton later became a Swedenborgian, but he remained close to Emerson, and was admired by Bronson Alcott as well. This undated edition of his most important literary work appears to have been printed for private circulation in a very small number of copies. Only two others are located, at Yale and at the British Library. The Yale copy is no. 7, and is inscribed by Sutton to James Martineau (in 1886). The copy at the British Library is no. 20, and was given to F. T. Palgrave, who noted that he received it in 1889. There is no doubt some connection between this gift and the fact that Palgrave anthologized poem 21 ("How Beautiful It Is to Be Alive") in his *Golden Treasury of Sacred Song*, published the same year by

318

the Oxford University Press. This newly discovered copy was the author's own; on the verso of a blank leaf at the front, in Sutton's hand, is "This is No. 1." The copy is further enhanced by the insertion of an illuminated title page, following the printed title; this is done in mock-medieval style, and is signed "B. P. 1896." Sixteen further pages of text have been decorated with delicate and very attractive hand-drawn illustrations, some in color. The illustrator has not as yet been identified. Acquired in 2010.

HENRY TAYLOR (1800–1886)

620. Taylor, Henry. The eve of the conquest, and other poems. London: Edward Moxon, 1847. 8vo, original green cloth.

> A slim volume of verse by an admirer of Wordsworth, but a poet who pursued an active life in and around Downing Street, as opposed to the seclusion of the Lake District. Taylor was a close friend of Tennyson and spent much time in his circle. This copy is inscribed by the author on the half-title, "Gilbert Elliot from H. Taylor, Mortlake, 3d Nov., 1847." The recipient may have been Lord Minto. Acquired in 2004.

621. Taylor, Henry. The poetical works of Henry Taylor, D.C.L. London: Chapman and Hall, 1864. Three vols., 8vo, original blue cloth.

> This set is inscribed by the author to W. E. H. Lecky, the eminent historian. With the recipient's bookplate in each volume. Acquired in 1976.

CHARLES TENNYSON, LATER TURNER (1808–1879)

622. Tennyson, Charles. Sonnets and fugitive pieces. Cambridge: published by B. Bridges, 1830. 8vo, original purple cloth.

> The first book by Tennyson's older brother, preceded only by his contributions to *Poems, by Two Brothers* (1827; no. 420) and a hitherto unknown prize poem printed in 1828 (see under Arthur Hallam, no. 669). These sonnets were noticed and praised by a select few, most notably Coleridge, whose annotated copy is extant. Charles Tennyson had talent, but published little; his next book appeared after a gap of thirty-four years, by which time he had changed his surname to Turner, having in the 1830s succeeded to the small property of a great-uncle. This copy is in a secondary binding; the earliest copies were issued in boards. Remarkably, bound in at the front is an Edward Moxon catalogue dated March 1856. Tipped in at the back are two manuscript poems, both signed "C. T. T." The first, entitled

"Autumn," consists of four six-line stanzas, and appears to be unpublished. The second, "On Seeing at Sunrise the Shadow of a Lattice and Leaves Cast on a Bedroom Wall," was published in *Sonnets* (1864; no. 623) as "The Lattice at Sunrise," with several slight textual variants. Acquired in 1984.

623. Turner, Charles [Tennyson]. Sonnets. London and Cambridge: Macmillan and Co., 1864. Sm. 8vo, original bright green cloth.

> The author's second book. He is identified on the title page as vicar of Grasby, Lincoln. Acquired in 1987.

624. Turner, Charles [Tennyson]. Sonnets, lyrics, and translations. London: Henry S. King & Co., 1873. Sm. 8vo, original blue cloth.

> The author's last book, dedicated to Alfred Tennyson. This copy is inscribed by him on the front flyleaf to the poet William Allingham ("with my kind regards"). Acquired in 1977.

625. Turner, Charles Tennyson. Collected sonnets: old and new. London: C. Kegan Paul & Co., 1880. 8vo, original dark blue cloth.

> The most complete collection of the author's poetry, published shortly after his death. Edited by Hallam Tennyson, who has contributed a memoir; there is also a memorial poem by Alfred Tennyson. This copy belonged to Turner's goddaughter, Susan Jane Hannam, née Haddesley. On the title page she has signed her name, with the date of her godfather's death and a notice of their relationship. On the flyleaves she has transcribed five pages of verse composed between 1834 and 1841. The first of the poems is "To Susan J. Haddesley," and the second is called "Translations of a Clerical Godfather"; both appear to be unpublished. Hannam has also made a few interesting annotations in the text, adding to Hallam Tennyson's notice, for example, the rather charming fact that her godfather trained his horses to respond to his commands in Greek. She also notes that one lyric was written at the joint request of herself and Cecilia Tennyson. Acquired in 1980.

FREDERICK TENNYSON (1807–1898)

626. Tennyson, Frederick. The isles of Greece: Sappho and Alcaeus. London and New York: Macmillan and Co., 1890. 8vo, original dark blue cloth.

> An epic poem, based on surviving fragments of Greek verse, by Tennyson's eldest brother. Acquired in 1982.

627. Tennyson, Frederick. Poems of the day and year. London: John Lane; Stone and Kimball (Chicago), 1895. 8vo, original vellum, stamped in gilt.

> A special copy, as is explained by a printed note on the verso of the half-title: "Twenty-five vellum bound copies of the first edition were printed for private circulation of which this is No. 12." This was one of a number of titles co-published by John Lane and the imaginative Chicago firm of Stone and Kimball; surprisingly, in his exceptionally thorough bibliography of Stone and Kimball's books (1940), Sidney Kramer makes no mention of this limited issue. Acquired in 1988.

628. Tennyson, Frederick. Poems of the day and year. London: John Lane; Stone and Kimball (Chicago), 1895. 8vo, original orange buckram cloth.

> This copy, in the trade binding, is inscribed at the front, "To Edmund Neel [?] Esq. C. P. E. With Capn. J. Tennyson's & the Author's compliments, Feb. 4th, 1898." Below, in a very shaky hand, is the signature "F. Tennyson." Frederick Tennyson died on February 26, 1898. His oldest child, Julius, was a captain in the army. Acquired in 1977.

MARTIN FARQUHAR TUPPER (1810–1889)

629. Tupper, Martin Farquhar. A batch of war ballads. London: T. Bosworth, 1854. Sm. 8vo, original pink printed wrappers.

> Martin Tupper was one of Queen Victoria's favorite writers. His *Proverbial Philosophy*, first published in 1838, became one of the most popular of all Victorian books, going through numerous editions and regularly selling at least five thousand copies a year. Acquired in 1991.

630. Tupper, Martin Farquhar. Martin F. Tupper on rifle-clubs. Some verse and prose about national rifle-clubs. London and New York: Routledge, Warnes, & Routledge, 1859. Sm. 8vo, original green printed wrappers.

> Tupper feared an invasion from France, and advocated the formation of bands of armed citizenry. This pamphlet is very rare; the only copies located are at the British Library, the Bodleian, Cambridge, and the National Library of Scotland (all copyright-deposit libraries). Acquired in 1991.

631. Tupper, Martin Farquhar. The anti-ritualistic satire. "Tupper's directorium": or plan of the ritualistic campaign; being secret instructions to our Anglican clergy. Guildford: published by J. W. Barfoot, n.d. [1867]. Sm. 8vo, original pale green printed wrappers.

A pamphlet of poems in opposition to High Church practices. This original printing is apparently unrecorded; the NUC, WorldCat, and Copac list only a "new edition," published in London by Simpkin, Marshall & Co. in 1868. This copy is inscribed by the author on the front wrapper in 1875 to W. J. Mercer. Tupper has himself added "scarce." Acquired in 1991.

THOMAS WADE (1805–1875)

632. Wade, Thomas. A volume containing three plays. London: 1829–1830. Three vols. in one, 12mo, contemporary green cloth.

The author's entire dramatic output. "Throughout his career, whether in his poetry, his dramatic productions, or his journalistic work, Wade's writing is fired by a reformist zeal and progressive temper, an energy which was inspired by Shelley, who to the last remained Wade's ideal."–*Oxford DNB*. Included here are the following:

(a) [Wade, Thomas.] Woman's love; or, the triumph of patience. A drama, in five acts. First performed at the Theatre Royal, Covent Garden, on Wednesday, December 17th, 1828. Second edition. London: Smith, Elder and Co., 1829.

(b) Wade, Thomas. The phrenologists: a farce, in two acts. By Thomas Wade, author of "Woman's Love," a drama; &c. First performed at the Theatre Royal, Covent Garden, on Tuesday, January 12th, 1830. London: sold by J. Onwhyn; and may be had of all booksellers, 1830.

(c) Wade, Thomas. The Jew of Arragon; or, the Hebrew queen. A tragedy, in five acts. By Thomas Wade, author of "Duke Andrea; or, Woman's Love," a drama. Performed at the Theatre Royal, Covent Garden, on Wednesday, October 20th, 1830. London: Smith, Elder and Co., 1830.

Each play is inscribed by Wade on the title page, "Serle, Esqr.–with the author's complts." The recipient was no doubt the dramatist, novelist, and theater manager Thomas James Serle (1798–1889), who himself published half a dozen plays in the 1830s. This volume has the bookplate of H. Buxton Forman, with his characteristic initials on a front flyleaf. Buxton Forman has listed the three titles, and added, "All good copies with author's autograph." Buxton Forman–and because of him T. J. Wise as well–was a great enthusiast of Wade. In 1895 he gathered together a number of Wade's scattered poems from manuscripts and journals, and published them with a long tribute as "Wade: The Poet and His Surroundings," in vol. 1 of his *Literary Anecdotes of the Nineteenth Century*. Forman's praise was unstinting: "With the sole exception of Thomas Lovell Beddoes, no nineteenth-century English poet whose merit equals that of Thomas Wade has been so liberally neglected." Buxton Forman was not quite so enthusiastic about the literary quality of *The Phrenologists*, but he did recognize its scarcity: "If the little book were as excellent as it is rare, it would indeed be a treasure. So hard is it to find that Wade's widow was unable to say if it had ever been published or not." Acquired in 2008.

DAVID WINGATE (1828–1892)

633. Wingate, David. Lily Neil: a poem. Edinburgh and London: William Blackwood and Sons, 1879. 8vo, original green cloth.

> The third of this Scottish poet's four books of verse. This copy is inscribed on the verso of the dedication leaf, "To Kenneth McLachlan from David Wingate." Acquired in 1984.

THOMAS WOOLNER (1825–1892)

634. Woolner, Thomas. My beautiful lady. London: Macmillan and and Co., 1863. 8vo; original brown pebbled cloth.

> The author's first book. While still in his early twenties and a struggling sculptor, Woolner made the acquaintance of Rossetti, and before long he became an original member of the influential circle of English artists who styled themselves the Pre-Raphaelite Brotherhood. Two small portions of the present volume had been contributed to the first number of *The Germ*, published in 1850 and for a brief time the chief repository of Pre-Raphaelite literature. Woolner went on to become a major artist of the Victorian era, noted chiefly for his portrait sculptures. Acquired in 1981.

635. Woolner, Thomas. Silenus. London: Macmillan and Co., 1884. 8vo, original dark blue cloth.

> The artist's third book, a long poem on classical themes. Acquired in 2001.

OTHER POETRY, MAJOR AND MINOR, OF THE MID-NINETEENTH CENTURY

WILLIAM HARRISON AINSWORTH (1805–1882)

636. [Ainsworth, William Harrison.] The maid's revenge; and A summer evening's tale; with other poems. By Cheviot Ticheburn [pseud.]. London: G. & W. B. Whittaker, 1823. 8vo, original brown wrappers.

> The author's first book. Second issue, with a cancel title page. These sheets first appeared in 1822 as *Poems by Cheviot Ticheburn*, with the imprint of John Arliss; according to Wise, the only surviving example is in the Manchester Reference Library (none is listed in WorldCat or Copac). This copy is signed on the inside front wrapper by W. J. P. Aston; at the top of the front flyleaf is the signature "Wm. P. Aston." In 1826, Ainsworth published his first work of fiction, *Sir John Chiverton*, and launched his career as a highly successful writer of historical novels. That book, published anonymously, was written in collaboration with a school friend, John Partington Aston (1805–1882). Acquired in 1978.

GEORGE BORROW (1803–1881)

637. Borrow, George, translator. Romantic ballads, translated from the Danish; and miscellaneous pieces. Norwich: printed and published by S. Wilkin, 1826. 8vo, contemporary half blue calf.

> George Borrow's second book, preceded only by an anonymous prose translation from the German. Borrow had 500 copies of this early work printed in Norwich, and 200 were issued with an imprint from that city. The remainder were sent to John Taylor, of Taylor and Hessey, the publisher of such authors as Keats and Clare, and some of these were eventually sent on to Wightman and Cramp; both London firms replaced the original title page with one of their own. Copies of the two London issues do not contain the three-page list of subscribers for 161 copies with which this first issue concludes. The Simon Nowell-Smith copy. Acquired in 2002.

638. Borrow, George, translator. Targum. Or metrical translations from thirty languages and dialects. St. Petersburg: printed by Schulz and Beneze, 1835. 8vo, half dark green morocco, by Zaehnsdorf.

The first and more substantial of two collections of verse printed by Borrow in Russia in 1835, during his two-year stay there, when he supervised the printing of a translation of the Bible into the Manchu dialect (under the auspices of the British and Foreign Bible Society). Included are poems translated from Arabic, Turkish, Chinese, Greek, Russian (including one by Pushkin), Portuguese, and Anglo-Saxon. With the signature on the flyleaf of Edwin H. Abbot. Acquired in 1992.

ITEM 638

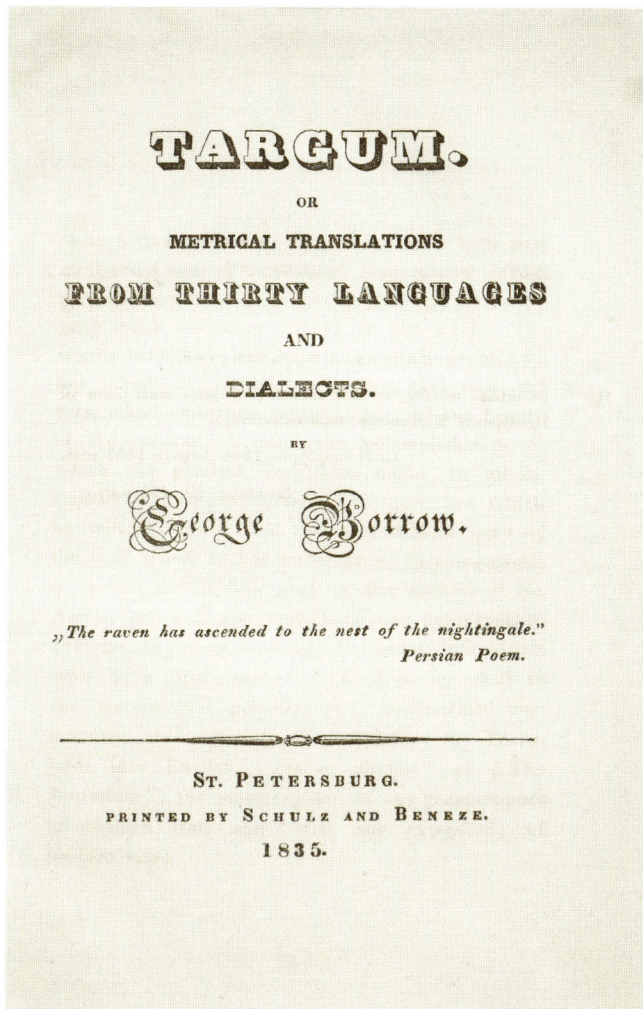

TARGUM.

OR

METRICAL TRANSLATIONS

FROM THIRTY LANGUAGES

AND

DIALECTS.

BY

George Borrow.

„*The raven has ascended to the nest of the nightingale.*"
Persian Poem.

St. Petersburg.

PRINTED BY Schulz AND Beneze.

1835.

639. [Borrow, George, translator.] The talisman. From the Russian of Alexander Pushkin. With other pieces. St. Petersburg: printed by Schulz and Beneze, 1835. 8vo, folded, as issued.

> The smaller of two collections of poetry printed by Borrow while he was in Russia. Included in this fourteen-page pamphlet are two poems by Pushkin ("The Talisman" and "The Mermaid"), three "ancient Russian songs," an "ancient ballad" (from the Malo-Russian), and "The Renegade," from the Polish of Adam Mickiewicz. This copy is from the library of Henry Cabot Lodge (1850–1924), the noted Republican senator from Massachusetts, who was an enthusiastic collector of rare books in the manner popularized by T. J. Wise; laid in is a catalogue slip in Lodge's hand. Acquired in 1984.

CHARLOTTE BRONTË (1816–1855), EMILY BRONTË (1818–1848), AND ANNE BRONTË (1820–1849)

640. [Brontë, Charlotte, Emily, and Anne.] Poems by Currer, Ellis, and Acton Bell [pseuds.]. London: Aylott and Jones, 1846. 8vo, green morocco, by Sangorski & Sutcliffe, original cloth covers and spine bound in at the end.

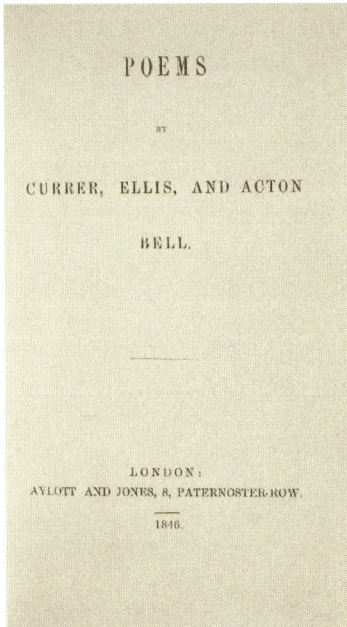

ITEM 640

The first publication of the Brontë sisters, and in its earliest form one of the most sought-after rarities of Victorian literature. The original printing, as organized by Charlotte Brontë, consisted of a thousand copies, but after a year the publishers had sold only two. Several more had been sent to the copyright-deposit libraries and eventually a few others were given away. After the appearance of *Jane Eyre* in 1847, the publishers, Smith, Elder and Co., took over the remaining 961 sets of sheets and reissued the volume with their own title page. This first issue, with the Aylott and Jones imprint, is described by Wise as "one of the most elusive objects of the collector's search." Twenty copies or more of this first issue can now be located, but examples have now pretty much vanished from the market. Acquired in 1977.

326

641. [Brontë, Charlotte, Emily, and Anne.] Poems by Currer, Ellis, and Acton Bell [pseuds.]. London: Smith, Elder and Co., 1846 [1848]. 8vo, original green cloth.

> The second issue, with a cancel title page. Included is an errata slip, which does not appear in Aylott and Jones copies (and is not always present in the reissue). Acquired in 1972.

642. [Brontë, Charlotte, Emily, and Anne, contributors.] Spice islands passed in the sea of reading. Seventy-three selections from the poets of Yorkshire. Bradford: published by Abraham Holroyd, 1859. 12mo, original red cloth.

> A rare provincial anthology originally published in six numbers for a penny each, and here bound up with a general title page and index. Included are five poems by the Brontë sisters, one by Charlotte ("Frances," from the *Poems* of 1846), two by Emily ("Immortality" and "A Death-Scene"), and two by Anne ("Resignation" and "The Consolation"). With the signature on the dedication page of Edwin Ridings, Clayton House. Acquired in 1983.

PATRICK BRONTË (1770–1861)

643. Brontë, Patrick. Cottage poems, by the Rev. Patrick Brontë, B.A. minister of Hartshead-cum-Clifton, near Leeds, Yorkshire. Halifax: printed and sold by P. K. Holden, for the author; sold also by B. Crosby and Co. (London); F. Houlston and Son (Wellington); and by the booksellers of Halifax, Leeds, York, &c., 1811. Sm. 8vo, original pale blue printed boards, rebacked.

> The first collection of poems by the father of the Brontë sisters, preceded only by a very rare twenty-three-page poem called *Winter-Evening Thoughts*, printed in Wakefield in 1810, a revised version of which appears here as "Winter-Night Meditations." This copy is from the library of H. Buxton Forman, and has his bookplate, penciled initials, and date of acquisition. Acquired in 1981.

644. Brontë, Patrick. The phenomenon; or, an account in verse, of the extraordinary disruption of a bog, which took place in the moors of Haworth, on the 12th day of September, 1824: intended as a reward-book for the higher classes in Sunday-schools. Bradford: printed and sold by T. Inkersley; and by F. Westley (London), 1824. 12mo, old wrappers.

A rare poem for young readers. WorldCat lists only a copy at the British Library, to which Copac adds another at York Minster. Acquired in 1983.

EDWARD GEORGE BULWER LYTTON (1803–1873)

645. Bulwer Lytton, Edward George. Ismael; an oriental tale. With other poems. . . . Written between the age of thirteen and fifteen. London: printed for J. Hatchard and Son, 1820. 12mo, original light blue boards, printed paper label.

> The author's first book, published when he was seventeen; the influence of Byron is apparent throughout. Included is a dedicatory poem to Sir Walter Scott, who sent a polite acknowledgment of the copy offered to him. There is a preface by the "editor" Charles Wallington, who signs himself, in Greek, as "Philomousos." Wallington, a schoolmaster in Ealing, was a private tutor to Bulwer Lytton for the better part of three years, and thought him a genius. His student soon developed into one of the major writers of his generation. A small remainder of this book appeared on the market many years ago, which accounts for the survival of copies in fine original condition; these copies have long since vanished from the market. This copy, however, is not from that cache, but was acquired from a later dispersal of books and other objects from Knebworth, Bulwer Lytton's ancestral estate. Acquired in 2003.

646. Bulwer Lytton, Edward George. Ismael; an oriental tale, with other poems. London: printed for T. and J. Hoitt, 1821. 12mo, original drab boards, printed paper label.

> "Second edition." In fact a reissue of the sheets of the first edition, published by Hatchard the year before, with a new title page, from which the reference to the author's age was removed. This copy was also acquired from the dispersal of books and other objects from Knebworth. Acquired in 2003.

647. [Bulwer Lytton, Edward George.] Delmour; or, a tale of a sylphid. And other poems. London: printed for Carpenter and Son; by C. Whittingham (Chiswick), 1823. 8vo, original pale blue wrappers.

> Bulwer Lytton's second book, published anonymously when he was twenty-one. Bulwer Lytton had a rather morbid streak when he was a young man, and was nicknamed "Childe Harold" by one of his acquaintances; his early poetry is indeed Byronic. Acquired in 1993.

648. [Bulwer Lytton, Edward George.] Weeds and wildflowers by E. G. L. B. Paris: not published, 1826. 8vo, original green printed wrappers.

> Bulwer Lytton's third book of verse, privately printed at the age of twenty-three, while he was living the life of a dandy amid the fashionable society of France. As in the case of *Ismael* (no. 645), a remainder of this book appeared on the market many years ago, and these copies, too, are in fine original condition. Again, this copy is not from that cache, but was acquired from the later dispersal of books and other objects from Knebworth. Acquired in 2003.

649. [Bulwer Lytton, Edward George.] The sea-captain; or, the birthright: a drama in five acts. By the author of "The Lady of Lyon," "Richelieu," &c. London: Saunders and Otley, 1839. 8vo, original dark green cloth.

> The author's fourth play, in blank verse; his plays were generally successful on the stage. With the bookplate of Lionel Ames. Acquired in 1993.

HENRY LYTTON EARLE BULWER (1801–1872)

650. [Bulwer, Henry Lytton Earle.] Ode on the death of Napoleon; lines upon the Neapolitan revolution; and other poems. London: published by Gossling and Egley, 1822. 8vo, contemporary turquoise calf, covers elaborately stamped in blind with gilt borders, spine gilt, red morocco label, m.e.

> The author's first book, published when he was twenty-one. He was the older brother of the novelist Edward George Bulwer Lytton, to whom the book is dedicated. He went on to become a successful diplomat, particularly in Washington, DC, where he was very popular. This title is occasionally listed as if Bulwer Lytton's authorship were uncertain, but it is confirmed here by a neat contemporary inscription (dated 1822) on a front flyleaf, possibly in the hand of the dedicatee (as suggested by the ornate gift binding). Acquired in 2003.

THOMAS BURBIDGE (1816–1892)

651. Burbidge, Thomas. Poems, longer and shorter. London: William Pickering, 1838. 8vo, original dark green cloth, printed paper label.

> The author's first book. Burbidge is now largely a forgotten figure, but he is of interest as an intimate friend of A. H. Clough, one of five schoolmates

to whom this book is dedicated; his only other book was, in fact, jointly published with Clough in 1849 (*Ambarvalia*; no. 485). Included here are two poems addressed to Wordsworth, and one on a portrait of him in King's College, Cambridge. This copy is inscribed, "From the Author" on the front flyleaf. John Sparrow's copy, with his book label. Acquired in 1993.

ISABELLA CRAIG, LATER CRAIG-KNOX (1831–1903)

652. [Craig, Isabella, editor.] Poems: an offering to Lancashire. Printed and published for the art exhibition the relief of distress in the cotton districts. London: Emily Faithfull, printer and publisher in ordinary to Her Majesty, Victoria Press, 1863. Sm. 8vo, original green cloth.

> This slim collection was printed in an edition of one thousand copies for charity. Included are fourteen poems, mostly original, including a long poem by Christina Rossetti ("A Royal Princess") and a shorter one by Dante Gabriel Rossetti ("Sudden Light"); there are also contributions by George MacDonald, William Bell Scott, William Allingham, Richard Monckton Milnes, and Frederick Locker. The editor, usually known as Isa Craig, who also contributed a poem ("Brothers"), was born in Scotland but moved to London in 1857, where she became involved with feminist groups. This copy has the bookplate of H. Buxton Forman, and his penciled note of acquisition, dated October 20, 1877. Acquired in 1985.

AUBREY THOMAS DE VERE (1814–1902)

653. De Vere, Aubrey. The Waldenses, or the fall of Rora: a lyrical sketch. With other poems. Oxford: John Henry Parker; Rivingtons (London), 1842. 8vo, original dark claret cloth.

> The poet's first book, a collection of lyrics and meditations on religion. The third and last edition of the *CBEL* (1999) gives priority to *A Song of Faith* (1842), but this is in fact a collection of poems by de Vere's father. The revision of this volume of the *CBEL* introduced a startling numbers of errors of this sort. This copy is from the library of Roger Senhouse, with his book label and signature. This was the copy shown at John Hayward's 1947 exhibition of English poetry at the National Book League, which served as a guide to many book collectors. For some reason, as Hayward notes in his catalogue, a leaf following the title page has been excised from this copy; it bore a dedication to the mathematician and astronomer William Rowan Hamilton. Acquired in 1974.

654. De Vere, Aubrey. The search after Proserpine, recollections of Greece, and other poems. Oxford: John Henry Parker; Rivingtons (London), 1843. 8vo, original purple cloth.

> The poet's second book. De Vere sent a copy to Walter Savage Landor, whom he had long admired. "Landor did not read the book for five years but when he did heaped praise upon it, and hailed de Vere as breathing the 'pure fresh air' of Greece."–*Oxford DNB*, citing Henry Taylor's *Autobiography* (1885). This is, in fact, Landor's copy, copiously annotated. At one point, Landor calls a sonnet "worthy of Milton," which is high praise indeed, as Milton was Landor's literary idol. The notes here seem to have been done at different times, and can be divided into two groups: (1) those on inserted onionskin slips, clearly in Landor's hand; (2) those penciled directly onto the pages, possibly in another hand, though the language and sentiments are consistent. There is an early note on the front pastedown, which reads, "The words & marks on the margins of this book come from the hand of Walter Savage Landor." Acquired in 1975.

655. De Vere, Aubrey. Picturesque sketches of Greece and Turkey. London: Richard Bentley, 1850. Two vols., 8vo, original red cloth.

> This book is based upon de Vere's experiences in the course of a tour of the Mediterranean in 1843–44. The first volume is largely devoted to an account of Athens, and the second deals mostly with Constantinople. De Vere had mixed feelings about the Greeks, whom he described as "a false people . . . never ashamed of being detected in a lie." With the penciled signature of R. L. Whelford (?) on the front flyleaf of vol. 1, and the later book labels of John Taylor. Acquired in 2006.

656. De Vere, Aubrey. The legends of Saint Patrick. London: Henry S. King & Co.; McGlashan and Gill (Dublin), 1872. 8vo, original dark green cloth.

> A collection of versified episodes from the life of Ireland's patron saint, describing his conversion to Christianity; with a long preface on Irish legends in general. The book is dedicated to the memory of Wordsworth. This copy is inscribed on a front flyleaf, "Henry Reeve Esq. from the author." The recipient was a prominent literary and political journalist. Acquired in 1982.

657. De Vere, Aubrey. Alexander the Great. A dramatic poem. London: Henry S. King & Co.; McGlashan and Gill (Dublin), 1874. 8vo, original green cloth.

This copy is inscribed by the author to the historian W. E. H. Lecky, and bears his bookplate. Acquired in 2000.

658. De Vere, Aubrey. St. Thomas of Canterbury: a dramatic poem. London: Henry S. King & Co., 1876. 8vo, original dark green cloth.

This copy is inscribed on the half-title, "E. V. Monsell from her affectionate uncle Aubrey de Vere, Oct. 25, 1876." Acquired in 1983.

659. De Vere, Aubrey. Antar and Zara: an eastern romance. Inisfail and other poems meditative and lyrical. London: Henry S. King & Co., 1877. 8vo, original green cloth.

This copy is inscribed by the author on a front flyleaf (August 7, 1881) to the Earl of Lytton, that is, Edward Robert Bulwer Lytton, a popular poet who wrote under the pen name "Owen Meredith." Acquired in 1979.

660. De Vere, Aubrey. The foray of Queen Maeve and other legends of Ireland's heroic age. London: Kegan Paul, Trench, & Co., 1882. 8vo, original green cloth.

This copy is inscribed on the front flyleaf, "His Excellency James Russell Lowell from A. de V., London June 21, 1882." Lowell's signature is on the half-title; he was at the time the US minister to England. Acquired in 1986.

661. De Vere, Aubrey. Medieval records and sonnets. London: Macmillan & Co., 1893. 8vo, original dark green cloth.

This copy is inscribed by the author on the title page to Juliet Pollock (1894). Juliet Creed, Lady Pollock, published a book on the actor and theater manager William Charles Macready and another called *Amateur Theatricals*, along with several books for children. With the book label of Edward Sandford Burgess. Acquired in 1975.

BENJAMIN DISRAELI (1804–1881)

662. Disraeli, Benjamin. The revolutionary epick. The work of Disraeli the younger, author of "The Psychological Romance." London: Edward Moxon, 1834. [With:] The revolutionary epick. . . . Books II and III. Containing the plea of Lyridon, the genius of federalism; and the first part of the conquest of Italy. London: Edward Moxon, 1834. Two vols., 4to, original gray boards, printed paper side labels.

An ambitious poem of some four thousand lines, in which the future Tory prime minister contrasts feudal and federal systems of government from early times to the triumphs of Napoleon. A substantially revised version was published in 1864, in the dedication to which Disraeli says that only fifty copies of the first edition were printed; this statement has often been repeated since that time, but is clearly false. Despite the unusually large format, this was a normal Moxon imprint; the side labels indicate that the first volume was sold for 9s. 6d. in boards, and that the price of the second volume was optimistically raised to 12 s. This set is inscribed on the front flyleaf of the first volume, "The Right Hon. the Earl of Shaftesbury from the Author"; the inscription is not in Disraeli's hand, and was no doubt inserted at his request by the publisher, Moxon. The Simon Nowell-Smith copy. Acquired in 2002.

AMELIA ANN BLANDFORD EDWARDS (1831–1892)

663. [Edwards, Amelia.] Ballads. By the author of "Barbara's History." London: Tinsley Brothers, 1865. 8vo, original green cloth.

The author's only book of original verse. Amelia Edwards was for a time a successful novelist, and she contributed many ghost stories to the Christmas numbers of Dickens's *Household Words* and *All the Year Round*. She later became an intrepid traveler and a passionate Egyptologist. On the front flyleaf of this copy the author has penned a very warm sixteen-line love poem, "To Lucy Renshaw," dated July 11, 1872; at the end of the text is another manuscript poem, of twenty lines, entitled "On the Rose She Gave Me." Tipped in to face the title page is a signed photograph. At the time Amelia Edwards presented this volume, Lucy Renshaw was her closest friend. This was the year the two women undertook an adventure in the Dolomites, an area then largely unknown and inaccessible; Edwards described the trip the following year in *Untrodden Peaks and Unfrequented Valleys*, a book that did much to open the region to tourism. At about the same time, Edwards and Renshaw set out for Egypt, after which they went on to Syria, crossed the Lebanese ranges to Damascus and Baalbeck, whence they proceeded on to Constantinople. But it was their experiences among the archaeological excavations in Egypt, particularly at Abu Simbel, that set the course of the last twenty years of Amelia Edwards's life. Acquired in 1981.

GEORGE ELIOT [MARY ANN EVANS (1819–1880)]

664. Eliot, George. Agatha. London: Trübner & Co., 1869. 8vo, sewn, as issued.

> A Thomas J. Wise forgery of a true rarity. George Eliot wrote this poem after a visit to a peasant's cottage at Sankt Märgen, in Germany's Black Forest, in the summer of 1868, and it was first published in the United States, in *The Atlantic Monthly*, in August 1869. To protect the British copyright, a small number of copies were printed in London in pamphlet form. This is one of only a handful of genuine titles forged by Wise, whose normal method was to invent a plausible but nonexistent first edition, as with the *Reading Sonnets* of Elizabeth Barrett Browning (see no. 464). The two printings are not textually identical; Wise's forgery may be easily identified by the presence of a comma after the word "behind" on p. 11, l. 16. In the Ashley catalogue, Wise explains the "minute variants" by concocting a story involving Buxton Forman's youthful involvement with seeing the poem into print: "Of the first edition twenty copies only were printed. These, however, proved insufficient to meet the demands of friends who clamoured for them, and a second batch of fifty copies were ordered. But the types had already been distributed, and were set up afresh for the second printing. Mr. Forman claimed that these later copies were a 'second issue of the first edition'; but as the types from which they were printed were re-set, they undoubtedly form a *second edition* of the poem." For the intricacies of this episode, see John Carter, "George Eliot's *Agatha* 1869–and after," *The Book Collector*, vol. 6, no. 3 (Autumn 1957), pp. 244–52. Exactly how many copies survive of the genuine first edition of this poem is a bit difficult to determine. With the bookplate of William Garth. Acquired in 1987.

665. [Eliot, George.] Brother and sister sonnets by Marian Lewes. London: for private circulation only, 1869. 8vo, original pale blue printed wrappers.

> This is a conventional Wise forgery; the poems are genuine, but there was no prior separate printing of them. Copies of this fabrication first appeared on the market about 1888. With the bookplate of William Garth. Acquired in 1987.

666. [Eliot, George.] Brother and sister sonnets by Marian Lewes. London: for private circulation only, 1869. 8vo, original gray printed wrappers.

> A forgery of a forgery. This counterfeit can be easily distinguished from the

Wise printing by the presence of fleurs-de-lis at the corners on the front wrapper. Circumstantial evidence, notably the appearance of copies in the book trade, suggests that this reprint was produced in the United States, possibly without any knowledge that the earlier printing was a fake; there is no reason to think that Wise was involved. Acquired in 1981.

SAMUEL FERGUSON (1810–1886)

667. Ferguson, Samuel. Poems. Dublin: William McGee; George Bell and Sons (London), 1880. 8vo, original blue cloth.

The author was one of the leading forerunners of the Irish literary renaissance. An antiquary as well as a poet, Ferguson made great efforts to create modern poetry from ancient Irish legends; some of the verses in this volume, published when the author was seventy, treat subjects later used by Yeats. At the end of the volume is an elegy to Sir William Wilde, Oscar Wilde's father. The copy is inscribed on the front flyleaf, "Mrs. Bernard, with sincere regards, from the Author. Dublin, June 1880." On the front pastedown is the inscription "Bessie E. Lyster, from her father, James Lyster." Acquired in 1976.

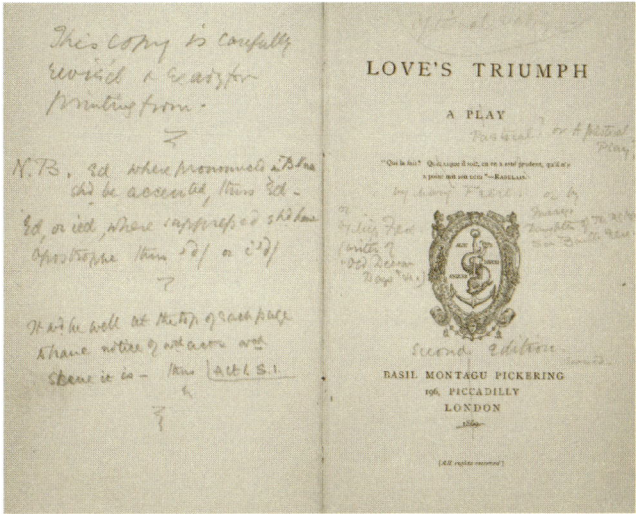

MARY ELIZA ISABELLA FRERE (1845–1911)

668. [Frere, Mary Eliza Isabella.] Love's triumph: a play. London: Basil Montagu Pickering, 1869. 8vo, original green cloth.

A verse play in the seventeenth-century manner. Mary Frere was the daughter of the prominent British statesman Sir Bartle Frere. She spent much of her early life in India, when her father was governor of Bombay, and she developed an interest in Hindu folklore that led to the publication in 1868 of *Old Deccan Days*, a collection of southern Indian fairy tales that achieved some popularity. This is the author's own copy of her play; it has been heavily revised in manuscript throughout for a second edition that never appeared. With the book label of Simon Nowell-Smith. Acquired in 1977.

ARTHUR HENRY HALLAM (1811–1833)

669. [Hallam, Arthur Henry.] Timbuctoo. [Cambridge: 1829.] 8vo, bound sixth in a volume of twenty-three separate pieces, later nineteenth-century half maroon morocco.

Arthur Hallam's first separate publication, an anonymous private printing of a poem submitted for a university prize that was won by Tennyson. "It was over the submission of their poems in April [1829] that Tennyson and Hallam first became friends."–Robert Bernard Martin, *Tennyson: The Unquiet Heart* (1980), p. 69. Only three copies of this seven-page pamphlet are recorded, at Harvard, Yale, and Princeton. The present copy is inscribed, "From the Author" on the first page, and is no doubt the copy given by Hallam to Richard Monckton Milnes, who has added Hallam's name in the upper corner. The poem forms part of a volume assembled by Monckton Milnes at a later date and consisting entirely of pieces relating to his days at Trinity College, Cambridge, where he belonged to the celebrated

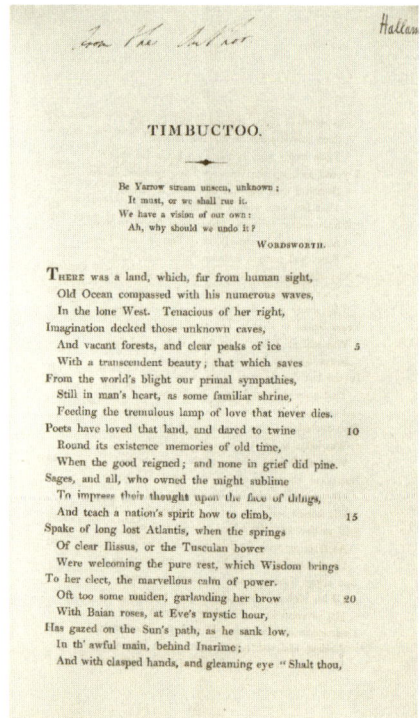

ITEM 669

336

undergraduate club called the Apostles, whose membership of twelve included Hallam and Tennyson. Most of the substantial Monckton Milnes library was inherited by his son, Robert Offley Ashburton Crewe-Milnes, Marquess of Crewe; a fair number of books from Crewe Hall appeared at an auction at Christie's East in London in 1997, where this remarkable volume was acquired. This volume also includes the following titles:

(a) Shelley, Percy Bysshe. Adonais. An elegy on the death of John Keats, author of Endymion, Hyperion, etc. Cambridge: printed by W. Metcalfe, and sold by Messrs. Gee & Bridges, 1829.

Second edition, the first printed in England; preceded by the original printing at Pisa in 1821. "It was this second edition of *Adonais*, brought out by Arthur Hallam, Monckton Milnes, and their friends, that was chiefly responsible for the first general enthusiasm over Shelley."—Ruth S. Granniss, *Shelley* (1923), p. 73. The short, unsigned note here, which follows the title page, is, in fact, by Hallam. Curiously (and regrettably), Shelley's four-page preface (pp. v–viii) is not present in this copy. Whether it was removed by Monckton Milnes, or merely dropped out at some point, cannot be determined; a slight ink offset indicates that it was once there.

(b) [Anon.] The invasion of Russia, by Napoleon Buonaparte. [Colophon:] Cambridge: Harwood & Hall, printers, n.d. [1828].

A poem no doubt submitted in the competition for the Chancellor's Medal at the Cambridge commencement of 1828; the medal was won by Christopher Wordsworth's poem on the same theme. No other copy of this ten-page poem has been located.

(c) [Tennyson, Charles, later Turner.] The expedition of Napoleon Buonaparte into Russia. [Cambridge: 1828.]

Another ten-page poem for the same competition, and also apparently unrecorded. The manuscript attribution to Charles Tennyson on the title page is in the hand of Monckton Milnes.

(d) Venables, George Stovin. The attempts made of late years to find a North-West Passage. A poem, which obtained the Chancellor's Medal at the Cambridge commencement, M.DCCC.XXXI. Cambridge: printed by H. Talbot, n.d. [1831].

A private printing, and very rare; the only copies located are at Cambridge and Illinois. Venables was also one of the Apostles; he went on to become a very successful barrister and journalist.

(e) Tennyson, Alfred. Timbuctoo. A poem, which obtained the Chancellor's Medal at the Cambridge commencement, M.DCCC.XXIX. [Cambridge: 1829.]

An extract from the forty-one-page *Prolusiones Academicæ*; for the remaining sheets of this collection, see below; there were also a small number of copies separately issued as offprints. Tennyson's second publication.

(f) [Venables, George Stovin.] [Caption title:] Byzantium. [Colophon:] Cambridge: printed by Talbot and Ladds, n.d. [1830].

An unsuccessful prize poem, privately printed. The author's name has been noted in manuscript on the first page. With a couple of very small ink corrections on the last page. Two copies are recorded, at the British Library and Cambridge.

(g) [Lushington, Henry.] Delphi. . . . A poem. [Cambridge: 1833.]

An unsuccessful prize poem, privately printed. The author's name has been noted in manuscript on the first page. His older brother Edmund Lushington was another member of the Apostles; he later married Tennyson's sister Cecilia. Two copies are located, at the British Library and Harvard.

(h) Wordsworth, Christopher. The invasion of Russia by Napoleon Buonaparte. A poem, which obtained the Chancellor's Medal at the Cambridge commencement, M.DCCC.XXVIII. [Cambridge: 1828.]

An extract from *Prolusiones Academicæ*, but bound separately by Monckton Milnes (see next item).

(i) [Prize poems.] Prolusiones academicæ præmiis annuis dignatæ et in curia Cantabrigiensi recitatæ comitiis maximis A. D. M.DCCC.XXVIII. Cambridge: typis Academicis excudit Joannes Smith, (1828).

The general title page and concluding section of this annual collection of prize poems.

(j) [Prize poems.] Prolusiones academicæ præmiis annuis dignatæ et in curia Cantabrigiensi recitatæ comitiis maximis A. D. M.DCCC.XXIX. Cambridge: typis Academicis excudit Joannes Smith, (1829).

The general title page and concluding section of this annual collection of prize poems; for the other section, see item (e), above.

(k) [Cambridge University.] [Docket title:] Baccalaurei quibus sua reservatur Senioritas Comitiis Posterioribus, 20 Mar. 1828. [Cambridge: 1828.]

Evidently some sort of program for a degree ceremony; the docket title is followed by a ranked list of twenty-four students, with the names of their colleges. The recto of each leaf contains a long Latin poem, and the author of each has been noted in manuscript. The first is by Brome of Trinity College, and the second by Selwyn of Saint John's, that is, George Augustus Selwyn (1809–1878), who later became bishop of New Zealand.

(l) [Cambridge University.] [Docket title:] Baccalaurei quibus sua reservatur Senioritas Comitiis Posterioribus, 21 Feb. 1828. [Cambridge: 1828.]

Similar to the preceding, but with a much longer roster of student names (sixty-three). The first Latin poem here is entitled "Bibliomania," and deals in a light way with the excesses of book collecting; there are references to Aldines (and Renouard's bibliography), the Shakespeare first folio, the "issue point" in Pine's Horace, and similar matters. This poem is identified as by "Wordsworth" of Trinity College, that is, Christopher Wordsworth (1807–1886), nephew of the poet. The other poem, untitled, is identified as by Herbert of Caius.

(m) [Tennyson, Frederick.] [Caption title:] Ægææ insulæ. [Cambridge: before 1830.]

A six-page poem in Greek, no doubt printed privately. No other copy has been located. The name of the author has been provided in manuscript by Monckton Milnes on the first page.

(n) [Anon.] Epilogue to Shakespeare's comedy of "Much Ado about Nothing"; performed Friday, 19th March, 1830, and printed at the request of the performers. Cambridge: printed by James Hodson, 1830.

The Apostles and their friends were keen on amateur theatricals. "There were intimate productions and readings of Shakespeare, in which Tennyson was especially good as Malvolio. In *Much Ado about Nothing* Hallam played Verges, Kemble was Dogberry, and Milnes was an overweight Beatrice, whom Kemble said he played 'like a languishing trull.' At one point the sofa on which Milnes sat collapsed, and he fell with his petticoats over his head, saying aloud a short vulgarity that Shakespeare had not provided for the 'elegant and high-minded Beatrice.'"—Robert Bernard Martin, *Tennyson: The Unquiet Heart* (1980), p. 128. Monckton Milnes is also listed as the stage manager of the production. "Jack" Kemble was the

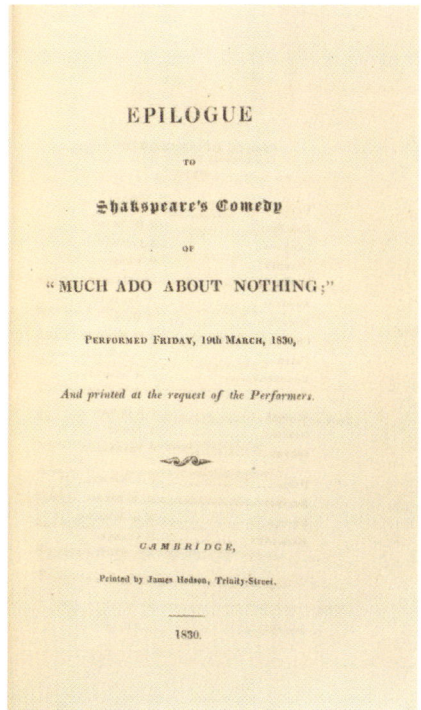

EPILOGUE

TO

𝕾𝖍𝖆𝖐𝖘𝖕𝖊𝖆𝖗𝖊'𝖘 𝕮𝖔𝖒𝖊𝖉𝖞

OF

"MUCH ADO ABOUT NOTHING;"

PERFORMED FRIDAY, 19th MARCH, 1830,

And printed at the request of the Performers.

CAMBRIDGE,

Printed by James Hodson, Trinity-Street.

1830.

ITEM 669 (n)

brother of the actress Fanny Kemble, with whom Hallam was for a time infatuated. Laid in is an amusing letter written in 1879 to Monckton Milnes by another member of the cast, Lord Ailesbury, who reminisces about the production fifty years earlier, and describes a recent meeting with Fanny Kemble, who had just turned seventy. Two other copies of this seven-page pamphlet have been located, at the Morgan Library and Folger.

(o) [Kinglake, Alexander William.] The post.... Wednesday, December 19, 1832. [Colophon:] Cambridge: W. Hatfield, (1832). Sm. 4to, folded in to fit the volume.

Presumably the only issue of this humorous periodical, though a face-tious note implies that another had preceded; no copy of any issue has been located. Monckton Milnes has identified Kinglake as the author; he also attended Trinity, and was friendly with both Tennyson and Thackeray. In 1844 he published *Eothen*, one of the classics of Victorian travel literature. Kinglake and Monckton Milnes remained friends for many years. The text of this little paper consists of comic sketches and poems, along with mock notices containing references to Kemble, James Spedding, and other members of the author's circle.

(p) A single leaf with facetious clippings pasted on, the first called "Scien-tific Intelligence," and the other an extract from a book, headed, "More Guesses at Truth."

The significance of these is not immediately apparent, though perhaps Monckton Milnes had a hand in them. *Guesses at Truth*, "by two broth-ers," that is, Julius Charles Hare and Augustus William Hare, had been published in 1827; this collection of aphorisms inspired by Wordsworth and Coleridge had attracted great attention.

(q) Grant, Robert. Cambridge University election. Copy of a letter to a member of the Senate of the University of Cambridge, from Robert Grant, Esq. M.P., fellow of Magdalene College. [Cambridge: ca. 1830.] Sm. 4to, broadside, folded.

Favoring the candidacy of a Mr. Cavendish. It is not clear why this broad-side has been included, nor has any record of it been found.

(r) [Cambridge University.] Prizemen of Trinity College for 1829. [Cam-bridge: 1829.] Single sheet.

Monckton Milnes is listed as the winner of the "English Essay" prize; he also won the second prize for "English Declamation" (after Sunderland). Dated December 16 at the end. Pasted on the verso is a manuscript slip reading, "Ascended Mr. Milnes, May 19, 1829. Mr. Whewell."

(s) [Sunderland, Thomas.] [Caption title:] The Revolution of 1688. A decla-mation delivered in the Chapel of Trinity College, Cambridge. [Colophon:] Cambridge: printed by Weston Hatfield, n.d. [1829].

A prize-winning oration, privately printed. Sunderland was perhaps the most earnest of the Apostles: he often complained that his friends were not serious enough. Sunderland and Tennyson rather disliked each other; Tennyson even wrote a satirical poem about Sunderland called "A Charac-ter." The authorship of this fifteen-page pamphlet is noted in manuscript by Monckton Milnes; no other copy has been located.

(t) [Cambridge University.] Laws and transactions of the Union Society, revised and corrected to March, M.DCCC.XXXIV, to which is annexed a list of the members and officers, from its formation in M.DCCC.XV. And a list of the periodical and other works taken in by the Society. Cambridge: printed by J. Hall, 1834.

The Union Society was an undergraduate debating club in which a number of the Apostles participated. Milnes, Kemble, and Sunderland were frequent speakers, and Kemble was even president for a term; Hal-lam spoke on two occasions, but the Tennyson brothers seem not to have been involved (though Charles is listed as a member). The text provides a full record of the debates, with the names of speakers pro and con for each question, and the final votes. One gets an occasional glimpse of the atmosphere, as in the entry for the debate on November 25, 1828, over the question "Is Mr. Wordsworth or Lord Byron the greater poet?" The debate had to be postponed: "No discussion took place on this question as the President [Kemble] deemed it necessary to dissolve the meeting in consequence of the turbulent state of the Society."

(u) [Cambridge University.] Laws of the Cambridge Literary Society. M.D.CCC.XXVIII. [On verso of title:] Cambridge: Harwood &' Hall, printers, (1828).

The rules of an undergraduate club devoted to the reading of members' essays; membership was limited to thirty. There is no list of members here, but presumably Monckton Milnes belonged.

(v) [Cambridge University.] Excerpta è statutis Academiæ Cantabrigiensis præfectorum interpretationibus, Senatûs decretis, et literis Regiis, ad schol-arium officia pertinata. Cambridge: typis academicis excudit J. Smith, 1819. A handbook of university rules and regulations for undergraduates, peri-odically updated; this would have been the version in print when Monck-ton Milnes, Tennyson, and Hallam were in attendance.

670. Hallam, Arthur Henry. Poems. [London: 1830.] 12mo, contemporary black morocco.

Privately printed, without a proper title page; the first leaf is a kind of half-title, reading simply, "Poems by A. H. Hallam, Esq." This collection had been intended to form part of a joint publication with poems by Tennyson, but at the last minute, with the poems set in type and the preface written, Hallam's father, the historian Henry Hallam, raised objections, and the venture was abandoned; Tennyson then issued his own poems as *Poems, Chiefly Lyrical* (no. 421).

His [Henry Hallam's] reluctance to let Arthur devote himself to literature was undoubtedly at the base of his objections, but he may also have taken exception to the love poems to Anna Wintour, for he said that some of the short poems were "unfit even for the limited circulation they might obtain, on account of their unveiling more of emotion than, consistently with what is due to him and to others, could be exposed to view." Hallam put a brave face on his disappointment and claimed that withdrawing the poems had been his own idea. . . . The cancellation of their joint publication was particularly frustrating to Tennyson and Hallam because the volume had been intended 'as a sort of seal' of their friendship. -- Robert Bernard Martin, *Tennyson: The Unquiet Heart* (1980), pp. 105–6.

About a dozen copies of this book can now be located; a handful of others are known without the title page and lacking the final six pages of text (pp. 169–74). This complete copy has on the front pastedown the armorial bookplate of Henry Monteith (1765–1848) of Carstairs, a cotton magnate and owner of huge textile mills. He had fourteen children, but his only surviving son was Robert Monteith (1811–1884), who, after beginning his studies at Glasgow University, proceeded to Trinity College, Cambridge, where he became a member of the Apostles, along with Tennyson and Hallam. Tennyson was later quite close to the Monteith family, and paid a number of visits over the years to Carstairs. It seems highly likely that it was Robert who first acquired, or was given, this copy of Hallam's *Poems*. Robert Monteith eventually inherited his father's great wealth and pursued an active career as a politician and philanthropist; in 1846 he was received into the Roman Catholic church by John Henry Newman. Acquired in 2010.

671. Hallam, Arthur Henry. Remains, in verse and prose. N.p. [London]: printed by W. Nicol, 1834. 8vo, brown morocco, by Riviere.

The author's major book, privately printed shortly after his untimely death at the age of twenty-two. The volume was edited, with a long biographical preface, by Hallam's father. This copy is inscribed, "From the Editor" on a preliminary blank leaf. With the bookplate of Violet Leconsfield. The H. Bradley Martin copy. Acquired in 1990.

ABRAHAM HAYWARD (1801–1884)

672. [Hayward, Abraham.] Verses of other days. (Printed for friends.) London: 1847. 12mo, original green cloth.

> The only book of poems by a prominent essayist, literary critic, and political journalist. "Extremely commonplace."–*DNB*. This copy is inscribed by Hayward on the front flyleaf to Mary Shelley; there are a fair number of published letters between the two that indicate a warm and informal relationship between them. Acquired in 1990.

673. Hayward, Abraham. Verses of other days. . . . (Reprinted, with additions, for friends.) [Colophon:] printed by Ballantyne, Hanson and Co., Edinburgh and London: 1878. 8vo, original blue-gray cloth.

> Second edition; first published in 1847. This copy is inscribed on the front flyleaf, "Mrs. Ford–from the writer, with best regards, A. H." Acquired in 2005.

674. Hayward, Abraham. Verses of other days. . . . (Reprinted, with additions, for friends.) N.p. [London]: 1882. 8vo, original green cloth.

> Third edition, enlarged; preceded by similar private printings in 1847 and 1878. This copy is inscribed by Hayward on the title page to the Countess of Roseberry. The recipient has identified some of the anonymous addressees of these poems, including the young Lillie Langtry. Acquired in 1990.

HENRY HOGG (1831–1874)

675. Hogg, Henry. Poems. London: Whittaker and Co.; J. Howitt (Nottingham), 1852. 8vo, contemporary green morocco, covers elaborately decorated in gilt with central panels stamped in blind, spine gilt, a.e.g.

> Hogg was born in Nottingham, where this volume was printed; he practiced as a solicitor there until his death in 1874. "He devoted himself to writing poetry from youth. . . . His poems, though chiefly echoes of Tennyson, show taste and artistic skill."–*DNB*. The versification is occasionally unconventional, as in the rather prosy opening to a poem called *Ellen*: "Walter

loved Ellen, and for many years / Had lived in the same village. . . ." This is the dedication copy, inscribed on a front flyleaf, "To Sarah J. Treffry, to whom this, the author's first volume, is dedicated. Présent d'amour. Henry Hogg." The book does not have a printed dedication, but the inscription is unambiguous, and the special binding is appropriate to the occasion. Acquired in 1997.

HENRY LUSHINGTON (1812–1855), AND GEORGE STOVIN VENABLES (1810–1888)

676. [Lushington, Henry, and George Stovin Venables.] Joint compositions. [London: 1848.] Sm. 8vo, contemporary red morocco.

A volume of three long poems, privately printed by two members of the Tennyson circle for distribution to friends. Henry Lushington was an early and ardent admirer of Tennyson's poetical genius; the two first met in 1831 as members of the Apostles, and in 1847 Tennyson dedicated *The Princess* to him. Venables, Lushington's closest friend, was also one of the Apostles; he went on to become a prominent barrister. The authorship and date of publication of this small volume are revealed in a preface by Venables to Lushington's *The Italian War, 1848–9* (1859). For youthful poems by the two friends, see no. 669 (d), (f), and (g). Acquired in 1991.

THOMAS BABINGTON MACAULAY (1800–1859)

677. Macaulay, Thomas Babington. Evening. A poem which obtained the Chancellor's Medal at the Cambridge commencement, July 1821. [Cambridge: 1821.] 8vo, original blue wrappers.

The historian's second publication, preceded only by another prize poem, *Pompeii*, printed two years earlier. With the contemporary signature "Edward Higginson, Jun." Acquired in 1981.

678. Macaulay, Thomas Babington. Lays of ancient Rome. London: Longman, Brown, Green, and Longmans, 1842. Sm. 4to, original brown cloth.

Macaulay's only volume of poetry, and one of the most popular books of the Victorian era; by 1875 more than a hundred thousand copies had been sold. Included here are many old favorites, such as "Horatius," which tells how the hero "kept the bridge." Acquired in 1981.

DENIS FLORENCE MACCARTHY (1817-1882)

679. MacCarthy, Denis Florence. Underglimpses, and other poems. London: David Bogue, 1857. 8vo, original green cloth.

> The author's second collection of original verse. MacCarthy was born in Dublin of Roman Catholic parents. He was educated at Maynooth, and was at first destined for the church, and then for a career in law, but his primary interests were literary and political; like many of his young contemporaries, he became involved in nationalist causes. Acquired in 2004.

680. MacCarthy, Denis Florence. The centenary of Moore. May 28th, 1879. An ode. . . . With a translation into Latin verse by the Rev. Julius Maxwell Blacker, A.M. London: printed for private circulation, 1880. 4to, original bright green glazed printed wrappers.

> A poem composed on the hundredth anniversary of the birth of the poet Thomas Moore. The text is printed throughout within a green border. Acquired in 1997.

GEORGE MACDONALD (1824-1905)

681. MacDonald, George. Scotch songs and ballads. Aberdeen: John Rae Smith, 1893. Sm. 8vo, original maroon cloth.

> A late collection of poems by a writer now best remembered for his children's books, especially *At the Back of the North Wind* (1871); he also published a good many three-decker novels. This copy is inscribed on a front flyleaf, "Susan Fisher Scott with much love from George MacDonald." Acquired in 1981.

JOHN WESTLAND MARSTON (1819-1890)

682. Marston, John Westland. The patrician's daughter. A tragedy, in five acts. London: C. Mitchell, 1841. 8vo, early half green calf.

> The author's first play, in blank verse, and based to some extent on his own recent courtship of Eleanor Jane Potts, the eldest daughter of the proprietor of a Cheltenham newspaper. The young lady's parents strongly opposed the match, as they had no confidence in her suitor's prospects, but in the end the wedding went ahead, and the marriage proved to be a happy one. John Marston published his play and then submitted it to the great actor

and theater manager William Charles Macready in October 1841. By the following spring, Marston and his clever young wife had moved to London and become part of Macready's circle. At the actor's dinners they met Thomas Carlyle, John Forster, Robert Browning, and, most notably, Charles Dickens, who was enthusiastic about the forthcoming production of Marston's drama, but felt it needed something to "get the curtain up with a dash, and begin the play with a sledge-hammer blow." The "blow," he suggested, should be a prologue by himself, which was duly written in November 1842, and was recited by Macready, who played the male lead, when the play opened on December 10. Marston was twenty-three when *The Patrician's Daughter* was first staged, and he was soon widely recognized as a writer of promise. "Marston's blank verse play with a contemporary and domestic setting quite naturally put him in the company of his friend Browning, also enamoured of poetic drama; R. H. Horne and Elizabeth Barrett's *A New Spirit of the Age* (1844) grouped the two writers together, and Barrett's *Lady Geraldine's Courtship* betrays the influence of Marston's play. Controversy erupted over the behaviour of the central character of Mordaunt, but *The Patrician's Daughter* was an undoubted success, and might have been a larger one had Marston taken Macready's advice and made the ending a happy one."–*Oxford DNB*. Marston went on to become a fixture of literary London, and for the better part of fifty years he was the chief author of such serious dramatic literature as actually reached the stage. In the end his work was eclipsed by the innovations of Shaw and Ibsen.

This is Marston's own copy, with about twenty corrections in the text, ranging from a few changes in punctuation to alterations of a word or phrase or revisions of the odd stage direction; in addition, a note has been added to the preface and the names of five actors included in the list of characters. Also bound in are the following, all in the author's hand: (a) A flyleaf at the front, with the text of a title page for the second edition of 1842, including the statement, "A prologue by Charles Dickens, Esq. is prefixed," which has been neatly crossed out. (b) A two-page letter, dated July 29, 1875, written from Boulogne-sur-Mer to an unknown correspondent, about the Dickens prologue: "No authorized version of Mr. Dickens's prologue to 'The Patrician's Daughter' has ever been published, though some incorrect renderings of it got abroad in one or two newspapers at the time. I have the original prologue in Mr. Dickens's handwriting (amongst other papers which I value) at home." (c) Four pages of manuscript, 4to, folded in, heavily corrected, containing a preface for a new edition, and a new dedication to Macready, much expanded from the printed dedication

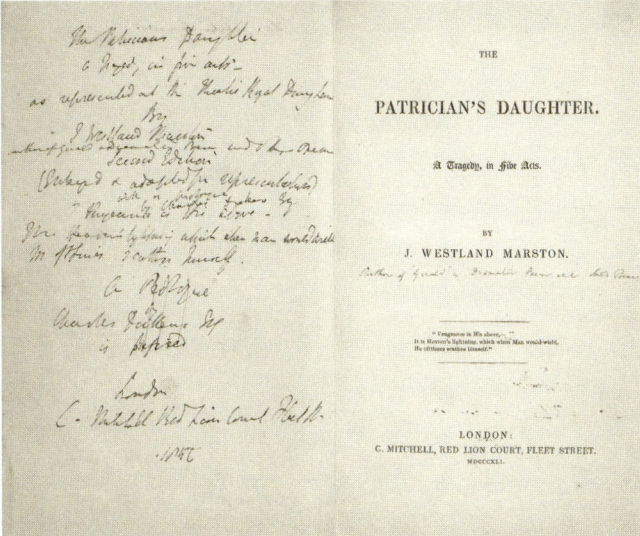

of this first edition. Included is a further acknowledgment of Dickens's prologue: "How shall I thank Mr. Dickens for his spontaneous kindness which has furnished me with so excellent a letter of introduction to the audience?" (d) A long statement about the play on the blank page facing the printed preface. (e) A one-page draft, bound at the back, of the opening lines of a new preface, much revised, with major portions crossed out. Acquired in 2006.

GEORGE MEREDITH (1828–1909)

683. Meredith, George. Poems. London: John W. Parker and Son, n.d. [1851]. 8vo, original purple cloth.

> The novelist's literary debut; the critical reception was lukewarm. This copy is inscribed on the half-title, "Howes! from his friend, G. M." Below this is a six-line manuscript poem, beginning, "Hail, Common Sense! most rare of all," and on the flyleaf opposite are three other short humorous poems (of four, six, and eight lines), all addressed to the recipient. "Howes" was Henry Howes, a fellow contributor, with Meredith, to "The Monthly Observer," a manuscript periodical composed for the amusement of the son and daughter of Thomas Love Peacock and their friends; it ran from March 1848 to July 1849. Meredith married Peacock's daughter, then a young widow (Mary Nicolls) some seven years his senior; this volume of poems

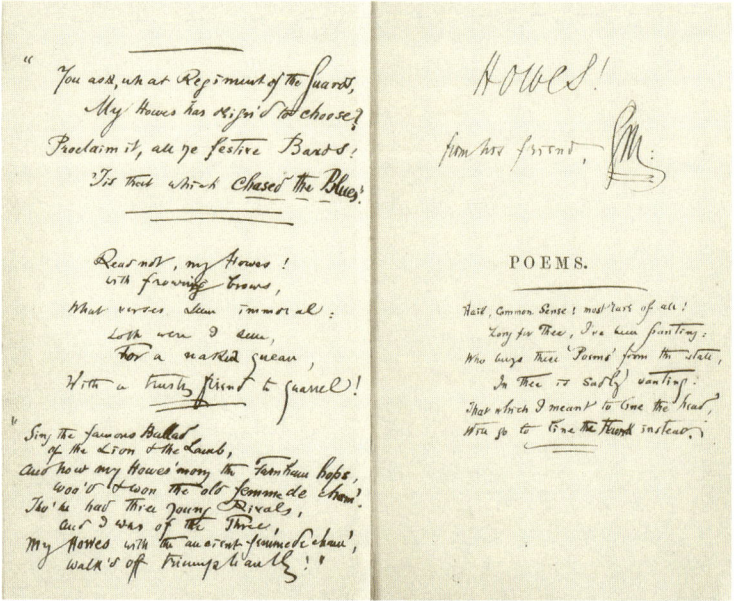

is dedicated to her father. The Simon Nowell-Smith copy. Nowell-Smith published the manuscript verses in *The Book Collector* in 1965, and they were later included in the edition of Meredith's poetry edited by Phyllis B. Bartlett in 1978. Acquired in 2002. Also in the collection is a copy of this book in a variant binding of green cloth, acquired in 1974.

684. Meredith, George. Modern love and poems of the English roadside, with poems and ballads. London: Chapman & Hall, 1862. 8vo, original green wavy-grain cloth.

Much of this collection is an account in verse of the breakup of Meredith's first marriage. This copy is inscribed on the title page, "Dante Gabriel Rossetti from his friend George Meredith." While the poems in this book were being written, and when it was published, Meredith lived in a village called Copsham, in Surrey, but he was much involved with Rossetti and Swinburne, who both urged him to come to London to share their house in Cheyne Walk. At the end of 1861, Meredith went so far as to take a room there, but Rossetti's bohemian manners were distasteful to him, and he ended up spending little time at the house; after three months he gave up paying rent. Meredith also gave a copy of his book of poems to Swinburne, with a similar inscription. That copy was sold at the Arthur Houghton sale in 1980, where

348

it was purchased by Blackwell for Simon Nowell-Smith. Curiously, there is another copy inscribed by Meredith to Rossetti, once part of T. J. Wise's collection and now in the British Library; the wording of that inscription is slightly different, and it seems likely that it was a later one. There are four ink corrections in the text in Meredith's hand; these same corrections were made in the copy given to Swinburne. Acquired in 1984. Also in the collection is a copy in a variant binding of bead-grain cloth, acquired in 1974.

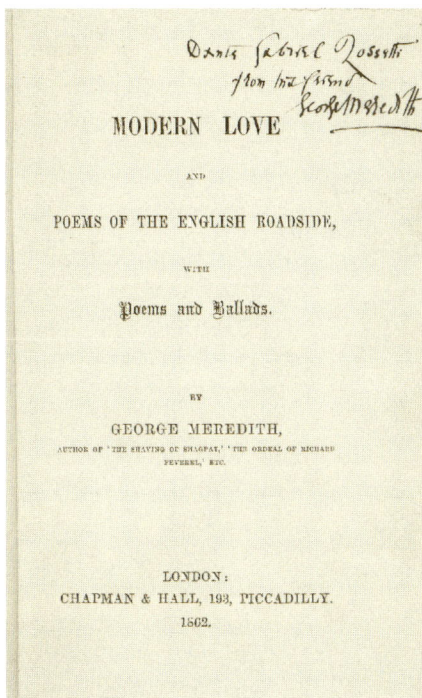

685. Meredith, George. Poems and lyrics of the joy of earth. London: Macmillan and Co., 1883. 8vo, original dark blue cloth.

Second edition, though not so designated; first printed earlier the same year. This important collec-

tion of poems has a slightly complicated publishing history. The first edition, printed by R. Clay, Sons, and Taylor, contained a number of misprints, much to Meredith's annoyance, but attempts to correct them by inserting new leaves in the text were unsatisfactory, so in the end it was decided to reprint the entire book, using a printer in Edinburgh, at Macmillan's expense. The two editions are sufficiently similar that for a long time the differences between them were not noticed; Wise, for example, lists his Edinburgh printing as the first edition. This copy is inscribed by Meredith on the half-title to "Miss Theresa Dent." There are manuscript corrections by Meredith on six pages of the text. With the bookplate of Theresa J. Marquoid, and the book label of Simon Nowell-Smith. Acquired in 1977.

JOHN HENRY NEWMAN (1801–1890)

686. [Newman, John Henry.] Verses on religious subjects. Dublin: James Duffy, 1853. 12mo, original dark blue cloth, printed paper label.

The author's first collection of verse, published anonymously at the time he was involved in the establishment of a new Catholic university in Ireland. Most of the poems were reprinted in *Verses on Various Occasions* (1868; no. 688). Acquired in 1986.

687. [Newman, John Henry.] The dream of Gerontius. London: Burns, Lambert, and Oates, 1866. 16mo, original maroon limp cloth.

One of the finest religious poems of the nineteenth century, written by Newman during a period of spiritual uncertainty. This tiny book, the smallest in the collection, was reprinted hundreds of times; the first edition has long been difficult to find. This copy is inscribed on the flyleaf facing the title page, "With the kindest regards of the author. Feby. 21 / '66." Above is the signature of the recipient, M. J. Roberts, who has added the following note: "The pencil marks [that appear several times in the text] are an exact copy of those in General Gordon's book, sent from Khartoum to his sister in England. The original was lent to me by Cardinal Newman, being sent to him for a few days by Gen. Gordon's sister." The massacre of General Gordon and his men in the Sudan by the forces of the Mahdi took place in 1885. The fact that he was reading Newman's poem as his end drew near is attested to by his last letter to his sister, and is a poignant detail included in all narratives of one of the

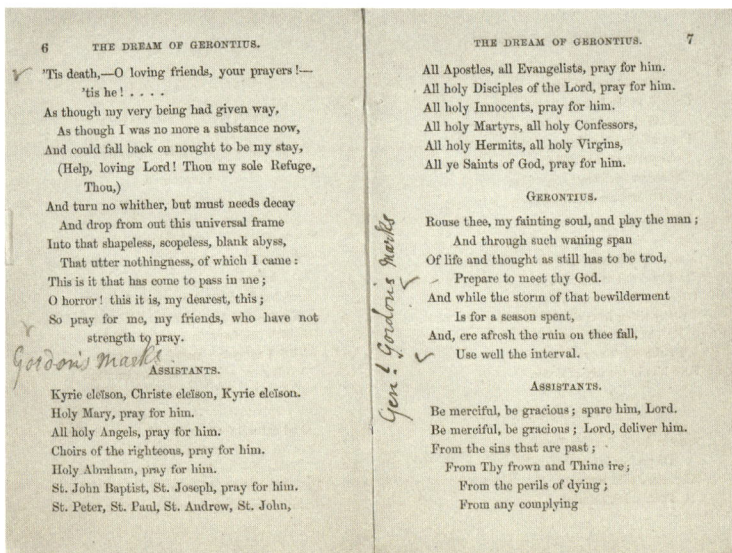

6 THE DREAM OF GERONTIUS.

'Tis death,—O loving friends, your prayers!—
 'tis he! . . . .
As though my very being had given way,
As though I was no more a substance now,
And could fall back on nought to be my stay,
 (Help, loving Lord! Thou my sole Refuge,
  Thou,)
And turn no whither, but must needs decay
 And drop from out this universal frame
Into that shapeless, scopeless, blank abyss,
 That utter nothingness, of which I came:
This is it that has come to pass in me;
O horror! this it is, my dearest, this;
 So pray for me, my friends, who have not
  strength to pray.

ASSISTANTS.

Kyrie eleïson, Christe eleïson, Kyrie eleïson.
Holy Mary, pray for him.
All holy Angels, pray for him.
Choirs of the righteous, pray for him.
Holy Abraham, pray for him.
St. John Baptist, St. Joseph, pray for him.
St. Peter, St. Paul, St. Andrew, St. John,

THE DREAM OF GERONTIUS. 7

All Apostles, all Evangelists, pray for him.
All holy Disciples of the Lord, pray for him.
All holy Innocents, pray for him.
All holy Martyrs, all holy Confessors,
All holy Hermits, all holy Virgins,
All ye Saints of God, pray for him.

GERONTIUS.

Rouse thee, my fainting soul, and play the man;
 And through such waning span
Of life and thought as still has to be trod,
 Prepare to meet thy God.
 And while the storm of that bewilderment
  Is for a season spent,
And, ere afresh the ruin on thee fall,
 Use well the interval.

ASSISTANTS.

Be merciful, be gracious; spare him, Lord.
Be merciful, be gracious; Lord, deliver him.
From the sins that are past;
From Thy frown and Thine ire;
From the perils of dying;
From any complying

ITEM 687

350

most famous incidents in British military history. The markings Gordon made in the text were transcribed in a number of copies of the poem, and one of these was given to Edward Elgar in 1889 as a wedding present. The location of the original has not been determined, nor is it clear which printing General Gordon was reading; presumably it was not a first edition. Acquired in 1982.

688. [Newman, John Henry.] Verses on various occasions. London: Burns, Oates, & Co., 1868. 8vo, original orange cloth.

The author's major book of poetry. Though Newman's name does not appear on the title page, his authorship is clear enough from the dedication, which is signed with his initials. On the front flyleaf is the signature of E. S. Foot, dated 1868. With the later book labels of Elizabeth S. Rolt and Kenneth Lohf. Acquired in 1992.

JAMES PAYN (1830–1898)

689. Payn, James. Poems. Cambridge: Macmillan and Co., 1853. 8vo, original green cloth.

The author's second book, written while he was an undergraduate at Cambridge. Payn went on to become a prolific and successful novelist, and a close friend of Dickens. The pages of this copy are unopened; ironically, the first poem here is entitled "The Uncut Volume." Acquired in 1982.

JOHN RUSKIN (1819–1900)

690. [Ruskin, John.] Poems. J. R. N.p. [London]: collected 1850. 8vo, original purple cloth.

One of Ruskin's earliest books, a collection of poems written between the ages of fourteen and twenty-six. "It was not published, but merely printed for private circulation, and has now become the *Rara Avis* of Ruskin literature. The present value of an 'uncut' copy in original state is about £50."–T. J. Wise. For a full account of this book, see James S. Dearden's "The Production and Distribution of John Ruskin's *Poems 1850," The Book Collector*, vol. 17, no. 2 (Summer 1968): 151–67. Dearden provides evidence that the press run was fifty copies, of which he was able to locate sixteen, including this one. At least five others can now be located. This copy, in a perfect state of preservation, has the bookplates of Herchel V. Jones (sold at Anderson Galleries, Jan. 29, 1919) and Louis H. Silver (sold at Sotheby's, Nov. 9, 1965). It was purchased at the latter sale by Seven Gables Bookshop, bidding on behalf of H. Bradley Martin. Acquired at the Bradley Martin sale in 1990.

691. Ruskin, John. The Scythian guest; a poem. N.p. [London]: printed for the author, 1849 [1880s]. 4to, original light brown printed wrappers.

> A Wise forgery, in his characteristic manner. This poem was written in 1839 and first printed in an annual, *Friendship's Offering*, the following year; it reappeared in Ruskin's privately printed *Poems* in 1850. For this purported first edition Wise adopted his usual strategy of inventing a plausible private printing, though there is in fact no reason why Ruskin would have chosen to print this poem separately while his father, John James Ruskin, was already making preparations for a collected edition of his verse. The first paragraph of the preface here is essentially bogus. Acquired in 1981.

692. Ruskin, John. The poems of John Ruskin: now first collected from original manuscript and printed sources; and edited, in chronological order, with notes, biographical and critical, by W. G. Collingwood. With facsimiles of MSS. and illustrations by the author. Sunnyside, Orpington, and London: George Allen, 1891. Two vols., 4to, original half vellum and green cloth boards.

> A sumptuous edition, with much new material. This set is one of eight hundred copies on large paper, with the photogravure plates on India paper. Acquired in 1971.

STEPHEN EDMOND SPRING-RICE (1814–1865)

693. Spring-Rice, Stephen Edmond. Sonnets. [London: ca. 1870.] Sq. 8vo, contemporary brown morocco.

> The author's only collection of verse, posthumously printed on a handpress by his children, possibly in a single copy only; no other copy has been located. Stephen Spring-Rice was the eldest son of an Irish peer, Thomas Spring-Rice, 1st Baron Monteagle, who played a prominent role in public affairs. Monteagle's sister Mary was the wife of Sir Aubrey de Vere, and their son, the poet Aubrey de Vere, was born the same year as his cousin (1814). The two boys were close; this collection of sonnets is dedicated to Aubrey de Vere. Spring-Rice later attended Cambridge, where he became a good friend of Tennyson and of various members of Tennyson's circle. The genesis of

this volume is explained by a note on the front flyleaf, in the hand of one of the author's daughters: "This book of my father's sonnets was given to me by my brother Frank, Sept. 1895. My sister Lucy & I began to print them in 1863, & had done about half when our leaving home put a stop to the work. Frank has now had it completed. Aileen Arthur. P. S. My sister Theo also carried on the work after Lucy & I had left home in 1864 & 1866." Spring-Rice was by profession the deputy chairman of the Board of Customs, and he died in the course of a voyage home from the Mediterranean in 1865. The fifty-nine sonnets here are printed in chronological order of composition, beginning with a poem of 1837, and ending with two sonnets penned in La Spezia in 1865 (one of them about the US Civil War). Precisely which sonnets were printed when is not immediately clear. Of particular interest is the fact that Aubrey de Vere reprinted twenty-four of these sonnets in 1877, as part of a volume called *Antar and Zara* (no. 659); possibly de Vere also owned a copy of this collection, but it has never surfaced. Acquired in 2005.

CHARLES HENRY TIMPERLEY (1795?–1861)

694. [Timperley, Charles Henry, editor.] Songs of the press and other poems relative to the art of printers and printing; also of author, books, booksellers, bookbinders, editors, critics, newspapers, etc. Original and selected. With notes, biographical and literary. London: Fisher, Son, & Co., 1845. Sm. 8vo, original rose cloth.

> Second edition, enlarged (though not so designated); first published in 1833. The editor, some of whose own poems are included in this collection, was a noted typographer and author of the well-known *Dictionary of Printers and Printing* (1839). Acquired in 1972.

ITEM 700

The Late Nineteenth Century

WILLIAM MORRIS (1834–1896)

695. Morris, William. The defence of Guenevere, and other poems. London: Bell and Daldy, 1858. 8vo, original purple cloth.

> The author's first book, printed by C. Whittingham at the Chiswick Press, and dedicated to Dante Gabriel Rossetti. This copy is inscribed by Morris (Christmas 1861) to his friend George Francis Campfield. Campfield was a pupil of Ruskin at the Working Men's College and the first employee to enter the service of Morris, Faulkner, Marshall & Co., a firm jointly founded by Morris, Ford Madox Brown, Edward Burne-Jones, Charles Faulkner, Dante Gabriel Rossetti, P. P. Marshall, and Philip Webb to create and sell handcrafted objects for the home. Campfield also contributed designs for the Kelmscott Press. Acquired in 1976.

696. Morris, William, and Eiríkr Magnússon, translators. Völsunga saga. The story of the Volsungs & Niblungs with certain songs from the Elder Edda. Translated from the Icelandic. London: F. S. Ellis, 1870. 8vo, original green cloth, elaborately decorated in gilt.

> One of the first of Morris's translations from Icelandic saga literature; Magnússon was his tutor. The ornate cloth binding was designed by Morris himself. This copy is inscribed on the front flyleaf, "G. F. Campfield from his friend William Morris" (see no. 695). Acquired in 1996.

697. Morris, William. Love is enough: or the freeing of Pharamond: a morality. London: Ellis & White, 1873. 8vo, original dark green cloth.

> This copy was inscribed by Morris in November 1872 to George Francis Campfield (see no. 695). Laid in are four pages of preliminary proofs for the book, with decorations sketched in pencil and ink; these reveal that Morris had originally planned a more elaborate design for the volume than he eventually used. The sketches are probably by Morris himself, but they may be in the hand of Edward Burne-Jones; possibly Campfield had something to do with them as well. Also laid in is a proof, on onionskin, of a woodblock design for decorating the text (or possibly the binding); this, too, was not used. Acquired in 1976.

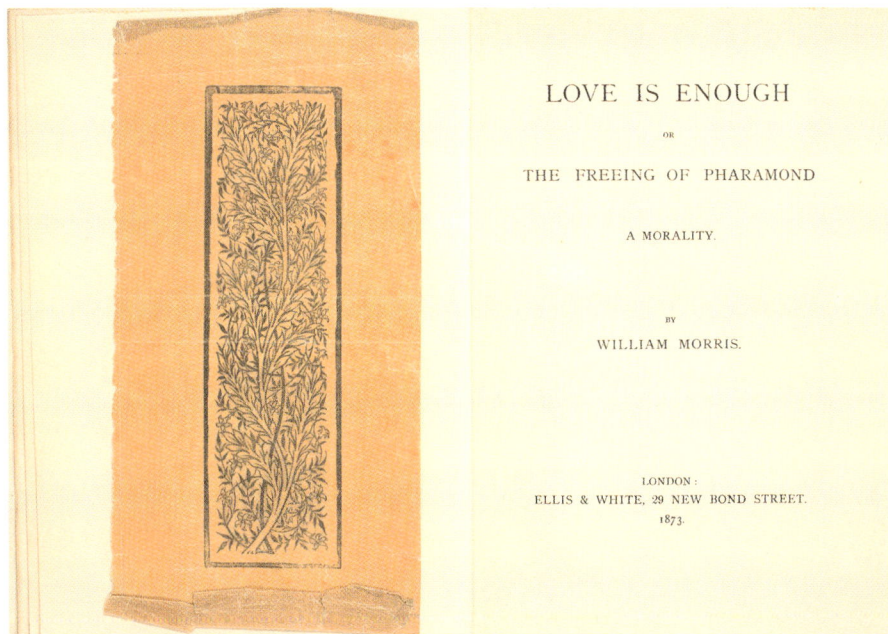

698. Morris, William. Love is enough: or the freeing of Pharamond: a morality. London: Ellis & White, 1873. 8vo, original slate blue boards, white paper backstrip, printed paper label.

> This is one of twenty-five copies printed on large Whatman's handmade paper; the limitation is on the verso of the title page. In this issue a final leaf with the Morris bookmark has been substituted for a leaf of advertisements in the trade edition. Acquired in 1981.

699. Morris, William. Chants for socialists. Contents: 1. The day is coming. 2. The voice of toil. 3. All for the cause. 4. No master. 5. The march of the workers. 6. The message of the March wind. London: published at The Socialist League Office, 1885. 8vo, folded, as issued.

> The first of these poems had been separately printed in 1884, under the same imprint; this was followed shortly by nos. 2 and 3, in a second pamphlet. This sixteen-page pamphlet was sold for a penny; the decorative factotum at the head of the title was designed by Walter Crane. Acquired in 1983.

700. Morris, William. The roots of the mountains: wherein is told somewhat of the lives of the men of Burgdale their friends their neighbours the foemen and their fellows in arms. London: Reeves and Turner, 1890. Sm. 4to, original chintz cloth, decorated in red, white, blue, and black.

> A fine-paper copy, one of 250 printed on Whatman's handmade paper. The remarkable binding was designed and manufactured by Morris at his own crafts company. Acquired in 1983.

701. Morris, William. Poems by the way. Hammersmith: 1891. Sm. 4to, original stiff vellum, yapp edges, silk ties.

> One of 300 numbered copies of an edition of 310, printed by Morris at the Kelmscott Press. This copy is inscribed, "To Phyllis Marion Ellis from William Morris, October 21st, 1891." The recipient was the daughter of F. S. Ellis, a successful dealer in rare books and manuscripts who was also a publisher on a small scale, and brought out works by Morris and Rossetti, with both of whom he was very friendly. With the bookplate of Willis Vickery. The Doheny copy. Acquired in 1989.

702. Morris, William. Poems by the way. London: Reeves and Turner, 1891. Sm. 4to, original black buckram cloth.

> First trade edition, printed by the Chiswick Press. Acquired in 1962.

ALGERNON CHARLES SWINBURNE (1837–1909)

703. Swinburne, Algernon Charles. The Queen-Mother. Rosamond. Two plays. London: Basil Montagu Pickering, 1860. 8vo, original slate cloth, printed paper label.

> The first issue of Swinburne's first book, with Pickering's title page and advertisements. After a small number of copies had been sold—Wise says fewer than twenty but this number seems too low—the sheets were turned over to Edward Moxon, and most copies surviving from the original press run have his cancel title page. With the bookplate of Walter T. Shirley II. Acquired in 1991.

704. [Gordon, Mary, later Mrs. Disney Leith.] The children of the chapel. A tale. By the author of "Mark Dennis." London: Joseph Masters, 1864. 8vo, original red cloth.

This little novel is by Swinburne's cousin. The text includes a "Morality Play" in verse, called "The Pilgrimage of Pleasure," and performed by "children," which is entirely by Swinburne. This copy is signed on the title page by Dante Gabriel Rossetti, who has identified the author as "Miss Gordon," and has further noted, "The Interlude by Algernon C. Swinburne." From the library of Jerome Kern. Acquired in 1985.

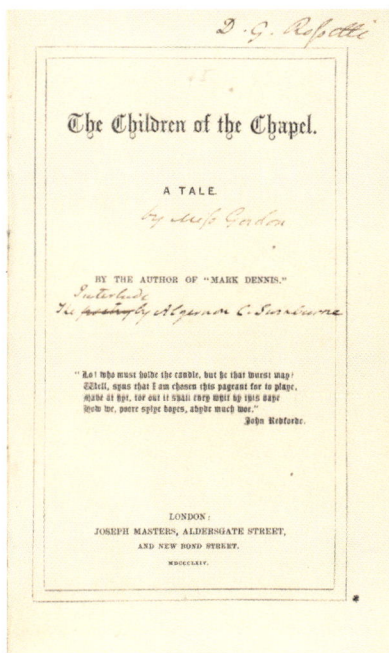

ITEM 704

705. Swinburne, Algernon Charles. Atalanta in Calydon. A tragedy. London: Edward Moxon and Co., 1865. 4to, original cream buckram cloth.

One of three hundred copies printed (not one hundred, as traditionally stated). The covers were designed by Rossetti. There are two states of this book. This copy is the rarer second state, with last-minute corrections, including the canceled form of pp. 85–86, to correct "made made" in l. 6 on p. 86. On the front pastedown is the signature of the Greek scholar and bibliophile Ingram Bywater (1840–1914), who has marked various passages throughout the book; Bywater and Swinburne became friends as undergraduates at Queen's College, Oxford. Acquired in 1980.

706. [Swinburne, Algernon Charles.] "O virgin mother of gentle days and nights." [London: 1865.] Folio, lithographed broadside.

A sonnet written by Swinburne for a painting by the Pre-Raphaelite artist Frederick Sandys, exhibited at the Royal Academy in 1865. The text has been printed in quasi-facsimile manuscript. Whether the printing was arranged by Sandys, or by Swinburne himself, it seems in any case to have been rather tentative, as a blank space has been left in the penultimate line for the word "ungrown." A note in an early hand at the top reads, "This lithographed copy of a poem by Swinburne was found amongst the papers of T. A. Sandys." This printing was unknown to Wise. It was first mentioned in Dodd and Livingstone's *First Editions of Swinburne* (1913), where a copy was described as "probably unique." At least one other copy is now known, in the Widener Collection at Harvard. From the collection of Halsted B. Vander Poel. Acquired in 2004.

358

707. Swinburne, Algernon Charles. Poems and ballads. London: Edward Moxon & Co., 1866. 8vo, original green cloth.

> This copy is an example of the first issue, with all the necessary leaves uncanceled; quite early in the print run many leaves were canceled and various errors corrected. The eight pages of advertisements are also in the first state, with the review notice of *Atalanta in Calydon* misplaced among the reviews of *Chastelard*. "An absolutely genuine example with every leaf . . . in the original state is of extreme rarity and is very seldom to be met with."–T. J. Wise. Acquired in 1972.

708. Swinburne, Algernon Charles. Laus veneris. London: Edward Moxon & Co., 1866 [ca. 1890]. 8vo, original sheets, folded.

> A classic T. J. Wise forgery. The poem had in fact appeared in 1866, in Moxon's edition of *Poems and Ballads*. Wise managed to convince Swinburne that a private printing of this one poem had been distributed to friends before the book's publication. In fact the printing was done about 1890, and a small "remainder" came to light, which Wise "traced" to the sale of surplus effects from Moxon's estate. The Jerome Kern copy. Acquired in 1977.

709. Swinburne, Algernon Charles. Siena. London: John Camden Hotten, 1868. 15 pp. Sm. 8vo, full dark blue morocco, by Riviere; original pale orange wrappers bound in.

> This is one of a very small number of copies printed in order to secure copyright for a poem first published in Philadelphia, in the June 1868 number of *Lippincott's Magazine*. Wise writes that he had been told by Swinburne that only six copies were printed, but the number may have been slightly larger, perhaps ten or twelve; the British Museum copy was received on May 27. As Wise points out, Hotten, whose relations with Swinburne were always less than straightforward, soon perceived that there was a demand for this pamphlet in the collector's market, even at that early date, and he therefore reprinted it, without Swinburne's knowledge. The spurious reprint is outwardly similar, but displays a fair number of typographical differences. Years later, Wise, who correctly describes the original printing as "one of the rarest of the first editions of Swinburne's writings," was unable to resist the temptation to make it a little more common, and at some point after 1890 he produced a very deceptive forgery of it. The forgery, however, may be easily detected, as it lacks the period after Hotten's address ("Piccadilly") in the imprint; the title page reproduced in Wise's

bibliography of Swinburne is that of the forgery. A close comparison also reveals that the fonts used are slightly different, with the forgery displaying certain letter forms that were not available in 1868.

The present copy of the genuine copyright printing has the bookplate of John A. Spoor, whose books were sold at auction in New York in 1939. Tipped in at the front is a four-page letter to Spoor, dated November 25, 1908, from the London booksellers B. F. Stevens and Brown, pointing out some of the differences between Hotten's two printings, and adding that only four other copies of the first were known, at the British Museum, and in the collections of Locker-Lampson, Buxton Forman ("in cream wrappers"), and Wise; the latter two at least were, of course, forgeries. The letter goes on to report that "Mr. Wise . . . was in keen search for a copy for a friend." This "friend" may well have been himself, as he seems never to have acquired a copy of the genuine first printing. From the collection of Halsted B. Vander Poel. Acquired in 2004.

710. Swinburne, Algernon Charles. Poems and ballads: second series. London: Chatto and Windus, 1878. 8vo, original dark blue-green cloth.

This book was issued in two sizes (one thousand copies of each were printed). The smaller size was bound in lighter green cloth to match *Poems and Ballads* (1866; see no. 707); the present copy is in the larger format used for many of Swinburne's later books. This copy is inscribed on the front flyleaf, "F. Boott from H. James Jun. Rome, Nov. 1878." The novelist Henry James used "Jun." after his surname until his father's death; beneath the inscription, apparently in the same hand, is his address in Rome, "44 Piazza di Espagna." The recipient was Francis Boott, a close friend, later used by James as a model for Gilbert Osmond in *Portrait of a Lady*. With the bookplate of John M. Cameron. Acquired in 1976.

711. Swinburne, Algernon Charles. A century of roundels. London: Chatto & Windus, 1883. 8vo, original dark blue cloth.

This copy is inscribed on the half-title, "J. W. Inchbold from his friend A. C. Swinburne." The recipient, John William Inchbold, was a painter whose work was much admired by Ruskin. Inchbold's pictures were unacceptable to the Royal Academy, and largely ignored by the general public, but he had many close friends in the literary world, especially Tennyson and Browning. He died in 1888, at the age of fifty-seven, from a heart attack, and Swinburne wrote a funeral ode for him, which was much praised. With the bookplate of Carroll A. Wilson; later in the collection of Halsted B. Vander Poel. Acquired in 2004.

712. Swinburne, Algernon Charles. A midsummer holiday and other poems. London: Chatto & Windus, 1884. 8vo, original dark blue cloth.

> This copy is from the library of Swinburne's close friend Edmund Gosse, with his bookplate. Tipped in is a four-page letter sent to Gosse on Sept. 4, 1884, by Theodore Watts (later Watts-Dunton) at The Pines, where he and Swinburne lived together for many years. The letter ends with a postscript referring to Tennyson: "I was talking of you and your work to a very illustrious man & rare genius not long since during a delightful country ramble." Gosse must have tipped in this letter because Swinburne's title poem, which is in nine parts and occupies the first thirty-eight pages here, is dedicated to Watts-Dunton. Acquired in 1994.

713. Swinburne, Algernon Charles. Marino Faliero: a tragedy. London: Chatto & Windus, 1885. 8vo, original dark blue-green cloth.

> From the library of John Quinn, whose extraordinary collection of modern literature was sold at auction in New York in 1923–24. With the bookplate of John M. Cameron. Acquired in 1976.

714. Swinburne, Algernon Charles. A study of Victor Hugo. London: Chatto and Windus, 1886. 8vo, original dark blue-green cloth.

> With the bookplates of John Quinn and John M. Cameron. Acquired in 1976.

715. Swinburne, Algernon Charles. Gathered songs. London: Charles Ottley, Landon, & Co., 1887. Sm. 4to, original pale green printed wrappers.

> A Wise fabrication. The four poems had first been printed in *The Times* (July 1, 1886) and in three issues of *The English Illustrated Magazine* (October 1885, December 1886, and February 1887); three of them were later collected in the Third Series of *Poems and Ballads* (1889). In his bibliography, Wise says that twenty-five copies were printed on paper, and four copies on vellum; these figures may be roughly correct. The date of publication, however, is less reliable, and the pamphlet could have been produced as late as 1891. Swinburne himself was incapable of keeping track of the various printings of his verse, and Wise used his confusion to create a number of such artificial rarities. With the bookplates of A. George Ulizio and Caroll A. Wilson; later in the collection of Halsted B. Vander Poel. Acquired in 2004.

716. Swinburne, Algernon Charles. The bride's tragedy. London: printed privately, 1889. 8vo, polished calf, by Riviere.

> A Wise fabrication. The poem was first printed in *The Athenæum* for March 9, 1889, and was collected later in the year in the Third Series of *Poems and Ballads*. Whether this separate printing is a piracy, printed in 1889, or a forgery, produced any time up to 1896, has not been determined. Wise's statement that forty copies only were printed may well be accurate. With the bookplate of John A. Spoor; later in the collection of Halsted B. Vander Poel. Acquired in 2004.

717. Swinburne, Algernon Charles. The brothers. N.p. [London]: printed 1889 [1892–96.] 8vo, polished calf, by Riviere.

> A Wise forgery. This poem first appeared in *The People*, no. 428 (December 22, 1889). Wise describes this separate edition as "a somewhat crude and rough-looking production," and says that "a few copies were printed off at the newspaper office for private distribution." Because this pamphlet differs typographically from Wise's other Swinburne fabrications, it was for a long time accepted, albeit with suspicion, as genuine. The poem was first collected in 1894, in *Astrophel and Other Poems*. With the bookplate of John A. Spoor; later in the collection of Halsted B. Vander Poel Acquired in 2004.

718. Swinburne, Algernon Charles. The ballad of Bulgarie. London: printed for private circulation, 1893. 8vo, polished calf, by Riviere (original plain buff wrappers bound in).

> A Wise piracy. "*The Ballad of Bulgarie* was written towards the close of 1876, in satire against the pro-Russian tendencies of Mr. Gladstone's Government, and the exploitation of what at the time were popularly termed 'the Bulgarian atrocities.' Swinburne made repeated efforts to get his ballad published . . . but his efforts met with no success."–T. J. Wise. Wise goes on to say that the original manuscript was lent by Swinburne to Edmund Gosse, who made a copy of it, from which this pamphlet was printed. Gosse asked that only "an exceedingly small number be printed," and that Swinburne not be told. Wise says that he treated the latter request as a joke, and that Swinburne looked upon the pamphlet with "considerable amusement and surprise." It now seems probable that Swinburne was not in fact informed. Wise claims to have printed only twenty-five copies, but the number was probably somewhat larger. With the bookplate of John A. Spoor; later in the collection of Halsted B. Vander Poel. Acquired in 2004.

719. Swinburne, Algernon Charles. Astrophel and other poems. London: Chatto & Windus, 1894. 8vo, original dark blue cloth.

This copy is inscribed by Swinburne on the half-title to W. H. Davenport Adams, presumably the son of the prolific miscellaneous writer of that name, who died in 1891. With a manuscript correction by Swinburne on p. 118. With the bookplate of Mark Samuels Lasner. Acquired in 1992.

720. Swinburne, Algernon. The tale of Balen. London: Chatto & Windus, 1896. 8vo, original blue cloth.

This copy is inscribed on the half-title, "Mary C. J. Leith from her affectionate cousin, A. C. Swinburne." The recipient was a writer as well; in 1864 she had published, under her maiden name, Mary Gordon, a little book called *The Children of the Chapel*, to which Swinburne had contributed a "Morality Play" in verse (no. 705). Acquired in 1997.

721. Swinburne, Algernon Charles. The Duke of Gandia. London: Chatto & Windus, 1908. 8vo, original dark blue cloth.

A large-paper copy, one of 110 printed, of which 100 were for sale; this is copy 3 of the 10 that were not for sale. This copy is inscribed on the front flyleaf, "Mary C. J. Leith from her affectionate cousin, A. C. Swinburne" (see no. 705). Acquired in 1997. Also in the collection is a second large-paper copy, one of the 100 that were for sale. Acquired in 1977.

722. Swinburne, Algernon Charles. The age of Shakespeare. London: Chatto and Windus, 1908. 8vo, original dark blue cloth.

This copy is no. 25 of 110 copies printed on large paper, of which 100 were for sale. From the collection of John A. Spoor. Acquired in 1976.

723. Swinburne, Algernon Charles. A record of friendship. [London: printed for private circulation, 1910.] 8vo, original pale green wrappers.

A proof copy of one of Wise's Swinburne pamphlets, giving Swinburne's account of a meeting with Rossetti. On the front cover are printing instructions written and signed by Wise; he is requesting that the title page, not yet set in type at this point, replace the half-title as copy for the front cover. Also stamped on the front wrapper is the oval mark of Richard Clay & Sons, the printers of many of Wise's forgeries. Laid in at the beginning is the original manuscript of the preface to the pamphlet, composed by Edmund Gosse; the printed version is also included, as well as a note signed with initials by Gosse to the effect that he can find no errors to correct in the proofs. This pamphlet was eventually issued by Wise in an edition purportedly limited to twenty copies; the color of the wrappers was changed from light green to light blue. Acquired in 1975.

JAMES THOMSON (1834–1882)

724. Thomson, James. The city of dreadful night, and other poems. London: Reeves and Turner, 1880. 8vo, original dark green cloth.

> A copy of the trade issue; there were also copies on large paper. Acquired in 1994.

725. Thomson, James. Essays and phantasies. London: Reeves and Turner, 1881. 8vo, original green cloth. Acquired in 1993.

726. Thomson, James. Vane's story, Weddah and Om-el-Bonain, and other poems. London: Reeves and Turner, 1881. 8vo, original dark green cloth.

> A large-paper copy; the number of such copies printed is not stated, but the format matches that of large-paper copies of *The City of Dreadful Night*, whose press run is said to have been only forty. Acquired in 1994.

727. Thomson, James. Address on the opening of the new hall of the Leicester Secular Society. Sunday March 6th 1881. Delivered by Mrs. Theodore Wright. [London: 1881.]

> An address in verse. The text is printed in blue, within decorative brown borders. Acquired in 1973.

728. Thomson, James. A voice from the Nile and other poems. . . . With a memoir of the author by Bertram Dobell. London: Reeves and Turner, 1884. Large 8vo, original royal blue cloth.

> This copy is one of a small number issued on large paper (to match in size the large-paper copies of the poet's earlier books). This was Thomson's last book of poetry, published posthumously by the bookseller Bertram Dobell, who owned the poet's manuscripts. The Simon Nowell-Smith copy. On the verso of the front flyleaf is a penciled poem in an unidentified hand, presenting this copy to Nowell-Smith as a Christmas present in 1969; the donor was a fellow collector, who had ordered the book from a catalogue before Nowell-Smith was able to get to it. Acquired in 2002.

GERARD MANLEY HOPKINS (1844–1889)

729. Hopkins, Gerard Manley. Poems of Gerard Manley Hopkins now first published. Edited with notes by Robert Bridges, Poet Laureate. London: Humphrey Milford, 1918. 8vo, original pale blue paper boards, canvas spine, printed paper label. Acquired in 1979.

ROBERT SEYMOUR BRIDGES (1844–1930)

730. Bridges, Robert. Poems. London: Basil Montagu Pickering, 1873. 8vo, original light blue cloth, printed paper label.

> The author's first book. Acquired in 1984.

731. Bridges, Robert. The growth of love. Oxford: printed by H. Daniel, 1889. 4to, green morocco, by Morley of Oxford.

> Second edition, much revised. This collection of sonnets was first published anonymously in 1876; in the text printed here, ten sonnets have been dropped, six extensively rewritten, and many new ones added. This book was printed at the Daniel Press in an edition of twenty-two copies, of which this is no. 22. Daniel and Bridges were close friends. Laid in is a two-page letter from Emily Daniel, the printer's wife, offering this copy to the American collector H. W. Poor; at the front is Poor's bookplate. With the additional bookplate of Bruce, Staunton Hill. Acquired in 1980.

732. Bridges, Robert. Eden: an oratorio. London: Geo. Bell & Sons; Novello, Ewer and Co. (London and New York), 1891. Sm. 8vo, original white parchment boards.

> This copy is no. 7 of 110 copies on hand-made paper; there were also 1,015 issued on ordinary paper, in blue printed wrappers. With the book label of Michael Sadleir. Acquired in 1989.

733. [Bridges, Robert.] Founders Day. A secular ode on the ninth jubilee of Eton College. [Oxford: Daniel Press, 1893.] Sm. 4to, folded.

> This is a proof copy of the first edition, which was printed at the Daniel Press in an edition of only thirty copies. Bridges has made a number of corrections, including rewriting two lines of the poem. Acquired in 1980.

734. Bridges, Robert. Milton's prosody: an examination of the rules of the blank verse in Milton's later poems, with an account of the versifica-

tion of Samson Agonistes, and general notes. Oxford: at the Clarendon Press; Henry Frowde (London); Macmillan & Co. (New York), 1893. Sm. 4to, original magenta buckram cloth.

> This copy is one of 250 printed on large paper. It is signed on the front flyleaf by Hugh E. Seebohm (in October 1893), a classicist who was a friend of Bridges. Laid in is a two-page letter from Bridges to Seebohm (August 1893), sending him a copy of the book, but asking that it be returned, "as it is the last copy I have." Acquired in 1989.

735. Bridges, Robert. Eros & Psyche. London: George Bell and Sons, 1894. Sm. 8vo, original tan cloth.

> Second edition, though not so designated on the title page. On the leaf following the title page is a note explaining the significance of this printing: "This poem was first published in 1885. It has now been revised throughout, and parts of the first and second cantos rewritten. It is printed in the form originally intended, the divisions corresponding to seasons, months, and days." This copy is inscribed by Bridges on an initial blank leaf, "To Coventry Patmore with the author's compliments. Nov. 1894." Bridges and Patmore knew each other well and admired each other's work; Patmore was the first person whom Bridges tried, in 1883, to interest in the poems of their mutual friend Gerard Manley Hopkins. At about the same time, Bridges sent to Patmore a preliminary version of this long poem; in a letter to Hopkins, Patmore wrote that "his first draft of 'Eros and Psyche' is more complete than I could have made such a poem after years of correction." On the back pastedown is a penciled inscription from John Carter to Simon Nowell-Smith, dated 1950; the two were close friends and fellow bibliophiles. With Nowell-Smith's book label. Acquired in 2008.

736. Bridges, Robert. [The testament of beauty. Oxford: printed at the University Press, 1927–29.] Five parts, 4to, sewn, as issued.

> A private issue, printed in a limited edition "for the convenience of the author" as a basis for his revision of the poem; the published edition appeared in 1929. The colophon leaf at the end of the fifth part reveals that twenty-five copies were printed of parts 1–4, and twenty-one of part 5 (four in September and seventeen in October 1929); this set includes both variants of part 5, with the colophon of the earlier one mentioning only the September printing. The poem, intended as the author's magnum opus, was begun in 1926. It was "published on the poet's 85th birthday in 1929, and achieved an

instantaneous success both in England and the United States of America. *The Testament of Beauty* is a great poem, demanding too much intellectual effort ever to be popular, but full of passages which carry away any sensitive reader by their eloquence, wit, and beauty of sound and imagery. It is unique as the work of an octogenarian, able to sum up his aesthetic and spiritual experience in a poem surpassing all that he had previously written, not only in scope and significance but in vigour and freshness."–*DNB*. Bridges died the following year. This set belonged to Sir Herbert Warren, president of Magdalen College. Inserted is a two-page letter from Bridges to Warren, dated Chilswell, November 23 [1929], which reads in part: "I am sending you a copy of the end of the poem, the part written this year–the Press insisted on printing it (tho' it was of no possible use to me) in order to complete their magnificent setting up of the previous sections–which were an inestimable assistance to me in my work. I do not know if you have all the four preceding sections; if not, I could supply II, III, & IV." The set was later in the collection of Simon Nowell-Smith, who lent it to John Hayward's poetry exhibition in 1947. It was also exhibited in the *Festival of Britain Exhibition of Books*, arranged in 1951 by the National Book League at the Victoria and Albert Museum. Acquired in 2002.

FRANCIS THOMPSON (1859–1907)

737. Thompson, Francis. Poems. London: Elkin Mathews and John Lane; Copeland and Day (Boston), 1893. Sm. 4to, original decorated boards.

The author's first book of verse; one of apparently only twelve copies printed on Japan vellum. This one is inscribed by the author to his publisher John Lane. Below is a second inscription, a short poem by Monica Meynell, the daughter of Wilfrid Meynell; both inscriptions are dated January 19, 1895, and may have been penned on the occasion of the publication of Thompson's second book, *Sister-Songs*, of which Lane was the publisher and Monica Meynell one of the dedicatees. Acquired in 1988. Also in the collection is one of five hundred copies of the trade edition. Acquired in 1981.

738. Thompson, Francis. Sister-songs: an offering to two sisters. London: John Lane; Copeland and Day (Boston), 1895. Sm. 4to, original green buckram cloth.

The author's second book, designed by Laurence Housman. The sisters were Monica and Madeleine Meynell, daughters of Alice Meynell. Acquired in 1981

ALFRED EDWARD HOUSMAN (1859–1936)

739. Housman, Alfred Edward. A Shropshire lad. London: Kegan Paul, Trench, Trübner, & Co. Ltd., 1896. 8vo, original pale blue paper boards, white parchment spine, printed paper label.

> The author's first book of verse, preceded only by a privately printed lecture. One of 500 copies printed, of which 150 were exported to the United States, with a new title page, dated 1897. Acquired in 1984.

EDWIN ARNOLD (1832–1904)

740. Arnold, Edwin. Poems narrative and lyrical. Oxford: Francis Macpherson, 1853. 8vo, original claret cloth.

> The author's first book, preceded only by a Newdigate Prize poem. This copy is inscribed on the front flyleaf, "Revd. Robert Whiston from his old pupil the Author." The recipient was Arnold's schoolmaster in Rochester. Acquired in 1993.

741. Arnold, Edwin. Lotus and jewel: containing "In an Indian Temple," "A Casket of Gems," "A Queen's Revenge:" with other poems. London: Trübner & Co., 1887. 8vo, original olive green cloth.

> This copy is inscribed on the title page, "Viscount Cross G. C. B. from the Author: Oct. 1887." The recipient, Richard Asshton Cross (1823–1914), was a prominent political figure; he was in the India Office at the time he was given this book. Acquired in 1985.

ALFRED AUSTIN (1835–1913)

742. Austin, Alfred. The human tragedy. A poem. London: R. Hardwicke, 1862. 8vo, original brown cloth.

> This long poem received a lukewarm reception and was withdrawn from circulation; much-revised versions appeared in 1876 and 1889. This copy is inscribed on the half-title, "To one who will understand: from him who wrote this poem, before he understood. Christmas 1893." A penciled note at the front identifies the recipient as Violet Maxse (1872–1958), whose wedding to Edward Cecil, a son of Lord Salisbury, was attended by Austin in June 1894, along with a number of other literary figures, including Oscar Wilde and George Meredith. Salisbury named Austin Poet Laureate in 1896; the appointment was greeted with ridicule. Acquired in 2000.

MACKENZIE BELL (1856–1930)

743. Bell, Mackenzie. Spring's immortality: and other poems. London: Ward, Lock, and Bowden, Limited, 1893. 8vo, original dark blue-green cloth.

This copy is inscribed on the front flyleaf, "To William Poel, with Macken-zie Bell's good wishes. 19th Nov., 1893." The recipient was a distinguished English actor and theatrical producer. Acquired in 1981.

LAURENCE BINYON (1869–1943)

744. [Binyon, Laurence, and others.] A collection of prize poems and other pamphlets, including Laurence Binyon's first three publications. Together twelve titles in one volume, 8vo, half dark green morocco.

Acquired in 1993, this unusual volume is from the library of John Sparrow. Included are the following:

(a) Binyon, Robert Laurence. Niobe. Milton Prize Poem. . . . Apposition. St. Paul's School, July 20, 1887. [London: 1887.]

Binyon's first publication, a seven-page school-prize poem printed when he was seventeen. No other copy of this title has been located; it is not listed in either WorldCat or Copac, or any other likely source. Binyon became an art historian by profession, but is now best known for his verse.

(b) Binyon, Laurence. Persephone. The Newdigate Poem, 1890. Oxford: B. H. Blackwell; Simpkin, Marshall, & Co. (London), 1890. Original blue printed wrappers bound in.

(c) [Binyon, Laurence, et al.] Primavera: poems, by four authors. Oxford: B. H. Blackwell, 1890. Original gray-brown printed front wrapper bound in.

Included are three poems by Binyon, four by Stephen Phillips, five by Manmohan Ghose, and three by Arthur S. Cripps.

(d) Alexander, Sidney Arthur. Sakya-Muni: the story of Buddha. Newdigate Prize Poem, 1887. Oxford: A. Thomas Shrimpton and Son; Simpkin, Mar-shall, and Co.; Hamilton, Adams and Co. (London), 1887. Original cream printed wrappers bound in.

(e) Hall, Frederick William. Gaisford Prize, 1887. Hexameter verse. Oxford: B. H. Blackwell, 1887. Original printed wrappers bound in.

Inscribed by the author to Ch. Cookson. Lines from Milton translated into Greek verse.

(f) Hall, Frederick William. Praemium Gaisfordianum. "De Origine Mali." Dialogum Graecum ad exemplar Platonicum scripsit. Oxford: B. H. Black-well, 1888.

Inscribed by the author to C. Cookson.

(g) Du Pontet, René L. A. Gaisford Prize, 1889. Hexameter verse. Oxford: B. H. Blackwell, 1889. Original printed wrappers bound in.

A poem in Greek about Columbus.

(h) Geldart, William Martin. Gaisford Prize–Greek verse, 1890. Shakespeare, Henry V, Act II, Scene III, translated into comic iambics. Oxford: B. H. Blackwell, 1890.

This copy is signed by the author with initials.

(i) Du Pontet, René L. A. Alaricus: carmen Latinum: cancellarii præmio donatum et in Theatro Sheldoniano recitatum die Junii XXV MDCCCXC. Oxford: B. H. Blackwell, 1890. Original printed wrappers bound in.

This copy is inscribed, "From the author" on the title page.

(j) [Anon.] Mors Marmionis. N.p.: n.d. [ca. 1890].

A three-page Latin poem, signed at the end with what appear to be the initials *J. H. S.*

(k) Cook, Arthur Bernard. Windsor Castle. A poem, which obtained the Chancellor's Medal at the Cambridge commencement, MDCCCLXXXIX. Cambridge: typis Academicis, 1889.

(l) Fleming, Edward Vandermere. Poema Latinum: numismate annuo dignatum et in curia Cantabrigiensi recitatum comitiis maximis A.D. M.DCCC. XCI. Cambridge: typis Academicis, 1891.

WILFRID SCAWEN BLUNT (1840–1922)

745. [Blunt, Wilfrid Scawen.] Sonnets and songs. By Proteus. London: John Murray, 1875. Sm. 8vo, original lemon cloth.

> The author's first book. This copy was inscribed forty-six years after publication on the half-title, "Lucy Chew in memory of a too short visit from Wilfrid Scawen Blunt. Newbuildings, August 23, 1921." Laid in is a typed letter from the poet and critic Louis Untermeyer to Professor Samuel G. Chew, explaining why Blunt had been left out of his anthology of modern British poetry, and apologizing for the omission. Acquired in 1983.

746. [Blunt, Wilfrid Scawen, and Charles Meynell.] Proteus and Amadeus: A correspondence. Edited by Aubrey de Vere. London: C. Kegan Paul & Co., 1878. 8vo, original orange-brown cloth.

> Blunt's second book. Acquired in 1990.

747. Blunt, Wilfrid Scawen. In vinculis. London: Kegan Paul, Trench and Co., 1889. 8vo, original white cloth, decorated in green.

This copy is inscribed by Blunt on the half-title, "To my dear friend, neighbour and literary ally Frederick Locker. Crabbet, March 1889." Frederick Locker-Lampson was himself a poet of some distinction, but is perhaps now best remembered as a keen book collector. Acquired in 1976.

748. Blunt, Wilfrid Scawen. A new pilgrimage, and other poems. London: Kegan Paul, Trench & Co., 1889. 8vo, original green cloth.

This copy is inscribed by Blunt on the half-title, "To my dear friend and Sussex neighbour Frederick Locker Lampson. Crabbet, March 1889." Acquired in 1976.

749. [Blunt, Wilfrid Scawen.] Griselda: a society novel in rhymed verse. London: Kegan Paul, Trench, Trübner, & Co. Ltd., 1893. Sm. 8vo, original olive green cloth.

A long poem, published anonymously. This copy is inscribed by Blunt on the front flyleaf (in June 16, 1919) to the younger poet Siegfried Sassoon. Acquired in 1996.

FRANCIS WILLIAM BOURDILLON (1852–1921)

750. Bourdillon, Francis William. Among the flowers, and other poems. London: Marcus Ward and Co.; and Royal Ulster Works (Belfast), 1878. 8vo, original white cloth.

The author's first book. This copy is inscribed on the front flyleaf, "With the author's best wishes. Cumberland Lodge: Windsor Park. July, 1878." Tipped in is a four-page letter dated July 27, 1878, sending this copy to a Miss Van de Weyer as a present for her forthcoming marriage: "Is Bach finished for this season yet? If he is, I suppose you have plenty of music to do still, equally advanced and equally appalling to the uninitiated eye. Shall you ever condescend to 'The Hardy Horseman' or the other time-honoured favourites of our Penny Readings again?" Bourdillon is now remembered, if at all, for a single poem, "The Night Has a Thousand Eyes." There is no entry for him in either the *DNB* or the *Oxford DNB*. Acquired in 1984.

751. [Bourdillon, Francis William.] The mountain's brow: a lay of the climbing of Helvellyn. Sept. 4th, 1883. [Ipswich: 1883.] Folio, sewn, as issued.

This piece of light verse in twenty-seven four-line stanzas describes four young couples on a climbing party in Cumbria. Bourdillon had an abiding interest in mountain climbing. An inserted plate, signed with the initials *H. J. F.*, and with the imprint of Cowell's Anastatic Press in Ipswich, shows several humorous scenes from the excursion. Only one other copy of this poem has been located, at Yale. Acquired in 2003.

752. [Bourdillon, Francis William.] Love-in-a-mist. Oxford: published by B. H. Blackwell, 1892. Sm. square 8vo, blue-green morocco.

> A set of proof sheets for the second of two small collections of verse by Bourdillon issued anonymously by Blackwell. The most obvious difference between this copy and the published version is that Bourdillon decided to remove the hyphens from the book's title. Whether or not there are other changes in the text has not been determined. This copy was acquired from a small archive of books and papers belonging to Bourdillon himself, though there is no indication of this; the binding was done especially for him. Acquired in 2003.

ROBERT WILLIAM BUCHANAN (1841–1901)

753. Buchanan, Robert William. Poems and love lyrics. Glasgow: Thomas Murray and Son; Sutherland and Knox (Edinburgh); Hall, Virtue, and Co. (London), n.d. [1858]. 8vo, original gray-green cloth.

> The author's first book. This copy is inscribed on the front flyleaf, "To Mrs. Charles Rice, with the best respects of her obedient servant the Author." Acquired in 1979.

754. [Buchanan, Robert William.] Saint Abe and his seven wives: a tale of Salt Lake City. London: Strahan and Co., 1872. 8vo, original blue cloth. Acquired in 1980.

MARY ELIZABETH COLERIDGE (1861–1907)

755. [Coleridge, Mary Elizabeth.] Fancy's following by Ἄνοδος. Oxford: Daniel, 1896. 8vo, original gray printed wrappers.

> The author's first book of verse, printed in an edition of 125 numbered copies at the Daniel Press. Mary Coleridge was the great-granddaughter of Samuel Taylor Coleridge's elder brother, James Coleridge. As a young woman she was the disciple of her father's friend William Johnson Cory, who taught her and helped her to develop the literary gifts she had shown

at a very early age. These poems were published at the instigation of Robert Bridges, some of whose works were also printed at the Daniel Press. Mary Coleridge went on to publish several novels; she taught literature at the Working Women's College, and died in 1907, at the age of forty-six. Acquired in 1992.

RICHARD WATSON DIXON (1833–1900)

756. Dixon, Richard Watson. Christ's company and other poems. London: Smith, Elder and Co., 1861. 8vo, original blue cloth.

> The author's first book of poems; preceded only by a prize essay of 1858. "The poems . . . though largely upon religious subjects, are not strictly religious poetry; they are works of picturesque imagination rather than of devotional feeling."–*DNB*. The Hayward exhibition catalogue states that this volume was, in 1947, still in print at the Oxford University Press; those copies, however, were in a different binding, and had an OUP slip pasted over the imprint. Acquired in 1992.

757. Dixon, Richard Watson. S. John in Patmos. Oxford: T. & G. Shrimpton; Smith, Elder, and Co. (London), n.d. [1863]. 8vo, original chocolate printed wrappers.

> At the head of the title page these verses are identified as "The Prize Poem on a sacred subject [at Oxford], for 1863." Acquired in 1992.

758. Dixon, Richard Watson. Historical odes and other poems. London: Smith, Elder and Co., 1864. 8vo, original purple cloth.

> The author's second book of poems. Acquired in 1977. Also in the collection is a copy of a remainder issue, with a tipped-in imprint slip of Humphrey Milford, Oxford University Press; according to Simon Nowell-Smith (*The Book Collector*, vol. 10, no. 3 [Autumn 1961], pp. 222–28) copies with this slip were issued after 1913, which indicates just how slowly Dixon's poetry sold. Acquired in 1992.

759. Dixon, Richard Watson. Lyrical poems. Oxford: printed by H. Daniel, Fellow of Worcester College, 1887. Sm. 4to, original gray printed wrappers.

> One of 105 copies privately printed at the Daniel Press. Acquired in 1975.

DIGBY MACKWORTH DOLBEN (1848–1867)

760. Dolben, Digby. The poems of Digby Mackworth Dolben. Edited with a memoir by Robert Bridges. London, New York, Toronto and Melbourne: Henry Frowde, Oxford University Press, 1911. 8vo, original light blue boards, canvas spine, printed paper label; in a light blue printed dust wrapper.

> The first collection of Dolben's verse; nothing was published during his lifetime. At Eton, Dolben became fag to his cousin Robert Bridges, whom he had not previously met. In 1865, during a brief visit to Oxford, Dolben was introduced to Gerard Manley Hopkins, who was four years his elder. The two young men never met again, but they remained in close touch for the next two years and greatly influenced each other's verse. Laid into this copy is a two-page letter from Bridges to an unnamed recipient in Cambridge, who had evidently requested a copy from the publishers: "This book was not sent out to any of the reviews. Only one copy was sent to 'The Times,' but I am sending you a presentation copy herewith, as I consider your request as coming from the sister university, and I have no doubt that many of my friends would be glad that it should be noticed in your journal." Bridges has also noted several errata on the front flyleaf (signed with initials); a more complete list of errata was later printed as a four-page leaflet, and a copy of this is laid in. Acquired in 1982.

ERNEST CHRISTOPHER DOWSON (1867–1900)

761. Dowson, Ernest. Verses. London: Leonard Smithers, 1896. 8vo, original white parchment boards, front cover decorated in gilt with a design by Aubrey Beardsley.

> One of three hundred copies printed; there were also thirty large-paper copies on Japan vellum. The author's first book of poems, preceded by one three-decker novel (a collaboration), one book of stories, and several translations from the French. Dowson was a prominent figure in the fin-de-siècle London literary set, but his reputation was such that in 1900, when he died impoverished at the age of thirty-three, the *DNB* neglected to provide an entry for him. Acquired in 1992.

762. Dowson, Ernest. Decorations: in verse and prose. London: Leonard Smithers and Co., 1899. 8vo, original white parchment boards, decorated in gilt (remains of glassine dust wrapper).

This copy is inscribed on the front flyleaf, "To Robbie Ross in memory of Ernest Dowson, Leonard Smithers, March 1900." The recipient, Robert Baldwin Ross, was one of the key literary figures of the nineties, particularly known for his close association with Oscar Wilde. This is one of about 350 copies printed at the Chiswick Press; the front cover design is by Pickford Waller, and the back cover design is by Althea Gyles. The Simon Nowell-Smith copy. Acquired in 2002.

MICHAEL FIELD [KATHARINE HARRIS BRADLEY (1846–1914) AND EDITH EMMA COOPER (1862–1913)]

763. [Bradley, Katharine Harris, and Edith Emma Cooper.] Field, Michael [pseud.]. Noontide branches: a small sylvan drama interspersed with songs and invocations. [Colophon:] Oxford: printed by Henry Daniel at Worcester House, September 13, 1899. 4to, original dark blue printed wrappers.

> This book was privately printed at the Daniel Press in an edition of 150 copies, of which this is no. 14. "Michael Field" was the pseudonym adopted by Katharine Harris Bradley and her niece Edith Emma Cooper, who collaborated on many verse plays and volumes of poetry from 1875 to the beginning of World War I. Acquired in 2001.

NORMAN GALE (1862–1942)

764. [Gale, Norman.] Marsh marigolds. Rugby: George E. Over, 1888. 8vo, original white printed wrappers, glassine dust wrapper.

> One of sixty numbered copies privately printed at the Rugby Press. This is the author's third book of verse, preceded by *Unleavened Bread* (1885) and *Primulas and Pansies* (1886). With the bookplate of W. MacDonald MacKay. Acquired in 1975.

DAVID GRAY (1838–1861)

765. Gray, David. The Luggie: and other poems.... With a memoir by James Hedderwick, and a prefatory notice by R. M. Milnes, M.P. Cambridge and London: Macmillan and Co., 1862. 8vo, original green cloth.

> The author's only book, published shortly after his death at the age of twenty-three. The introductory essay, by Richard Monckton Milnes, tells a

376

romantic tale. David Gray first wrote to Milnes from Scotland in 1860, enclosing some poems that showed great promise. Receiving encouragement, Gray came to London to see Milnes, but he spent his first night in Hyde Park and caught a cold, which soon settled in his lungs. Milnes advised the young poet to go back to Scotland, but Gray was determined to stay, and was given some light literary work. His health began to deteriorate, however, and in January 1861, he returned north, where he lingered on for the rest of the year, composing a series of sonnets and other short poems; he died a day after seeing a proof of a page of the title poem, "The Luggie," named after the stream flowing past his birthplace. Milnes did not hesitate to compare Gray's early death with that of others of greater ability: "The public mind will not separate the intrinsic merits of the verses from the story of the writer, any more than the works and fate of Keats or of Chatterton." Gray himself identified closely with Keats, as can be vividly seen in his sonnet sequence: "Last night, on coughing slightly with sharp pain, / There came arterial blood, and with a sigh / Of absolute grief I cried in bitter vein, / That drop is my death-warrant: I must die." It is not entirely clear why the *CBEL* classifies Gray as a late nineteenth-century poet. Acquired in 2001.

JOHN GRAY (1866–1934)

766. Gray, John. Silverpoints. London: Elkin Mathews and John Lane, 1893. Tall narrow 8vo, original green cloth, decorated in gilt.

This copy is inscribed by the author on the front flyleaf, "Lady Gregory from John Gray, April 1893." The recipient's large and striking bookplate is on the front pastedown. Lady Gregory was a leading figure in the Anglo-Irish literary world, particularly known for her close association with Yeats and for her role in founding the Abbey Theatre in Dublin in 1904. This is one of 250 copies printed (of which 200 were for sale), with the limitation notice printed on the verso of the title page filled in by hand (this being copy 116). There were also 25 copies on thick paper, bound in vellum, as well as an unknown number of copies without the note of limitation. This volume, the author's first publication, has long been considered one of the most beautiful books of the 1890s; the covers and layout were designed by Charles Ricketts.

As a young man Gray was a fastidious dandy and a disciple of the French Symbolists. Among the dedicatees of the various poems here are Paul Verlaine, Oscar Wilde, Jules Laforgue, Ernest Dowson, and Frank Harris; there are also imitations of Mallarmé and Baudelaire. Oscar Wilde paid for the production of this book; Gray, who later became a priest, never allowed the text to be reprinted, and is said to have bought up copies to "immobilise" them whenever he saw the opportunity. With book labels of Michael Sadleir and Simon Nowell-Smith. Acquired in 2002.

767. [Gray, John.] The fourth and last blue almanack. 1898. London: printed by R. Folkard and Son, n.d. [1897]. 16mo, original plain blue wrappers.

> The last in a series of small booklets, "privately printed and not for general distribution." This pamphlet is in the form of an almanac, with an original poem or carol for each month. Four copies are located, at the British Library, the Bodleian, Manchester, and the New York Public Library. Acquired in 1978.

WILLIAM ERNEST HENLEY (1849–1903)

768. Henley, William Ernest. A book of verses. London: published by David Nutt, 1888. Large 8vo, original stiff white wrappers, printed in gold (remains of tissue dust wrapper).

> The author's first book of poems; Henley's published writing had hitherto been largely confined to dramatic collaborations with Robert Louis Stevenson. This copy is on large paper, one of either fifty or seventy-five so issued (authorities differ); there were also twenty copies on Japan vellum. It is signed by the author at the end of the text (not all large-paper copies were so signed). The volume contains "Invictus," one of the most widely quoted poems in all English verse ("I am the master of my fate, / I am the captain of my soul"). From the library of the actor H. Beerbohm Tree, with an inscription to him on the front flyleaf, possibly by the author, dated August 28, 1890. With the later bookplates of Richard Till Worthington and Kenneth A. Lohf. Acquired in 1992.

769. Henley, William Ernest. London voluntaries: the song of the sword, and other verses. London: published by David Nutt, 1893. 8vo, original green cloth.

> Second edition, revised, with a new title; first published earlier the same year as *The Song of the Sword*. This copy is inscribed by Henley in 1895 on the front flyleaf to the Marchioness of Granby ("with gratitude"). There are numerous penciled alterations in the author's hand, largely changing punctuation and other accidentals, but in a number of cases making

substantive revisions. There were no further editions of this book; the text includes many of Henley's best poems. With the bookplate of Diana Duff Cooper. Acquired in 1994.

770. Henley, William Ernest. Hawthorn and lavender, with other verses. London: published by David Nutt, 1901. 8vo, original green cloth.

This copy is inscribed by the author, "To T. G. with affection, sympathy, & praise. 20 / 11 / 1901." Tipped onto the front endpaper is a photograph of the author, also inscribed to "T. G." Acquired in 1974.

771. Henley, William Ernest. I. M. Reginae Dilectissimae Victoriae. 24th May 1819: 22nd January 1901. [Colophon:] Worthing, Feb. 1, 1901. Folio, two leaves, folded, as issued.

A privately printed poem on the death of Queen Victoria. Acquired in 2001.

EDMOND GORE ALEXANDER HOLMES (1850–1936)

772. Holmes, Edmond Gore Alexander. Poems. London: Henry S. King & Co., 1876. 8vo, original maroon cloth.

The author's first book, a collection of poems on spiritual themes published when he was twenty-six. Holmes was Irish by birth, and the last four sonnets relate to the coast of County Clare. In later years he published widely on philosophical, religious, and educational subjects; he also had an interest in the poetry of Walt Whitman, and edited a selection, with commentary, in 1902. By his death in 1936, Holmes's reputation had faded to the point where he was not thought worthy of an entry in the *DNB*. This copy is inscribed on the half-title, "M. J. Barrington Ward from E. G. A. H., Nov. 1877"; the recipient was Mark James Barrington Ward, a fellow inspector of schools and later rector of Duloe, in Cornwall. Acquired in 2000.

LIONEL JOHNSON (1867–1902)

773. Johnson, Lionel. Sir Walter Raleigh in the Tower. [Chester: Phillipson and Golder, printers, 1885.] 4to, sewn, as issued.

The poet's first publication, a prize poem for which he won a medal at Winchester College, at the age of eighteen. At Oxford, Lionel Johnson came under the influence of Walter Pater; he converted to Catholicism, and became a characteristic aesthete of the fin de siécle. This poem is of the greatest rarity; the only copy located is at British Library. From the library of Oliver Brett, Viscount Esher; later in the collection of H. Bradley Martin. Acquired in 1990.

774. Johnson, Lionel. Poems. London: Elkin Mathews; Copeland and Day (Boston), 1895. 8vo, original brown buckram cloth.

> The author's first and most important book of poems. The first issue, one of only 25 copies numbered and signed by the author on the page facing the half-title. The second, or trade, issue had the first and last gatherings reimposed, with some changes in design; of this issue 750 copies were printed. This copy has the bookplate of the great collector and patron of the arts John Quinn; later it was in the collection of James Gilvarry. Acquired in 1993.

EDWARD CRACROFT LEFROY (1855–1891)

775. Lefroy, Edward Cracroft. [Wrapper title:] Echoes from Theocritus. A cycle of sonnets. Blackheath: H. Burnside, n.d. [1883]. Sm. 8vo, original tan printed wrappers,

> The first of four small collections of sonnets published by the author over the course of 1883–84; each has the same Blackheath imprint. Lefroy was a clergyman whose verse was admired by Tennyson, Christina Rossetti, Edmund Gosse, and, most notably, John Addington Symonds, who published his appraisal of Lefroy's work in an edition of his poems, with a biographical account, in 1897. Lefroy is now classed as one of the "Uranian" (homosexual) poets of the late nineteenth century. For an account of his publications, see Timothy D'Arch Smith, "Some Uncollected Authors XXX," *The Book Collector* 10, no. 4 (Winter 1961), pp. 442–45. D'Arch Smith describes the four sonnet collections as follows: "These little pamphlets are extremely rare; the only set I have seen is in the British Museum and is bound in leather." Four other copies of this collection can now be located, at Leeds, British Columbia, the University of San Francisco, and Cornell. The Simon Nowell-Smith copy; the pamphlet itself is contained in later plain brown wrappers, with the author, title, and imprint, below which Nowell-Smith has written, "The above is in the hand of Michael Sadleir, who gave the book to me in 1950." Acquired in 2002.

ALFRED COMYN LYALL (1835–1911). *See below, under "Anglo-Indian Verse."*

EDWARD ROBERT BULWER LYTTON, 1ST EARL OF LYTTON (1831–1891)

776. Lytton, Edward Robert Bulwer, 1st Earl of. Glenaveril; or, the metamorphoses. London: John Murray, 1885. Six vols., sm. 8vo, contemporary limp red morocco, gilt rules, front covers lettered in gilt, spines gilt, a.e.g.

> A long novel in verse by one of the most popular of all Victorian poets, whose life as a man of letters was combined with that of a scholar, diplomat, magistrate, and courtier. This volume was printed for binding up in two cloth volumes; copies were first issued, however, in six parts with printed wrappers, and it is no doubt from one of these sets that the present copy, in what is clearly a kind of presentation binding, derives. This copy is inscribed on a front flyleaf by the author's daughter, Lady Elizabeth Balfour ("Betty"), to his granddaughter Eve S. Balfour. Acquired in 1997.

ALICE MEYNELL (1847–1922)

777. Meynell, Alice. Poems. London: Elkin Mathews and John Lane, 1893. Tall 8vo, original brown buckram cloth.

> This is no. 29 of fifty copies on large paper, signed by the author; the first edition, on ordinary paper. was published earlier in the year. Some of the poems here had appeared in 1875 in *Preludes*, the author's first book and the only one she published under her maiden name (Thompson). The Simon Nowell-Smith copy. Acquired in 2002.

LEWIS MORRIS (1833–1907)

778. [Morris, Lewis.] Songs of two worlds. By a new writer. London: Henry S. King & Co., 1871. 8vo, original green cloth.

> The author's first book; Morris went on to become one of the most prominent Welsh poets of his day. This copy is inscribed on the half-title, in January 1872, to Mr. and Mrs. W. T. Malleson. Elizabeth Malleson was a prominent figure in the women's suffrage movement; her husband presided over the meeting at which John Stuart Mill first spoke to Westminster electors, in June 1865. With the book label of Simon Nowell-Smith. Acquired in 1977.

HENRY JOHN NEWBOLT (1862–1937)

779. [Newbolt, Henry John.] A fair death. London: Simpkin, Marshall, and Co.; Walsall: W. Henry Robinson, n.d. [1882]. 8vo, original white printed wrappers.

> The author's first book. Newbolt is one of those poets now chiefly associated with the height of the British Empire. Acquired in 1976.

JOHN PAYNE (1842–1916)

780. Payne, John. The masque of shadows: and other poems. London: Basil Montagu Pickering, 1870. 8vo, original black cloth.

> The author's first book. This copy is inscribed on the half-title by the author to W. C. B. Wyse ("a token of friendship"); the recipient was a writer with a particular enthusiasm for Provençal poetry. As a young man, Payne was a close friend of the Irish poet Arthur O'Shaughnessy, to whom this book is dedicated. Through O'Shaughnessy he gained entrée to Pre-Raphaelite circles, and his early books were highly praised by Rossetti and Swinburne; some of the poems here have a dreamlike atmosphere that clearly echoes much Pre-Raphaelite poetry, especially the works of William Morris. In later years Payne turned to translating, especially from Persian and Arabic; he also formed a close friendship with Mallarmé. By the time of his death his reputation had suffered such a decline that no entry was provided for him in the *DNB*; he remains unnoticed by the *Oxford DNB*. Acquired in 1992.

781. Payne, John. Intaglios: sonnets. London: Basil Montagu Pickering, 1871. 8vo, original black cloth.

> The author's second book. This copy is inscribed on the half-title, "The Right Honourable Lord Lytton with the author's compliments." The recipient was Edward Robert Bulwer Lytton, the popular poet who published under the pseudonym "Owen Meredith." Tipped in is John Payne's calling card, with the address corrected in his hand. With the book label of John Sparrow. Acquired in 1994.

JAMES LOGIE ROBERTSON (1846–1922)

782. Robertson, James Logie. Poems. Dundee: printed by John Leng & Co., 1878. 8vo, original bright green cloth.

The author's first book. Robertson went on to publish a number of other volumes of poetry, as well as literary criticism and texts on English literature for young students. This copy is inscribed on the front flyleaf, "With the author's compts." Acquired in 1992.

JANET LOGIE ROBERTSON (FL. 1880)

783. [Robertson, Janet Logie.] Blossoms: a series of child-portraits. By Jessie Simpson [pseud.]. N.p. [London?]: printed for private circulation, n.d. [1880]. 8vo, original ocher limp cloth.

> A privately printed collection of twenty poems describing children. This copy is signed on the front flyleaf, on December 7, 1880, by James Logie Robertson, who has added significant annotations. Robertson has identified the name on the title page as an "alias" of his sister, Janet Logie Robertson. He has also named the printer as Burness ("printer to H. M. the Queen"), and has given the print run as 250 copies. In the text he has made a fair number of comments about the quality of the individual poems, and has provided clues to the identity of the children portrayed; the subject of "Katharine," for example, is noted as follows: "A similar character bearing the same name in Bowring's Russian Poetry." Robertson's annotations here must have been made after 1882, as he names his sister as the coauthor of *Our Holiday among the Hills*, published at Edinburgh in that year. The true identity of "Jessie Simpson" is not revealed in either WorldCat or Copac. Acquired in 2001.

JOSEPH SKIPSEY (1832–1903)

784. Skipsey, Joseph. Poems. Blyth: printed by William Alder, 1871. 8vo, original green cloth.

> This copy is inscribed on the front flyleaf, "Dec. 18 / 71. Old Newsham, Blyth. To Joseph Knight Esq. with the compliments of the author." This is the author's third surviving book of verse; a collection of poems published in 1859 is referred to in the preface to a later volume, but no copy appears to have been located. Joseph Skipsey was the youngest of eight children of a Northumberland coal miner who was shot in a fight between pitmen and special constables during a period of labor disturbances. Skipsey went to work in the coalpits at the age of seven; he had no schooling, but managed to teach himself to read, though until the age of fifteen he had access to no

other book than the Bible. Subsequently he studied Shakespeare, Milton, Burns, and translations of Heine, Goethe, and the Greek and Latin classics. He soon began to write verse of his own, and became friendly with another working-class poet, Thomas Dixon, to whom Ruskin addressed the letters of his *Time and Tide in Tyne and Wear*. One of the first notices of Skipsey's verse outside the local press was published in *The Athenæum* by the recipient of this copy, Joseph Knight, a drama critic and later the biographer of Dante Gabriel Rossetti. Rossetti himself was the first major literary figure to take notice of Skipsey's abilities, and others soon followed; Oscar Wilde likened some of his poems about the coalpits to the work of William Blake. In 1880, Dixon brought Skipsey to London, and introduced him to Burne-Jones, who obtained for him a civil pension of £10 a year (later raised to £25). In 1889, Skipsey and his wife were named custodians of Shakespeare's birthplace at Stratford, but he soon tired of the drudgery of attending to tourists, and in October 1891, he resigned; the incident was the subject of a short story by Henry James called "The Birthplace," published in *The Better Sort* in 1903. "Skipsey's poems were mainly lyrical, although he occasionally attempted more sustained flights, and they show the influence of Burns and Heine. He is at his best in the verse which was prompted by his own experience as a pitman."–*DNB*. A number of the poems in this volume have to do with the coal mines, including "Bereaved" (about a pit disaster) and "The Young Collier." Skipsey's first three books, published before he achieved wider notice, are all extremely rare. This title is said to have been printed in an edition of three hundred copies; WorldCat and Copac together now record five copies, at the British Library, Newcastle, the National Coal Mining Museum, the Brooklyn Public Library, and Oberlin College. Acquired in 2001.

JAMES KENNETH STEPHEN (1859–1892)

785. [Stephen, James Kenneth.] Lapsus calami. By J. K. S. Cambridge: Macmillan and Bowes, 1891. 8vo, original light blue cloth, printed paper label.

This copy is inscribed on the half-title, "J. A. Blaikie from J. K. Stephen, 'by way of chop, swap, barter or exchange,' Apr. 22, '91"; the recipient was John Arthur Blaikie, who published volumes of poetry in 1870 and 1890. This was the author's first book of poems, published a year before he died, at the age of thirty-two. Stephen was educated at Eton, and then at Cambridge, where he was one of the Apostles. He was Virginia Woolf's cousin. Acquired in 2001.

384

ARTHUR SYMONS (1865–1945)

786. Symons, Arthur. Silhouettes. London: Elkin Mathews & John Lane, 1892. 8vo, original gray printed boards.

> The author's second book of poems, of which 250 copies were printed. To this copy Symons has added a manuscript poem of twelve lines on the front flyleaf (signed at the end), entitled "At Dieppe: A Colour Study." These verses relate to the first six poems of the book itself, which are grouped under the heading "At Dieppe." Symons was a sensitive young man who became a disciple of Walter Pater. He later was much involved with the literature and art of France, where he knew Verlaine, Mallarmé, Rodin, and many other prominent writers and artists of the day. Acquired in 1992.

JOHN BYRNE LEICESTER WARREN, 3RD BARON DE TABLEY (1835–1895)

787. [Warren, John Byrne Leicester, 3rd Baron de Tabley.] Praeterita. By William Lancaster [pseud.]. London; and Cambridge: Macmillan and Co., 1863. 8vo, original bright green cloth.

> While a student at Christ Church, Oxford, Warren had already published several books under the pseudonym "G. G. Preston." He succeeded his father to the title baron de Tabley in 1887. Acquired in 1981.

788. Warren, John Byrne Leicester, 3rd Baron de Tabley. Poems dramatic and lyrical. . . . With illustrations by C. S. Ricketts. London: Elkin Mathews and John Lane; Macmillan and Co. (New York), 1893. 8vo, original vellum, decorated in gilt with an allover pattern of rose petals in diagonal rows, and a gilt angel within a heart at the upper right of each cover.

> This copy is one of one hundred printed on Japan vellum. The special binding, with the monograms of Charles Ricketts and Charles Shannon, is one of the most famous of the 1890s. The volume includes an etched frontispiece and four other plates by Ricketts; an additional plate shows the author's bookplate, designed by William Bell Scott. The poems for this collection were largely selected by the younger writer Richard Le Gallienne, whose judgment Lord de Tabley seems to have trusted. Acquired in 2000.

789. Warren, John Byrne Leicester, 3rd Baron de Tabley. Poems dramatic and lyrical. . . . With illustrations by C. S. Ricketts. London: Elkin Mathews and John Lane, 1893. 8vo, original light green cloth, decorated in gilt.

The trade edition; there was also a limited edition on Japan vellum (no. 788). This copy is inscribed on the front flyleaf, "Clara Grant Duff from her Godfather. June 1893." Tipped onto the pastedown opposite is a letter to the recipient: "My dear godchild, I am sending you a copy of my long delayed and rather ineffectual book. You are in the same line, so you will make allowance. Don't trouble to write to acknowledge, for I well know the nuisance of having such letters to write. Yours sincerely, De Tabley." Acquired in 1996.

WILLIAM WATSON (1858–1935)

790. Watson, William. Ode on the day of the coronation of King Edward VII. London & New York: John Lane, 1902. 8vo, green morocco, by Zaehnsdorf.

Watson, an enemy of modernism, was a strong contender for the Poet Laureateship after the death of Tennyson in 1892; ten years later his reputation was on the wane, but his coronation ode was widely acclaimed. This copy is inscribed by Watson to the poet and critic Richard Garnett (June 13, 1902). Also bound in are the following: (1) A three-page letter from the publisher John Lane to Garnett, thanking him for his suggested revisions of the poem, of which Watson had availed himself; (2) two sets of page proofs of the text, both with significant alterations in Watson's hand; (3) a carbon copy of a typescript of the poem, representing yet another early version of the text. At the front is a note in Garnett's hand, and the later bookplate of Roderick Terry. Acquired in 1980.

HILAIRE BELLOC (1870–1953)

791. Belloc, Hilaire. Verses and sonnets. London: Ward and Downey, Limited, 1896. 12mo, original green cloth.

> The author's first book. This copy was inscribed in April 1961, by Belloc's daughter Eleanor Jebb to Siegfried Sassoon. Acquired in 1983.

ARTHUR CHRISTOPHER BENSON (1862–1925)

792. Benson, Arthur Christopher. Lord Vyet and other poems. London and New York: John Lane, the Bodley Head, 1897. Sm. 8vo, original light brown buckram cloth.

> The author's fourth book of poems. This copy is inscribed on the front flyleaf, "Edmund Gosse from Arthur C. Benson. Eton College, Oct. 2, 1897." Gosse was thirteen years Benson's senior, and well established as a critic; Benson was teaching at Eton. With an inscription on the half-title, "Alan Lubbock from Philip Gosse. Wepham, Nov. 29, 1937." Acquired in 1993.

GILBERT KEITH CHESTERTON (1874–1936)

793. Chesterton, Gilbert Keith. The wild knight and other poems. London: Grant Richards, 1900. 8vo, original light blue boards, parchment spine.

> With the signature on the front flyleaf of M. J. Evans, dated March 30, 1903. Acquired in 1984.

SAMUEL RUTHERFORD CROCKETT (1860–1914)

794. [Crockett, Samuel Rutherford.] Dulce cor: being the poems of Ford Berêton [pseud.]. London: Kegan Paul, Trench and Co., 1886. 8vo, original green cloth.

> The author's first book. Crockett had just become a minister of the Free Church of Scotland. This copy is inscribed on the half-title, "Harry Furniss, Esq., with the author's compts. and thanks for much pleasure given. S. R. Crockett. Penicuick. 17.2.89." The recipient was a well-known political cartoonist and caricaturist. Acquired in 1978.

795. Dobson, Austin. "The Drama of the Doctor's Window." A brief state-ment concerning that poem since its appearance in "St. Paul's Magazine," for February, 1870; with appendices respecting its "earlier history." By Austin Dobson, the author of the verses in question. [London: 1872.] 8vo, sewn, as issued.

> The author's first separately published, original publication, preceded only by a translation from French that had appeared in 1866. This pamphlet gives details of a bizarre dispute between Dobson and Richard Everard Webster, a contemporary who later became Viscount Alverstone. Webster was convinced that a poem published under initials only in St. Paul's Magazine was not in fact by "A. D.," as Dobson signed himself, but by an unspecified woman who occasionally published verse as "A. B." Dobson did his best to disabuse Webster of his mistaken impression, but to no avail; Webster withdrew all claims of his lady friend to authorship of the poem, but refused to give unequivocal credit to Dobson. The exchanges between Dobson and Webster are given in an opening statement dated July 19, 1872. This is followed by a first draft of the poem, under the title "A Story of Pyra-mus and Thisbe," followed by the full text of the poem itself. At the end, in an appendix, are various letters in support of Dobson's authorship, most notably from the editor of the magazine, Anthony Trollope. Trollope's first letter, dated November 8, 1869, is quite long, and offers specific suggestions for revisions; the second letter, sent a week later, transmits proofs (under the title "Pyramus and Thisbe"). At the head of the title page is printed, "For private circulation only." Dobson elsewhere states that thirty copies only were printed. This is one of several copies discovered in an archive of Dobson's papers. Acquired in 2006.

796. Dobson, Austin. Proverbs in porcelain and other verses. London: Henry S. King & Co., 1877. 8vo, original green cloth.

> Dobson's second and best book of verse. This copy is inscribed on the half-title, "To A. H. Japp, with the kind regards of Austin Dobson. May 17, 1877." Alexander Hay Japp was an essayist and publisher and a close friend of Robert Louis Stevenson. Tipped in at the front is a touching two-page letter from Dobson to Japp, presenting the book and expressing doubt about Dobson's own poetical abilities: "Personally, I am rather puzzled as to which road to take. I am tired of vers de société, indeed I was never

thoroughly in sympathy with them, and I fear, honestly, that my wing is hardly strong enough, nor my equipment sufficient, for classical 'high-falutin.'" Also present is a broadside poem, possibly a proof of a piece in a periodical, entitled "The Dance of Death." The poem is signed at the end by Dobson, who has made a couple of small corrections; it is accompanied by a brief letter to Japp, sending the poem and expressing concern that it might be "tedious." Acquired in 1978.

CHARLES LUTWIDGE DODGSON (1832–1898)

797. [Dodgson, Charles Lutwidge.] The deserted parks. N.p. [Oxford]: May, 1867. 4to, two leaves, folded.

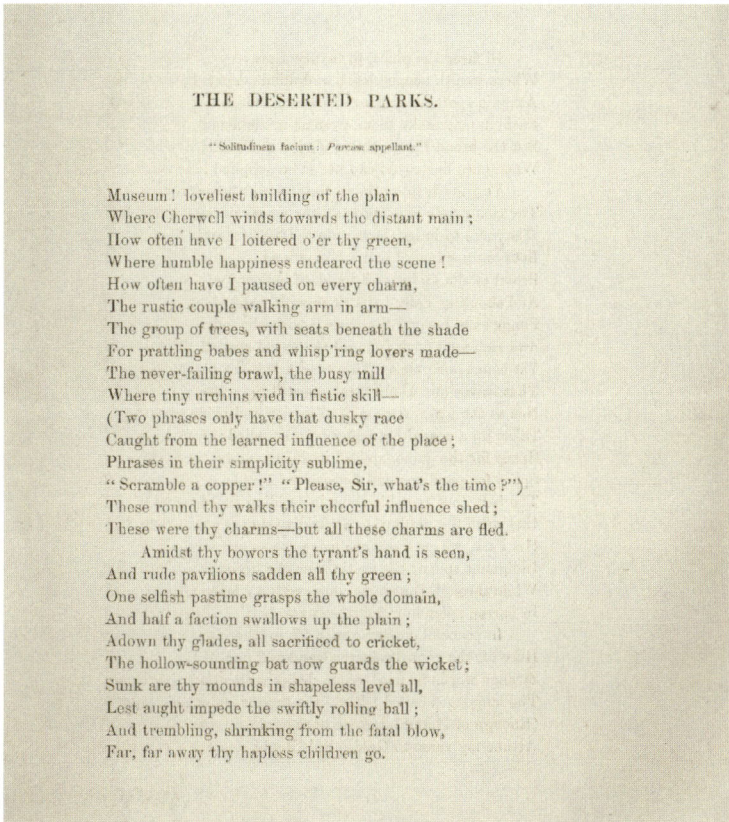

THE DESERTED PARKS.

"Solitudinem faciunt : *Parcas* appellant."

Museum! loveliest building of the plain
Where Cherwell winds towards the distant main ;
How often have I loitered o'er thy green,
Where humble happiness endeared the scene !
How often have I paused on every charm,
The rustic couple walking arm in arm—
The group of trees, with seats beneath the shade
For prattling babes and whisp'ring lovers made—
The never-failing brawl, the busy mill
Where tiny urchins vied in fistic skill—
(Two phrases only have that dusky race
Caught from the learned influence of the place ;
Phrases in their simplicity sublime,
"Scramble a copper!" "Please, Sir, what's the time ?")
These round thy walks their cheerful influence shed ;
These were thy charms—but all these charms are fled.
    Amidst thy bowers the tyrant's hand is seen,
And rude pavilions sadden all thy green ;
One selfish pastime grasps the whole domain,
And half a faction swallows up the plain ;
Adown thy glades, all sacrificed to cricket,
The hollow-sounding bat now guards the wicket ;
Sunk are thy mounds in shapeless level all,
Lest aught impede the swiftly rolling ball ;
And trembling, shrinking from the fatal blow,
Far, far away thy hapless children go.

ITEM 797

389

A 104-line parody of Oliver Goldsmith's *Deserted Village*, written to oppose the restriction of portions of Oxford's parks to college cricket matches. The poem was written on May 22, 1867. Only one hundred copies were printed, half of which Dodgson distributed among Oxford common rooms. This poem is now very rare; there is no copy listed in the NUC, WorldCat, or Copac. A copy is cited in the Parrish catalogue, but this does not appear in the Princeton online catalogue; another copy is apparently at Christ Church, Oxford. Acquired in 1977.

798. [Dodgson, Charles Lutwidge.] Phantasmagoria and other poems. By Lewis Carroll [pseud.]. London: Macmillan and Co., 1869. 8vo, original blue cloth.

> This copy is inscribed on the half-title, "Miss M. B. Smedley, with the author's affectionate regards. Jan. 1869." Dodgson records in his diary for Jan. 7, 1869, "Called on Macmillan and sent off twenty-eight copies of *Phantasmagoria*"; this is presumably one of those copies. The recipient was the poet Menella Bute Smedley (1819–1877), one of Dodgson's cousins, to whom he was very close. Smedley gave him much advice on his early writings; he in turn is recorded as having read everything she wrote. With the signature of Major Minter on the half-title and at the top of the title page. From the library of Mrs. J. Insley Blair. Acquired in 2004.

799. [Dodgson, Charles Lutwidge.] The hunting of the snark: an agony, in eight fits. By Lewis Carroll [pseud.]. . . . With nine illustrations by Henry Holiday. London: Macmillan and Co., 1876. 8vo, original white cloth, elaborately decorated in gilt.

> This copy is inscribed on the half-title in Dodgson's familiar purple ink, "Presented to Bennie by the Author, Mar. 1, '77"; the recipient, undoubtedly a child, has not been identified. The book was first printed in an edition of ten thousand copies, in a buff cloth binding with the blocking in black. Dodgson also, however, had a number bound in other colors for his own use; in a letter to Macmillan on March 21, 1876, he asks for "100 in red and gold, 20 in dark blue and gold, 20 in white vellum and gold," along with "four miscellaneous covers to be used in binding 4 copies for me." The following year he described these special bindings in a letter to Maud Standen: "I have had them bound in various coloured cloths with a ship and bell-buoy in gold: e.g. light blue, dark blue, light green, dark green, scarlet (to match Alice), and, what is perhaps prettiest of all,

ITEM 799

white i.e. a sort of imitation vellum which looks beautiful with the gold." The present copy is one of the last of these. The Simon Nowell-Smith copy. Acquired in 2002.

EDMUND GOSSE (1849–1928)

800. Gosse, Edmund. King Erik. London: Chatto and Windus, 1876. Sm. 8vo, original white cloth, decorated in gilt.

> This copy is inscribed on the half-title in February 1876 from Gosse to his close friend Austin Dobson, with a poem that reads as follows:
>
>> Whether like porcelain, delicately Dresden,
>> Daintiest verse-form tempt you to bewitch us,
>> Or, more stern, satirico-didactic
>> Measures Horatian,
>> Still we are charmed, and still are we delighted!
>> Lo! this blander dowry of the Muses,
>> Lo! this rapier keener than a sword is,
>> Scorn not and blunt not!
>> Thou no mouth of a thundering Olympus,
>> Thou no seer made frantically Delphic,
>> Yet with the brand of the service of Apollo
>> Sealed where the brows bend!
>
> Dobson was nine years older than Gosse, but the two men were colleagues at the Board of Trade. Gosse's poem, neatly penned in his characteristic purple ink, seems to foreshadow the appearance of Dobson's second book of poems, *Proverbs in Porcelain*, first published in 1877. This verse play is Gosse's third literary work. He went on to become one of England's leading men of letters, and a close friend of such noted writers as Swinburne, Thomas Hardy, Robert Louis Stevenson, and Henry James. This play reflects an abiding interest in Scandinavian literature; Gosse is especially remembered for having introduced the works of Ibsen to the English public. Acquired in 1994.

801. Gosse, Edmund. Firdausi in exile and other poems. London: Kegan Paul, Trench and Co., 1885. Sm. 8vo, original olive green cloth.

> This copy is inscribed by Gosse on the front flyleaf, "Miss Alice Boyd with the Author's affectionate regards." With the book label of Simon Nowell-Smith. Acquired in 1984.

802. Gosse, Edmund. On viol and flute. London: Kegan Paul, Trench, Trübner & Co., Ltd., 1890. 8vo, blue-green morocco, by Riviere.

> Second edition, preserving thirty-three poems from the edition of 1873, and adding thirty-six other poems ("all that the author desires to preserve of such of his verses as were published, up to the year 1879"). This is the author's own copy, one of fifty printed on large paper and signed by the printer Charles Whittingham of the Chiswick Press; with Gosse's bookplate. Tipped in is a five-page letter from the book's dedicatee, Viscountess Wolseley, expressing her gratitude: "I cannot sufficiently thank you for associating my name with what will help others, as it has me, to forget . . . the tiresome turmoil of life." With the book label of Simon Nowell-Smith. Acquired in 1984.

THOMAS HARDY (1840–1928)

803. Hardy, Thomas. Wessex poems and other verses. With thirty illustrations by the author. London and New York: Harper and Brothers, 1898. 8vo, original dark green cloth.

> Hardy's first book of poetry. The book has a frontispiece, twelve full-page illustrations, and eighteen head- and tailpieces, all after drawings by Hardy himself. Acquired in 1984.

RICHARD LE GALLIENNE (1866–1947)

804. Le Gallienne, Richard. My ladies' sonnets and other "vain and amatorious" verses, with some of graver mood. N.p. [Liverpool]: privately printed, 1887. Sq. 12mo, original blue-gray boards, parchment spine, printed paper label.

> The author's first book. Le Gallienne grew up in Liverpool and was apprenticed by his father to a firm of chartered accountants, but he found the work tedious and failed his examinations. Turning to literature, he received encouragement from Oliver Wendell Holmes, and he became a conspicuous figure in the world of letters of the nineties. This small book, printed in Liverpool by W. and J. Arnold, was issued privately with the financial assistance of his office friends. This copy is inscribed by the author on the front flyleaf, "To the Editor of 'The Century Guild Hobby Horse,' from Richard Le Gallienne. 16, ix, '87." The recipient was Arthur Heygate Mackmurdo (1851–1942), architect, designer, and social reformer,

who founded the Century Guild in 1882 to promote such arts and crafts as cabinetmaking, decorative metalwork, and the design of fabric and wallpaper; *The Hobby Horse* was the guild's periodical. Acquired in 2004.

THOMAS STURGE MOORE (1870–1944)

805. Moore, Thomas Sturge. The vinedresser and other poems. London: At the Sign of the Unicorn, 1899. 12mo, original light green cloth.

> The author's first collection of poetry, preceded only by *Two Poems*, privately printed in 1893. This copy is inscribed on the front flyleaf, "To Marie with love from Tom." The recipient was Moore's cousin Marie Appia, the daughter of a Lutheran minister who lived in France. Moore had long been in love with Appia, but in 1893 she became engaged to his younger brother Harry. Harry, however, was training to be an Anglican clergyman, and was sufficiently disturbed by his fiancée's Nonconformity that he soon broke off the engagement. Moore declared his love in June 1897, but was refused; he persisted nonetheless, and the two finally married in 1903. This copy was acquired from a small collection of Moore's books in the possession of descendants of Moore's French in laws. Laid in is a four page souvenir for the baptism of Daniel Charles Sturge-Moore [sic], the poet's first child, who was born in London in November 1905, and baptized in Paris in May 1906. The godfather is named: he was the well-known artist Charles Ricketts, with whom Moore had studied in the late 1880s, and who was later much involved in various literary and theatrical projects. Acquired in 2007.

STEPHEN PHILLIPS (1864–1915)

806. Phillips, Stephen. Orestes and other poems. London: printed for private circulation, 1884. Sm. 4to, original yellow glazed printed wrappers.

> The author's first book, published when he was twenty. Phillips was a cousin of Laurence Binyon, and appeared with him in *Primavera* (1890), a small collection of poems by four young writers printed in Oxford (no. 744). With the book label of W. Van R. Whitall. The Simon Nowell-Smith copy. Acquired in 2002.

WILLIAM SHARP (1855–1905)

807. Sharp, William. The human inheritance, the new hope, motherhood. London: Elliot Stock, 1882. 8vo, original dark blue cloth.

The author's first book, published after he had spent several years living with Gypsies, and pursuing romantic adventure in Australia. In 1894, Sharp began to publish fiction under the pseudonym "Fiona MacLeod," an identity he kept secret until his death in 1905; it is for these novels and stories that he is today chiefly remembered. This copy is inscribed on the title page, "To W. M. Rossetti, with the great regard & esteem of the author, 1882." Sharp had a year earlier first met the recipient's brother Dante Gabriel Rossetti. Acquired in 2002.

GEORGE ROBERT SIMS (1847–1922)

808. Sims, George Robert. The dagonet ballads. (Chiefly from the Referee). London: E. J. Francis & Co., 1879. 8vo, original gray cloth.

Probably the author's most enduring publication, if only for the fact that it includes the line "It is Christmas Day in the workhouse." This copy is inscribed on the title page, "With kind regards, Geo. R. Sims." Acquired about 2005.

ROBERT LOUIS STEVENSON (1850–1894)

809. Stevenson, Robert Louis. A child's garden of verses. London: Longmans, Green, and Co., 1885. 12mo, original bright blue cloth. Acquired in 1981.

810. Stevenson, Robert Louis. Ballads. London: Chatto & Windus, 1890. 4to, original white buckram cloth.

This copy is one of one hundred on large paper, signed by the printers, R. & R. Clark. The two longest poems here, "A Song of Rahéro" and "The Feast of Famine," are set in islands in the South Seas, Tahiti and the Marquesas, respectively. Acquired in 1992.

JOHN ADDINGTON SYMONDS (1840–1893)

811. Symonds, John Addington. The Escorial. A prize poem, recited in the Theatre, Oxford, June 20, 1860. Oxford: T. and G. Shrimpton, 1860. 8vo, original white printed wrappers.

The author's first publication, printed when he was twenty. Symonds went on to become a noted poet and critic, and was one of the first English writers to deal in print with the subject of homosexuality. With the book label of Kenneth A. Lohf. Acquired in 1992.

JOHN TODHUNTER (1839–1916)

812. Todhunter, John. Alcestis: a dramatic poem. London: C. Kegan Paul & Co., 1879. 8vo, original olive green cloth.

> Todhunter was involved with the Irish literary revival at the end of the nineteenth century, and was closely associated with the Yeats family. This copy is inscribed on the dedication page to Olive Cockerell, "with kind regards." Todhunter has corrected the text in manuscript on virtually every other page; the changes range from small corrections to a word or phrase to major additions and deletions running to many lines. Acquired in 1980.

813. Todhunter, John. Notes on Shelley's unfinished poem "The Triumph of Life." London: printed for private circulation, 1887. 8vo, original pale blue printed boards. [With:] Shelley and the marriage question. London: printed for private distribution, 1889. 8vo, original blue printed boards.

> Two private printings of papers read before the Shelley Society. Each title was limited to twenty-five copies only (in addition to three copies printed on vellum). Acquired in 1996.

OSCAR WILDE (1854–1900)

814. Wilde, Oscar. Newdigate prize poem. Ravenna. Recited in the Theatre, Oxford, June 26, 1878. Oxford: Thomas Shrimpton and Son, 1878. 8vo, original gray printed wrappers.

> Wilde's first publication. Acquired in 1981.

WILLIAM BUTLER YEATS (1865–1939)

815. Yeats, William Butler. The wanderings of Oisin and other poems. London: Kegan Paul, Trench and Co., 1889. Sm. 8vo, original dark blue cloth.

> The author's first book, preceded only by a single pamphlet poem, *Mosada*, which is very rare. One of two hundred copies printed. Acquired in 1979.

816. Yeats, William Butler. The Celtic twilight. Men and women, dhouls and faeries. London: Lawrence and Bullen, 1893. Sm. 8vo, original olive green cloth.

> Yeats's fifth book. Acquired in 2005.

817. Yeats, William Butler, editor. The poems of William Blake. Edited by W. B. Yeats. London: Lawrence & Bullen; Charles Scribner's Sons (New York), 1893. Sm. 8vo, original light blue cloth.

> Yeats had an editorial role, along with Edwin John Ellis, in a three-volume collected works of Blake published earlier the same year. This more modest selection was issued as a volume in the Muses' Library. Yeats wrote the introduction (pp. [xv]–liii), a list of acknowledgments (p. [liv]), and a section of notes (pp. [235]–51). Acquired in 2005.

818. Yeats, William Butler. Poems. London: published by T. Fisher Unwin; Boston: Copeland and Day, 1895. 8vo, original tan cloth, elaborately decorated in gilt.

> This copy is the American issue, with a cancel title page naming the Boston publisher, and with the name of Copeland and Day added to the foot of the spine. The print run consisted of 750 copies, of which perhaps two hundred sets of sheets were sent to America. Acquired in 1978.

819. Yeats, William Butler. Poems. London: T. Fisher Unwin, 1899. 8vo, original dark blue cloth, elaborately decorated in gilt after a design by Althea Gyles.

> Second edition (though not so designated); first published in 1895 (no. 818). This edition has a new preface, explaining that the poems have been rearranged and substantially revised. Acquired in 2005.

The City of Palaces;

A FRAGMENT.

AND

Other Poems.

By James Atkinson, Esq.

CALCUTTA:
PRINTED AT THE GOVERNMENT GAZETTE PRESS.

1824.

ITEM 820

JAMES ATKINSON (1780–1852)

820. Atkinson, James. The city of palaces; a fragment. And other poems. Calcutta: printed at the Government Gazette Press, 1824. 8vo, contemporary half black calf.

> James Atkinson studied medicine at Edinburgh and London, and in 1805 took a post as a medical officer in the Bengal service. His duties in India were not arduous, and he devoted himself to the study of Persian and other Oriental languages, with considerable success. "Atkinson's Persian translations are his chief title to fame, and those of his selections from the 'Shâh Nâmeh' of Firdausi are the most notable, inasmuch as they were the first attempt to make the great Persian 'Epic of Kings' familiar to English readers."–*DNB*. Atkinson also had ability as a writer of original verse. This collection displays throughout the influence of Byron, most particularly in a long piece entitled "Peer Mahommud; The Moralist," written in ottava rima, the verse form of *Don Juan*. The title poem is a vivid description of Calcutta, based upon the author's own observations. Three other poems have to do with Lord Minto, the former governor-general, who much admired Atkinson's linguistic attainments. Five copies of this book are recorded, at the British Library, the Bodleian, Manchester, Newberry, and Illinois. Acquired in 1999.

MAJOR HENRY COURT (1843–1892?)

821. Court, Major Henry, translator. Selections from the Kulliyat or complete works of Mirza Rafi-oos-Sauda being the parts appointed for the high proficiency examination in Oordoo. Simla: printed by J. Elston, "Station Press," 1872. 8vo, contemporary red morocco.

> This copy is inscribed on the front flyleaf, "Presented to H. E. Lord Northbrook Viceroy and Govr. Gen. of India with the translator's humble compliments." Major Court was Northbrook's official interpreter. With the later library label on the spine of Lord Lytton (Northbrook's successor). Acquired in 1986.

SHOSHEE CHUNDER DUTT (1824–1885)

822. Dutt, Shoshee Chunder. Miscellaneous verses. Calcutta: printed by Sanders, Cones and Co., 1848. 8vo, contemporary half purple morocco.

> This is probably the dedication copy, as it was acquired from a group of books belonging to James Ramsay, 1st Marquess of Dalhousie, who had been governor-general of India; the printed dedication is to his wife. Shoshee Chunder Dutt converted to Christianity, and went on to write many other books about India; he was one of the first Indian writers to publish fiction in English. Of this youthful work three copies are recorded, at Cambridge, Kansas State, and the Library of Congress. Acquired in 1981.

HENRY BAILY WADE GARRICK (FL. 1889)

823. Garrick, Henry Baily Wade. India, a descriptive poem. London: Trübner & Co., 1889. 8vo, original orange cloth.

> This copy is inscribed on the verso of the half-title, "To the Earl of Lytton, with the author's comps. and best wishes. 17th March, 1919." The recipient was the son of the poem's dedicatee, the 1st Earl Lytton, poet, statesman, and viceroy and governor-general of India; his son was born in Simla in 1876, and himself had a long involvement with Indian affairs, including a term as governor of Bombay, beginning in 1922. H. B. W. Garrick was a government archaeologist in India; his long poem in Spenserian stanzas narrates the history of the country in which he spent many years of his life. Acquired in 2000.

HENRY BARKLEY HENDERSON (1793–1862)

824. [Henderson, Henry Barkley.] Satires in India. Calcutta: printed for the author, by P. Crichton, 1819. 8vo, contemporary half calf.

> A collection of seven poems, consisting of character sketches drawn from Anglo-Indian social and military circles. According to a brief introduction, all but one of these satires were first published in *The Asiatic Mirror* in 1817: "The author . . . is said to be a Subaltern of Native Infantry; any thing further relating to him can scarcely be deemed necessary here, but to his few friends and acquaintances, it is certain, that he never attempted to conceal the heinous indiscretion of his having employed some of his frequent leisure hours in such composition. When these first appeared, it

SATIRES

IN

INDIA.

OMNES HI METUUNT VERSUS —— ODERE POETAS.

HOR. *Sat.* l.

ALL DREAD THE SATIRE—AND DETEST THE BARD.

CALCUTTA.

PRINTED FOR THE AUTHOR,

By P. Crichton.

1819.

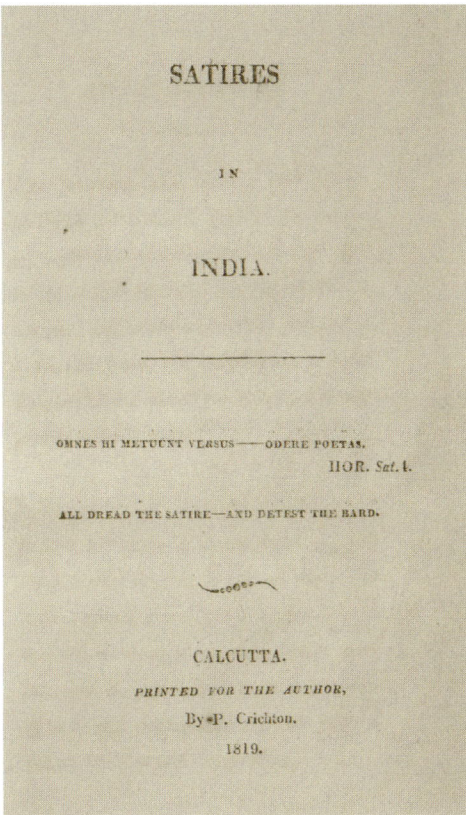

is mentioned that several individuals applied some of the more satirical illustrations of character to themselves, and were even silly enough to evince their sense of such application." WorldCat lists three copies of this book, at the British Library, the Bodleian, and UCLA. These are all listed with no indication of the author's identity, but in fact the same poems were reprinted in 1829 in London, by Smith, Elder, and Co., in a volume called *The Bengalee: Or, Sketches of Society and Manners in the East,* where they are interspersed among a number of prose pieces. The author of that volume has reliably been identified as Henry Barkley Henderson (1793–1862), who had also published two other slim volumes of verse in Calcutta, *The Goorkah, and Other Poems* (1817) and *Violanthe: A Tale of the Twelfth Century* (1818). This copy of his third work has frequent light penciled notes by a contemporary reader (often corrections and alterations of the text, but not authorial). Acquired in 2000.

401

ROBERT FRANCIS HODGSON (FL. 1850)

825. Hodgson, Robert Francis. Selections from the French poets of the past and present century, rendered into English verse. Calcutta: W. Thacker and Co.; Smith, Elder and Co. (London), 1850. 8vo, contemporary red straight-grained morocco.

> This is an elegant copy, in what is almost certainly an Indian binding; it is very likely the dedication copy, as it was acquired from the library of the dedicatee, James Ramsay, 1st Marquess of Dalhousie, who was the governor-general of India. The author served in the Bengal Civil Service. The book was printed in Calcutta at the Military Orphan Press. Acquired in 1983.

HENRY GEORGE KEENE (1825–1915)

826. Keene, Henry George. Peepul leaves. Poems written in India. London: W. H. Allen and Co., 1879. 8vo, original green cloth.

> The author was the son of a noted scholar, also named Henry George Keene (1781–1864), who was professor of Arabic and Persian at the East India College at Hailesbury (see the *DNB*). The younger Keene, born in 1825, worked most of his life as an administrator in India, and published numerous historical volumes, guidebooks, reminiscences, and other prose works, as well as several other volumes of verse. With the armorial bookplate of Reuben David Sassoon. Acquired in 2000.

MARY ELIZA LESLIE (B. 1834)

827. Leslie, Mary Eliza. Ina, and other poems. Calcutta: W. Newman and Company, 1856. 12mo, contemporary red morocco, decorated in gilt, a.e.g.

> The author's first book. Mary Leslie was the daughter of a Baptist missionary in India, where she spent virtually her entire life. She went on to publish several other collections of verse, including a sonnet sequence about her experiences during the Indian Mutiny, and accounts of her involvement in educational and missionary affairs. This copy of her first book is in a beautifully preserved Indian binding of the period. Only one copy is recorded by WorldCat and Copac, at the British Library. Acquired in 1981.

ALFRED COMYN LYALL (1835–1911)

828. [Lyall, Alfred Comyn.] Verses written in India. (A. C. L.) N.p. [Simla?]: n.d. [probably 1880]. Sm. 4to, contemporary calf, original stiff printed wrappers bound in.

> The first edition, clearly printed in India, of the author's only book of verse; a revised version of these poems was later printed in London, and became extremely popular (no. 830). This copy is inscribed on the front wrapper, "Fred. Roberts from A. C. L. Simla, October, 1880." The recipient was Frederick Sleigh Roberts, later Field Marshal Earl Roberts of Kandahar. In 1880, Roberts acquired glory and achieved fame; his exploits in the Afghanistan campaign and his march on Kandahar in August caught the public imagination at home and transformed him into a popular hero. Alfred Comyn Lyall, who was at the time foreign secretary to the Indian government, was one of the chief negotiators in the Kabul and Kandahar talks that followed Roberts's victory. A comparison of the text with a subsequent Indian printing (no. 829) reveals that all the poems here have been preserved (with additions), except for one piece, the lines on Badminton that form the second part of poem 12. Two copies of this book are recorded, at Cambridge and Florida State University (both assigned the date 1882). Acquired in 1980.

829. [Lyall, Alfred Comyn.] Verses written in India. (A. C. L.) N.p. [Simla?]: n.d. [1883?]. 8vo, original half cloth and light blue printed boards.

> Apparently the third edition, though not so designated, with eighty-five pages, as opposed to sixty-three in the earliest printing (no. 828), and seventy-one in an edition of which three copies are recorded (British Library, Yale, Morgan Library). The text contains poems written up to 1882. The paper is not watermarked, but in the margin of p. 19 is a faint impression that reads, "Indian Empire / Simla, the [illegible] August, 1881." No other copy of this edition has been located. Acquired in 1977.

830. Lyall, Alfred Comyn. Verses written in India. London: Kegan Paul, Trench and Co., 1889. 8vo, contemporary green morocco, by Roger de Coverly.

> The first published edition. This is no. 33 of fifty copies printed on large paper, and signed by the printers, Charles Whittingham and Co. Lyall's signature appears on the title page. Of the twenty-five poems in the preceding Indian edition, three have been omitted, and two new poems have been added;

virtually all the original poems show some signs of revision. Acquired in 1978. Also in the collection is a copy of the trade edition, in green cloth, with an autograph letter of Lyall tipped in at the front. Acquired in 1978.

JOHN MALCOLM (1769–1833)

831. [Malcolm, John.] Miscellaneous poems. By Sir J–– M––. Bombay: printed at the American Mission Press, (not published), 1829. 8vo, contemporary maroon morocco.

> John Malcolm was one of England's great administrators in India. Acquired in 1984.

JULIA MERCADO (FL. 1858)

832. [Mercado, Julia.] "Wild flowers." Dedicated to friends, and patrons. By the author of "Heath Flowers." Calcutta: printed and published by D'Rozario & Co., 1858. 12mo, contemporary brown morocco.

> A collection of Anglo-Indian poems and sketches. At the front is a presentation leaf, printed in gold, and filled out by the author for a Mr. Forrester. Neither this title nor the other mentioned on the title page has been located in the NUC, WorldCat, or Copac. Acquired in 1992.

JOHN BRUCE NORTON (1815–1883)

833. [Norton, John Bruce.] Folia opima. By J. B. N. of Merton College, Oxford. Madras: J. B. Pharoah, 1843. 8vo, contemporary half red morocco.

> The author's first book. John Bruce Norton was advocate-general of Madras. This copy is inscribed on the title page to Sir Robert Cunliffe (1808–1855), of the Bengal civil service. There are numerous corrections in the author's hand, mostly of misprints; at one point, however, he has added four lines of verse. WorldCat lists five copies of this book, at the British Library, Cambridge, Harvard, Princeton, and Texas. With the bookplate of Robert Cunliffe. Acquired in 1980.

RONALD ROSS (1857–1932)

834. Ross, Ronald. The deformed transformed. Bangalore: printed at the Spectator Press, 1890. 12mo, original tan printed wrappers.

The author's second book, preceded by a novel called *The Child of Ocean*, published in London in 1889. This is one of fifty copies printed in India for private circulation; this copy is signed at the top of the title page, and marked "Author's Copy." Laid in is a printed slip giving a "reduction of the play for representation." Ross was a physician who entered the Indian Medical Service in 1881, and arrived in Bombay in October of that year. He subsequently achieved considerable fame as the discoverer of the mosquito cycle in malaria. Ross had a lifelong interest in literature, and continued to publish poetry and fiction until his death in 1932. The origin of this play, much of it in verse, is explained in the preface: "This story is founded on two very old legends. The former, appearing originally in the Books of Genesis and Tobit, has lately been touched by Coleridge, treated by Byron, and been made the subject of an opera of Rubinstein's, to which I am much indebted, and which is founded on a poem by Lermantoff [*sic*]. The other is, in its latest form, the story of Byron's *Deformed Transformed*, which he states to be founded partly on a novel called *Three Brothers*, and partly on *Faust*." The play was reprinted in London in 1892, by Chapman and Hall. Acquired in 2003.

STEPHEN HENRY SHARMAN (FL. 1858)

835. Sharman, Stephen Henry. The relief of Lucknow, and other poems. London: Hamilton, Adams, and Co.; J. Fry (Chelmsford), 1858. 8vo, original dark red cloth.

> The title poem deals with one of the most dramatic episodes of the Indian Mutiny, which had just taken place. The author, who was evidently a schoolmaster in Great Baddow, near Chelmsford (where the book was printed), was not himself in India, but his verse represents the great outpouring of feeling with which Victorian England responded to the unsettling events in "the Jewel in the Crown." The book is dedicated, with permission, to Lady Havelock, widow of one of the military heroes of the Mutiny. With a five-page list of subscribers. Inscribed on the front flyleaf, "Dorothy E. Bell, from Auntie Croxon." Acquired in 2001.

Author Index

The numbers below refer to catalogue entries.

Set in Comenius types. Designed by Jerry Kelly.